Lecture Notes in Computer Science 9331

Commenced Publication in 1973
Founding and Former Series Editors:
Gerhard Goos, Juris Hartmanis, and Jan van Leeuwen

More information about this series at http://www.springer.com/series/7410

Sara Foresti (Ed.)

Security and Trust Management

11th International Workshop, STM 2015
Vienna, Austria, September 21–22, 2015
Proceedings

 Springer

Editor
Sara Foresti
Dipartimento di Informatica
Università degli Studi di Milano
Crema
Italy

ISSN 0302-9743   ISSN 1611-3349   (electronic)
Lecture Notes in Computer Science
ISBN 978-3-319-24857-8   ISBN 978-3-319-24858-5   (eBook)
DOI 10.1007/978-3-319-24858-5

Library of Congress Control Number: 2015949450

LNCS Sublibrary: SL4 – Security and Cryptology

Printed on acid-free paper

Springer International Publishing AG Switzerland is part of Springer Science+Business Media
(www.springer.com)

Preface

These proceedings contain the papers selected for presentation at the 11th International Workshop on Security and Trust Management (STM 2015), held in Vienna, Austria, during September 21–22, 2015, in conjunction with the 20th European Symposium on Research in Computer Security (ESORICS 2015).

In response to the call for papers, 38 papers were submitted from 23 different countries. Each paper was reviewed by three members of the Program Committee, who considered its significance, novelty, technical quality, and practical impact in their evaluation. As in previous years, reviewing was double-blind, that is, the identities of reviewers were not revealed to the authors of the papers and identities of authors were not revealed to the reviewers. The Program Committee's work was carried out electronically, yielding intensive discussions over a period of one week. Of the submitted papers, the Program Committee accepted 15 full papers (resulting in an acceptance rate of 39.5%) and 4 short papers for presentation at the workshop. Besides the technical program including the papers collated in these proceedings, the workshop featured an invited talk by the winner of the ERCIM STM WG 2015 Award for the best PhD thesis on security and trust management.

The credit for the success of an event like STM 2015 belongs to a number of people, who devoted their time and energy to put together the workshop and who deserve acknowledgment. First of all, I wish to thank all the members of the Program Committee and all the external reviewers, for all their hard work in evaluating all the papers in a short time window, and for their active participation in the discussion and selection process. I would like to express my sincere gratitude to the ERCIM STM Steering Committee, and its chair, Pierangela Samarati, in particular, for their guidance and support in the organization of the workshop. Thanks to Giovanni Livraga, for taking care of publicity. I would also like to thank Javier Lopez (ESORICS Workshop Chair), Günther Pernul (ESORICS General Chair), and Yvonne Poul (ESORICS Local Organizer) for their support in the workshop organization and logistics.

Last but certainly not least, thanks to all the authors who submitted papers and to all the workshop's attendees. I hope you find the proceedings of STM 2015 interesting and of inspiration for your future research.

September 2015   Sara Foresti

Organization

Program Chair

Sara Foresti   Università degli Studi di Milano, Italy

Publicity Chair

Giovanni Livraga   Università degli Studi di Milano, Italy

STM Steering Committee

Theo Dimitrakos	British Telecom, UK
Javier Lopez	University of Málaga, Spain
Fabio Martinelli	National Research Council, Italy
Sjouke Mauw	University of Luxembourg, Luxembourg
Stig F. Mjølsnes	NTNU, Norway
Pierangela Samarati (Chair)	Università degli Studi di Milano, Italy
Ulrich Ultes-Nitsche	University of Fribourg, Switzerland

Program Committee

Ken Barker	University of Calgary, Canada
David W. Chadwick	University of Kent, UK
Jorge Cuellar	Siemens AG, Germany
Sabrina De Capitani di Vimercati	Università degli Studi di Milano, Italy
Theo Dimitrakos	British Telecom, UK
Josep Domingo-Ferrer	Universitat Rovira i Virgili, Spain
Carmen Fernández-Gago	University of Málaga, Spain
José-Luis Ferrer-Gomila	University of the Balearic Islands, Spain
Joaquin Garcia-Alfaro	Telecom SudParis, France
Ehud Gudes	Ben-Gurion University, Israel
Michael Huth	Imperial College London, UK
Christian D. Jensen	Technical University of Denmark, Denmark
Florian Kerschbaum	SAP, Germany
Costas Lambrinoudakis	University of Piraeus, Greece
Javier Lopez	University of Málaga, Spain
Evangelos Markatos	University of Crete, Greece
Stephen Marsh	University of Ontario, Institute of Technology, Canada
Fabio Martinelli	National Research Council, Italy
Sjouke Mauw	University of Luxembourg, Luxembourg

Catherine Meadows	Naval Research Laboratory, USA
Stig F. Mjølsnes	NTNU, Norway
Charles Morisset	Newcastle University, UK
Stefano Paraboschi	Università degli Studi di Bergamo, Italy
Siani Pearson	HP, UK
Günther Pernul	University of Regensburg, Germany
Marinella Petrocchi	National Research Council, Italy
Silvio Ranise	FBK, Italy
Carsten Rudolph	Huawei European Research Centre, Germany
Pierangela Samarati	Università degli Studi di Milano, Italy
Mohammad Torabi Dashti	ETH, Switzerland
Vicenç Torra	University of Skövde, Sweden
Claire Vishik	Intel Corporation, UK
Edgar Weippl	Vienna University of Technology, Austria
Nicola Zannone	TU/e, The Netherlands

External Reviewers

Mahdi Alizadeh
Alberto Blanco-Justicia
Joshua Daniel
Malik Imran Daud
Riccardo De Masellis
Daniel Ricardo Dos Santos
Alexandru Ionut Egner
Ludwig Fuchs
Jordi Herrera-Joancomarti
Hugo Jonker
Aljosha Judmayer
Ali El Kaafarani
Yin Li

Martina Lindorfer
Stefan Meier
Michael Netter
David Nuñez
Pramod Pawar
Nikolaos Pitropakis
Jordi Ribes-González
Ali Sajjad
Johannes Sänger
Andrea Saracino
Giada Sciarretta
Rolando Trujillo-Rasua

Contents

Security Metrics and Classification

Digital Waste Sorting: A Goal-Based, Self-Learning Approach to Label Spam Email Campaigns

Mina Sheikhalishahi[1]([✉]), Andrea Saracino[2], Mohamed Mejri[1],
Nadia Tawbi[1], and Fabio Martinelli[2]

[1] Department of Computer Science, Université Laval, Québec City, Canada
mina.sheikh-alishahi.1@ulaval.ca
{mohamed.mejri,nadia.tawbi}@ift.ulaval.ca
[2] Istituto di Informatica e Telematica, Consiglio Nazionale delle ricerche, Pisa, Italy
{andrea.saracino,fabio.martinelli}@iit.cnr.it

Abstract. Fast analysis of correlated spam emails may be vital in the effort of finding and prosecuting spammers performing cybercrimes such as phishing and online frauds. This paper presents a self-learning framework to automatically divide and classify large amounts of spam emails in correlated labeled groups. Building on large datasets daily collected through honeypots, the emails are firstly divided into homogeneous groups of similar messages (campaigns), which can be related to a specific spammer. Each campaign is then associated to a class which specifies the goal of the spammer, i.e. phishing, advertisement, etc. The proposed framework exploits a categorical clustering algorithm to group similar emails, and a classifier to subsequently label each email group. The main advantage of the proposed framework is that it can be used on large spam emails datasets, for which no prior knowledge is provided. The approach has been tested on more than 3200 real and recent spam emails, divided in more than 60 campaigns, reporting a classification accuracy of 97 % on the classified data.

1 Introduction

At the end of 2014, emails are still one of the most common form of communication in Internet. Unfortunately, emails are also the main vector for sending unsolicited bulks of messages, generally for commercial purpose, commonly known as *spam*. The research community has investigated the problem for several years, proposing tools and methodologies to mitigate this issue. However, a definitive solution to the problem of spam emails still has to be found. In fact, according to *McAfee Report* [19], unsolicited emails, constitute more than 70 percent

This research has been partially supported by EU Seventh Framework Programme (FP7/2007–2013) under grant no 610853 (COCO Cloud), MIUR-PRIN Security Horizons and Natural Sciences and Engineering Research Council of Canada (NSERC).

S. Foresti (Ed.): STM 2015, LNCS 9331, pp. 3–19, 2015.
DOI: 10.1007/978-3-319-24858-5_1

of total amount of email messages in 2014. Moreover, *Cisco Report* [26] shows that spam volume increased 250 percent from January 2014 to November 2014. Unfortunately, the problem of spam emails is not only related to unsolicited advertisement. Spam emails have become a vector to perform different kinds of cybercrimes including phishing, cyber-frauds and spreading malware.

Motivation: Trying to filter spam emails at the user end, actually is not enough to fight this kind of attacks, which moves the effect of unsolicited spam emails from illicit to real crime. Finding the spammers becomes important not only to tackle at the source the problem of spam emails, but also to legally prosecute the responsible of cybercrimes brought by spam emails different from undesired advertisement. To identify spammers, the early analysis of huge amount of messages to find correlated spam emails with the specific spammer purpose is vital. Several papers in the literature observed that the forensic analysis, which plays a major role in finding and persecuting spammers for cybercrimes, needs a proactive mechanism or tool which is able to perform a fast, multi-staged analysis of emails in a timely fashion [9,10,14,29]. To this end, large amounts of spam emails, generally collected through honeypots should be at first divided in similar groups, which could be related to the same spammer (i.e., spam campaigns). Afterward to each campaign should be assigned a label describing the purpose of spammer. This goal-based labeling facilitates for investigators the analysis of spam campaigns, eventually directed toward a specific cybercrime. However, this analysis generally appears to be a challenging task. In fact, considering the number of produced spam emails and their variance, spam email datasets are huge and very difficult to handle. In particular, human analysis is almost impossible, considering the amount of spam emails daily caught by a spam honeypot [28,29]. On the other hand, an automated and accurate analysis requires the usage of correctly trained computational intelligence tools, i.e. *classifiers*, whose training requires accurately chosen datasets, which presents to the classifier a good reality description in which it will be employed. Moreover, due to the high variance of spam emails, a valid training set may become obsolete in few weeks, and a new up-to-date training set must be generated in a short period of time.

Though previous work largely improved the state of the art in analysis of spam emails for forensic purposes, more improvement is still needed. In particular, previous work either focuses on a specific cybercrime only, especially phishing [11], or exploit in the analysis a small set of features not effective in identifying some cybercrime emails. For example, the analysis of email text words [14], link domains [10] is not effective in identifying emails used to distribute malware, which often do not contain text [20] , or spam emails with dynamic links [5].

Paper Contribution: In this paper we propose Digital Waste Sorter (DWS), a framework which exploits a self learning *goal of the spammer*-based approach for spam email classification. The proposed approach aims at automatically classifying large amount of raw unclassified spam emails dividing them into campaigns and labeling each campaign with its spammer goals. To this end, we propose five class labels to group spammer goals in five macro-groups, namely *Advertisement, Portal Redirection, Advanced Fee Fraud, Malware Distribution* *and Phishing*. Moreover, a set of 21 categorical features representative of email structure is proposed to perform a multi-feature analysis aimed at identifying emails related to a large range of cybercrimes. DWS is based on the cooperation of unsupervised and supervised learning algorithms. Given a set of *classes* describing different spammer goals and a dataset of non classified spam emails, the proposed approach at first automatically creates a valid training set for a classifier exploiting a *categorical* clustering algorithm, named CCTree (Categorical Clustering Tree). In more detail, this clustering algorithm divides the dataset into structurally similar groups of emails, named spam campaigns [7]. DWS is built on the results of CCTree , which is effective in dividing spam emails in homogeneous clusters. Afterward, significant spam campaigns useful in the generation of the training set are selected through similarity with a small set of known emails, representative of each spam class. Hence, a classifier is trained using the selected campaigns as training set, and will be used to classify the remaining unclassified emails of the dataset.

To further meet the needs of forensic investigators, which have limited time and resource to perform email examinations [9], the DWS methodology does not require a prior knowledge of dataset, except the desired classes (i.e. spammer goals) and a small set of emails representative of each class. It is worth noting that this email set cannot be used to train the classifier. In fact, this set contains a small number of emails not belonging to the dataset to be classified, being thus not necessarily descriptive of the reality in which the classifier will operate.

In the following, we will describe in details the DWS framework, explaining the process of division in campaigns, training set generation and campaigns classification. The framework effectiveness has been evaluated against a set of 3200 recent raw spam emails extracted by a honeypot. DWS reported a classification accuracy on this preliminary dataset of 97.8 %. Furthermore, to justify the classifier selection, an analysis of performances on different classifiers is presented.

The rest of the paper is organized as follows. Section 2 reports related work on email classification. Section 3 presents the DWS framework and work-flow in details, also it gives brief background information on the clustering algorithm. Section 4 presents the results of the analysis on a real dataset of spam emails, as well as a comparison on the classification results of four different classifiers. Finally Sect. 5 briefly concludes reporting planned future extensions.

2   Related Work

In the literature, the spam campaigns are usually labeled based on characteristic strings (keywords) representing individual campaign types as in [10,18] and [13]. These approaches are weak against the kind of spam emails which do not contain keywords or that use word obfuscation techniques. Pathak et al. [21] label spam campaigns on the base of URLs, phone number, Skype ID, and Mail ID used as contact information. This methodology is effective only against emails reporting contacts, which are only a subset of all the spam emails found in the wild.

There are several approaches in the literature in which the spammer goal is considered. However, these approaches are mainly focused on detecting phishing emails, not considering other spammer purposes. Fette et al. [11] applied 10 email features to discern phishing emails from ham (good) emails. Bergholz et al. [6] propose a similar methodology with additional features to train a classifier in order to filter phishing emails. Almomani et al. [3] provide a survey on different techniques in filtering phishing emails, while Gansterer et al. [12] compare different machine learning algorithms in phishing detection. Furthermore, the authors propose a technique which refines the previous phishing filtering approaches. In this work, three types of messages, named *ham, spam* and *phishing* are distinguished automatically. Nevertheless, the category of emails containing *spam*, is not precisely characterized. In [8] a methodology to detect phishing emails based on both machine learning and heuristics is proposed. These approaches report accuracy ranging from 92% to 96%, where the classifiers have been trained through labeled datasets. On the contrary, DWS generates the training set on the fly, without requiring a pre-trained classifier. Notwithstanding, in the performed experiments DWS shows comparable accuracy.

3   Digital Waste Sorting

DWS is a framework which takes as input datasets of unclassified spam emails. Hence, DWS divides the emails in campaigns by mean of a hierarchical clustering algorithm, then labels each campaign through a classifier. The classifier is trained on the fly, through a training set generated by DWS directly from the unlabeled input dataset, exploiting the knowledge generated by the clustering algorithm.

This section describes in details the DWS framework and methodology. First, we will present the classes used to label each spam campaign. Then, we present the feature extraction process from raw emails, discussing the features relevance in describing structural elements of an email and their relation to each spam class. The framework is then presented, briefly introducing the clustering algorithm and the methodology for the generation of the training set. Finally the classification process is presented.

3.1   Definition of Classes

As anticipated, spam emails can be sent with different intentions, spanning from the common advertisement to vectors of different cybercrimes. We argue that spam emails can be divided in five well-known macro-groups which represent the main target of spammers, and can thus be used to label spam campaigns.

Advertisement: The *advertisement* class contains those emails whose target is convincing a user to buy a specific product [17]. Advertisement emails embody the most typical idea of spam messages, advertising any kind of product which could be of interest of companies or private users. Generally these emails only constitute a hindrance to the users that have to spend time removing them from the inbox. The main requirements for a commercial email to be legal according to

Federal Trade Commission [2], is that it uses no deceptive subject lines, provides correct complete header information, real physical location of the business, offers an opt-out choice, and honors opt-out requests in 10 business days. In this paper, we consider as advertisement emails both the ones which comply with the legal requirements and the ones that does not, given that their purpose is clearly advertising a product.

Portal Redirection: *Portal redirection* spam emails are the enablers of an evolved advertisement methodology. This spam emails are characterized by a minimal structure generally reporting one or more links to one or more websites. Once the user clicks on the link, she is redirected several times to different pages whose address is dynamically generated. The final target page is mostly an advertisement portal with several links divided by categories, generally related to common user needs (e.g., medical insurance). This strategy is useful in reducing the legal responsibility on spam emails of the companies which are advertising a product. The rationale is that the advertised company cannot be sued because another website, i.e. the portal, links to it. As an example, the opt-out clause of advertisement emails [16] does not apply. Moreover, the multi-redirection with dynamic links strategy makes difficult to track the responsible websites. The strategy of portal redirection emails, is also used to redirect users on websites with the intention of defrauding the users, or to distribute malicious code.

Advanced Fee Fraud: An *advanced fee fraud* or *confidence trick* spam email (synonyms include *confidence scheme* or *scam*) attempts to defraud a person after first gaining their confidence, used in the classical sense of trust [15]. Confidential trick spam exploits social engineering to trick the user in paying, by her own will, a certain amount of money to the spammer. Scammers may use several techniques to deceive the user in paying money, generally exploiting sentimental relations or promising a large amount of money in return. The confidential trick emails, mostly are written in a friendly long text, to convince the victim the interactions. These kinds of emails, usually, do not redirect the users to other web pages, mainly contain an email address.

Malware: Emails are an important vector for spreading malicious software or *malware*. Generally the malware is sent as email attachment, while the email structure is very simple, with a small text which encourages the reader to open the attachment or no text at all [20]. Once opened, the malware infects the user device, showing different possible malicious behaviors. Often the malicious file is camouflaged, inserted in a zip file or with a modified extension, which allows to deceive basic anti-virus control implemented by some spam filters.

Phishing: *Phishing* emails attempt to redirect users to websites, which are designed to obtain credentials or financial data such as usernames, passwords, and credit card detail illegally [3]. Generally, these emails pretend to be sent by a banking organization, or coming from a service accessible through username and password, e.g. social networks, instant messaging etc., reporting fake security issues that will require the user to confirm her data to access again the service. To this end, phishing emails are mostly very well presented with a well organized structure, even reporting contact informations such as phone numbers and email. The representative structure of phishing emails we applied in this research, contain short well written text, providing the victim some important news. Mostly there exists one link, which direct the user to a very well designed fake website of a bank, which asks the victim to provide her credit card information.

3.2   Feature Extraction

DWS parses raw spam emails (`eml` files) extracting a set of 21 categorical features building a numerical vector readable by clustering and classification algorithms. The extracted features are reported in Table 1, with a brief description, whilst the values which each feature may assume is reported in [25]. The "number of recipients" which are in the To and Cc fields of the email differentiate between emails which should look strictly personal, e.g. communications from a bank (phishing) and those that pretend to be sent to several recipients, such as some kind of frauds or advertisement. The structure of links in the email text gives several information useful in determining the email goal. Portal redirections emails and advertisement generally show a high "Number of links", in the first case to redirect the user to different portal websites, in the second one to redirect the user to the website where she can buy the products. Generally, fraud emails do not report links except for "IP based links". These links are expressed through IP addresses, without reporting domain names, to reduce the

Table 1. Features extracted from each email.

Attribute	Description
RecipientNumber	Number of recipients addresses.
NumberOfLinks	Total links in email text.
NumberOfIPBasedLinks	Links shown as an IP address.
NumberOfMismatchingLinks	Links with a text different from the real link.
NumberOfDomainsInLinks	Number of domains in links.
AvgDotsPerLink	Average number of dots in link in text.
NumberOfLinksWithAt	Number of links containing "@".
NumberOfLinksWithHex	Number of links containing hex chars.
NumberOfNonAsciiLinks	Number of links with non-ASCII chars.
IsHtml	True if the mail contains html tags.
EmailSize	The email size, including attachments.
Language	Email language.
AttachmentNumber	Number of attachments.
AttachmentSize	Total size of email attachments.
AttachmentType	File type of the biggest attachment.
WordsInSubject	Number of words in subject.
CharsInSubject	Number of chars in subject.
ReOrFwdInSubject	True if subject contains "Re" or "Fwd".
SubjectLanguage	Language of the subject.
NonAsciiCharsInSubject	Number of non ASCII chars in subject.
ImagesNumber	Number of images in the email text.

likelihood of being tracked or to make the email text, generally discussing about secret money transaction, more legitimate. The "number of domains in links" represents the number of different domains globally found in all the links in the email text. Phishing and advertisement emails generally have just a single domain respectively of the website where to buy the advertised product and the website of the authority which the message pretends to be sent from. On the other hand portal redirection may contain several domains to redirect the reader to different portal websites. Moreover, links in portal redirection emails generally have a high "average number of dots in links" (i.e. sub-domains) and being dynamically generated are likely to contain hexadecimal or non ASCII - characters. Non ASCII characters in the links are also typical of some advertisement emails redirecting to foreign websites. It is worth noting that all these link-based features consider the real destination address, not the clickable text shown to the user. If the clickable text (hyper-link) shows an address ("click here"-like text is not considered) different from the destination address, the link is considered mismatching and counted through the feature "mismatching links". Phishing and portal redirection emails make extensive use of mismatching links to deceive the user. For a further insight, a sample for each class is shown in Fig. 1. Advertisement and phishing emails may appear like a web-page. In this case, the email contains HTML tags. On the other hand, fraud, malware and portal emails rarely are presented in HTML format. The size of an email is another important structural feature. Confidential trick and portal redirections generally are quite small in size, considering they are raw text. Advertisement, malware and some kind of phishing emails generally have a more complex structure, including images and/or attachments, which makes the message size to noticeably grow. "Attachment Number", "Attachment Size" and "Attachment Type" are structural features mainly used to distinguish between the attachment of malware emails and those of advertisement and phishing emails, which attach to the email images for a correct visualization. The "Number of Images" in an email determines the global look of the message. Images are typical of some advertisement emails and phishing ones. Finally three features are used for the analysis of the subject. For example, some advertisement emails use several one-character words or non ASCII characters in emails to deceive typical spam detection techniques based on keywords [22]. It is worth noting that rarely non ASCII characters are used in phishing emails, to make them look more legit. Moreover, some fraud and phishing emails send deceiving mail subject with the "Re": or "Fwd": keyword to look like part of a conversation triggered by the victim. Furthermore, some fraud emails are characterized by the difference between the email "Language" and the "Subject Language". Many scam emails are, in fact, translated through automatic software which ignore the subject, causing this language duality.

3.3 DWS Classification Workflow

After the email features have been extracted, the resulting feature vectors are given as input to the DWS classification workflow. This process aims at dividing the unclassified spam emails in campaign and label them through a classifier

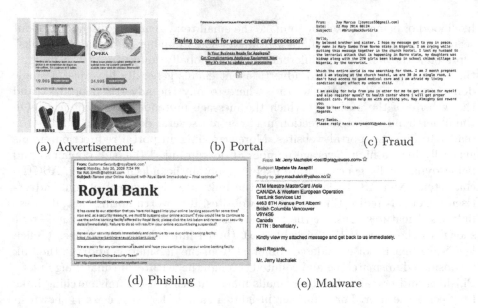

(a) Advertisement   (b) Portal   (c) Fraud

(d) Phishing   (e) Malware

Fig. 1. Spam emails representing five categories of spammer goals.

trained on the fly. The workflow is depicted in Fig. 2. The main part of the workflow is aimed at generating a valid training set from the dataset of unclassified emails, applying hierarchical clustering algorithm to divide email in campaigns (step 1 in Fig. 2). The chosen algorithm, named *Categorical Clustering Tree* (CCTree) generates a tree-like structure (step 2) which is exploited to associate a campaign to each email coming from a small dataset of labeled emails. The campaign receives the label of the email associated to it (step 3). Thus, this set of campaigns is used as training set for a classifier (step 4), successively used to label all the remaining campaigns (steps 5 and 6).

In the following the six steps of the DWS workflow are described in detail.

Phase 1: Clustering Spam Emails into Campaigns. The first step performed by the DWS framework is to divide large amounts of unclassified spam emails (constituting the set $\mathcal{D}$) into smaller groups of similar messages (steps 1 and 2 in Fig. 2). Emails are clustered by structural similarity exploiting the CCTree algorithm.

CCTree Algorithm: CCTree is a categorical clustering algorithm, constructed iteratively through a decision tree-like structure. The root of the CCTree contains all the elements to be clustered. Each element is described through a set of *categorical* attributes, such as the *Language* of a message. Being categorical each attribute may assume a finite set of discrete values, constituting its domain. For example the attribute *Language* may have as domain: {*English, French, Spanish*}. At each step, a new level of the tree is generated by splitting the nodes of the previous levels, when they are not homogeneous enough. *Shannon Entropy* [23] is used both to define a homogeneity measure called *node purity*, and to select

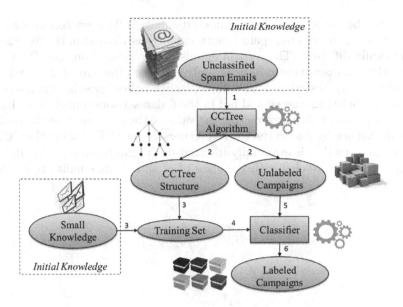

Fig. 2. DWS Workflow.

the attribute used to split a node. In particular non-leaf nodes are divided on the base of the attribute yielding the maximum value for Shannon entropy. The separation is represented through a branch for each possible outcome of the specific attribute. Each branch or edge extracted from parent node is labeled with the selected feature which directs data to the child node. Finally the leaves of the tree are the desired clusters. We refer the reader to [24] for details on the CCTree algorithm.

The CCTree algorithm has already proven to be effective in clustering spam emails into campaigns, as shown in [25]. When used on large dataset with the same set of features presented in Sect. 3.2, the CCTree algorithm generates highly homogeneous clusters, where all emails inside the same cluster belong to the same campaign. As other clustering algorithms which aim at maximizing the cluster homogeneity, the CCTree algorithm is likely to generate some clusters with only one element. Generally these clusters contain outlier emails, i.e. messages not belonging to any specific campaign. DWS discards these clusters not using them in the following steps of algorithm.

Phase 2: Training Set Generation. In order to label the campaigns, it is necessary to train a classifier to recognize emails coming from the five predefined spam classes (steps 3 and 4 in Fig. 2). To this end, it is necessary to provide to the classifier a good training set, which has to be representative of the reality in which the classifier has to operate. For this reason the training set will be extracted from the unclassified emails dataset $\mathcal{D}$ itself. More specifically, the CCTree structure generated in previous step is exploited to label a small number of generated spam campaigns. To this end, small number of campaigns are labeled with the use of a small set of labeled emails $\mathcal{C}$. This set contains a small number of manually selected spam emails, equally distributed in the five classes, all structurally different. These spam emails do not come from the $\mathcal{D}$ set. The emails in the $\mathcal{C}$ dataset have to be accurately chosen on the base of the email that investigator are interested in. For example, Italian police investigators interested in following a phishing case should put in the $\mathcal{C}$ dataset some emails with Italian text and bank names. After extracting the value of the features from the email in $\mathcal{C}$, they are fed one by one to the CCTree generated on $\mathcal{D}$. Following the CCTree structure each email c_i is eventually inserted in the campaign C_j (Fig. 3). Thus the campaign C_j is labeled with the class of c_i and all its emails are added to the training set.

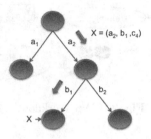

Fig. 3. Insert new instance X in a CCTree

If the same spam campaign is reached by two or more emails of different classes, the campaign is discarded and the emails are re-evaluated to be sent to other campaigns. It is worth noting that such an event is unlikely due to the high homogeneity of the clusters generated through CCTree. Furthermore, in the event that an email in $\mathcal{C}$ does not reach to any campaign, i.e. a specific attribute value of the email is not present in the CCTree, the email is inserted in the more similar campaign. To this end, the node purity of each campaign is calculated before and after the insertion of the email c_i. The email is thus assigned to the campaign in which the difference between the two purities, weighted by the number of elements, is lesser.

Phase 3: Labeling Spam Campaigns. Feeding the training set to the classifier, we are able to classify all remaining campaigns generated by the CCTree (steps 5 and 6 in Fig. 2). To this end, each campaign resulted from CCTree is given to the classifier. The classifier labels each email of received campaign on the base of spammer purpose. Under two conditions DWS considers a spam campaign as non classified. Firstly, it is possible that emails belonging to the same campaign receive different labels, e.g. phishing and portal redirection. In such a case, calling as "majority class" the label with more emails in the cluster, the campaign is considered non classified if the emails of the majority class amount to less than 90 % of all the emails in the campaign. The second condition is instead related to the *prediction error* reported by the classifier on each element of a campaign. The predicted error, computed as $1 - P(e_i \in \Omega_j)$, where $P(e_i \in \Omega_j)$ is the probability that the element e_i belongs to the class Ω_j, i.e. the label assigned to the element e_i. DWS framework considers a campaign as non classified, if the average predicted error is more than 30 %. If the non classified campaigns are a consistent percentage, it is possible to restart the classification process running the CCTree algorithm with tighter criteria for node purity.

4   Results

This section presents the experimental results of the DWS framework. First we discuss the classifier selection process, exploiting two small datasets of manually labeled spam emails. Afterward, we present the results for a real use case of the DWS framework on a recent dataset of spam emails.

4.1   Classifier Selection

In this first set of experiments we compare the performance of three different classifiers. To this end, two sets of real spam emails are provided to be used as training and test sets. These two datasets are extracted from emails collected by the untroubled honeypot [1] in February and January 2015. The emails have been manually analyzed and labeled for standard supervised learning classification and performance evaluation. The manual analysis and labeling process has been performed rigorously analyzing text and images, and following the links in each email. Only the emails for which the discovered class was *certain* have been inserted to the datasets. For a spam email, the label is certain if it matches the label description given in Sect. 3.1 and the label is verified through manual analysis. For example, Portal Redirection emails are *certainly* labeled if the links really redirect to a portal website. The first dataset, used as training set, is made of 160 spam emails, the second one, used as test set, is made of 80 emails.

Experiments have been run on all the classifiers offered by the WEKA library to classify categorical data. For the sake of brevity and clarity we only report the classifier with the better results for each classifier group. More specifically, the chosen classifiers are the K-Star from the *Lazy* group, the Random Tree Forest from the *Tree* group and the Bayes Network from the *NaiveBayes* group. Among these three classifiers, the best one has been used by the DWS framework.

Dataset Dimensioning: The process of manual analysis and labeling is time consuming. However, it is necessary to have a dataset well balanced, without duplicates and representative of the five classes, needed to correctly assess classifier performances. Given the complexity of manual analysis procedure, it is not possible to choose training and testing set of extremely large dimension. Thus, standard dimensioning techniques have been used, for both training and testing set. A general rule to assess the minimum size for a training set is to dimension it as six times the number of used features [27]. It is worth noting that the training set of 160 elements already matches this condition ($6 \times 21 < 160$). However, in multi-class problem, the dimension of data should provide well result in terms

Table 2. Classification results evaluated with K-fold validation on training set.

Algorithm	K-star	RandomForest	BayesNet
True Positive Rate	0.956	0.937	0.95
False Positive Rate	0.01	0.019	0.013
Area Under Curve	0.996	0.992	0.996

of sensitivity and specificity, i.e. true positive rate (TPR) and (1 - false positive rate (FPR)) respectively, when K-fold validation is applied [4]. This must be done keeping balanced the relative frequencies of data in various classes. As shown in the following, the provided testing set returns for K-fold validation a value of Receiver Operating Characteristic's Area Under Curve (ROC-AUC or AUC for short) higher than 90 % for all tested classifiers.

Concerning the test set, it is important the null intersection with the training set and the balanced relative frequencies of the various classes. In [4], the minimum size for a testing set to provide meaningful results, in a problem of classification with five classes, is estimated to be 75, which is smaller than the test set of 80 spam emails provided.

Classification Results: We report now the classification results for the three tested classifiers on the two aforementioned datasets. The first set has been used as training set for the classifiers. According to the methodology in [4], a first performance evaluation has been done through the K-fold (K=5) validation method, classifying the data for K times using each time $K - 1/K$ of the dataset as training set and the remaining elements as testing set. The used evaluation indexes are the True Positive Rate (TPR), False Positive Rate (FPR) and Receiver Operating Characteristic Area Under Curve (ROC-AUC or simply AUC). The AUC is defined in the interval $[0, 1]$ and measures the performance of a classifier at the variation of a threshold parameter T, proper of the classifier itself, according to the following formula:

$$AUC = \int_{-\infty}^{\infty} TPR(T) \cdot FPR'(T)dT$$

where $FPR' = 1 - FPR$. When the value of AUC is equal to 1, the classifier is considered "good" for the classification problem.

Table 2 reports TPR, FPR and AUC of the three classifiers, i.e. the number of correctly classified elements between the five classes for both the K-fold test on the first dataset (160 spam emails). As shown, all classifiers return an accuracy higher than 90 %. Afterward, the whole first dataset has been used to train the three classifiers, whilst the second dataset has been used as test set. Table 3 reports the detailed classification results, where classifiers are trained with training set (160 emails) and evaluated with test set (80 emails). The result is reported on the classes for TPR, FPR and AUC. For a further insight, we report in Fig. 4 the comparison of the ROC curves of the three classifiers for the five classes,

Table 3. Classification results evaluated on test set.

Algorithm	K-star			RandomForest			BayesNet		
Measure	*TPR*	*FPR*	*AUC*	*TPR*	*FPR*	*AUC*	*TPR*	*FPR*	*AUC*
Advertisement	1.000	0.031	0.998	1.000	0.000	1.000	1.000	0.031	0.967
Portal	0.786	0.000	0.996	0.786	0.016	0.985	0.929	0.000	0.998
Fraud	1.000	0.016	0.992	1.000	0.016	0.951	1.000	0.016	0.928
Malware	0.938	0.016	0.995	0.938	0.016	0.908	0.938	0.016	0.957
Phishing	0.947	0.017	0.977	0.947	0.051	0.963	0.842	0.017	0.907
Average	0.9342	0.016	0.9916	0.9342	0.019	0.9614	0.9418	0.016	0.9514

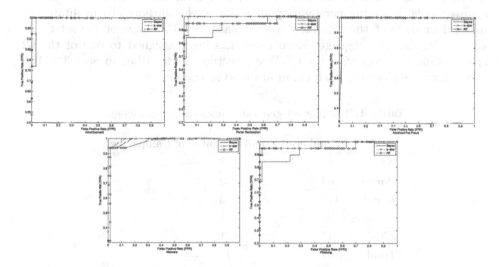

Fig. 4. ROC curves for the five classes labeling on test set.

measured on the test set. It is worth noting that in all cases the area under the ROC curve is close to 1, hence, in general the classifiers show good performances on the testing set for each class.

As can be observed in Table 2, on the average the K-star and Bayes Net classifiers give slightly better K-fold results. However, the K-star classifier yields the better results in terms of AUC in average, evaluated with test set (see Table 3). Therefore, K-star is the classifier used in the DWS framework.

4.2   DWS Application

The second set of experiments aims at assessing the capability of the framework to cluster and label large amounts of spam emails. To this end the DWS framework has been tested on set of 3230 recent spam emails. The spam emails have been extracted from the collection of the honeypot in [1], related to the first week of March 2015. The emails have been manually analyzed and labeled for performance analysis.

Phase 1: Clustering with CCTree: In the first step CCTree has been used to divide the emails in campaigns. The CCTree parameters have been chosen finding the optimal values for number of generated clusters and homogeneity, using the knee method described in [25]. 135 clusters have been generated of which 73 only contains one element. Generated clusters with a single element have not been considered. These emails are, in fact, outliers which do not belong to any spam campaign. The remaining 3149 emails divided in 62 clusters have been used for the following steps.

Phase 2: Training Set Generation: To generate the training set, we used a small dataset made of three representative emails for each of the five classes. These 15 emails have been manually selected from different datasets of real spam emails, including personal spam inbox of the authors. To facilitate the manual analysis of the classified spam emails, the 15 emails of the set C are written in English language. Each email has been assigned to one of the 62 spam campaigns, following the CCTree structure, as described in Sect. 3.3. The campaigns associated to each email are used as training set.

Table 4. Training set generated from small knowledge.

Class	Number of Emails	Number of Campaigns
Advert.	29	2
Portal	66	3
Fraud	113	3
Malware	27	1
Phishing	17	1
Total	252	10

The generated training set (Table 4) is composed of 252 emails, contained in 10 campaigns. It is worth noting that the 15 emails have not been added to the associated cluster after the CCTree classification, to not alter the decision on the following emails.

Phase 3: Labeling Spam Campaigns: After training the classifier with the generated training set, we label the remaining (52 out of 62) unlabeled spam campaigns of CCTree. The classification results are reported in Table 5. The table reports for each class the amount of campaigns and corresponding email classified correctly or incorrectly. Moreover, we report for the emails the statistics on TPR, FPR and Accuracy (i.e., the ratio of correctly classified elements). The global accuracy, (last row of the table) is of 97,82 %. However, we point out that, due to the conditions on predicted error reported in Subsect. 3.3, 8 campaigns out of 62, containing 344 spam emails are considered unclassified. For the sake of accuracy, considering these 8 campaigns as misclassified, the total accuracy for emails on the dataset is of 87,14 %. The accuracy is in line with previous works on classification emails into phishing and ham [6,8,11].

Table 5. DWS classification results for the labeled spam campaigns.

Class	Campaigns		Emails		TPR	FPR	Accuracy
	Correct	Wrong	Correct	Wrong			
Advert.	5	0	137	0	1	0	1
Portal	26	0	1331	0	1	0.03	0.9935
Fraud	10	2	1032	43	0.96	0.01	0.9788
Malware	3	0	31	0	1	1	1
Phishing	7	1	213	18	0.915	0	0.994
Total	51	3	2744	61	0.975	0.008	0.9782

Concerning the 8 non classified campaigns, 3 campaigns containing 68 spam emails were correctly labeled as portal. However, they are considered unclassified since the average predicted error is higher than 30 % in all the 3 campaigns. 4 campaigns containing 258 spam emails have been classified as phishing. 2 of them with 116 messages, were correctly identified but did not match the predicted error condition. The other 2 campaigns have been incorrectly classified as fraud. However, they are considered as unclassified due to high predicted error. The last campaign with 18 elements is in the advertisement class, but incorrectly classified as fraud, though the predicted error condition again is not matched. It is worth noting how the condition on predicted error is useful in increasing the overall accuracy on classified data.

From Table 5 it is possible to infer what a large portion of spam messages belongs to portal and fraud classes. Even if these preliminary results are related to a relatively small dataset, they are indicative of the current trend of spam emails distribution, which may provide to the spammer the greatest result with the smallest risk.

5   Conclusion and Future Directions

Spam emails constitute a constant threat to both companies and private users. Not only these emails are unwanted, occupy storage space and need time to be deleted, also they have become vectors of security threat and used to perform cybercrimes, such as phishing and malware distribution. In this paper, we have presented a framework, named DWS, for analysis of large amounts of spam emails collected through honeypots. We argue that DWS can provide a helpful tool for police and investigators in forensic analysis of spam emails. In fact DWS automatically clusters and classifies large amount of spam emails in labeled campaigns, to eventually help investigator to focus on campaigns for a specific cybercrime, filtering out the non-interesting spam emails. Moreover DWS is self learning, not requiring any preexistent knowledge of the dataset to analyze.

Preliminary tests performed on a first dataset of more than 3200 emails showed a good accuracy of the framework. More extensive experiments on larger datasets have been planned as future work, including performance analysis and an eventual refinement of the spam campaign labels, to include sub-groups such as *pharmacy-advertisement* or additional classes such as *propaganda*. To improve the effectiveness of DWS, we plan to detect and add more email representative features. Furthermore, application of dataset balancing techniques could be used to increase the quality of the generated training set.

References

1. Spam archive. http://untroubled.org/spam/
2. Federal trade commission (2009). http://www.consumer.ftc.gov
3. Almomani, A., Gupta, B.B., Atawneh, S., Meulenberg, A., Almomani, E.: A survey of phishing email filtering techniques. IEEE Commun. Surv. Tutorials **15**(4), 2070–2090 (2013)
4. Beleites, C., Neugebauer, U., Bocklitz, T., Krafft, C., Popp, J.: Sample size planning for classification models. Anal. Chim. Acta **760**, 25–33 (2013)
5. Benczur, A.A., Csalogany, K., Sarlos, T., Uher, M.: Spamrank-fully automatic link spam detection work in progress. In: Proceedings of the First International Workshop on Adversarial Information Retrieval on the Web (2005)
6. Bergholz, A., PaaB, G., Reichartz, F., Strobel, S., Birlinghoven, S.: Improved phishing detection using model-based features. In: CEAS (2008)
7. Calais, P., Douglas, E.V.P., Dorgival, O.G., Wagner, M., Cristine, H., Klaus, S.: A campaign-based characterization of spamming strategies. In: CEAS (2008)
8. Chen, T.C., Stepan, T., Dick, S., Miller, J.: An anti-phishing system employing diffused information. ACM Trans. Inf. Syst. Secur. **16**(4), 16:1–16:31 (2014)
9. da Cruz Nassif, L., Hruschka, E.: Document clustering for forensic analysis: An approach for improving computer inspection. IEEE Trans. Inf. Forensics Secur. **8**(1), 46–54 (2013)
10. Dinh, S., Azeb, T., Fortin, F., Mouheb, D., Debbabi, M.: Spam campaign detection, analysis, and investigation. Digit. Invest. **12**(1), S12–S21 (2015)
11. Fette, I., Sadeh, N., Tomasic, A.: Learning to detect phishing emails. In: Proceedings of the 16th International Conference on World Wide Web, pp. 649–656. ACM (2007)
12. Gansterer, W.N., Pölz, D.: E-Mail classification for phishing defense. In: Boughanem, M., Berrut, C., Mothe, J., Soule-Dupuy, C. (eds.) ECIR 2009. LNCS, vol. 5478, pp. 449–460. Springer, Heidelberg (2009)
13. Gao, H., Hu, J., Wilson, C., Li, Z., Chen, Y., Zhao, B.: Detecting and characterizing social spam campaigns. In: Proceedings of the 10th ACM SIGCOMM Conference on Internet Measurement, IMC 2010, pp. 35–47. ACM, New York (2010)
14. Hadjidj, R., Debbabi, M., Lounis, H., Iqbal, F., Szporer, A., Benredjem, D.: Towards an integrated e-mail forensic analysis framework. Digit. Invest. **5**(34), 124–137 (2009)
15. Henderson, L.: Crimes of Persuasion: Schemes, Scams, Frauds : how Con Artists Will Steal Your Savings and Inheritance Through Telemarketing Fraud Investment Schemes and Consumer Scams. Coyoto Ridge Press, Azilda (2003)
16. Kanich, C., Kreibich, C., Levchenko, K., Enright, B., Voelker, G.M., Paxson, V., Savage, S.: Spamalytics: An empirical analysis of spam marketing conversion. In: Proceedings of the 15th ACM Conference on Computer and Communications Security, CCS 2008, pp. 3–14. ACM, New York (2008)

17. Kanich, C., Weavery, N., McCoy, D., Halvorson, T., Kreibichy, C., Levchenko, K., Paxson, V., Voelker, G., Savage, S.: Show me the money: Characterizing spam-advertised revenue. In: Proceedings of the 20th USENIX Conference on Security, SEC 2011. USENIX Association, Berkeley (2011)
18. Kreibich, C., Kanich, C., Levchenko, K., Enright, B., Voelker, G., Paxson, V., Savage, S.: Spamcraft: An inside look at spam campaign orchestration. In: Proceedings of the 2nd USENIX Conference on Large-scale Exploits and Emergent Threats: Botnets, Spyware, Worms, and More, LEET 2009. USENIX Association, Berkeley (2009)
19. Labs, M.A.: Mcafee threats report: 2015 (2015). http://mcafee.com
20. Narang, S.: Cryptolocker alert: Millions in the uk targeted in mass spam campaign. (2013). http://www.symantec.com/connect/tr/blogs/cryptolocker-alert-millions-uk-targeted-mass-spam-campaign
21. Pathak, A., Qian, F., Hu, Y.C., Mao, Z.M., Ranjan, S.: Botnet spam campaigns can be long lasting: Evidence, implications, and analysis. SIGMETRICS Perform. Eval. Rev. **37**(1), 13–24 (2009)
22. Seewald, A.K.: An evaluation of naive bayes variants in content-based learning for spam filtering. Intell. Data Anal. **11**(5), 497–524 (2007)
23. Shannon, C.E.: A mathematical theory of communication. SIGMOBILE Mob. Comput. Commun. Rev. **5**(1), 3–55 (2001)
24. Sheikhalishahi, M., Mejri, M., Tawbi, N.: Clustering spam emails into campaigns. In: 1st International Conference on Information Systems Security and Privacy (2015)
25. Sheikhalishahi, M., Saracino, A., Mejri, M., Tawbi, N., Martinelli, F.: Fast and effective clustering of spam emails based on structural similarity (2015). http://goo.gl/zlzHNl
26. Tillman, K.: How many internet connections are in the world? right. now (2013). http://blogs.cisco.com/news/cisco-connections-counter
27. Viola, P., Jones, M.: Rapid object detection using a boosted cascade of simple features. In: Proceedings of the 2001 IEEE Computer Society Conference on Computer Vision and Pattern Recognition, CVPR 2001, vol. 1, pp. I-511–I-518 (2001)
28. Wang, D., Irani, D., Pu, C.: A study on evolution of email spam over fifteen years. In: 2013 9th International Conference on Collaborative Computing: Networking, Applications and Worksharing (Collaboratecom), pp. 1–10, October 2013
29. Wei, C., Sprague, A., Warner, G., Skjellum, A.: Mining spam email to identify common origins for forensic application. In: Proceedings of the 2008 ACM symposium on Applied computing, SAC 2008, pp. 1433–1437. ACM, New York (2008)

Integrating Privacy and Safety Criteria into Planning Tasks

Anna Lavygina, Alessandra Russo, and Naranker Dulay$^{(\boxtimes)}$

Department of Computing, Imperial College London, London SW7 2RH, UK
{a.lavygina,a.russo,n.dulay}@imperial.ac.uk

Abstract. In this paper we describe a new approach that uses multi-criteria decision making and the analytic hierarchy process (AHP) for integrating privacy and safety criteria into planning tasks. We apply the approach to the journey planning using two criteria: (i) a willingness-to-share-data (WSD) metric to control data disclosure, and (ii) the number of unsatisfied safety preferences (USP) metric to mitigate risky journeys.

Keywords: Personal safety · Information privacy · Multi-criteria decision making · Analytic hierarchy process · Smart city applications

1 Introduction

Smart cities aim to increase the quality of life in cities by addressing problems such as traffic congestion, air pollution, and energy consumption. To help achieve this, information and communication technologies need to be integrated into the infrastructure of the city, to improve its functionality and efficiency [8,20,23]. In this paper we consider the provision of transportation services that provide flexible transportation options to efficiently move people around the city. The challenge is to be able to provide individual journeys that are efficient in terms of city-level parameters (e.g. energy consumptions, environmental impact) as well as to satisfy individual preferences and constraints. The latter are typically modelled using a utility function defined over the cost and duration of journeys, and the preferred modes of transportation. However, there can be other considerations, such as, seeking journeys suitable for people with special needs (e.g. the elderly, disabled), avoiding particular areas of the cities (e.g. with a high crime rate, crowded or uncrowded, areas with high pollution levels), not wanting to be tracked (e.g. by video surveillance cameras, MAC address tracking by public WiFi hotspots), not wanting to disclose unnecessary private data (e.g. date of birth to service providers). Such preferences may also be contextual - only apply in particular situations. The aim is to be able to fuse context information with user requirements and then to use the resulting knowledge to make *smart* (automatic or semi-automatic) decisions for users.

Our overall contribution is to demonstrate that the analytic hierarchy process (AHP), a multi-criteria decision making approach, is able to integrate privacy

S. Foresti (Ed.): STM 2015, LNCS 9331, pp. 20–36, 2015.
DOI: 10.1007/978-3-319-24858-5_2

and safety[1] criteria into planning tasks. We demonstrate this for the classical journey planning task taking into account the traditional utility of the journey plus two additional user-defined criteria, newly introduced in this paper: (i) a novel willingness-to-share-data (WSD) metric that reflects the users perceived sensitivity of their personal data and (ii) the number of unsatisfied safety preferences (USP) which allows users to minimize safety risks.

This paper is organised as follows. Section 2 describes related work. Section 3 outlines our approach to decision making for planning tasks incorporating privacy and safety criteria. Section 4 introduces AHP and shows how to apply it to the journey planning task. The decision making criteria we use (utility, USP, and WSD) are discussed in Sect. 5. This section also provides detailed examples of setting up the criteria and evaluating them for the journey planning task. Section 6 describes a study on how different ratios of the importance of criteria affect the final ranking of journey alternatives. Possible extentions and modifications of the USP and WSD criteria are discussed in Sect. 7 . Finally, Sect. 8 concludes the paper and outlines our future work.

2 Related Work

Privacy and Safety in Smart Cities. Research related to privacy and safety of individuals in smart city services has focused on what the city infrastructure, technology and management can do to ensure an individual's privacy and safety. For example, utilising video surveillance systems to detect and identify abnormal activities, which can help to reduce the level of crime and speed up the response of emergency services [7,21].

In [12] quantitative risk assessment is used to support the design of physical security systems by optimizing the coverage of protection mechanisms. The features that influence fear of crime (e.g. low lighting, desolation, lack of opportunities for surveillance by the general public, etc.), and the ways of reducing the levels of crime and fear of crime (e.g. criminal justice systems, problem-oriented policing, environmental criminology, situational crime prevention) are identified and discussed in [16]. These are important problems for cities to solve. However, they all address the problem "in the large", by reducing the overall levels of crime and harassment (hence, the risk and fear to become a victim), rather then helping individuals to satisfy their personal safety requirements which may differ from those of the city in kind and/or in degree.

Ferraz and Ferraz [11] identify nine risks associated with information sharing including access to information from applications, information tracking, citizen tracking, and user/citizen data loss. Martinez-Balleste et al. [19] define a citizens' privacy model based on five dimensions: identity privacy, query privacy, location privacy, footprint privacy and owner privacy. For each dimension they show how existing privacy enhancing techniques (e.g. statistical disclosure control, private information retrieval, privacy-preserving data mining, etc.) can be used

---

[1] We use term safety to encompass physical security, physiological harm (pollution), physical harm (attack), psychological fear (crowding), etc.

to maintain citizens' privacy. De Cristofaro and Di Pietro [9] focus on query privacy in urban sensing systems. These papers focus on protecting information that is already collected from sensors, users and mobile devices, rather than controlling which data can be sensed, collected, or shared at the first place. The need for usable privacy policies and user interfaces that maximise user control based on their perception of privacy risks is highlighted in [6].

Criteria for Journey Planning. There are a growing number of studies dedicated to understanding travellers' attitudes and criteria for evaluating service quality from a user's perspective (see e.g. [1,5,10,18]). Eboli and Mazzulla [10] report on the importance of service quality indicators, such as reliability, punctuality, pollution, and comfort. In [18] 29 different criteria of users perception of a bus service are grouped into service design, access to service, operation, information and facilities, ticket price and safety. Lynch and Atkins discovered high levels of perceived insecurity for walking at night, in parks and subways and when waiting for public transport services in isolated areas [17] . These studies highlight the importance of user's perceptions of city services. However, none of them show how the considered criteria can be applied in practice, for the evaluation and selection of journeys in a given context. Existing journey planners do not allow any other criteria apart from the preferred modes of transport (e.g. bus, metro), maximum walking time or the need for step free access. Furthermore, they only use these criteria to filter out journey alternatives and rank journeys by travel time only.

The use of utility functions for evaluating and ranking journeys is explored in [2,15] where different types of utility functions are used based on travel time and cost. Kim et al. [14] proposes a more complex utility function based on various latent variables, such as comfort, convenience, environmental preferences, that is used for building a general choice modelling framework for analysing travellers' choice behaviour rather than planning of an individual journey.

3 Approach

Our approach accounts for both privacy and safety criteria in the decision making process for planning tasks, particularly for journey planning. This approach allows the user to address two crucial aspects: (i) what personal data is sensitive and the degree of data sensitivity, and (ii) what situations are consider as safe/unsafe and which level of safety should be achieved.

The approach can be generalised into any user privacy and safety criteria and any planning task. Our overall approach is shown in Fig. 1. Given a user query and a set of criteria, a set of alternative plans satisfying the query are generated by a planner and passed to ranking process that evaluates all generated plans according to the criteria, for example, the utility of the plan, safety, privacy, reliability, comfort. After ranking, an ordered list of the plans is returned to the user alongside values of metrics that represent the quality of the plans and that can help the user (or user's agent) to select or reject plans.

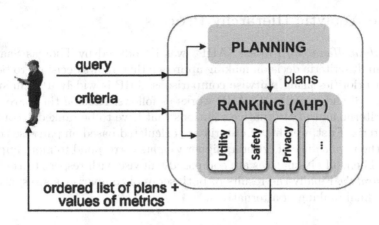

Fig. 1. Multi-criteria planning

As an example, consider a user query "Find the best journey from A to B" and a set of privacy and safety criteria defined by the user. Based on the request, the journey planner generates a list of alternative journeys from A to B that fulfil the user query. We then use AHP to evaluate and rank journey alternatives according to the following three criteria:

- *utility* of a journey based on the time and ticket price (see Sect. 5.1)
- *number of unsatisfied safety preferences* (USP) that allows users to avoid areas with high-crime rates, crowded buses, providers with a bad safety record (see Sect. 5.2)
- *value of a willingness-to-share-data metric* (WSD) that reflects willingness of a customer to share personal information required by a service provider in order to provide a requested service (see Sect. 5.3)

Sections 5.2 and 5.3 also provide the details on how users can define privacy and safety criteria, respectively.

This problem can be tackled using composite objective functions as the weighted sum of all objectives. However, this approach have two major disadvantages. First, solutions are very dependent on the weight-vectors used and in different situations different weight-vectors have to be used [24]. Secondly the values of composite objective functions are often difficult to interpret for complex problems with many criteria. We address these issues by considering all criteria separately and using AHP (see Sect. 4) for ranking alternative solutions. Using AHP in our approach provides (i) means of deriving the weights of the criteria from a series of pairwise comparisons that are more understandable by users - this is importance because the overall ranking is dependent on the relative importance of criteria w.r.t. to the goal (ii) tolerance to minor inconsistencies in defining criteria importance, (iii) the ability to deal with both qualitative and quantitative criteria based on either subjective user opinion or actual measurements, (iv) an elegant method to incorporate diverse criteria, such as privacy, safety, comfort level and punctuality.

4 The Analytic Hierarchy Process

The *Analytic Hierarchy Process* (AHP) was introduced by Thomas Saaty [22] and is a multi-criteria decision making approach that allows decisions to be made based on priorities using pairwise comparisons. AHP is widely used in supplier selection [13] and logistics [4]. AHP works as follows: Assume there are n evaluation criteria, and m alternative solutions that have to be ranked according to these criteria. First, weights of criteria are calculated based on pairwise comparisons of the importance of criteria; higher weights correspond to more important criteria. Then, all alternatives are compared pairwise with respect to *each criterion separately*. Finally the results of both series of comparisons are synthesised to give a final ranking of alternatives.

4.1 AHP Hierarchy

The first step in AHP involves decomposition of the problem into a hierarchy of criteria and alternatives. In the AHP hierarchy for planning a journey (see Fig. 2), the goal is to choose the best journey. We consider the following criteria for decision making:

- utility of a journey for the user (to be maximized);
- number of unsatisfied safety preferences (USP) (to be minimized);
- value of the willingness-to-share-data (WSD) metric (to be minimized).

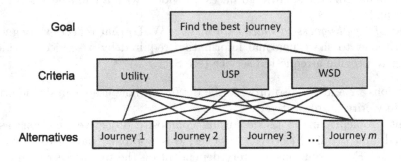

Fig. 2. AHP hierarchy for journey selection.

4.2 Relative Importance of Criteria

To capture the relative importance of criteria, a matrix **C** of pairwise comparisons of criteria is created. The matrix $\mathbf{C} = (c_{jk})$ is of dimension $n \times n$, where n is a number of criteria and each element c_{jk} is the relative importance of the jth criterion to the kth criterion with respect to the goal. The elements c_{jk} satisfy the constraint

$$c_{jk} \times c_{kj} = 1, \tag{1}$$

Table 1. Scale of relative importance of criteria

Level of relative importance	Definition
1	Equal importance
3	Moderate importance
5	Essential or strong importance
7	Very strong importance
9	Extreme importance (the highest possible)
2, 4, 6, 8	Intermediate values
1.1, 1.2,1.3,	Very close importance

where $c_{jk} > 1$ indicates that the jth criterion is more important than the kth criterion. Consequently, in the case where the jth criterion is less important than kth criterion, we have $c_{jk} < 1$, and if the two criteria are indifferent we have $c_{jk} = 1$; which also implies that $c_{jj} = 1$. Saaty [22] suggests a numerical scale between 1 and 9 to express the importance of one criterion over another (see Table 1). Pairwise comparisons can be done by the user when defining criteria for journey planning.

A useful advantage of AHP is that it tolerates minor inconsistencies in the comparisons. For example, assume we have three criteria where criterion #1 is slightly more important than criterion #2, and criterion #2 is slightly more important than criterion #3. If the user asserts that criterion #1 is much more important than criterion #3, then these comparisons are consistent. A minor inconsistency can be induced if the user asserts that criterion #1 is slightly more important then criterion #3; AHP would tolerate this inconsistency. An unacceptable inconsistency would be one where the user asserts that criteria #1 and #3 are indifferent.

Once the criterion importance matrix $\mathbf{C}$ has been established, it can be used to derive the *criteria weight vector* $\mathbf{w}$ using the equation

$$w_j = \frac{\sum_{l=1}^{n} \bar{c}_{jl}}{n} \qquad (2)$$

where $\bar{c}_{jl} = c_{jl} / \sum_{k=1}^{n} c_{kl}$ is the normalized relative importance.

4.3   Ranking of Alternative Plans

At this step we have to score all generated alternative plans with respect to *each criteria*. To derive these scores we calculate a matrix of pairwise comparisons of alternative plans $\mathbf{B}^j = (b_{ih}^j)$, where b_{ih}^j is the evaluation of the ith alternative plan compared to the hth alternative plan with respect to the jth criterion.

Let x_i^j and x_h^j be the values of the jth criterion for alternative plans i and h respectively.

If the jth criterion has to be maximized, then for all alternative plans i and h with $x_i^j \geq x_h^j$, the element b_{ih}^j can be computed as

$$b_{ih}^j = 8\frac{x_i^j - x_h^j}{x_{max}^j - x_{min}^j} + 1 \tag{3}$$

where x_{max}^j and x_{min}^j are the maximum and minimum values of the jth criterion.

Similarly, if the jth criterion has to be minimized, then for all alternative plans i and h with $x_i^j \leq x_h^j$, the element b_{ih}^j can be computed as

$$b_{ih}^j = 8\frac{x_h^j - x_i^j}{x_{max}^j - x_{min}^j} + 1 \tag{4}$$

Similar to the criterion importance matrix $\mathbf{C}$, the elements of alternative comparison matrix $\mathbf{B}^j$ have to satisfy the constraint $b_{ih}^j \times b_{hi}^j = 1$.

Having obtained $\mathbf{B}^j$, we can now calculate the score vectors $\mathbf{y}^j$ for alternative plans with respect to each criterion $j \in [1, n]$. This calculation is done using Eq. 2 but replacing the terms c_{jl} with b_{ih}^j.

The score vectors are then used to create a score matrix $\mathbf{Y} = [\mathbf{y}^1, \mathbf{y}^2, ..., \mathbf{y}^n]$, from which a plan ranking vector $\mathbf{v} = (v_i), i \in [1, n]$, is calculated by

$$\mathbf{v} = \mathbf{Y} \cdot \mathbf{w} \tag{5}$$

The greater the value v_i, the more preferable the ith alternative plan is.

5   Criteria

We demonstrate application of our approach for the classic journey planning task. In this section we describe three criteria we use to evaluate journey alternatives generated by the journey planner: utility of a journey alternative, the USP and WSD metrics. Detailed examples of setting up the privacy and safety preferences and evaluating the USP and WSD criteria are also included.

5.1   Utility

Journey planners typically rank journeys based on either journey time, walking distance or number of changes. For example, in [2] the authors use a utility function for journey ranking and selection: for each journey i generated by the journey planner, the utility function value is calculated based on the total travel time and ticket price:

$$u_i(t, T_i, c_i) = \frac{e^{(t-T_i)/60}}{e^{|t-T_i|/60 + c_i/100}} \tag{6}$$

where $u_i(t, T_i, c_i) \in [0, 1]$ is the utility, t the desired travel time as defined by the user, T_i the travel time of the ith journey, and c_i the total cost of the ith journey. The objective is to find a journey with the highest utility. In this formula if $t - T_i > 0$ (i.e. the traveler arrives in time), then the utility is constant with respect to T_i. If $t - T_i < 0$ (i.e. the traveler arrives late), then the travelers utility decreases as T_i increases.

In this paper we introduce a penalty for longer journeys even if the traveler is on time, hence our revised utility is:

$$u_i(t, T_i, c_i) = \frac{1}{e^{T_i/t+c_i/100}} \tag{7}$$

Of course, one could devise a more complex utility function. However, we kept the function simple, because AHP uses pairwise comparisons of the journey alternatives with respect to this criteria rather than a very accurate value of the utility function for each alternative plan.

5.2 Unsatisfied Safety Preferences (USP)

Consider the following. Alice is traveling late at night. Suppose that there are two alternative journeys with similar ticket price and travel time, but the first alternative includes walking through an undesirable area. If Alice is aware of this area and concerned about her safety, then she is likely to choose the second option. However, if Alice is not familiar with this area, then she might choose the undesirable area but would have preferred the other alternative.

To address this kind of requirement we propose to include personal safety preferences to other requirements the user can set when starting or changing a journey. For example:

(i) avoiding areas with high-crime rates, or are sparsely-lit or sparsely-populated,
(ii) avoiding using trains or buses carrying a low number of passengers for fear of attack,
(iii) avoiding crowded areas or crowded trains or buses,
(iv) avoiding service providers with poor safety records or a bad reputation.

All solutions generated by the journey planner have to be evaluated with respect to all safety preferences defined by the user. The *number of unsatisfied safety preferences* (USP) is then used as an *criterion* in the ranking of alternative plans and choice of a journey.

Example 1

Alice arranges a dinner with a friend for 8pm next to Paddington train station. Because she is travelling alone, she wants to avoid crowded areas and crowded transportation as well as sparsely populated areas and transportation. She sends a request to the Journey Planning Service with the following data:

- Starting point: : 180 Queen's Gate, London SW7 2RH, UK
- Destination point: Paddington Station, Praed St, London W2, UK
- Arrival time: 20:00
- Safety preferences: (i) Avoid sparsely populated areas & transport (ii) Avoid crowded areas & transport

Table 2. List of journey alternatives

Alternative 1 7:28 PM–7:51 PM 23 min, cost £3.80	(1) walk – 5 min – Hixley Bldg to Royal Albert Hall (2) bus 9 – 5 min – Royal Albert Hall to High Street Kensington (3) walk – 3 min – from High Street Kensington to High Street Kensington Underground station (4) the Underground, Circle line – 6 min – High Street Kensington Underground station to Paddington
Alternative 2 7:28 PM–7:57 PM 29 min, cost:£1.50	(1) walk – 2 min – Huxley Bld to Imperial College Elvaston Pl (2) bus 70 – 17 min – Imperial College Elvaston Pl to Queensway Westbourne Grove (3) walk – 10 min – Queensway Westbourne Grove to Paddington Station
Alternative 3 27 min, cost: £0	(1) walk – 27 min – from Huxley Bld to Paddington Station via Queens Gate
Alternative 4 30 min, cost: £0	(1) walk – 30 min – from Huxley Bld to Paddington Station via Queens Gate
Alternative 5 27 min, cost: £0	(1) walk – 27 min – from Huxley Bld to Paddington Station via Queens Gate
Alternative 6 13 min, cost: £0	(1) cycle – 13 min – from Huxley Bld to Paddington Station via Broad Walk
Alternative 7 13 min, cost: £0	(1) cycle – 13 min – from Huxley Bld to Paddington Station via W Carriage
Alternative 8 9 min, cost: £11	(1) taxi – from Huxley Bld to Paddington Station
Alternative 9 9 min, cost: £7–9	(1) Uber – from Huxley Bld to Paddington Station

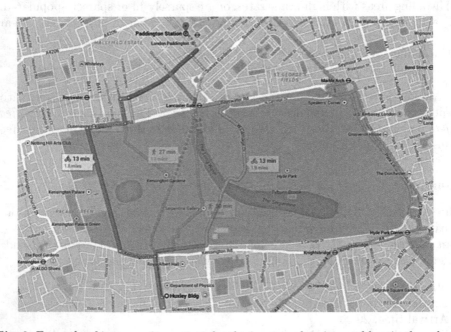

Fig. 3. Example of journey alternatives for the journey planning problem in the urban mobility scenario

We simulated the result of this request using Google Maps, taxi services and the Uber application. The generated list of journey alternatives is presented in Table 2.

Alternatives 1, 2, 7, 8 and 9 satisfy both safety preferences. Alternatives 3–6 do not satisfy "Avoiding sparsely populated areas/transport" as all of them are passing through a big park area (Kensington Gardens) as shown in Fig. 3. This area is sparsely populated at the time the request was made because it gets dark early at that time of the year. Hence, alternatives 1, 2, 7, 8 and 9 are preferable to alternatives 3–6 if satisfaction of safety preferences is important for Alice.

5.3   Willingness-to-Share-Data (WSD)

The willingness-to-share-data (WSD) metric is used to control the disclosure of personal data to others, e.g. to service providers. We define the sensitivity of personal data by how much a person values the data in case of a possible harm due to misuse, loss or disclosure by a recipient of the data, such as service provider. We allow different data attributes to be of different sensitivity (for example, a person can define an email address as less sensitive than a phone number or a postal address). Moreover, sensitivity may be dependent on a recipient: the user may trust some recipient to handle their data more than others, and thus may be more willing to provide it.

We define the sensitivity of a certain data attribute as a function $s : (a, p) \rightarrow [0, 1]$, where a is a data attribute and p is a recipient (service provider). Higher values of sensitivity correspond to data that the user prefers not to share.

Given the sensitivity levels for all personal data attributes defined by the user, we define a willingness-to-share-data (WSD) metric that indicates the sensitivity of the whole set of attributes requested by a service provider in order to complete a transaction when ordering a service. We propose the following metric:

$$d_c(\mathbf{a}, \mathbf{r}, p) = \frac{1}{m} \sum_{j=1}^{m} s(a_j, p) \times r_j \tag{8}$$

where $\mathbf{a} = (a_1, ..., a_m)$ is a vector of data attributes (e.g. name, address, etc.) that can be possibly requested by a service provider p in order to provide a service, and $s(a_j, p) \in [0, 1]$ is a user-specified level of sensitivity of sharing information related to the jth data attribute with a provider p. The vector $\mathbf{r} = (r_1, ..., r_m)$ represents the data request mask, and consists of values $r_j = 1$ if the jth data attribute is requested by a provider p, and $r_j = 0$ otherwise.

Users can define the sensitivity of their personal data by completing a form on a mobile application. For this the user has to select a degree of sensitivity ranging from "not sensitive" to "extremely sensitive" (see Table 3 for possible degrees of sensitivity) that are then translated to a value in the range [0,1]. For *each* information attribute, the user can assign a configuration of providers using *one* of the following options:

Table 3. Scale of data sensitivity

Sensitivity	Definition
0	not sensitive
0.25	slightly sensitive
0.5	sensitive
0.75	very sensitive
1	extremely sensitive

1. Apply a specified sensitivity level to all service providers.
2. Define *different* levels of sensitivity for two of the following categories of service providers based on a certain level of trust:
   - level of trust greater or equal to x;
   - level of trust lower than x;
   Levels of trust x are specified in the range $[0,1]$, where higher values correspond to more trustworthy service providers. The trustworthiness of each service provider is calculated based on feedback of all registered users. For the first category of service providers the level of sensitivity must be higher than for the second category.
3. Define a sensitivity level for a specified list of providers (the user has to create the list herself), and set a *different* sensitivity level for other service providers that do not belong to this list.

Note that the WSD metric can be used to express a user's preferences in the case where *data sharing is negotiable*. If the user does not want to share any data attributes, hard constraints need to be introduced. If a particular journey alternative contains any violation of these constraints, then it is discarded immediately.

Example 2

In this example we calculate the values of the WSD metric s for the scenario described in Example 1. Assume the data attributes $\mathbf{a} = (a_1, ..., a_m) = \{$name, date of birth, email, phone number, postal code, address, GPS location data, payment details$\}$ to be the personal data attributes that could possibly be requested. The following service providers p are available to fulfil Alice's request: the bus service, the Underground, taxis, and Uber. Suppose, regardless of the service provider p, Alice defines her date of birth, address and phone number as sensitive data, her phone number, GPS location and payment details as very sensitive, and all other attributes she defines as not sensitive. For Table 3 this will yield the following sensitivity levels:

$$s(name, p) = s(email, p) = s(postal\ code, p) = 0,$$
$$s(date\ of\ birth, p) = s(address, p) = 0.5$$
$$s(phone\ number, p) = s(GPS, p) = s(payment\ details, p) = 0.75$$

Some services, such as the bus service and the Underground, do not require any personal data about passengers. For these, we have a data request mask of $\mathbf{r} = (0,0,0,0,0,0,0,0)$ and a WSD metric of $d_c(\mathbf{a},\mathbf{r},Underground) = d_c(\mathbf{a},\mathbf{r},bus) = 0$.

A taxi service typically requires the phone number to be provided, or $\mathbf{r}^{taxi} = (0,0,0,1,0,0,0,0)$. Therefore, $d_c(\mathbf{a},\mathbf{r}^{taxi},taxi) = (0\cdot0+0.5\cdot0+0\cdot0+0.75\cdot1+0\cdot0+0.5\cdot0+0.5\cdot0+0.5\cdot0)/8 \approx 0.094$.

Uber requires name, email, the phone number, postal code, payment details and GPS location data to register to their service. Hence, for this service we have $\mathbf{r}^{Uber} = \{1,0,1,1,1,0,0,0\}$ and the WSD metric of $d_c(\mathbf{a},\mathbf{r}^{Uber},Uber) = (0\cdot1+0.5\cdot0+0\cdot1+0.75\cdot1+0\cdot1+0\cdot0+0.5\cdot0+0.75\cdot1+0.75\cdot1)/8 \approx 0.281$.

Example 3

Bob lives in a city with smart transportation system that allows people to use the following transportation modes: (i) public transport (public buses, trams, taxis), (ii) FlexiBuses whose routes and stops are determined by passenger requirements, and (iii) car pooling with people sharing a car to save fuel costs and/or gain access to car pooling lanes [3].

Assume the data attributes are the same as for the previous example: $\mathbf{a} = (a_1,...,a_m) =$ {name, date of birth, email, phone number, postal code, address, GPS location data, payment details}

Bob defines the sensitivity of his data as follows:

- name – not sensitive regardless of the provider: $s(name,p) = 0$;
- date of birth – sensitive regardless of the provider: $s(date\ of\ birth,p) = 0.5$;
- email – slightly sensitive regardless of the provider: $s(email,p) = 0.25$;
- phone number – very sensitive for providers a level of trust greater than or equal to 0.8 and extremely sensitive for providers with a level of trust lower than 0.8:

$$s(phone\ number,p) = \begin{cases} 0.75, & \text{if trust}(p) \geq 0.8 \\ 1, & \text{if trust}(p) < 0.8 \end{cases}$$

- postal code, address and payment details – extremely sensitive regardless of the provider: $s(postal\ code,p) = s(address,p) = s(payment\ details,p) = 1$;
- GPS location data – slightly sensitive for the taxi and FlexiBus providers and extremely sensitive for all other providers:

$$s(GPS,p) = \begin{cases} 0.25, & \text{if } p \in \{taxi,\ FlexiBus\} \\ 1, & \text{otherwise} \end{cases}$$

For this example assume that there are only two providers, FlexiBus (with trust level 0.9) and car pooling (with trust level 0.75) able to fulfill Bob's request. FlexiBus requires name, email, phone number, GPS data, and car pooling provider requires name, phone number and GPS data. The WSD metric values for these two providers are as follows:

For FlexiBus : $d_c(\mathbf{a},(1,0,1,1,0,0,1,0),FlexiBus) = 0\cdot1+0.5\cdot0+0.25\cdot1+0.75\cdot1+1\cdot0+1\cdot0+0.25\cdot1+1\cdot0 = (0.25+0.75+0.25)/8 \approx 0.156$

For car pooling: $d_c(\mathbf{a}, (1, 0, 0, 1, 0, 0, 1, 0), car\ pooling) = 0 \cdot 1 + 0.5 \cdot 0 + 0.25 \cdot 0 + 1 \cdot 1 + 1 \cdot 0 + 1 \cdot 0 + 1 \cdot 1 + 1 \cdot 0 = (1 + 1)/8 = 0.25$

We can see that although the FlexiBus service is more demanding in terms of the personal data wanted, Bob is more willing to provide his data to this company rather than to the car pooling provider that requires less data but is less trustworthy.

6   The Influence of Criteria Importance Ratios

Based on the scenario described in Examples 1 and 2 we conducted a small study on how different ratios in criteria importance affect the final ranking of journey alternatives. We considered the following cases:

Case 0: Only the utility value is used for decision making. For AHP this means that a single criterion, or $n = 1$, is used for ranking journey alternatives.

Case 1: Utility is *very much more important* than USP and WSD, which have *equal importance*.

Case 2: All criteria are of *equal importance*.

Case 3: All criteria are of *equal importance*.

Case 4: Utility is *slightly less important* than USP but *equally important* to WSD. USP is *equally important* to WSD (this is a case of moderate inconsistency in criteria ranking).

Case 5: Utility is *much less important* than USP and WSD, while USP and WSD are of *equal importance*.

Case 6: Utility is *very much less important* than USP and WSD, while USP and WSD are of *equal importance*.

For all cases, the utility values of all alternatives are calculated based on Eq. 7. For alternatives 5 to 8, the USP value is equal to 1, while it is equal to 0 for the other alternatives. The values of the WSD metric were calculated as explained in Example 2. The final vectors of global scores of all journey alternatives and considered cases are presented in Table 4.

We can see from the results that both cycling alternatives (alternatives 6 and 7) have the best (highest) scores when ranking is done based on the utility values only (case 0). This is because they are fast journeys and do not involve any cost. However, when the importance of the USP metric rises (see cases 1 to 6), then the ranking of alternative 6 (also 3 to 5) drops down as it has one unsatisfied preference (which is avoiding an empty area/transport). Similarly, while alternatives 8 and 9 have the same (low) score for case 0 (they are the most expensive alternatives), alternative 8 outperforms alternative 9 as the WSD metric becomes more important. This pattern is due to alternative 8 (taxi) requesting less data from the user to provide a service.

As expected, the scores of alternatives 1 and 2 grow as the importance of utility is decreasing compared to two other criteria. This is due to the fact that these alternatives satisfy the safety preferences specified by the user and do not require any personal information. Nevertheless, these alternatives have lower

Table 4. Global scores of alternatives for the journey planning problem with changing criteria importance

	Global scores of alternatives								
	1	2	3	4	5	6	7	8	9
case0	0.021	0.033	0.123	0.108	0.123	0.248	0.248	0.019	0.019
case1	0.039	0.049	0.112	0.099	0.112	0.214	0.225	0.031	0.029
case2	0.060	0.068	0.098	0.089	0.098	0.173	0.197	0.045	0.041
case3	0.087	0.091	0.081	0.076	0.081	0.123	0.163	0.062	0.055
case4	0.100	0.102	0.069	0.065	0.069	0.097	0.151	0.076	0.069
case5	0.111	0.112	0.066	0.065	0.066	0.078	0.132	0.078	0.068
case6	0.115	0.116	0.064	0.063	0.064	0.070	0.127	0.080	0.070

scores than alternative 7 because utility, yet very low in importance, is still used in the calculation of the final scores.

Interesting results are the final scores of alternatives 4 and 9 for cases 4 to 6. Alternative 9 has a higher final score than alternative 4, although alternative 9 has the worst scores with respect to both the first (utility) and the third (value of the WSD metric) criteria, while alternative 4 is the worst with respect to the second criterion (USP) only. Moreover, the second and the third criteria have the same importance, and feature values of $b_{9,4}^2 = b_{4,9}^3 = 9$ in the pairwise comparison matrices. Nevertheless, the reason that alternative 9 has a higher final score than alternative 4 is due to the way the score vectors of alternatives are calculated (the sum of the scores of all alternatives for each criterion is equal 1), as the difference in scores with respect to the second criteria is greater than first and the third combined.

7 Discussion

Our approach advocates the use of privacy and safety criteria into decision making in planning alongside the common utility of the solutions. Of course, the criteria used for ranking of alternatives can be modified and extended.

The preferences used for calculating the USP metric are related to personal safety. However, there can be various other reasons why a particular user might want to avoid (or not avoid) certain areas or transport. For example, a tourist may want to pass as many places of interest as possible. Similar preferences could also be used for other applications where safety preferences are beneficial, such as hotel booking or choosing a neighbourhood to live in. Moreover, the preferences can be of different importance (for example, for a particular commuter avoiding unsafe areas is more important than avoiding crowded areas). In these cases the weighted sum can be used instead of number of unsatisfied preferences. By using AHP for ranking of alternative solutions there is no need for normalization of the criteria, because all alternatives are compared to each other with respect to *each criteria separately* (see Eqs. 3 and 4). Learning user preferences and their relative importance based on the decisions (the final selections) made by a user can further improve the quality of ranking alternatives where there are hidden or context-dependant preferences. We can also organise criteria into a hierarchy to reduce the number of pairwise comparisons.

One can also think about an alternative to the WSD metric to control the information shared with service providers. WSD (see Eq. 8) reflects an "average harm" of sharing all requested by a provider data and might not be effective in cases when providers request not many, but very sensitive data attributes. Using $\max_j s(a_j, p) \times r_j$ in such situations would help to protect the most sensitive data attributes by giving in the less sensitive attributes.

8   Conclusion and Future Work

In this paper we proposed an approach for directly incorporating the privacy and safety criteria into decision making in planning. The approach was illustrated using the classic journey planning task. Our approach allows a user to define their own criteria and their relative importance. AHP was used to rank solutions incorporating two criteria, the number of unsatisfied safety preferences (USP) and a willingness-to-share-data (WSD) metric, plus a utility. The combination of these criteria helps users to find the safer journeys and to control the information they share with providers as well as achieve the required utility. Applying AHP allows to produce not only the ranked list of alternative plans, but also scores for those alternative plans, which can help users to understand why some alternatives are preferable to others, and in some cases select the alternative not from the top of the list.

To conduct some user trials we plan to develop a mobile phone application that combines the approach and criteria we described in this paper with existing journey planning services (e.g. The Google Directions API). For this integration we need to define parameters and contextual data associated with journey alternatives that can be used to calculate USP metric, in particular: assign safety levels to areas and routes, define context-dependent sparseness/crowdedness of areas and routes.

Acknowledgements. This work is supported by the 7th Framework EU-FET project ALLOW Ensembles (grant 600792).

References

1. André, P., et al.: Journey planning based on user needs. In: CHI 2007 Extended Abstracts on Human Factors in Computing Systems, pp. 2025–2030. ACM (2007)
2. Andrikopoulos, V., et al.: A game theoretic approach for managing multi-modal urban mobility systems. In: Proceedings of the 5th International Conference on Applied Human Factors and Ergonomics (AHFE 2014). CRC Press/Taylor & Francis, Kraków, Poland, July 2014

3. Andrikopoulos, V., Bucchiarone, A., Gómez Sáez, S., Karastoyanova, D., Mezzina, C.A.: Towards modeling and execution of collective adaptive systems. In: Lomuscio, A.R., Nepal, S., Patrizi, F., Benatallah, B., Brandić, I. (eds.) ICSOC 2013. LNCS, vol. 8377, pp. 69–81. Springer, Heidelberg (2014)
4. Barker, T.J., Zabinsky, Z.B.: A multicriteria decision making model for reverse logistics using analytical hierarchy process. Omega **39**(5), 558–573 (2011)
5. Beirão, G., Cabral, J.S.: Understanding attitudes towards public transport and private car: a qualitative study. Transp. Policy **14**(6), 478–489 (2007)
6. Breaux, T.: Privacy requirements in an age of increased sharing. IEEE Softw. **31**(5), 24–27 (2014)
7. Calavia, L.: A semantic autonomous video surveillance system for dense camera networks in smart cities. Sens. **12**(8), 10407–10429 (2012)
8. Caragliu, A., et al.: Smart cities in europe. J. Urban Technol. **18**(2), 65–82 (2011)
9. De Cristofaro, E., Di Pietro, R.: Adversaries and countermeasures in privacy-enhanced urban sensing systems. IEEE Syst. J. **7**(2), 311–322 (2013)
10. Eboli, L., Mazzulla, G.: A methodology for evaluating transit service quality based on subjective and objective measures from the passengers point of view. Transp. Policy **18**(1), 172–181 (2011)
11. Ferraz, F.S., Ferraz, C.A.G.: Smart city security issues: depicting information security issues in the role of an urban environment. In: 2014 IEEE/ACM 7th International Conference on Utility and Cloud Computing, pp. 842–847. IEEE (2014)
12. Flammini, F., Gaglione, A., Mazzocca, N., Pragliola, C.: Quantitative Security risk assessment and management for railway transportation infrastructures. In: Setola, R., Geretshuber, S. (eds.) CRITIS 2008. LNCS, vol. 5508, pp. 180–189. Springer, Heidelberg (2009)
13. Ho, W., et al.: Multi-criteria decision making approaches for supplier evaluation and selection: a literature review. Eur. J. Oper. Res. **202**(1), 16–24 (2010)
14. Kim, J., et al.: Hybrid choice models: principles and recent progress incorporating social influence and nonlinear utility functions. Procedia Environ. Sci. **22**, 20–34 (2014)
15. Koppelman, F.S.: Non-linear utility functions in models of travel choice behavior. Transp. **10**(2), 127–146 (1981)
16. Loukaitou-Sideris, A., Eck, J.E.: Crime prevention and active living. Am. J. Health Promot. **21**(4s), 380–389 (2007)
17. Lynch, G., Atkins, S.: The influence of personal security fears on women's travel patterns. Transp. **15**(3), 257–277 (1988)
18. Mahmoud, M., Hine, J.: Using AHP to measure the perception gap between current and potential users of bus services. Transp. Plann. Technol. **36**(1), 4–23 (2013)
19. Martinez-Balleste, A., et al.: The pursuit of citizens' privacy: a privacy-aware smart city is possible. IEEE Commun. Mag. **51**(6), 136–141 (2013)
20. Nam, T., Pardo, T.A.: Conceptualizing smart city with dimensions of technology, people, and institutions. In: Proceedings of the 12th Annual International Digital Government Research Conference: Digital Government Innovation in Challenging Times, pp. 282–291. ACM (2011)
21. Patsakis, C., Solanas, A.: Privacy-aware event data recorders: cryptography meets the automotive industry again. IEEE Commun. Mag. **51**(12), 122–128 (2013)
22. Saaty, T.L.: What is the analytic hierarchy process? In: Mitra, G., Greenberg, H.J., Lootsma, F.A., Rijkaert, M.J., Zimmermann, H.J. (eds.) Mathematical Models for Decision Support. NATO ASI Series, vol. 48, pp. 109–121. Springer, Heidelberg (1988)

23. Schaffers, H., et al.: Smart cities and the future internet: towards cooperation frameworks for open innovation. In: Domingue, J., et al. (eds.) FI. LNCS, vol. 6656, pp. 431–446. Springer, Heidelberg (2011)
24. Srinivas, N., Deb, K.: Muiltiobjective optimization using nondominated sorting in genetic algorithms. Evol. Comput. 2(3), 221–248 (1994)

Security Metrics, Secure Elements, and Operational Measurement Trust in Cloud Environments

Teemu Kanstrén$^{(\boxtimes)}$ and Antti Evesti

VTT, Oulu, Finland
{teemu.kanstren,antti.evesti}@vtt.fi

Abstract. Operational security assurance evaluation requires building security metrics models to express the expected security status of the system, and collecting data from the operational system to express the current state against these models. Many factors impact the confidence we can have in these metrics and their reported status. One major factor is the trust we can put in the provided measurement data. This paper describes the properties of a trusted measurement base, use of secure element functions and different probe form factors, and their impact on defining confidence levels for the measurement data. A way of quantifying this confidence level and using it as part of security metrics models is defined. Cloud computing is used as a domain to illustrate these concepts and the process of their application. The cloud environment is especially challenging for this type of assurance due to mixed ownership and potentially limited visibility into the infrastructure.

Keywords: Security assurance · Security metrics · Secure element · Measurement trust · Confidence

1 Introduction

With the ever-increasing pervasiveness, connectivity and criticality of software intensive systems, providing high level of security assurance for them is critical in itself. Having trust (high confidence) in the security status of the system requires also having high confidence in the evidence of this security. In this paper, we focus on providing such confidence in the context of cloud-based systems, which provide both unique challenges (due to distributed ownership and access) but also unique opportunities (due to potential supporting cloud-based services). We previously presented an overall process for operational security assurance in [5]. In this paper we extend this work by integrating the concept of operational measurement trust into the security metrics.

We specifically define a set of confidence levels for the measurements based on three factors; the concept of a trusted monitoring base (TMB), use of secure elements, and the different measurement probe form factors. While the concept of security metrics is extensively covered in previous works from various viewpoints

© Springer International Publishing Switzerland 2015
S. Foresti (Ed.): STM 2015, LNCS 9331, pp. 37–51, 2015.
DOI: 10.1007/978-3-319-24858-5_3

(see, e.g., [13] for an overview), the concept of *confidence* in the measurement data is, to our knowledge, not considered. The measurement data is used to evaluate the operational status of the target system against the security metrics model, meaning the data is critical to have correct and up-to-date view into the operational security status of the system. The term *confidence* in this case refers to our confidence in these properties (correctness and timeliness) for our security monitoring data.

This is an especially tricky question in the context of modern highly distributed systems (e.g., internet of things, cloud computing), where ownership of the hosting infrastructure may be with a different party than the one performing the security assurance monitoring. A specifically challenging environment is the domain of (public) cloud computing, where we (as a cloud customer) are hosting parts of our infrastructure as virtualized elements on the physical infrastructure of a cloud provider. In such case, many properties of the security status and configurations of the physical hosting infrastructure are also very relevant for the operational security status of the overall system for the cloud customer. Misconfigurations, vulnerabilities and compromises of different elements of the infrastructure can all impact the security status.

In this paper we describe the impact of various properties on this measurement data confidence. This includes the use of secure elements (SE) such as trusted platform module (TPM) for measurement data and infrastructure assurance, techniques for providing a trusted monitoring base (TMB), and different form factors of measurement probes. A set of confidence levels for the measurement data is defined depending on the level of TMB achieved, the availability and use of SE features for measurement data assurance, and properties of different probe form factors used. This is also the main contribution of this paper; defining the previously missing property of *confidence in measurement data* in the context of operational security assurance, and integrating it with the process of using security metrics. This approach has been implemented as part of a metrics visualization tool and prototyped with the use of TPM based approaches in a private cloud environment.

The rest of the paper is structured as follows. Section 2 reviews related work. Section 3 defines the threat model we are addressing. Section 4 presents our definition for operational measurement trust, and the relation of secure elements to this concept. Section 5 defines a set of trust levels for the measurement data depending on various properties. Section 6 describes how we have used these levels in building operational security assurance metrics. Section 7 discusses the operational confidence in a broader context. Finally, conclusions end the paper.

2   Background and Related Work

In this section, we define our terminology and review different viewpoints into confidence in security assurance and how this has been addressed in related work.

2.1   Terminology

We borrow terminology from [13] and define *security metrics* as depicting security-level, -performance, -indicators or -strength for the System under Investigation (SuI). Similarly, we also define the term *measurement* based on [6] as a process of experimentally obtaining quantitative information for (the magnitude of) a specific property. Finally, following [12] we define *measurement result* as representing data for a specific point in time for a specific factor being measured, and a *metric* representing higher level data derived from these measurements and used to support decision making.

We use the term system under investigation (SuI) to refer to the overall system whose security assurance is being monitored and evaluated. We use the term target of measurement (ToM) to refer to parts of this SuI (e.g., single host) from which we collect measurements.

Security metrics modelling in this paper refers to the process of analyzing the security properties of the SuI, defining what are the relevant security properties for that system, and creating a model representing these properties. The metrics are typically composed of several lower level properties, where the properties are composed into more abstract metrics, and also decomposed into concrete measurements that can be collected using available probes. This is a part of an overall security assurance process we have described in [5].

In this process, the raw measurement data collected is called *base measures (BM)*, interpretations of this as higher level measures are called *derived measures (DM)*, and combinations of these to high-level indicators for abstract security assurance concepts. A BM is a raw measure such as a specific property value for a property in a configuration file. An example of a DM from this is a check whether the BM matches a specific expected value, and providing a boolean result from this check. A metric on the other hand is a higher level combination of several such measures, summing up a set of these values. For example, one metric can sum up the authentication status of the system. The metrics can be hierarchically composed of several layers, and the BM and DM can be shared across several metrics.

Operational security assurance takes these metrics models, collects matching measurements for relevant infrastructure elements using the probes, and presents an evaluation of the security metrics model to the users. The result of this evaluation tells the operational security assurance status of the SuI at (current) measurement time. The security measurement data we discuss in this paper is used for this operational evaluation of security metrics.

In [13] a set of 19 quality properties for security metrics are presented based on an extensive literature review. Considering the topic of this paper, the most relevant ones of these is *correctness*, which indicates whether the security metric is correctly implemented and error-free. In the context of security metrics, this refers to the metric properly reflecting what a security expert sees as important properties for the security of the SuI.

To our knowledge, the concept of measurement data *confidence* as discussed in this paper is not part of any of these previously existing quality attributes for security metrics. We assume this is due to how this concept is less relevant in traditional operational infrastructure assurance, where we can assume to have full visibility and control over the physical infrastructure. In a cloud-based environment this does not hold and the trust needs to be set on a wider base, as the infrastructure ownership is distributed between the cloud operator (physical host) and customer (virtual guest).

We use the term secure element (SE) to refer to a component that is tamper-resistant and capable of securely hosting both cryptographic functionality (e.g., signing) and data (e.g., keys and measurement registers). These components can be either software (SW) or hardware (HW), although typically to achieve high trust, a HW based SE is required to provide a root of trust for a SW based SE. We have used the Trusted Platform Module (TPM), which is a HW based dedicated secure cryptoprocessor commonly found in new PCs and laptops. For TPM details we refer the reader to references such as [15] and [16]. A SW extension of this is called the virtual TPM (vTPM) [2]. Other potential SE such as the Amazon CloudHSM [1] can be used as well.

In this paper, we focus on the measurement confidence impact of different features enabled by using a SE as part of security metrics infrastructure and measurements, as well as different probe form factors. For details on potential features of SE form factors we refer the reader to our previous work on associated security measurement architecture [7] and SE usage scenarios in this context [8]. In this paper, we extend these previous works to consider the confidence in security assurance measurements and infrastructure as enabled by the a measurement architecture making use of the SE in different scenarios, and with different types of probes.

2.2 Related Work

Composing trust values regarding distributed system security is discussed in [14]. In this case, the trust is seen as composed of a logical composition of the probability for a given component to fulfill its security requirements. These probabilities are assumed to be given based on information such as historical analysis of component issues. In our case we do not make such assumptions but base the confidence measure on the properties of the measurement infrastructure and the use of different features of secure elements for providing higher security assurance. As high confidence in measurement results does not mean there are no security vulnerabilities in the SuI, these types of approaches can be seen as orthogonal and addressing complementary aspects of security assurance.

A taxonomy of quality metrics for assessing security assurance status is presented in [11]. The main parameters of this taxonomy are rigor, depth, coverage, and independence of verification of the security assurance. The taxonomy is intended to support decision-making process in making use of available security assurance metrics. This is done by evaluating the quality of the security assurance metrics and the measurement data/infrastructure they are based on. While [11] presents a comprehensive set of properties and gives good foundations for why those are selected, it is also lacking the element of confidence in the data as presented in this paper. We see the taxonomy presented in [11] and the concept of security assurance confidence presented in this paper as complementary in providing a possibility to extend the security metrics quality assurance by incorporating the concept of measurement confidence.

The probe quality part of the taxonomy is discussed deeper in [10]. This again includes the four categories of coverage, depth, rigor and independence of verification. Coverage measures the number of functionalities of the security mechanism covered by the probe. Depth is how extensively each of these is investigated. Rigor measures the formalization level of the requirements for the checks over the mechanism. Independence measures the distance from the deploying and using entity to the evaluating entity. [10] further presents a process and risk attributes to consider in performing value assignments for such metrics. However, as before, the trust of the measurement data is not considered.

A security metrics evaluation tool called Metrics Visualization System (MVS) is presented in [9] and another one discussed in [5]. We have used the MVS tool in our prototyping. As discussed in [9], this tool supports the modelling expert in defining their confidence in the model. This confidence is intended to reflect how effectively and fully the expert feels the model is capturing the actual security properties of the SuI. This paper extends this with a new confidence value for operational measurements.

3   Threat Model

We consider two types of general attackers on the system, malicious insiders and external attackers. From the viewpoint of the work discussed in this paper, the assets we are interested in protecting are the correctness and availability of the monitoring information. Indirectly we are interested in protecting the security assets themselves through providing assurance for having high-confidence security assurance measurement results.

Malicious insider may have access to the host or the guest, performing unauthorized actions. These can be from both the cloud provider and cloud customer side. The changes may be intended (malicious actor) or unintended (mistake or misunderstanding). In these cases, we are interested to know that some unauthorized operations have been performed, and a property of interest being monitored has been modified. The threat from the attacker is to tamper with the system and hide or forge this information. We further assume that the cloud provider is not fully malicious but may contain one or more malicious individuals.

An external attacker who gains access to the cloud provider infrastructure may access the guest instances information for the cloud customer and/or modify their configurations. An external attacker who gains access to the cloud customer VM instances is able to access the data inside the specific VM and perform unauthorized actions. Again, we are interested in detecting such actions, and the threat being addressed in this case is in the attacker hiding or forging this information.

Additionally, we have to consider the possibility of a man-in-the-middle type attacks, where the monitoring data being provided to us from the different ToM's is modified before we receive it.

4 Operational Measurement Trust

4.1 Trusted Monitoring Base

We presented the term Trusted Monitoring Base (TMB) in [8]. This relates to defining all the HW and SW elements that are relevant to have trust in our monitoring infrastructure and monitoring data collected with it. The TMB from a cloud-type systems viewpoint is illustrated in Fig. 1. The lower levels of this pyramid need to be assured for us to have higher trust in the high levels. In this paper, we do not focus on these techniques but rather rely on existing techniques to achieve these properties (as described, e.g., in [7] and [8]), and consider how their use impacts the confidence we have on the measurement data. However, in the following, we briefly summarize techniques related to different levels to support further discussion.

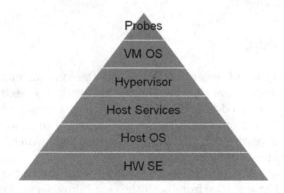

Fig. 1. Trusted Monitoring Base

Techniques such as trusted boot and scaled attestation [3] can be used to provide assurance that the operating system and services we are using have not been tampered with. This is based on HW SE such as TPM. From the viewpoint of a virtualized environment (the cloud), this can also be used to verify that the virtualization environment (the hypervisor) is not tampered with.

Once the host is considered trusted in this way, it can be used to provide trusted services for the virtualized environment (the VM instances). This type of a service is called a virtual SE (vSE). For example, in [3] the vTPM is used in this way to verify that the SW on the VM is not tampered with. The vSE service can also be used by the cloud customer through the vSE interface for their own purposes.

This forms a chain of trust from the VM side all the way to the host HW SE. As the host SW (including the vSE) is verified using the HW SE and the VM SW using the vSE, the chain is considered trusted. There is no direct way from the VM side to forge the measurements done on the host side, and it is not possible to forge the measurement data stored on the HW SE outside physical access to the HW SE itself. This is discussed in more detail in our previous works [7] and [8].

The cloud environment also provides a unique opportunity to provide special services for trusted measurements against the VM environment as discussed in [7]. Interfaces such as the standard virtual machine introspection (VMI) interface can be used to provide access for tools and services on the host side to provide trusted measurements to the VM side (the cloud customer).

These techniques do not offer 100 % security, e.g., against fully malicious cloud provider or nation state adversary with massive resources, in-depth information on the system, and full exploits available in all levels. However, they do offer significant added protection against most adversaries, malicious insiders, and also make the attacks by highly resourced and skilled attackers much harder.

4.2 Secure Elements and Measurement Data

Besides having trust in the measurement infrastructure (the TMB) as discussed in Sect. 4.1, we also need to consider trust in the actual measurement data being correct and up-to-date. This requires means to verify that the data is coming from the correct target of measurement (ToM) where the TMB applies. We also need assurance that the data is fresh, not tampered with, and represents the current SuI status.

Means to achieve this using different SE features is discussed in our previous works [7] and [8], and we briefly summarize this here. To assure the data is coming from the correct ToM and is tamper-free, the data can be signed with the SE only available at the SuI. To assure the data is fresh, SE based timestamp functionality can be used. To provide assurance no data is missing or changed over time, SE measurement registers (hash-chains) can be used. Together these provide high confidence in having untampered data from the correct ToM, both in a timely manner when required and tamper-free over time when longer history is considered.

5 Levels of Operational Trust

In this section, we discuss the different levels of confidence we can have in relation to our operational security assurance measurements in cases where different levels of the TMB are achieved, or different SE features mentioned in Sect. 4.2 are utilized. We also discuss different measurement probe form factors and the impact of their properties on this confidence.

5.1   Trusted Monitoring Base

In relation to confidence in the measurement infrastructure, the best we can achieve is to have all levels of the TMB described in Sect. 4.1 in place. In case the full TMB is not achieved, different considerations are needed.

Even when no HW SE is available as a basis for the HW root of trust, access to a vSE service on the host side can still be useful for the guest VM side. Such a service roots the trust outside the VM scope, meaning that a potential attacker would have to be able to break out from the hypervisor and tamper with the vSE instance on the host side. From the in-VM viewpoint we can still gain added trust from such features even if reduced in relation to having full HW rooted trust on the host side as well.

Another scenario is the case where we have a HW SE available in the cloud, but it is not linked to the hosts we run our guest instance on. This is the case, for example, with the Amazon CloudHSM [1], and in the case of the cloud based TPM (cTPM) as described in [4]. In these cases, the SE functionality is provided as a separate cloud-based and HW rooted service, to be used over a network interface and only accessible within the cloud customers virtual private network. This alone does not provide the TMB but provides means to use the SE for the measurements. From the conceptual viewpoint, this provides another distribution of the trust elements, requiring an adversary to compromise multiple points to forge the SE based measurements. However, it is also lacking the TMB at the ToM itself, and potentially the strongest possible link of the SE to the ToM itself.

Considerations for such cloud-based SE service include having it rooted in HW or not (which can still be useful in both cases, similar to host-side vSE services). The cloud provider may also provide access logs and other assurance to these services (e.g., secured with a SE as for the Amazon CloudHSM [1]), providing another mechanism that can be used to increase confidence in the SE not being used improperly. We take these elements also into account in considering our confidence in the security measurements.

The use of HW SE at the cloud hosting provider side needs to be also considered in relation to the trust against host-side tampering. While the bare vSE instances and similar cloud-provider hosted services can be useful for the virtual machine side from the viewpoint of threats from an external attacker, they do not protect from malicious insiders at the cloud provider. For this, techniques such as trusted boot and its extensions such as [3] are needed.

5.2   Probes

The base of trust for the probe instances themselves are in the TMB. If attestation techniques such as [3] are applied to the full TMB stack from the host HW SE to the VM side software (including the probes), we can have higher confidence in running untampered probes. If SE are available but not fully applied for the TMB, we can still use the SE features for signatures, measurement tracing and timestamping.

When SE signatures are used, we can have confidence in where the data has originated from and not being tampered with since signing. If only a vSE or cSE is available with no HW root of trust at ToM, the confidence is higher than without it but not as high as with full TMB.

SE measurement register tracing can be used to attest that we have received all measurement data. This gives us confidence that no data has been removed that should have been delivered to us. This is important for current measurements and also for historical audits.

Timestamps can be used to provide confidence that the data stream being current, and that the stream is not tampered with (e.g., replay-attacks or sequence tampering). Full TMB and SE based timestamping provides the highest confidence. Such timestamps cannot be forged outside access to the SE at the ToM (or the cSE).

Another point to consider is probe form factors and their context. We consider two types of form factors and contexts: VM-internal and VM-external. VM-internal probes run in the context of the ToM, making it possible for anyone who has access to the ToM to also tamper with the probes. This can be an issue in a compromised ToM. VM-external probes run in a separate context from the ToM and as such compromising the ToM alone is not sufficient to compromise the measurement probes, providing higher measurement trust. A traditional example is a separate network monitoring device/tool such as intrusion detection system (IDS).

In a cloud-based environment there are also special opportunities for VM-external probe form factors. Interfaces such as the virtual machine introspection interface (VMI), can be used to access data about the VM state from the cloud host side (external to the VM). As discussed in [7] and [8], such features can be used for providing trusted external-context monitoring services for cloud customers. Potential services for this include virus and malware scanners, intrusion detection systems and similar generic tools (as opposed to in-VM service specific logging). Such external probes have higher confidence in requiring compromise of the cloud-provider infrastructure to tamper with the probes and measurement data, in addition to compromising the virtualized guest infrastructure.

5.3 Quantifying Overall Confidence

In the above, we have identified several elements affecting the confidence in our measurements:

- TMB level
- SE use
- Probe form factor

That is, the level of TMB achieved, potential use of a SE to tamper-proof a measurement, and the type of probe used. The following detail each of these.

We roughly split the TMB into two categories in our confidence evaluation:

1. Host verification
2. Guest (VM) verification

Host verification refers to having applied attestation methods such as trusted boot and scalable attestation discussed in [3]. When this is achieved, host side probes can be seen to have achieved their TMB trust goal. Guest verification refers similarly to the VM side verification using host-side services. In cases where found necessary, more details of the TMB can be used for finer-grained analysis.

To classify the use of SE functionality, we follow a simple classification:

1. SE features used
2. SE features not used

In this case these refer to using the relevant features of the SE for the probe. Currently, these include the SE based signatures, timestamps, and measurement registers. However, these could be extended with new features as more advanced SE and related services become available. We use this type of high-level definition as it is generic and applicable to all measurements and probes. More detailed classification would require more probe-specific analysis and is out of the scope for this paper.

We classify the probe type to three categories:

1. Context: Internal vs External
2. Black-box (host/external)
3. White-box (VM)

As discussed, we consider external-context probes more trusted with regards to data tampering due to additional layers of security separating it from an external attacker. We classify a probe as a black-box depending on our visibility into it and knowledge of its working. For example, if the probe interface is given from the cloud provider but no details on how it is implemented (e.g., Amazon CloudTrail [1]), we can only trust the word of the provider related to the probe functionality. If we have high visibility into the probe implementation and inner workings (e.g., open source) and deploy it ourselves, we classify it as white-box with higher confidence in the provided data.

The combinations of these different levels are illustrated in Table 1. In this table, SE refers to availability and use of SE for a probe, I/E refers to internal/external probe, B/W refers to black-/white-box probe, and TMB to achieving the trusted monitoring base.

Quantifying all these variables into a single factor to calculate overall operational measurement trust is difficult. We can score each of these depending on their properties. However, scoring each of these in relation to one another is more difficult. For example, we can say that having an external white-box probe (N=1-2,9-10 in Table 1) is better than having an external black-box probe (N=3-4,11-12 in Table 1). However, it is not clear whether having an internal white-box probe (N=5-6,13-14 in Table 1) is better than having an external

Table 1. Confidence levels

N	SE	I/E	B/W	TMB
1	+	E	W	+
2	+	E	W	-
3	+	E	B	+
4	+	E	B	-
5	+	I	W	+
6	+	I	W	-
7	+	I	B	+
8	+	I	B	-
9	-	E	W	+
10	-	E	W	-
11	-	E	B	+
12	-	E	B	-
13	-	I	W	+
14	-	I	W	-
15	-	I	B	+
16	-	I	B	-

black-box probe (N=3-4,11-12 in Table 1). This is further complicated by the use of the SE and the application of TMB in each of these cases.

For this reason, we simply define the preference for each attribute and use these as a way to express different attributes about the probe confidence in each case. Our preference is to have the SE used (SE=+ in Table 1), use an external white-box probe (I/E=E and B/W=W in Table 1), and have full TMB applied (TMB=+ in Table 1).

However, for display in our visualization tool (MVS [9]), we do sum this up to a single value where each of the preferred values from Table 1 adds one to the overall score. This is illustrated in Eq. 1, where E refers to value of each element from Table 1 ($E_1 = SE$, $E_2 = I/E$, $E_3 = B/W$, $E_4 = TMB$). Similarly, W_i refers to the weight given to each of these elements.

$$\sum_{i=1}^{4} (E_i \cdot W_i) \tag{1}$$

Each of the elements is given a value of 0 to 1, weighted by the observed importance. In our case, we have simply used 1 for the weights, but have also observed that in practice this requires some tuning depending on various factors, such as trust in the cloud operator and the type of external probes used. We then normalize this value to between 0 and 1, where 1 means all preferred values are met. This is intended only to support quick visual evaluation. For more detailed exploration, the user can open the confidence indicator and see the status of all the elements forming that score.

6   Operational Measurement Trust and Security Metrics

We have now defined a set of properties for probes and the confidence in their measurement values. However, for the measurements to be useful, we must apply them for some purpose. In our case this is the evaluation of security assurance metrics. Previous work has described a process for security assurance metrics evaluation based on operational measurement data [5] as a six step process of service modelling, metrics selection, measurement, aggregation, evaluation and presentation. Considering these steps, we see the application of the operational security assurance measurement data confidence value as follows for each of these steps.

In the first step (service modelling), we have to take into account what type of information and at what confidence we can have available from each relevant ToM. In this case, the confidence in the distributed (cloud) monitoring and operating infrastructure is a new value to incorporate.

In Step 2 (Metric selection), we should also consider how the confidence in our measurement results impacts our security assurance metrics and out trust in the results, as well as how we can then use these results better. If we have several potential metrics to choose from, measurement confidence can be used as one property for selection.

In Step 3 (Measurement), we need also to consider the confidence of the probes and associated SE features available. We may wish to deploy specific probe types or SE features as part of the measurement infrastructure to increase the measurement data confidence.

In Steps 4-5 (Aggregation and Evaluation), the measurement confidence needs to be taken into account as part of the metrics aggregation and evaluation process. The measurement confidence can affect how much trust we put in our measurement, but the related features may also produce new information for evaluation. For example, if the SE signature is not valid we have to provide a suitable alarm to check for security incidents and tampering with the probes and/or measurement data provided.

In Step 6 (Presentation) we must consider how to show the confidence values we have for each probe, how high it should be able to go, and how high it is in practice. We must also be able to visualize any issues in the confidence (e.g., tamper-evidence) for the user. These may be new types of alerts or other ways to display issues. In our case, we visualize this as issues in specific parts of the metrics model (highlighted (red) elements in the metric tree hierarchy), and as failed entries shown in the measurement log and associated log visualizations.

The confidence values presented in this paper (Sect. 5) are the enabler to make these features possible. How these are realized in different tools and security assurance cockpits depends on the design choices for each of those cockpits and the supporting measurement framework.

7   Discussion

Our summary quantification for the confidence is limited in not taking into account detailed variation within a single property. It is also possible to split some of these further, such as setting several levels for the host verification or VM verification itself as illustrated in Fig. 1.

For example, as noted before, TMB can be split to several levels depending on the granularity of interest. One might set a higher value for the TMB based on whether all SW in the full system stack is verified using techniques such as those presented in [3], whether host operating system is verified, whether all host software is verified (including probes), whether VM software is verified, and so on. On the other hand, as also discussed, these measures are not exclusive in relation to each other (e.g., one can apply some level of VM verification from host services, even if full trusted boot is not applied).

Similarly, the type of external probe can be further classified such as external to the ToM context such as a separate IDS system, or external to the monitoring entity (e.g., cloud customer vs cloud provider hosted). This can impact the trust in the external probe, and may need to be reflected further in these confidence values. For the white-/black-box probe types, the classification can also be taken further in considering the level of information available. For example, a probe or monitoring service can be based on well-known open-source software but customized and extended by a probe provider or by a cloud-provider as their customized service. Different detail levels may also be available for different services depending on various factors, such as the willingness of a cloud-provider to provide details of their internal service operation and available audit data.

The form of SE is also relevant for the granularity of the confidence value. If cloud based SE services (e.g., Amazon CloudHSM are used instead of specific ones for each ToM (e.g., TPM), they can be seen to increase the confidence in being external to the ToM context. However, they can also be seen as a weaker point in providing a single point of compromise. Compromising any single ToM and gaining access to the cSE through it potentially allows an adversary to access the same SE from the viewpoint of all the different targets of measurement in the SuI. From the cloud point of view, this type of an approach can also be necessary to address specific cloud properties such as elasticity and auto-scaling if not otherwise supported by the cloud provider infrastructure.

In our case, we have used the overall confidence level measure more as an informal indicator to quickly give an overview of our trust indicators for different probes. However, these indicators can be extended where found relevant by splitting and weighting different elements at a finer granularity.

The confidence levels we described in this paper allow us to better quantify and make visible to different trust elements in measuring security assurance in a cloud-based environment. They also provide mechanisms for making it harder for external adversaries and cloud-provider insiders to compromise our system, and to tamper with the measurement data. We still have to trust the cloud provider as they have full physical access to infrastructure. However, this trust is not blind when these techniques are applied, and it makes tampering by an isolated malicious insider much more difficult (vs. fully malicious cloud provider).

In relation to cloud provider assurance providing a specific level of TMB for their services, the cloud customer typically has to trust the services provided as it is unlikely that every cloud customer is able to arrange an audit of the cloud provider infrastructure and the physical aspects of their TMB. One approach to increase this trust is if the cloud provider has certificates stating auditing has been performed on their infrastructure to verify these services.

Finally, although techniques such as scalable attestation [3] can be used to provide the TMB, and assurance over tamper-free infrastructure, they are limited to attestation of static SW elements. As noted in [3], they do not currently protect against runtime vulnerabilities, meaning the system can still be compromised after the trusted software has been loaded. As usual, no technique can be seen to provide 100 % trust but as means to increase the confidence in the results.

While we discuss the confidence values in this paper from the cloud environment perspective, we see them also as applicable in a wider context of operational security assurance measurements. The same types of confidence increasing techniques can also be applied in traditional (in-house) operational infrastructure, and used as part of the security metrics evaluation. The increasing use of virtualization in this context also makes these techniques more generally relevant. We have focused here on the cloud environment, which we see as the most challenging due to distributed ownership and limited visibility into the physical infrastructure.

8   Conclusion

Traditionally we define a set of security metrics, deploy a set of possible probes, and evaluate their operational status against the security metrics model. In addition to collecting this data, we have to consider how much confidence we have in its correctness. With the work presented in this paper, we take a step towards having knowledge on the confidence we put on our measurements. In the future we hope to see this better integrated as part of cloud-based services to make it easily deployable.

References

1. Amazon, AWS CloudHSM. http://aws.amazon.com/cloudhsm/. Accessed May 2015
2. Berger, S., Cáceres, R., Goldman, K., Perez, R., Sailer, R., van Doorn, L.: vTPM: virtualizing the trusted platform module. In: Proceedings of the 15th USENIX Security Symposium (2006)
3. Berger, S., et al.: Scalable attestation: a step toward secure and trusted clouds. In: IEEE International Conference on Cloud Engineering (2015)

4. Chen, C., Raj, H., Saroiu, S., Wolman, A.: cTPM: a cloud TPM for cross-device trusted applications. In: Proceedings of the 11th USENIX Conference on Networked Systems Design and Implementation (NSDI) (2014)
5. Haddad, S., Hecker, A., Marquet, B., Dubus, S., Kanstrén, T., Savola, R.: Operational security assurance evaluation in open infrastructures. In: 6th IEEE International Conference on Risk and Security of Internet and Systems (CRISIS), Timisoara, Romania, 26–28 September 2011
6. ISO/IEC Guide 99:2007, International vocabulary of metrology e basic and general concepts and associated terms (VIM), International Organization for Standardization and the International Electrotechnical Commission (2007)
7. Kanstrén, T., Lehtonen, S., Savola, R., Kukkohovi, H., Hatonen, K.: Architecture for high confidence cloud security monitoring. In: Proceedings of IEEE International Conference on Cloud Engineering (IC2E) (2015)
8. Kanstrén, T., Lehtonen, S., Kukkohovi, H.: Opportunities in using a secure element to increase confidence in cloud security monitoring. In: Proceedings of the 8th IEEE International Conference on Cloud Computing (CLOUD) (2015)
9. Latvala, O-M., et al.: A tool for security metrics modeling and visualization. In: Proceedings of the European Conference on Software Architecture Workshops (2014)
10. Ouedraogo, M., et al.: Appraisal and reporting of security assurance at operational systems level. J. Syst. Softw. 8(1), 193–208 (2012)
11. Ouedraogo, M., et al.: Taxonomy of quality metrics for assessing assurance of security correctness. Softw. Qual. J. 21, 67–97 (2013)
12. Savola, R.: A security taxonomization model for software-intensive systems. J. Inf. Process. Syst. 5(4), 197–206 (2009)
13. Savola, R.: Quality of security metrics and measurements. Comput. Secur. 37, 78–90 (2013)
14. Schryen, G., Volkamer, M., Ries, S., Habib, S.-M.: A formal approach towards measuring trust in distributed systems. In: Proceedings of the ACM Symposium on Applied Computing, (SAC) (2011)
15. Tomlinson, A.: Introduction to the TPM. In: Smart Cards, Tokens, Security and Applications, pp. 155–172. Springer, Heidelberg (2008)
16. Trusted Computing Group, TPM Main Specification Version 1.2 Level 2, Revision 116 (2011)

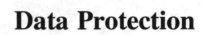

Data Protection

A Declarative Framework for Specifying and Enforcing Purpose-Aware Policies

Riccardo De Masellis[1]([⊠]), Chiara Ghidini[2], and Silvio Ranise[2]

[1] Trento RISE, Via Sommarive 18, 38123 Trento, Italy
r.demasellis@trentorise.eu
[2] Bruno Kessler Foundation, Via Sommarive 18, 38123 Trento, Italy
{ghidini,ranise}@fbk.eu

Abstract. Purpose is crucial for privacy protection as it makes users confident that their personal data are processed as intended. Available proposals for the specification and enforcement of purpose-aware policies are unsatisfactory for their ambiguous semantics of purposes and/or lack of support to the run-time enforcement of policies.

In this paper, we propose a declarative framework based on a first-order temporal logic that allows us to give a precise semantics to purpose-aware policies and to reuse algorithms for the design of a run-time monitor enforcing purpose-aware policies. We also show the complexity of the generation and use of the monitor which, to the best of our knowledge, is the first such a result in literature on purpose-aware policies.

1 Introduction

An important aspect of privacy protection is the specification and enforcement of purposes, i.e. users should be confident that their data are processed as intended. For instance, email addresses are used only for billing but not for marketing purposes. Unfortunately, as already observed several times in the literature (see, e.g., [21] for a thorough discussion), both specifying and enforcing purposes turn out to be difficult tasks.

Specification. Following the seminal paper [36], the specification of privacy constraints consists of establishing when, how, and to what extent information about people is communicated to others. In the context of IT systems, this amounts to define policies governing the release of personal data for a given purpose. From a technological point of view, these policies are usually mapped to access control policies augmented with purpose constraints, which we call *purpose-aware policies* (sometimes called privacy-aware access control policies in the literature, see, e.g., [11]). In this paper, we do not consider the problem of deriving purpose-aware policies from the high-level and heterogenous privacy requirements . We assume that this has been done and focus instead on the basic building blocks of the models and specification languages underlying the policies. As observed in [20,21], such building blocks are data-centric and rule-centric policies. In the former, every piece of information is associated with

© Springer International Publishing Switzerland 2015
S. Foresti (Ed.): STM 2015, LNCS 9331, pp. 55–71, 2015.
DOI: 10.1007/978-3-319-24858-5_4

the purposes for which it can be used; examples are the policies in [9] or those expressed in the XACML Privacy Profile[1]. In the latter, rules specify under which conditions subjects can perform some action on a given piece of information for some purpose; examples are those in [11,25] and those expressed in EPAL[2]. For expressivity reasons, both data- and rule-centric policies should be supported for the specification of purpose-aware policies.

One of the most serious problems in purpose-aware policies is the lack of semantics for purposes, which are usually considered as atomic identifiers. This gives rise to arbitrariness in the interpretation of purposes; e.g., if the policy of a company states that emails of users are collected for the purpose of communication, this allows the organization to use emails for both billing and marketing when the majority of users has a strong preference for the first interpretation only. To solve this problem, several works have observed that *"an action is for a purpose if it is part of a plan for achieving that purpose"* [33]. Among the many possible ways to describe plans, one of the most popular is to use workflows, i.e. collections of activities (called tasks) together with their causal relationships, so that the successful termination of a workflow corresponds to achieving the purpose which it is associated to. We embrace this interpretation of purpose and avoid ambiguities in its specification by using a temporal logic which allows us to easily express the causal relationships among actions in workflows associated to purposes. Additionally, the use of a logic-based framework allows us to express in a uniform way, besides purpose specifications, also authorization (namely, data- and rule-centric) policies together with authorization constraints, such as Separation/Bound of Duties (SoD/BoD). While temporal logics have been used before for the specification of authorization policies (see, e.g., [26]) and of workflows (see, e.g., [13]), it is the first time—to the best of our knowledge—that this is done for both in the context of purpose-aware policies. In particular, the capability of specifying SoD or bod constraints—which are crucial to capture company best practices and legal requirements—seems to be left as future work in the comprehensive framework recently proposed in [21].

Enforcement. Enforcing purpose-aware policies amounts to check if (**C1**) a user can peform an action on a certain data for a given purpose and (**C2**) the purpose for which a user has accessed the data can be achieved.

(**C1**) is relatively easy and well-understood being an extension of mechanisms for the enforcement of access control policies (see, e.g., [14] for an overview) by considering the combined effect of rule- and data-centric policies.

(**C2**) is much more complex than (**C1**) as it requires to foresee if there exists an assignment of users to tasks that allows for the successful termination of the workflow. This is so because—as discussed above—a purpose is associated to a workflow so that its successful execution implies the achievement of the purpose. The problem of checking (offline) if a workflow can successfully terminate, known as the Workflow Satisfiability Problem (WSP), is already computationally expensive with one SoD [34], and moreover, the on-line monitoring

---

[1] docs.oasis-open.org/xacml/3.0/xacml-3.0-privacy-v1-spec-cd-03-en.pdf.
[2] www.w3.org/Submission/2003/SUBM-EPAL-20031110.

of authorization constraints requires to solve several instances of the WSP [12]. For purpose-aware policies, this implies that it is necessary to solve an instance of the WSP per user request of executing a task in the workflow associated to a given purpose.

Contributions. The paper provides the following contributions:

- The *specification* of a comprehensive framework for expressing purpose-aware policies which are a combination of data- and rule-centric policies together with workflows augmented with authorization constraints (Sect. 3 and, in particular, Fig. 1). To the best of our knowledge, this is the first time authorization constraints are considered and naturally integrated in a purpose-aware setting.
- The *semantic formalization* of purpose-aware policies as formulas in first-order temporal logic (Sect. 3.1).
- The provision of *formal techniques* not only for the (on-line) enforcement of purpose-aware policies, but also for their (off-line) analysis, together with decidability and complexity results (Sect. 4). Proofs of theorems can be found in the full-length version of the work [17].

A running example (Sect. 2) introducing the main issues related to purpose-aware policies is used throught the paper to illustrate the main concepts of our framework. Related work and conclusions are also discussed (Sect. 5).

2 Running Example

We describe a running example, based on *Smart campus*[3], which will be used throughout the paper. Smart campus is a platform in which citizens, institutions and companies can communicate with each other by exchanging data and services. It provides functionalities to access information about transportations, social services, education, and user profiles. These services allow companies to build new applications and thus offer new services to citizens. In this kind of scenario, users should be confident that the services access only the data required to their needs and use them for the right purposes. Additionally, service providers should comply with laws, regulations, and best practices in handling data mandated by local governments, the European Union, and enterprises. In other words, access to personal data must be mediated by appropriate authorization policies augmented with purpose constraints so that only authorized subjects have the right to access certain data for a given purpose. Following an established line of works (see, e.g., [21] for an overview), we assume that the purpose of an action is determined by its relationships with other, interrelated, actions.

For concreteness, we illustrate these ideas by considering the situation in which some personal data of users in the Smart campus platform (namely, the work experience and the academic transcripts) is accessed by JH, a job hunting company, for the purpose of finding jobs to students. JH has deployed in the

---

[3] http://www.smartcampuslab.it.

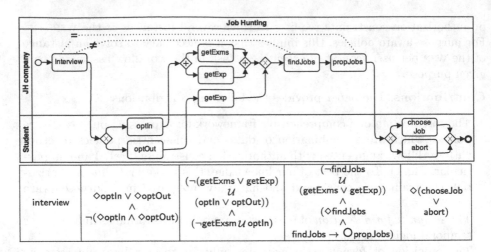

Fig. 1. The JobHunting workflow expressed in BPMN (upper half) and as a (partial) set of LTL formulae (lower half).

Smart Campus platform the service depicted of Fig. 1 (upper half), specified in the Business Process Model and Notation (BPMN). The swim lane labelled 'Student' contains the activities (also called tasks) that must be executed under the responsibility of the data owner and the swim lane labelled 'JH company' shows the activities that employees of JH are supposed to perform for the purpose of finding some jobs to the data owner. First of all, an employee of JH performs an interview to the student to understand his/her job preferences. Then, the student decides to give or not his/her consent for JH to access his/her academic transcripts by executing either task optIn or task optOut, respectively (the empty diamond before the two tasks in Fig. 1 is an exclusive-or gateway). If he/she opts in, an employee of JH can access both his/her academic transcripts and past experience (by executing both getExms and getExp since the diamond containing the plus sign before the two tasks in Fig. 1 is a parallel gateway); otherwise, only the student past experiences can be accessed. Based on the interview and the collected personal information, an employee of JH search for jobs the student can be interested in (task findJobs) and some other employee proposes him/her some of them (task propJobs). Finally, the students decides if choosing one of the jobs or to abort the process (tasks chooseJob and abort, respectively). Further authorization constraints are imposed on which employees can execute task interview, findJobs, and proposeJobs: the first two must be executed by different employees to keep the overall process unbiased—this is called a Separation of Duty (SoD) constraint—whereas the first and last tasks must be executed by the same employee so that the student gets in contact with the same person of JH—this is called a Bind of Duty (BoD) constraint. (In Fig. 1, these constraints are shown as dotted lines connecting the tasks labelled by the distinct ≠ or equal = sign in case of SoD or BoD, respectively.)

To summarize, the workflow specification is used to specify the purpose of an activity (task) with respect to all the others that must be executed for achieving the given purpose. From now on, we assume that a workflow is uniquely associated to a purpose or, equivalently, that the semantics of a purpose is its associated workflow.

Since the tasks in the workflow are executed under the responsibility of a user (e.g., an employee of JH), he/she must have the right to access such data. For instance, the task getExp takes as input the list of past job experiences of the student. The employee of JH executing this task must have the right to access such a list and the student should have given the consent to access this information to (an employee of) JH. In other words, every time an employee of JH asks to execute an activity for the purpose of finding jobs, he/she not only must have the right to do so according to the authorization policy of the company but also the student (data owner) should agree to release the information for the purpose of finding jobs. In other words, there are two types of policies that must be taken into account when granting the right to execute a task to an employee: one is called *rule-centric*, and constrains access by considering subjects, actions, and data objects while the other is called *data-centric*, and is such that data owners constrain access to their data objects for certain purposes only. For instance, in the job hunting scenario, the rule-centric policy specifies that employee bob has the right to read the list of job experiencens of students and the data-centric policy specifies that student sam's academic transcripts can be accessed for the purpose of JobHunting.

Notice the subtle interplay between purposes, described by workflows, and authorization policies. For instance, the execution of certain tasks can modify both rule- and data-centric policies as it is the case of optIn and optOut in Fig. 1. When executing the latter, the execution of the task getExms is skipped in the current instance of the workflow despite the fact that sam has agreed to disclose such information according to the above data-centric policy (for which sam's academic transcripts can always be used for the purpose of jobHunting). This flexibility allows us to model certain data directive for privacy (see, e.g., [1]) in which the data owner must explicitly give his/her consent to access his/her personal data, every time it is requested.

Finally, observe that handling purposes in presence of authorization constraints (such as SoD or BoD) requires to solve, at run-time, the *Workflow Satisfiability Problem* (WSP) [12], i.e., to be able to answer the question: does there exist an assignment of authorized users (according to the rule- and data-centric policies) to workflow tasks that satisfies the authorization constraints (SoD or BoD)? The WSP is known to be a computationally expensive activity; it is already NP-hard with one SoD constraint [34]. To make things even more complex, at run-time, we need to solve several instances of the WSP, one per user request of executing a task in a workflow associated to a purpose. Indeed, the WSP returns one possible future execution sequence meeting the constraints and thus, each time the real execution diverges from that one, a new WSP problem taking into account the real evolution, must be solved. This may happen each time a new request is presented.

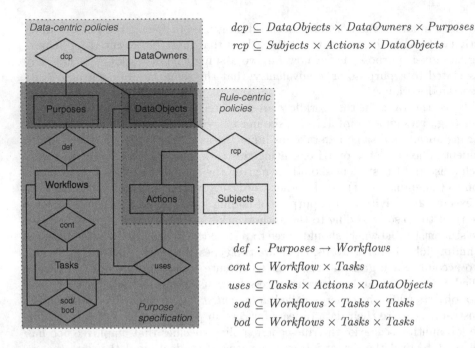

$$dcp \subseteq DataObjects \times DataOwners \times Purposes$$
$$rcp \subseteq Subjects \times Actions \times DataObjects$$

$$def : Purposes \rightarrow Workflows$$
$$cont \subseteq Workflow \times Tasks$$
$$uses \subseteq Tasks \times Actions \times DataObjects$$
$$sod \subseteq Workflows \times Tasks \times Tasks$$
$$bod \subseteq Workflows \times Tasks \times Tasks$$

Fig. 2. Conceptual representation of the data-, rule- and purpose-centric policies.

3   A Declarative Framework for Purpose-Aware Policies

On the left of Fig. 2, it is shown an entity-relationship diagram describing the conceptual organization of our framework (rectangles represent sets of entities and diamonds relationships among them). We have *DataOwners* who own *DataObjects* and decide the *Purposes* for which these can be accessed by means of a data-centric policy (relation *dcp*). *Subjects* can perform certain *Actions* on *DataObjects* according to a rule-centric policy (relation *rcp*). *Purposes* are defined (relation *def*) in terms of *Workflows* which are composed of *Tasks* (relation *cont*) and SoD or BoD constraints; each task can perform some *Actions* on *DataObjects* (relation *uses*).

On the right of Fig. 2, it is shown the formal characterization of the relationships as subsets of the cartesian products of the appropriate sets of entities. To illustrate, recall the running example in Sect. 2:

– the rule- and data-centric policies "bob has the right to read the list of job experiencens of students" and "sam's academic transcripts can be accessed for the purpose of JobHunting" can be specified by relations *rcp* and *dcp* which are such that[4] *rcp*(bob, read, jobExpList) and *dcp*(academicTranscript, sam, jobHunting);

---

[4] Given an *n*-ary relation R, we write $R(e_1, ..., e_n)$ for $(e_1, ..., e_n) \in R$.

- if φ is the specification of the workflow in the upper half of Fig. 1 (we explain below what is φ), then def(JobHunting) $= \varphi$ (notice that def is a total function from *Purposes* to *Workflows*, i.e. every purpose is associated to a workflow);
- the SOD and BOD contraints in Fig. 1 can be specified by relations sod and bod such that $sod(\varphi, \text{interview}, \text{findJobs})$ and $bod(\varphi, \text{interview}, \text{propJobs})$;
- the fact that, for example, tasks interview and optIn are part of the worflow specification φ can be specified by a relation $cont$ such that $cont(\varphi, \text{interview})$ and $cont(\varphi, \text{optIn})$;
- the fact that the task interview reads the user profile can be specified by a relation *uses* such that $uses(\text{interview}, \text{read}, \text{UserProfile})$;

We now explain how we specify workflows in our framework. Following the declarative approach in [2], we have chosen Linear-time Temporal Logic (LTL) as the specification language. The main reason for this is two-fold. First, well-known techniques (see, e.g., [22]) are available to translate procedural descriptions of workflows (e.g., that in the upper half of Fig. 1), and more in general concurrent systems, to LTL formulae. For instance, the lower half of Fig. 1 shows an (incomplete) set of LTL formulae (to be read in conjunction) corresponding to the BPMN workflow in the upper half. The first conjunct on the left means that interview must be the first task to be executed, formula $\neg\text{getExms} \, \mathcal{U}\text{optIn}$ in the third conjunct of the figure means that the academic transcripts cannot be accessed if the student has opted out. Formula $\neg\text{findJobs} \, \mathcal{U}(\text{getExms} \vee \text{getExp})$ in the fourth conjunct means that the execution of task findJobs must not happen before the execution of getExms or getExp.

The second reason for chosing LTL to specify workflows is that it allows us to derive a precise semantics of purpose-aware policies and to reuse available techniques for the off-line and on-line verification of formulae to support the analysis of policies at design-time and their enforcement at run-time. Such verification tasks are presented in Sect. 4. Here we focus on the semantics of purpose-aware policies, starting with the meaning of LTL formulae, which are expressions of the following grammar:

$$\varphi ::= a \mid \neg\varphi \mid \varphi_1 \wedge \varphi_2 \mid O\varphi \mid \varphi_1\mathcal{U}\varphi_2 \mid \Box\varphi \mid \Diamond\varphi \text{ with } a \in Prop$$

where *Prop* is a set of Boolean variables representing tasks. Intuitively, $O\varphi$ means that φ holds at the *next* instant, $\varphi_1\mathcal{U}\varphi_2$ means that at some future instant φ_2 will hold and *until* that point φ_1 holds, $\Box\varphi$ means that φ always holds, and its dual $\Diamond\varphi$ that φ eventually holds. Since we assume workflows to *eventually terminate*, we adopt the finite-trace semantics in [15, 16]. The only notable aspect of this semantics (with respect to the standard semantics as given in, e.g., [22]) is that $O\varphi$ is true iff a next state actually exists *and* it satisfies φ. The models of LTL formulae are finite sequences of Boolean assignments to the variables in *Prop* indexed over natural numbers, which represent instants of a linear and discrete time. The idea is that at a certain time instant, the Boolean variable representing a task is assigned to *true* iff the corresponding task has been executed. As customary in workflow specifications, we assume that one task only is executed at a time. By looking at a sequence of Boolean assignments satisfying a formula, we can thus understand which tasks have been executed and which are not. In other words, a sequence Π of Boolean assignments satisfying a formula φ, in symbols $\Pi \models \varphi$, correspond to a possible execution of the workflow described by φ (see [15,16] for a precise definition). The set of all sequences satisfying a formula φ, i.e. the set of all successful executions of the workflow described by φ, is called its *language* and is denoted by $\mathcal{L}(\varphi)$. It is possible to build an *automaton* (i.e., a finite-state machine) from a formula φ accepting exactly all the traces belonging to $\mathcal{L}(\varphi)$; see again [15,16] for the description of the procedure for doing this.

We can now define the notion of purpose-aware policy as a tuple

$$\mathcal{P} = (DataOwners, Subjects, DataObjects, Actions, Tasks,$$
$$Workflows, Purposes, dcp, rcp, sod, bod, cont, def)$$

whose components are as explained above.

As it is standard in access control models, we introduce the notion of a request as a tuple (wid, sub, tsk, do, p) where $sub \in Subjects$, $tsk \in Tasks$, $do \in DataOwners$, $p \in Purposes$, and wid belongs to the set Wid of workflow identifiers (allowing us to distinguish among different executions of possibly the same workflow). Intuitively, (wid, sub, tsk, do, p) means that subject sub asks the permission to execute task tsk on the data objects owned by the data owner do in the workflow instance wid for the purpose p. The relation $req \subseteq Wid \times Subjects \times Tasks \times DataOwner \times Purposes$ contains all possible requests.

3.1 Semantics of Purpose-Aware Policies

We explain how a request (wid, sub, tsk, do, p) is granted or denied according to a purpose-aware policy $\mathcal{P}$. The idea is to derive a first-order LTL formula from the LTL formula $def(p)$ constraining the ordering of requests such that the rule-, data-centric policies and SOD and BOD constraints are satisfied. Thus, instead of sequences of Boolean assignments, we consider first-order models which differ for the interpretation of requests only. For the sake of brevity, we do not give a formal semantics of first-order LTL on finite-traces but only some intuitions and refer the interested reader to [19] for the details.

First of all, we observe that every workflow instance can be considered in isolation since the framework presented above allows one to specify only constraints within a workflow instance and not accross instances. For this reason, we introduce an operator to identify requests referring to the same workflow instance wid out of a trace Π containing requests referring to arbitrary workflow instances, i.e. $\Pi|_{\text{wid}} = req_1(\text{wid}, sub_1, tsk_1, do_1, \text{p}), \ldots, req_n(\text{wid}, sub_n, tsk_n, do_n, \text{p})$ is the trace representing the evolution of the specific workflow instance wid. Notice that requests in $\Pi|_{\text{wid}}$ share the same workflow identifier wid and purpose p whereas subjects, tasks, and data owners may be different. Given a purpose-aware policy $\mathcal{P}$, for each purpose $\text{p} \in Purposes$ such that $def(\text{p}) = \varphi$, we build a (first-order) LTL formula $\Phi_{\text{p}} := \varphi \wedge \Lambda \wedge \Sigma \wedge B$ where

$$\Lambda := \bigwedge_{cont(\varphi,t)} t \leftrightarrow \exists sub, do. \left(\begin{array}{l} req(\mathsf{wid}, sub, t, do, \mathsf{p}) \wedge \\ \bigwedge_{uses(act,t,obj)} dcp(do, obj, \mathsf{p}) \wedge rcp(sub, act, obj) \end{array} \right)$$

$$\Sigma := \bigwedge_{sod(\varphi,t_1,t_2)} \xi(t_1, t_2, =) \wedge \xi(t_2, t_1, =)$$

$$B := \bigwedge_{bod(\varphi,t_1,t_2)} \xi(t_1, t_2, \neq) \wedge \xi(t_2, t_1, \neq)$$

$$\xi(t, t', \bowtie) := \Box \forall sub, sub'. \left(\begin{array}{l} \forall do.req(\mathsf{wid}, sub, t, do, \mathsf{p}) \wedge \\ \Diamond \forall do.req(\mathsf{wid}, sub', t', do, \mathsf{p}) \end{array} \right) \rightarrow sub \bowtie sub'.$$

Formula Λ says that in order to execute task t for purpose p, we need to check that subject sub who has requested to execute it is entitled to do so according to both the rule- and data-centric policies in $\mathcal{P}$, thus formalizing the check (**C1**) in the introduction. Formulae Σ and B encode the SoD and BoD constraints in $\mathcal{P}$, respectively, which are both derived from the same template formula $\xi(t, t', \bowtie)$, saying that if a request for executing t' is seen after that for executing t, then the two subjects performing such tasks must be either different (when $\bowtie$ is $\neq$, i.e., in case of a SoD) or equal (when $\bowtie$ is $=$, i.e., in case of a BoD). Formulae φ, Σ and B, thanks to their temporal characterization, formalize the check (**C2**) in the introduction. A sequence of requests $\Pi|_{\mathsf{wid}}$ for a purpose p and an instance wid of the workflow $def(\mathsf{p})$ *satisfies* the purpose-aware policy $\mathcal{P}$ iff $\Pi|_{\mathsf{id}} \models \Phi_{\mathsf{p}}$. By abusing notation, we write $\mathcal{L}(\varphi)$ for all such sequences. Given a sequence σ of (previous) requests, a (new) request $r = (\mathsf{wid}, sub, tsk, do, \mathsf{p})$ is *granted* by the purpose-aware policy $\mathcal{P}$ iff wid is an instance of the workflow $def(\mathsf{p})$ and there exists a sequence σ' of requests such that σ, r, σ' is in $\mathcal{L}(\varphi)$; otherwise, it is *denied*.

To illustrate some of the notions introduced above, let us consider the first-order LTL formula that can be derived from the example in Sect. 2. As already observed, the formula φ associated to the purpose JobHunting is the conjunction of the formulae in the lower half of Fig. 1. The conjunct in Λ for interview is

$$\mathsf{interview} \leftrightarrow \exists sub, do. \left(\begin{array}{l} req(\mathsf{wid}, sub, \mathsf{interview}, do, \mathsf{jobHunting}) \wedge \\ dcp(do, \mathsf{userProfile}, \mathsf{jobHunting}) \wedge \\ rcp(sub, \mathsf{read}, \mathsf{userProfile}) \end{array} \right).$$

The formula representing the SoD constraint between interview and findJobs is

$$\Box \forall sub, sub'. \left(\begin{array}{l} \forall do.req(wid, sub, \mathsf{interview}, do, \mathsf{jobHunting}) \wedge \\ \Diamond \forall do.req(wid, sub', \mathsf{findJobs}, do, \mathsf{jobHunting}) \end{array} \right) \rightarrow sub \neq sub' \wedge$$

$$\Box \forall sub, sub'. \left(\begin{array}{l} \forall do.req(wid, sub, \mathsf{findJobs}, do, \mathsf{jobHunting}) \wedge \\ \Diamond \forall do.req(wid, sub', \mathsf{interview}, do, \mathsf{jobHunting}) \end{array} \right) \rightarrow sub \neq sub'.$$

Notice that the second conjunct above can be dropped without loss of generality since, from $def(\mathsf{jobHunting})$, it is possible to derive that it is never the case that task findJobs is executed before task interview. From a complete specification of the purpose-aware policy $\mathcal{P}$ for the running example, it is not difficult to see that the request $r_0 = (\mathsf{wid}, \mathsf{bob}, \mathsf{interview}, \mathsf{sam}, \mathsf{jobHunting})$ is granted by applying the definition given above as follows. First, take σ to be the empty sequence as r_0 is the first request. Second, we can derive that task interview can be executed from the formula for interview above and the fact that $\mathcal{P}$ is such that $dcp(\mathsf{sam}, \mathsf{userProfile}, \mathsf{jobHunting})$, i.e. sam decided to release his user profile for the purpose of job hunting, and $rcp(\mathsf{bob}, \mathsf{read}, \mathsf{userProfile})$, i.e. bob has the right to read user profiles. Third, take $\sigma' = r_1, r_2, r_3, r_4, r_5$ for

$$r_1 := (\mathsf{wid}, \mathsf{sam}, \mathsf{optOut}, \mathsf{sam}, \mathsf{jobHunting}) \qquad r_2 := (\mathsf{wid}, \mathsf{bob}, \mathsf{getExp}, \mathsf{sam}, \mathsf{jobHunting})$$
$$r_3 := (\mathsf{wid}, \mathsf{adam}, \mathsf{findJobs}, \mathsf{sam}, \mathsf{jobHunting}) \qquad r_4 := (\mathsf{wid}, \mathsf{bob}, \mathsf{propJobs}, \mathsf{sam}, \mathsf{jobHunting})$$
$$r_5 := (\mathsf{wid}, \mathsf{sam}, \mathsf{choosJob}, \mathsf{sam}, \mathsf{jobHunting})$$

where r_1 corresponds to the fact that sam has opted out and only his past experiences can be released, r_2 to the fact that bob can retrive sam's past experiences (as said in Sect. 2), r_3 to the fact that the jobs for sam are found by adam, who is distinct from bob in order to satisfy the SoD constraint between interview and findJobs in Fig. 1 (indeed, we assume that bob can execute getExp according to $\mathcal{P}$), r_4 to the fact that the list of found jobs is proposed to sam by bob in order to satisfy the BoD constraint between interview and propJobs in Fig. 1, and r_5 to the fact that sam decides to pick a job from the proposed list.

We close the Section by remarking that this technique allows to discover inconsistencies as soon as they occur, i.e., at the earliest possible time. This is sometimes called *early detection* in the BPM literature, and it is a notable feature of temporal logics. To explain the concept, assume that, according to $\mathcal{P}$, *only* bob can perform the activities of jobHunting: when $r_0 =$ $(\mathsf{wid}, \mathsf{bob}, \mathsf{interview}, \mathsf{sam}, \mathsf{jobHunting})$ (or actually any other request for purpose jobHunting) is presented to the system, we are able to understand that no execution can ever successfully complete the workflow, as sooner or later task findJobs must be executed by someone different from bob which however does not have the rights to do it. As a result, r_0 is denied and hence bob is not granted to access the data even if, by observing the current state, there is no evidence yet of any violation.

The decidability and complexity of answering requests is studied in the following section.

4   Policies Verification

We now formalize, provide a solution and give complexity results to the following verification tasks:

Purpose achievement problem : given a purpose-aware policy $\mathcal{P}$ and a purpose p, is it possible to successfully execute workflow $def(\mathsf{p})$? That is to say: is it possible to assign tasks to subjects such that policy $\mathcal{P}$ is satisfied and the workflow successfully terminates?

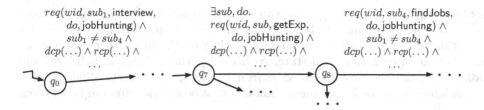

Fig. 3. An excerpt of the pre-automaton for formula $\Phi_{\text{jobHunting}}$.

Runtime policy enforcement : given a purpose-aware policy $\mathcal{P}$, the current work-flow execution trace π, and a new request r_i, can r_i be granted or must be denied in order for the workflow to eventually terminate (check (**C2**) in the introduction) and such that the sequence of granted request always satisfies $\mathcal{P}$ (check (**C1**))?

Due to space constraints, proofs have been omitted. We refer the interested reader to [17] for the full-length version of this work.

4.1 Purpose Achievement Problem

Technically speaking, this problem amounts to check, given a purpose p in a purpose-aware policy $\mathcal{P}$, if Φ_{p} is satisfiable, i.e., if there exists a trace $\Pi|_{\text{wid}}$ (where wid is a generic identifier for workflow $def(\text{p})$) such that $\Pi|_{\text{wid}} \models \Phi_{\text{p}}$.

   We adopt an automata-based approach to solve the problem, which consists in building the automaton for Φ_{p}, which we call A_{p}, and check if there exists a path to a final state. Since Φ_{p} is first-order, we exploit the modularity of our framework and the of symbolic techniques in [19] to build the automaton with a reasonable complexity. Figure 3 shows an excerpt of the automaton for $\Phi_{\text{jobHunting}}$, where for the sake of readability we abbreviated formulas on edges. Indeed, on each edge, along with formula $req(wid, sub, \text{t}, do, \text{p})$, taking care of the order of activities, constraint $\bigwedge_{act,obj \in uses(act,\text{t},obj)}(dcp(do, obj, \text{p}) \land rcp(sub, act, obj))$ is also present, checking that dcp and rcp policies are met. We notice that variables for subjects involved in SoD or BoD constraints are *free*, i.e., not bounded by any quantifier. Indeed, as tasks interview and jobHunting must be executed by different subjects (SoD), variables for such subjects, namely sub_1 and sub_4, are free and must be different.

Theorem 1. *Given a purpose-aware policy $\mathcal{P}$, and a purpose p with $def(\text{p}) = \varphi$, the construction of the automata A_{p} requires exponential space in the number of temporal operators of φ, sod and bod.*

Automaton A_{p} is a symbolic structure where we check whether there is a way to reach a final state—thus solving a workflow satisfiability problem— by trying to satisfy formulas on edges. Indeed, satisfy a formula (w.r.t. $\mathcal{P}$) precisely means assigning a task to a subject which is authorized by $\mathcal{P}$ to perform it. Consider, e.g., formula $\exists sub, do.req(wid, sub, \text{findJobs}, do,$

jobHunting) $\bigwedge_{uses(act,\text{findJobs},obj)} dcp(do, obj, \mathsf{p}) \wedge rcp(sub, act, obj)$ on edge from q_7 to q_8 in Fig. 3: assuming that bob has the rights to perform getExp, the substitution bob/sub satisfy the formula according to $\mathcal{P}$, and so that edge can be use to build a path to a final state. Analogously, the assignment bob/sub_1 and adam/sub_4 satisfies formulas on edges from q_0 and q_8 respectively. When no such an assignment can be found, the workflow cannot be successfully completed given policy $\mathcal{P}$.

Theorem 2. *Given a finite purpose-aware policy $\mathcal{P}$ and a purpose p with $def(\mathsf{p}) = \varphi$ the purpose achievement problem can be solved in exponential time in the size of φ, sod and bod.*

4.2   Runtime Policies Verification

Given a sequence π of (previous) requests and a new request r, should we allow r or not?

Traditional LTL semantics presented in the previous Section is not adequate for evaluating requests at runtime, as it considers the trace Π seen so far to be *complete*. Instead, we want to evaluate the current request by considering that the execution could still continue and this evolving aspect has a significant impact on the evaluation: at each step, indeed, the outcome may have a degree of uncertainty due to the fact that future executions are yet unknown.

Consider, e.g., that so far request r_0 has been granted, where $r_0 :=$ (wid, bob, interview, sam, jobHunting) is as in the previous Section. Assume that now request $r_1 :=$ (wid, sam, optOut, sam, jobHunting) is presented and must be evaluated: we may be tempted to use the traditional LTL semantics, which returns $\pi : r_0, r_1 \not\models \Phi_{\mathsf{p}}$ because some constraints have not been satisfied (such as: "eventually findJobs must be executed") but this is not a good reason to deny request r_1, as the workflow execution will not stop after r_1 (and actually any other single request different from r_1 would not have satisfied Φ_{p} anyway).

A more complex analysis is hence required, which assesses the capability of a partial trace to satisfy or violate a formula φ *in the future* by analyzing whether it belongs to the set of *prefixes* of $\mathcal{L}(\varphi)$ and/or the set of prefixes of $\mathcal{L}(\neg\varphi)$. Roughly speaking, let $\pi : r_0, r_1$ be as before: we want to check if there exists a possible sequence of future requests $\pi' : r_2, r_3, \dots r_n$ such that $\pi, \pi' \models \Phi_{\mathsf{p}}$ and, if this is the case, we grant request r_1. We can actually be more precise, and evaluate the current request in four different ways.

Given a (partial) trace π, a formula Φ_{p} and a new request r, we adopt the runtime semantics in [15] which is such that:

- $\pi, r \models [\Phi_p]_{\mathrm{RV}} = temp\_true$, when π, r *temporarily satisfies* Φ_p, i.e., π is currently compliant with Φ_p, but a possible system future prosecution may lead to falsify Φ_p;
- $\pi, r \models [\Phi_p]_{\mathrm{RV}} = temp\_false$, when that the current trace *temporarily falsify* Φ_p, i.e., π, r is not current compliant with Φ_p, but a possible system future prosecution may lead to satisfy Φ_p;
- $\pi, r \models [\Phi_p]_{\mathrm{RV}} = true$, when π, r *satisfies* Φ_p and it will always do, no matter how it proceeds;

– $\pi, r \models [\Phi_p]_{\mathrm{RV}} = false$, when π, r *falsifies* Φ_p and it will always do, no matter how it proceeds.

A new request r is *denied* if $\pi, r \models [\Phi_p]_{\mathrm{RV}} = false$, and *granted* otherwise.

Intuitively, every time a new request is presented, we check that: (*i*) from the current automaton state there exists an outgoing edge whose formula is satisfied by the current request (which corresponds to check (**C1**) in the introduction) and (*ii*) from the arrival state there exists a path to a final state, which is a WSP that exactly corresponds to check (**C2**). Such analyses are performed on an automaton which is different from the one presented in the previous Section, as it not only has to check prefixes of Φ_p, but also that of $\neg\Phi_p$, in order to distinguish among the four cases above (see [15] for details). However, the automaton technique shown in [19] can equally be used.

Once the automaton has been computed, the current sequence of requests is analyzed. Notice that, differently from the offline verification, assignment of users to tasks are partially given by the current and previous requests, and hence we have to check if such partial assignments can be extended, according to policy $\mathcal{P}$, in order to reach a final state. Consider again $r_0 :=$ (wid, bob, interview, sam, jobHunting) to be the already granted request and $r_1 :=$ (wid, sam, optOut, sam, jobHunting) to be the current one. Request r_0 provides the assignment bob/sub_1 which forces us to solve the WSP with the additional constraint of $sub_1 = $ bob. Actually, $r_0, r_1 \models [\Phi_p]_{\mathrm{RV}} = temp\_false$, as $r_0, r_1 \not\models \Phi_p$ but there exists a sequence of assignments of users to tasks that eventually satisfies it, which is sequence r_2, r_3, r_4, r_5 shown in the previous Section. We remark that a WSP instance must be performed each time a new request is presented. Indeed, the actual next request $\hat{r}_2$ (still unknown at the current time) is in general different from r_2, and hence sequence r_2, r_3, r_4, r_5 found at this step as a witness of a possible future execution is of no use as the system progresses. Notably, the fact that we discover inconsistencies at the earliest possible time (early detection) allows us to block workflow executions exactly when a possible successful path can still be followed. When this is not guaranteed, the online enforcement is inefficient as when the precise point of deviation from the right path is unknown: (*i*) possible several tasks are executed before realizing the inconsistency (hence several data are accessed thus breaking the security) and (*ii*) possibly it is too late to recover the execution.

Theorem 3. *Given a purpose-aware policy $\mathcal{P}$ and a purpose p with $def(\mathsf{p}) = \varphi$, the runtime policy verification requires, at each step, exponential time in the size of φ, sod and bod.*

5   Discussion and Related Work

We have presented a declarative framework to specify and enforce purpose-aware policies. In the literature, several proposals have attempted to characterize the notion of purpose in the context of security policies. Some of them (e.g., [10]) propose to manage and enforce purpose by self-declaration, i.e. subjects explicitly announce the purpose for accessing data. While this provides a first effort to embody purpose in access control policies, these approaches are not able to precent malicious subjects from claiming false purposes. Other works (e.g., [30]) propose to extend the Role Based Access Control model with mechanisms to automatically determine the purpose for which certain data are accessed based on the roles of subjects. The main drawback of these approaches is the fact that roles and purposes are not always aligned and members of the same role may serve different purposes in their actions. Other approaches (e.g., [11]) are based on extensions of (Attribute Based) Access Control models for handling personal data in web services or (e.g., [31]) on extensions of Usage Control models for the distributed enforcement of the purpose for data usage (see, e.g., [29]). The main problem of these approaches derives from the limited capability of the application initiating the handling of personal data to control it when this has been transferred to another (remote) application in the distributed system. Our framework avoids this problem by assuming a central (workflow-based) system acting as a Policy Enforcement Point (PEP) intercepting all requests of executing a particular action on certain data. Such an architecture for the PEP is reasonable in cloud-based environments (e.g., the Smart Campus platform briefly described in Sect. 2) in which services and applications are implemented via of Application Programming Interfaces (APIs) so that remote applications provide only the user interface while the control logic is executed on the cloud platform and can thus be under the control of the central PEP.

The common and more serious drawback of the approaches considered above is that they fail to recognize that the purpose of an action (or task) is determined by its position in a workflow, i.e. by its relationships with other, interrelated, actions. This observation has been done in more recent works—e.g., [21,28,33]—and is also the starting point of our framework in this paper. We share the effort of formalizing the notion of purpose as a pre-requisite of future actions. In future work, we would like to study how hierarchical workflows (i.e. workflows containing complex activities, specified in terms of lower level tasks) can be expressed in our framework so as to capture the specification of purposes as high-level activities as done in [21]. The main difference with previous works is our focus on run-time enforcement of purpose-aware policies while [28,33] on auditing. Furthermore, the formal framework adopted to develop these proposals are different from ours: [33] uses Markov Decision Processes, [28] a process calculus, and [21] an *ad hoc* modal logic. These choices force the authors of [21,28] to design algorithms for policy enforcement or auditing from scratch. For instance, [21] gives a model checking algorithm on top of which a run-time monitor for purpose-based policies can be implemented, without studying its complexity. In contrast, we use a first-order temporal logic which comes with a wide range of techniques to solve logical problems (see, e.g., [15]) that can be reused (or adapted) to support the run-time enforcement of purpose-aware policies. For instance, we were able to derive the first (to the best of our knowledge) complexity result of answering authorization requests at run-time under a given purpose-aware policy: exponential time in the number of authorization constraints (Theorem 3). This complexity is somehow intrisic to the problem when assuming that the purpose of an action is determined by its position in a workflow, as we do in this paper. As a consequence, achieving a purpose amounts to the succesful execution of the associated workflow, which is called the Workflow Satisfiability Problem (WSP) in the literature [12] and is known to be NP-hard already in the presence of one SoD constraint [34]. Several works have proposed techniques to solve both the off-line [27,34] and the on-line [6,8] version of the WSP but none considers purpose-aware policies as we do here.

Indeed, we are not the first to use first-order LTL for the specification of security policies. For example, [26] shows how to express various types of SoD constraints in the Role Based Access Control model by using first-order LTL. However, the paper provides no method for the run-time monitoring of such constraints and do not discuss if and how the approach can be used in the context of workflow specifications. Instead, the work in [13] uses (a fragment of propositional) LTL to develop algorithms for checking the successfull termination of a workflow. Both works do not discuss purpose-aware policies. To the best of our knowledge, only the approach in [4] shares with ours the use of first-order LTL to specify and enforce utility and privacy in business workflows. The main difference is in the long-term goal: we want to give rigorous foundation to specification and verification techniques for purpose-based policies, while [4] is seen as a first step towards to the development of a general, clear, and comprehensive framework for reducing high-level utility and privacy requirements to specific operating guidelines that can be applied at individual steps in business workflows. It would be an interesting future work to see if and how the two approaches can be combined together in order to derive purpose-aware policies from high-level privacy requirements typically found in laws, directives, and regulations.

Our choice of using a first-order LTL formula (Sect. 3.1) as the semantics of purpose has two main advantages. First, it allows us to reuse well-known techniques to specify access control policies, what we call data- and rule-centric policies, by using (fragments of) first-order logic (see, e.g., [3,23]). Second, it allows us to reuse the techniques for the specification and enforcement of workflows put forward by the declarative approach to business process specification in [2,24,35]. However, these works focus on tasks and their execution constraints, disregarding the security and privacy aspects related to accessing the data manipulated by the tasks. A first proposal of adding the data dimension to this approach is in [18], which has been from which we have borrowed the construction of the automata for off-line and on-line verification in this paper (Sect. 4). The choice of considering first-order LTL over finite instead of infinite traces goes back to [16] in which it is argued that this is the right choice for business process which are supposed to terminate as the workflows associated purposes, which can be achieved in this way. In general, monitoring first-order LTL formulae is undecidable [7] but, under the finite domain assumption, [19] shows decidability. Such an assumption is reasonable in our framework where subjects are usually employees of a company (e.g., the job hunting organization in Sect. 2) whose number is bounded. Our verification techniques are also related to mechanisms for enforcing security policies, such as [5,29,32]. However, these works mainly focus on access or usage control policies and are of limited or no use for purpose-based policies considered in this paper.

References

1. Directive 95/46/ec of the european parliament and of the council of 24 october 1995. http://eur-lex.europa.eu/LexUriServ/LexUriServ.do?uri=CELEX: 31995L0046:en:HTML
2. van der Aalst, W.M.P., Pesic, M., Schonenberg, H.: Declarative workflows: balancing between flexibility and support. CS - R&D **23**(2), 99–113 (2009)
3. Arkoudas, K., Chadha, R., Chiang, C.J.: Sophisticated access control via SMT and logical frameworks. Proc. ACM TISSEC **16**(4), 17 (2014)
4. Barth, A., Datta, A., Mitchell, J.C., Sundaram, S.: Privacy and utility in business processes. In: Proceedings of 20th IEEE Computer Security Foundations Symposium, July 2007
5. Basin, D., Klaedtke, F., Müller, S.: Monitoring security policies with metric first-order temporal logic. In: Proceedings of ACM SACMAT, pp. 23–34. ACM, New York, USA (2010)
6. Basin, D., Burri, S.J., Karjoth, G.: Dynamic enforcement of abstract separation of duty constraints. ACM TISSeC **15**(3), 13:1–13:30 (2012)
7. Bauer, A., Küster, J.-C., Vegliach, G.: From propositional to first-order monitoring. In: Legay, A., Bensalem, S. (eds.) RV 2013. LNCS, vol. 8174, pp. 59–75. Springer, Heidelberg (2013)
8. Bertolissi, C., dos Santos, D.R., Ranise, S.: Automated synthesis of run-time monitors to enforce authorization policies in business processes. In: Asia CCS. ACM (2015)
9. Byun, J.W., Bertino, E., Li, N.: Purpose based access control of complex data for privacy protection. In: Proceedings of the ACM SACMAT, pp. 102–110. ACM (2005)
10. Byun, J., Li, N.: Purpose based access control for privacy protection in relational database systems. VLDB J. **17**(4), 603–619 (2008)
11. Ardagna, C.A., Cremonini, M., De Capitani di Vimercati, S., Samarati, P.: A privacy-aware access control system. J. Comput. Secur. (JCS) **16**(4), 369–392 (2008)
12. Crampton, J.: A reference monitor for workflow systems with constrained task execution. In: Proceedings of ACM SACMAT, pp. 38–47. ACM (2005)
13. Crampton, J., Huth, M., Kuo, J.P.: Authorized workflow schemas: deciding realizability through LTL(F) model checking. Int. J. Soft. Tools Technol. Transf. (STTT) **16**(1), 31–48 (2014)
14. De Capitani di Vimercati, S., Foresti, S., Jajodia, S., Samarati, P.: Access control policies and languages. IJCSE **3**(2), 94–102 (2007)
15. De Giacomo, G., De Masellis, R., Grasso, M., Maggi, F.M., Montali, M.: Monitoring business metaconstraints based on LTL and LDL for finite traces. In: Sadiq, S., Soffer, P., Völzer, H. (eds.) BPM 2014. LNCS, vol. 8659, pp. 1–17. Springer, Heidelberg (2014)
16. De Giacomo, G., De Masellis, R., Montali, M.: Reasoning on LTL on finite traces: Insensitivity to infiniteness. In: Proceedings of AAAI Conference on AI, pp. 1027–1033 (2014)
17. De Masellis, R., Ghidini, C., Ranise, S.: A declarative framework for specifying and enforcing purpose-aware policies (2015). arxiv.org/abs/1507.08153
18. De Masellis, R., Maggi, F.M., Montali, M.: Monitoring data-aware business constraints with finite state automata. In: Proceedings of ICSSP, pp. 134–143 (2014)

19. De Masellis, R., Su, J.: Runtime enforcement of first-order LTL properties on data-aware business processes. In: Basu, S., Pautasso, C., Zhang, L., Fu, X. (eds.) ICSOC 2013. LNCS, vol. 8274, pp. 54–68. Springer, Heidelberg (2013)
20. Jafari, M., Safavi-Naini, R., Sheppard, N.P.: Enforcing purpose of use via workflows. In: Proceedings of WPES, pp. 113–116 (2009)
21. Jafari, M., Safavi-Naini, R., Fong, P.W.L., Barker, K.: A framework for expressing and enforcing purpose-based privacy policies. ACM Trans. Inf. Syst. Secur. **17**(1), 3:1–3:31 (2014)
22. Kröger, F., Merz, S.: Temporal Logic and State Systems. Texts in Theoretical Computer Science. An EATCS Series. Springer, Heidelberg (2008)
23. Li, N., Mitchell, J.C.: Datalog with constraints: a foundation for trust management languages. In: PADL 2003, pp. 58–73 (2003)
24. Maggi, F.M., Montali, M., Westergaard, M., van der Aalst, W.M.P.: Monitoring business constraints with linear temporal logic: an approach based on colored automata. In: Rinderle-Ma, S., Toumani, F., Wolf, K. (eds.) BPM 2011. LNCS, vol. 6896, pp. 132–147. Springer, Heidelberg (2011)
25. Masoumzadeh, A., Joshi, J.B.D.: PuRBAC: purpose-aware role-based access control. In: Meersman, R., Tari, Z. (eds.) OTM 2008, Part II. LNCS, vol. 5332, pp. 1104–1121. Springer, Heidelberg (2008)
26. Mossakowski, T., Drouineaud, M., Sohr, K.: A temporal-logic extension of role-based access control covering dynamic separation of duties. In: Proceedings of TIME-ICTL, pp. 83–90 (2003)
27. P. Yang, X. Xie, I.R., Lu, S.: Satisfiability analysis of workflows with control-flow patterns and authorization constraints. IEEE TSC 99 (2013)
28. Petković, M., Prandi, D., Zannone, N.: Purpose control: did you process the data for the intended purpose? In: Jonker, W., Petković, M. (eds.) SDM 2011. LNCS, vol. 6933, pp. 145–168. Springer, Heidelberg (2011)
29. Pretschner, A., Hilty, M., Basin, D.: Distributed usage control. Comm. ACM **49**, 39–44 (2006)
30. Qun, N., Elisa, B., Jorge, L., Carolyn, B., Karat, C.M., Alberto, T.: Privacy-aware role-based access control. TISSeC **13**, 1–31 (2010)
31. Rath, A.T., Colin, J.N.: Modeling and expressing purpose validation policy for privacy-aware usage control in distributed environment. In: Proceedings of ICUIMC, pp. 14:1–14:8. ACM (2014)
32. Schneider, F.B.: Enforceable security policies. TISSeC **3**, 30–50 (2000)
33. Tschantz, M.C., Datta, A., Wing, J.M.: Formalizing and enforcing purpose restrictions in privacy policies. In: IEEE Symposium on Security and Privacy, pp. 176–190 (2012)
34. Wang, Q., Li, N.: Satisfiability and resiliency in workflow authorization systems. TISSeC **13**, 40:1–40:35 (2010)
35. Westergaard, M., Maggi, F.M.: Declare: A tool suite for declarative workflow modeling and enactment. In: Proceedings of BPM (2011)
36. Westin, A.: Privacy and Freedom. Atheneum, New York (1968)

How to Trust the Re-use of Data

Erisa Karafili$^{(\boxtimes)}$, Hanne Riis Nielson, and Flemming Nielson

DTU Compute, Technical University of Denmark, Kongens Lyngby, Denmark
{erka,hrni,fnie}@dtu.dk

Abstract. Research in natural sciences and life sciences involve carrying out experiments to collect data as well as carrying out analysis to interpret the data. Increasingly data is being made available to other scientists in big databases. The scientific process builds on the idea that research results can be independently validated by other researchers. However, the concern about the correct re-use of data is also increasing. As illustrated by a currently evolving case of alleged scientific mispractice there is a need to support a reliable re-use of data. To solve this challenge we introduce an enriched coordination language based on Klaim, that can model the coordination of the re-use of data in the research community. We define the formal semantics of our language and develop a static analysis that can be used to check whether we have a trustable re-use of data.

1 Introduction

The sharing and re-use of data is becoming an important and normal procedure in the scientific community, where scientists use the data for proving their hypotheses. The reliability of the shared and re-used data is an important problem. One of the main causes of not having reliable data is because of their improper re-use. We introduce below a real case from the neuroscience research community, where there is an alleged mispractice of data re-use. In this case the same data are used for proving the same or related hypotheses, without checking the data or repeating the experiments with other sets of data. In this paper, we propose an IT solution for avoiding such problems during the re-use of data.

In the past, scientists were quite skeptical about sharing their data and re-use of other scientists' data. Some of their doubts concern the infrastructure where the data is collected or the quality of documentation of the collected data [10,15]. Other doubts of the scientific community concern ethical, privacy, and trust issues about the data [15]. An important issue during the re-use of data is its reliability. Reliable data should give reliable results, that can be reproduced by using disjoint data sets when using the same or different scientific methods. Deciding if a data set is reliable or not, is not trivial. During the re-use of data one should be careful about the hypothesis for which the data were previously used. Using the same data set for proving the same or similar results is not *good practice*. This is because the data set can be corrupted, or biased in a certain direction, or badly collected/documented, or there can be hidden errors,

© Springer International Publishing Switzerland 2015
S. Foresti (Ed.): STM 2015, LNCS 9331, pp. 72–88, 2015.
DOI: 10.1007/978-3-319-24858-5_5

which were not relevant for a certain scientific method, but quite important for another one, and also some of the data in the data set can be incorrect (written by dishonest or careless scientists). Thus, if the same data set is used for proving the same results, we cannot be sure that what we are proving is true.

The re-use of not disjoint data sets for proving the same results was the central problem in the *Penkowa case* [6]. This Danish scientist based a part of her research on some results obtained by re-using the same data set. Penkowa established different results, that were connected with each other, by using the same data set, without repeating the experiments with other sets of data, and in some cases without stating that the data she was using were the same as in some previous works. Everything came out, some years after, when some students were complaining of not being able to replicate the results by using different data sets. After several studies made by a scientific committee, it emerged that the results of these papers were based on a result that could not be replicated.

The economical, scientific, and ethical consequences of this case were quite severe. Some of Penkowa's papers were retracted, and the negative impact was extended also to the work of other scientists that used the results published in the retracted papers. Klarlund Pedersen, one of the senior authors of Penkowa's papers was also involved and had to deal with the negative effects of this case.

What started just by the re-use of the same data set for proving the same or similar results, became an avalanche of negative effects. This case created doubts in trusting the re-use of data. The scientific community seems to agree that corrupted data cannot be re-used and that special attention should be given to the re-use of data. This problem brought out that there is no IT support for avoiding the above scenario happening in the future. We know that there is no solution for avoiding the creation of corrupted data. However, it is possible to coordinate the re-use of data, in a way that does not permit the occurrence of other scenarios, as the one described above.

In this paper we develop an IT solution based on the coordination language Klaim [7,9], for defining a model that coordinates a reliable re-use of data between scientists. We decide to be based on Klaim because the language we want to construct has to model different locations that want to access to other locations or sets of locations, as is done in Klaim [8]. In this version of Klaim we use two non-blocking actions, that prevent the processes on being blocked. For coordinating the use of sets of data by scientists we add the notion of *goal* to our language. The goal represents the purpose for why the scientist is using the data set.

Our solution uses Flow Logic [12], which statically determines the behavior of different processes, where the processes are composed of the different actions that can occur in our model. Through the Flow Logic we developed a static analysis, which checks that different scientists use disjoint data sets for proving the same goal, and that the same scientists cannot use the same data sets for proving similar goals.

Through our language and the static analysis we can model the coordination of the re-use of data sets and solve the above problem, by ensuring a reliable re-use of data. Our solution helps in trusting the re-using and sharing of data. An obvious application of our language is in the coordination of the re-use of data in Big Data.

We now introduce some related work. There are different coordination languages that can be used for coordinating data accesses. One of them is BIP [3,4], that allows building complex systems by coordinating the behavior of a set of atomic components. Other interesting languages are REO [2], that enforces a channel-based coordination model, and other coordination languages based on Actor Model [1]. We decided to use Klaim in our work, as it permits us to naturally model distributed data repositories. Our extension of Klaim checks that the data are accessed for the right goal. If a location is accessing the data for a certain goal, then we expect that iy is going to use the data for that goal, but we do not check what is going on after we grant the access to the data. The work in [13] deals with this problem, and checks that the data have been used for the intended goal/purpose. For verifying the actual use of data, they use COWS [11], that is a process calculus used not just for web service orchestration, but also in flow graphs, and business process [14].

In Sect. 2, we introduce the syntax and the formal semantics of our language. In Sect. 3, we develop the static analysis and show how it can be applied through an example. In Sect. 4, we give some conclusions and future works.

2   Klaim with Goals

Our coordination language is based on Klaim. Whilst, in classic Klaim we had just the notion of *location*, for our language we decide to distinguish the locations from the data. We have single data and locations as well as sequence of them, called *tuple* of data and locations, denoted respectively by $\overrightarrow{d}$, and $\overrightarrow{l}$, where: $\overrightarrow{d} = \langle d_1, d_2, \cdots, d_n \rangle$ and $\overrightarrow{l} = \langle l_1, l_2, \cdots, l_m \rangle$. In the coming subsections we introduce the syntax and the semantics of our language.

2.1   Syntax

In Table 1, we present the syntax of our coordination language that is composed of nets, processes, and actions. Before explaining in detail the syntax, we present the syntactic categories of the basic elements we are going to use.

The first basic category is the set of data **Data**. If $b \in$ **Data**, then b can be a data constant, denoted by d, or an occurrence of a data variable, denoted by x. In case of data patterns, if $b^\lambda \in$ **DataPat**, then b^λ can be a data constant d, an occurrences of data variable $!x$, or an applied occurrences of a data variable x.

The other category is the set of locations **Loc**. If $\ell \in$ **Loc**, then ℓ can be a locality constant, denoted by l, or an occurrence of a locality variable, denoted by u. In case of locality patterns, we have that, if $\ell^\lambda \in$ **LocPat**, then ℓ^λ can be a locality constant l, an occurrence of locality variable $!u$, or an applied occurrence of a locality variable u.

Table 1. Syntax: nets, processes and actions

$$N \in \textbf{Net} \quad N ::= N_1 || N_2 \mid l :: P \mid l :: \overrightarrow{d}, \text{AC}$$

$$P \in \textbf{Proc} \quad P ::= P_1 | P_2 \mid \sum_i a_i.P_i \mid *P$$

$$a \in \textbf{Act} \quad a ::= \textbf{out}(\overrightarrow{b})@\ell \mid \textbf{in}(\overrightarrow{b^\lambda}, G)@\ell \mid \textbf{read}(\overrightarrow{b^\lambda}, G)@\ell \mid \textbf{noread}(\overrightarrow{b^\lambda}, G)@\ell \mid$$
$$\textbf{get}(\overrightarrow{b^\lambda}, G)@\ell \mid \textbf{noget}(\overrightarrow{b^\lambda}, G)@\ell$$

$$\text{AC} \in \textbf{AC} \quad \text{AC} ::= \{(G_1 : l_1), (G_2 : l_2), \cdots, (G_m : l_n)\} \mid \emptyset$$

$$\ell \in \textbf{Loc} \quad \ell ::= l \mid u \qquad\qquad \ell^\lambda \in \textbf{LocPat} \quad \ell^\lambda ::= \ell \mid !u$$

$$b \in \textbf{Data} \quad b ::= d \mid x \qquad\qquad b^\lambda \in \textbf{DataPat} \quad b^\lambda ::= b \mid !x$$

The last basic category is the set of goals $G \in \textbf{Goal}$ that a location wants to accomplish when performing certain actions. The goals can be in conflict between each other, denoted with $G_1 \# G_2$, where G_1 is in conflict with G_2. In reality, the conflict relation is a dependency relation between two goals. For the purpose of our work, this relation influences negatively the data accesses, this is why we call it conflictual relation, though the goals are not in conflict but dependent on each other. Two goals G_1 and G_2 are in conflict with each other when for proving G_1 we need to prove also some G' also needed for G_2, or vice versa. The conflict relation is an irreflexive, symmetric and transitive relation, (where if $G_1 \# G_2$ and $G_2 \# G_3$, then $G_1 \# G_3$ and we also have that $G_1 \neq G_3$). (We decided to have the transitivity property for the $\#$ relation.) We assume that the conflict relation is already given. The access control set AC for a given tuple of data is composed by couples goal-location, that represent the locations, that have accessed to the given data, with their goals. A tuple of data cannot be used by two different locations for the same goal. For every tuple of data its AC is initialized as empty ($\emptyset$), and is filled step by step as accesses are requested to it.

We introduce now the syntax in detail. A net is a parallel composition of located processes and/or located tuples of data and their AC. A process can be a parallel composition of processes, a guarded sum of action prefixed processes, or a replicated process (indicated by the $*$ operator); we shall write 0 for the empty sum. An action operates on tuples: a tuple can be output to, input from (read and delete the tuple), read from (read and keep the tuple), and get (read the first tuple that was not read before and keep it) from a location, respectively denoted by **out**, **in**, **read** and **get**. We also have other two extra actions: **noread**, used for checking that there does not exist any tuple that contains the data that the process is searching for, where the process has permission to access in it; and **noget**, used for checking that there is no tuple that the process has permission to access in it, and contains data the process is searching for and that it has not got yet. These two actions are executed when respectively **read** and **get** are blocked. Thus, for understanding that **read**/**get** is blocked, we have in parallel the action **noread**/**noget**. These two last actions are used for avoiding to have blocked processes, because they can be executed if the other actions are blocked. As shown in Table 1, the actions (except for **out**) are all related to a certain goal, this means that they are executed respectively for a certain goal.

Example 1. Let's go back to the problem described in the introduction. We are in the neuroscience research community[1]. Let's suppose that we have two researchers: Penkowa and Klarlund, we denote them as two locations, respectively l_P and l_K. The institute provides the locations l_1, l_2, l_3 that they can use and access. Suppose now that Penkowa runs her experiment, and decides to put the resulting data in l_1, represented as follows:

$$l_P :: \mathbf{out}(\vec{d_1})@l_1 | \mathbf{out}(\vec{d_2})@l_1 | \mathbf{out}(\vec{d_3})@l_1 | \mathbf{out}(\vec{d_4})@l_1.$$

Later, Penkowa decides to use the data of the experiment for proving: the production of a certain amount of proteins, denoted with G_1. Thus, she wants to access the data in l_1 for goal G_1: $l_P :: \mathbf{noread}(!x, G_1)@l_1.P_1$ | $\mathbf{read}(!x, G_1)@l_1.P_1'$. The $\mathbf{noread}$ action is used for checking if the searched data are in l_1 or not, in a way to not just wait for the $\mathbf{read}$ action. Meanwhile also Klarlund wants to use the data for the same goal, but she is looking for the data in l_3: $l_K :: \mathbf{noread}(!x, G_1)@l_3.P_3$ | $\mathbf{read}(!x, G_1)@l_3.P_3'$. In this case, we have a net formed by two processes (that are themselves composed by parallel processes):

$$l_P :: \mathbf{noread}(!x, G_1)@l_1.P_1 \mid \mathbf{read}(!x, G_1)@l_1.P_1' \parallel$$
$$l_K :: \mathbf{noread}(!x, G_1)@l_3.P_3 \mid \mathbf{read}(!x, G_1)@l_3.P_3'.$$

After reading the first occurrence of the data, Penkowa decides to get all the data of the experiment by using $*\mathbf{get}$. The $\mathbf{noget}$ action is used for understanding that she gets all the data, and just once[2].

$$l_P :: \mathbf{noget}(!x, G_1)@l_1.P_2 \mid *\mathbf{get}(!x, G_1)@l_1 \qquad\qquad \square$$

2.2 Semantics

The semantic is given by a one-step reduction relation on nets and actions. It makes use of a structural congruence on nets, which is an associative and commutative equivalence relation that is a congruence (with respect to $\parallel$) and with some additional rules defined in Table 2. It also makes use of an operation *match*, for matching input patterns to actual data, defined in Table 3.

The reaction rules are defined in Tables 4 and 5 and are straightforward for nets, where we denote with N_C the *context net*, and with N, M nets that are part of the context net. The rules and axioms should be straightforward: if the action is granted, then it will be executed; otherwise it will be replaced with the 0 process and the execution of the thread at this location terminates.

Table 2. Structural congruence

$$l :: P_1 | P_2 \equiv l :: P_1 \| l :: P_2 \quad\big|\quad l :: * P \equiv l :: P | * P$$
$$l :: P \equiv l :: P \| l :: 0 \quad\big|\quad \dfrac{N_1 \equiv N_2}{N \| N_1 \equiv N \| N_2}$$

---

[1] For our examples we were inspired by the *Penkowa case.*
[2] The processes P_i, P_i' can be sentinel processes, or real processes.

Table 3. Matching input patterns to data

$$match(!x, \overrightarrow{b^\lambda}; d, \overrightarrow{d}) = [d/x] \circ match(\overrightarrow{b^\lambda}; \overrightarrow{d}) \quad match(d, \overrightarrow{b^\lambda}; d, \overrightarrow{d}) = match(\overrightarrow{b^\lambda}; \overrightarrow{d})$$
$$match(\epsilon; \epsilon) \qquad\qquad = id \qquad\qquad match(\cdot; \cdot) \qquad\qquad = fail \text{ otherwise}$$

Table 4. Reaction semantics

$$\frac{N_C \cup \{N_2\} \vdash N_1 \rightarrow N_1'}{N_C \vdash N_1 || N_2 \rightarrow N_1' || N_2} \quad \frac{N \equiv M \quad N_C \vdash M \rightarrow M' \quad M' \equiv N'}{N_C \vdash N \rightarrow N'}$$

The **out** action when it is executed writes the tuple $\overrightarrow{b}$ in location l_t and goes on with the next process P. To execute the other actions (except for **noread** and **noget**) we should have a matching, in the location where we are looking in (l_t), between what we are looking for (the formal parameter $\overrightarrow{b^\lambda}$) and the data ($\overrightarrow{d}$), and the location that wants to execute the action for a certain goal G, has not accessed the data for another goal, G', that is in conflict with G. A location, for executing the **in** and **read** actions, needs also to have access to the data for goal G, and this means it already has accessed the data for G, or no other location have accessed them for G. For **get**, this condition is stronger because it requires that no location has accessed for G. The **noread** is executed if the data we are looking for do not exist, or l_t does not have access to them for G, or l_t has accessed the data for a goal G', that is in conflict with G. The **noget** action is executed if the data we are looking for do not exist, or l_t has already used the data for G, or another location has used the data for G, or l_t has accessed the data for a goal G', that is in conflict with G.

Example 2. Let's go back to the previous example and show how to use the reaction semantics. From Example 1, we had that Penkowa placed the data of the experiment in l_1: $l_P :: \mathbf{out}(\overrightarrow{d_1})@l_1|\mathbf{out}(\overrightarrow{d_2})@l_1|\mathbf{out}(\overrightarrow{d_3})@l_1|\mathbf{out}(\overrightarrow{d_4})@l_1$ that is reduced in:

$$l_1 :: \overrightarrow{d_1}, \emptyset || l_1 :: \overrightarrow{d_2}, \emptyset || l_1 :: \overrightarrow{d_3}, \emptyset || l_1 :: \overrightarrow{d_4}, \emptyset.$$

The two researchers want to access the data, but while l_P is looking for the data in l_1, l_K is looking for them in l_3, and the data are in l_1:

$$l_P :: \mathbf{noread}(!x, G_1)@l_1.P_1 \mid \mathbf{read}(!x, G_1)@l_1.P_1' ||$$
$$l_K :: \mathbf{noread}(!x, G_1)@l_3.P_3 \mid \mathbf{read}(!x, G_1)@l_3.P_3' || l_1 :: \overrightarrow{d_1}, \emptyset$$

and by using the reaction semantics rules is reduced in:

$$l_P :: \mathbf{noread}(!x, G_1)@l_1.P_1 || l_P :: P_1' || l_K :: P_3 ||$$
$$l_K :: \mathbf{read}(!x, G_1)@l_3.P_3' || l_1 :: \overrightarrow{d_1}, \{(G_1 : l_P)\}.$$

The $l_P :: \mathbf{noread}(!x, G_1)@l_1.P_1$ is left as it was because the data are in l_1, so it is just blocked. The **read** in l_1 is processed, and the AC of $\overrightarrow{d_1}$ in l_1 is updated with the permission for l_P to use the data for G_1. The $l_K :: \mathbf{noread}(!x, G_1)@l_3.P_3$ is

Table 5. Reaction semantics of actions

$$N_C \vdash (l_s :: \mathbf{out}(\overline{b})@\overrightarrow{l_t}.P + \cdots) \quad \rightarrow \quad l_s :: P \parallel l_t :: \overrightarrow{b}, \overrightarrow{\emptyset}$$

$$\frac{match(b^\lambda; \overrightarrow{d}) \overset{\rightarrow}{=} \theta \quad \forall l.(G:l) \in \mathrm{AC} \Rightarrow l = l_s}{\forall l, G'. \ (G':l) \in \mathrm{AC} \wedge G\#G' \ \Rightarrow \ l \neq l_s}{N_C \vdash (l_s :: \mathbf{in}(b^\lambda, G)@l_t.P + \cdots) \parallel (l_t :: \overrightarrow{d}, \overrightarrow{\mathrm{AC}}) \rightarrow l_s :: P\theta}$$

$$\frac{match(b^\lambda; \overrightarrow{d}) \overset{\rightarrow}{=} \theta}{\forall l.(G:l) \in \mathrm{AC} \Rightarrow l = l_s \qquad \forall l, G'.(G':l) \in \mathrm{AC} \wedge G\#G' \Rightarrow l \neq l_s}{N_C \vdash (l_s :: \mathbf{read}(b^\lambda, G)@l_t.P + \cdots) \parallel (l_t :: \overrightarrow{d}, \overrightarrow{\mathrm{AC}}) \rightarrow l_s :: P\theta \parallel l_t :: \overrightarrow{d}, \overrightarrow{\mathrm{AC}} \cup \{(G:l_s)\}}$$

$$\frac{\neg(\exists(\overrightarrow{d}, \overrightarrow{\mathrm{AC}}) \text{ s.t. } (l_t :: (\overrightarrow{d}, \overrightarrow{\mathrm{AC}}) \in N_C}{match(b^\lambda; \overrightarrow{d}) \overset{\rightarrow}{=} \theta \quad \forall l.(G:l) \in \mathrm{AC} \Rightarrow l = l_s}{\forall l, G'. \ (G':l) \in \mathrm{AC} \ \wedge \ G\#G' \ \Rightarrow \ l \neq l_s))}{N_C \vdash (l_s :: \mathbf{noread}(b^\lambda, G)@l_t.P + \cdots) \quad \rightarrow \quad l_s :: P}$$

$$\frac{match(\overrightarrow{b^\lambda}; \overrightarrow{d}) \overset{\rightarrow}{=} \theta \quad \not\exists l.(G:l) \in \mathrm{AC} \quad \forall l, G'.(G':l) \in \mathrm{AC} \wedge G\#G' \Rightarrow l \neq l_s}{N_C \vdash (l_s :: \mathbf{get}(b^\lambda, G)@l_t.P + \cdots) \parallel (l_t :: \overrightarrow{d}, \overrightarrow{\mathrm{AC}}) \rightarrow l_s :: P\theta \parallel l_t :: \overrightarrow{d}, \overrightarrow{\mathrm{AC}} \cup \{(G:l_s)\}}$$

$$\frac{\neg(\exists(\overrightarrow{d}, \overrightarrow{\mathrm{AC}}) \text{ s.t. } (l_t :: (\overrightarrow{d}, \overrightarrow{\mathrm{AC}}) \in N_C \quad match(b^\lambda; \overrightarrow{d}) \overset{\rightarrow}{=} \theta)}{\not\exists l.(G:l) \in \mathrm{AC} \quad \forall l, G'.(G':l) \in \mathrm{AC} \wedge G\#G' \Rightarrow l \neq l_s))}{N_C \vdash (l_s :: \mathbf{noget}(b^\lambda, G)@l_t.P + \cdots) \quad \rightarrow \quad l_s :: P}$$

processed and l_K goes on with P_3 as the data are not in l_3, while the **read** in l_3 is blocked.

Let's see how the other net is processed in case l_P wants to get all the data of the experiment:

$$l_P :: \mathbf{noget}(!x, G_1)@l_1.P_2 \mid *\mathbf{get}(!x, G_1)@l_1 \parallel l_1 :: \overrightarrow{d_1}, \{(G_1 : l_P)\} \parallel \cdots \parallel l_1 :: \overrightarrow{d_4}, \emptyset$$

that is reduced as follows because l_P gets the next data in l_1:

$$l_P :: \mathbf{noget}(!x, G_1)@l_1.P_2 \parallel l_P :: \mathbf{get}(!x, G_1)@l_1 \parallel l_P :: *\mathbf{get}(!x, G_1)@l_1 \parallel$$
$$l_1 :: \overrightarrow{d_1}, \{(G_1 : l_P)\} \parallel l_1 :: \overrightarrow{d_2}, \{(G_1 : l_P)\} \parallel l_1 :: \overrightarrow{d_3}, \emptyset \parallel l_1 :: \overrightarrow{d_4}, \emptyset$$

and is reduced step by step in:

$$l_P :: P_2 \parallel l_P :: *\mathbf{get}(!x, G_1)@l_1 \parallel l_1 :: \overrightarrow{d_1}, \{(G_1 : l_P)\} \parallel \cdots \parallel l_1 :: \overrightarrow{d_4}, \{(G_1 : l_P)\}.$$

$\square$

Below, we show how our semantics can capture the introduced problem.

Example 3. Previously, l_K was searching for the data in l_3. Suppose, she decides to search for them in l_1, and she has the same goal as l_P, G_1. As shown above, l_P has already accessed the data in l_1 for G_1:

$$l_K :: \mathbf{noread}(!x, G_1)@l_1.P_3 \mid \mathbf{read}(!x, G_1)@l_1 \parallel$$
$$l_1 :: \overrightarrow{d_1}, \{(G_1 : l_P)\} \parallel \cdots \parallel l_1 :: \overrightarrow{d_4}, \{(G_1 : l_P)\}.$$

The above net is reduced in:

$$l_K :: P_3 \parallel l_K :: \mathbf{read}(!x, G_1)@l_1 \parallel l_1 :: \overrightarrow{d_1}, \{(G_1 : l_P)\} \parallel \cdots \parallel l_1 :: \overrightarrow{d_4}, \{(G_1 : l_P)\}$$

where, **noread** is processed as the data have already been used by l_P for G_1. $\square$

Thus, our semantics do not permit the re-use of the same data set, by different locations, for the same goal.

Example 4. Suppose that l_P wants to use the same data, for proving that: a certain amount of produced proteins affects the receptor expression in contracting human skeletal muscle, denoted by G_2. The goal G_2 is in contradiction with G_1, because for proving G_2, we need first to prove G_1. The net is described below:

$$l_P :: \mathbf{noread}(!x, G_2)@l_1.P_1 \mid \mathbf{read}(!x, G_2)@l_1.P_2 \parallel$$
$$l_1 :: \overrightarrow{d_1}, \{(G_1 : l_P)\} \parallel \cdots \parallel l_1 :: \overrightarrow{d_4}, \{(G_1 : l_P)\}$$

and is reduced in:

$$l_P :: P_1 \mid \mathbf{read}(!x, G_2)@l_1.P_2 \parallel l_1 :: \overrightarrow{d_1}, \{(G_1 : l_P)\} \parallel \cdots \parallel l_1 :: \overrightarrow{d_4}, \{(G_1 : l_P)\}$$

where, l_P cannot access the data for G_2, as she had already accessed to those data for G_1, as $G_1 \# G_2$. $\square$

Our semantics model the coordination of the re-use of data in a way to do not permit the same researcher to re-use the same data set for proving results that are correlated between each other, as shown in Example 4. The above example represent, in a simple way, what happened in the *Penkowa case* and our language can enforce that it does not occur.

Example 5. Suppose that l_K decides to read the same data in l_1 but for a different goal G_3, and that l_P wants to access again the data in l_1 but for G_1:

$$l_K :: \mathbf{noread}(!x, G_3)@l_1.P_1 \mid \mathbf{read}(!x, G_3)@l_1.P_2 \parallel l_P :: \mathbf{noread}(!x, G_1)@l_1.P_3 \mid$$
$$\mathbf{read}(!x, G_1)@l_1.P_4 \parallel l_1 :: \overrightarrow{d_1}, \{(G_1 : l_P)\} \parallel \cdots \parallel l_1 :: \overrightarrow{d_4}, \{(G_1 : l_P)\}$$

that is reduced in:

$$l_K :: \mathbf{noread}(!x, G_3)@l_1.P_1 \parallel l_K :: P_2[d_1/x] \parallel l_P :: \mathbf{noread}(!x, G_1)@l_1.P_3 \parallel$$
$$l_P :: P_4[d_1/x] \parallel l_1 :: \overrightarrow{d_1}, \{(G_1 : l_P), (G_3 : l_K)\} \parallel \cdots \parallel l_1 :: \overrightarrow{d_4}, \{(G_1 : l_P)\}$$

$\square$

Our semantics permit the same researcher to re-use the data for the same goal, but not for goals that are in conflict between each other (it is not permitted to produce correlated results by re-using the same data).

3 Analysis

Our goal is to prohibit that the same data set is used for the same goal by different locations, and that the same location uses the same data set for proving different goals that are in conflict between each other. Our semantics accomplish this goal but just for direct accesses to the data, it does not deal with indirect accesses. The first case that is not captured by our semantics is when a location/agent[3] reads the data sets and puts them in another location, where they are accessed by another agent with the same goal. The second case that is not captured is when data are accessed by an agent that writes them in two different locations, and the data in the new locations are accessed by two different agents for the same goal.

Example 6. Let's go back to the examples introduced in Sect. 2. Suppose that, after reading the tuple of data $\vec{b}$ for G_1, l_P writes it in l_2. Now, l_K can read $\vec{b}$ for G_1 in l_2, because nobody else has accessed it in l_2 for G_1, and also l_P can use $\vec{b}$ for G', where $G_1 \# G'$, because we cannot keep track that $\vec{b}$ was accessed by l_P in l_1.

$$l_P :: \mathbf{read}(\vec{b}, G_1)@l_1.\mathbf{out}(\vec{b})@l_2$$
$$l_K :: \mathbf{read}(\vec{b}, G_1)@l_2 \ \| \ l_P :: \mathbf{read}(\vec{b}, G')@l_2$$

The second case that is not captured is when l_P reads the tuple of data $\vec{b}$ from l_1, and writes it in l_2 and l_3. Agent l_K can access to $\vec{b}$ in l_2 for G_2, and also Charlie (l_C), who is another researcher, can access to $\vec{b}$ in l_3 for G_2.

$$l_P :: \mathbf{read}(\vec{b}, G_1)@l_1.\mathbf{out}(\vec{b})@l_2.\mathbf{out}(\vec{b})@l_3$$
$$l_K :: \mathbf{read}(\vec{b}, G_2)@l_2 \ \| \ l_C :: \mathbf{read}(\vec{b}, G_2)@l_3$$

□

We show through this example how the same tuple of data is used by the same agent for goals that are in conflict between each other and how the same tuple of data can be accessed by two different agents for the same goal. For capturing these cases we extract certain information that keeps track of the *origin* of a given tuple of data. The notion of origin is used to express the location where the tuple of data was located the first time. In this case, we need to know the history of our data sets from the moment they were placed in the locations. This means that we are working with a history-sensitive static analysis that needs the history of the data sets and how they are used and moved. Through our analysis we do not need to bind the tuple of data to just one location, and even if the data is moved or copied, we can still keep track of who accessed it and with which goal.

---

[3] For sake of understandability we will call *agent* the location that is performing a process.

3.1   Over Approximation

We introduce the over approximation analysis used for the history of data sets and processes, that capture the information needed for avoiding the two above scenarios. As our language does not bind the data sets to their past locations, through our analysis we need to capture this relation. For doing this we use three relations: *valueof* (ρ), *record* (δ), and *contains* (χ).

The *valueof*: **DataVar** $\times$ **Loc** is a relation between data variables and locations, where **DataVar** is a subset of **Data** composed of all its data variables. It assigns to the variable a location where it could have come from, e.g., $\rho(\overrightarrow{x}, \overrightarrow{l})$ says that the tuple of data $\overrightarrow{x}$ could have been originated from location $\overrightarrow{l}$.

The *record* : **DataPat** $\times$ **Loc** is a relation between data patterns and locations. This relation gives the possible origin location of data pattern and is based on the *valueof* relation. Given a data pattern b^λ we can have three cases depending on b^λ, (1) it is a constant d, then $\delta(d, l) = $ true, it means that it is always true; (2) it is a data variable x, then $\delta(x, l) = $ true, it is always true; (3) it is an occurrence of a data variable $!x$, then $\delta(!x, l) = \rho(x, l)$, it means that the origin location of $!x$ is where this variable could come from.

The *contains* : **Loc** $\times \cup_{k \geq 1}$**Loc**$^k \times$ **Loc** $\times$ **Goal** is a relation between locations, agents and goals. It assigns to a given location a tuple of locations where the data of the location are originated from, and also the agents that accessed to these data with a certain goal. So, $\chi(l, \overrightarrow{l'}, l'', G)$ says that location l contains data originated from location $\overrightarrow{l'}$, that has been used by agent l'' for goal G.

These relations capture global information about the behavior of the process of interest and the different locations related to it, or that can be related to it in the future. We also need to capture local information of interest about our process, this is done by adding an *error* component. We have two types of errors. The first type is a triple composed of the location where the error occurs and the agent with the goal that already had accessed the data, $\varepsilon = \{(l', l_0, G)\}$. The second type is a quadruple composed of the location where the error occurs, the location that wanted to execute a given action and the agent with the goal that already had accessed to the data $\varepsilon = \{(l', l, l_0, G)\}$. The actions that can have an error are the **read**, **in** and **get** actions.

The analysis is specified by logical judgments, and it takes the form:

$$\chi, \rho \vdash_N N : \varepsilon.$$

This judgment expresses that χ, ρ and ε provide a valid analysis result for the behavior of N. We introduce the judgments of our analysis in Table 6, where we have a judgment for every form of nets, processes and actions. Let's take the **read** judgment, it says that for every location $\overrightarrow{l''}$ where the used data come from, the location where the data are taken, l', contains data from $\overrightarrow{l''}$, and l can use the data for G, if no other location has used the data for G and G is not in conflict with some other goal used by l to access l' (in these two last cases we have an error). The judgments for **get** and **in** are similar. The judgments

Table 6. Logical judgments of the flow logic

$$\chi, \rho \vdash_N N_1 \| N_2 : \varepsilon \qquad \text{iff } \chi, \rho \vdash_N N_1 : \varepsilon_1 \,\wedge\, \chi, \rho \vdash_N N_2 : \varepsilon_2 \,\wedge \qquad (1)$$
$$\varepsilon_1 \cup \varepsilon_2 \subseteq \varepsilon \text{ (where } \varepsilon_1, \varepsilon_2 \text{ fresh)}$$

$$\chi, \rho \vdash_N l :: P : \varepsilon \qquad \text{iff } \chi, \rho, l \vdash_P P : \varepsilon \qquad (2)$$

$$\chi, \rho \vdash_N l :: \vec{d}, \mathrm{AC} : \varepsilon \qquad \text{iff } \forall G, l''. \, (G : l'') \in \mathrm{AC} \,\wedge \qquad (3)$$
$$\nexists \vec{l'}. \, \chi(l, \vec{l'}, l'', G) \Rightarrow (l, l'', G) \in \varepsilon$$

$$\chi, \rho, l \vdash_P P_1 | P_2 : \varepsilon \qquad \text{iff } \chi, \rho, l \vdash_P P_1 : \varepsilon_1 \,\wedge\, \chi, \rho, l \vdash_P P_2 : \varepsilon_2 \,\wedge \qquad (4)$$
$$\varepsilon_1 \cup \varepsilon_2 \subseteq \varepsilon \text{ (where } \varepsilon_1, \varepsilon_2 \text{ fresh)}$$

$$\chi, \rho, l \vdash_P *P : \varepsilon \qquad \text{iff } \chi, \rho, l \vdash_P P : \varepsilon \qquad (5)$$

$$\chi, \rho, l \vdash_P \textstyle\sum_i a_i.P_i : \varepsilon \qquad \text{iff } \forall i \in I. \, \chi, \rho, l \vdash_A a_i : \varepsilon_i \,\wedge\, \chi, \rho, l \vdash_P P_i : \varepsilon_i' \,\wedge \qquad (6)$$
$$\varepsilon_i \subseteq \varepsilon \,\wedge\, \varepsilon_i' \subseteq \varepsilon \text{ (where } \varepsilon_i, \varepsilon_i' \text{ fresh)}$$

$$\chi, \rho, l \vdash_A \mathbf{read}(\vec{b^\lambda}, G)@l' : \varepsilon \qquad \text{iff } \forall \vec{l''}. \, \rho(\vec{b^\lambda}, \vec{l''}) \wedge \chi(l', \vec{l''}, l, G) \,\wedge \qquad (7)$$
$$(\forall l_0. \, \chi(l', \vec{l''}, l_0, G) \wedge l_0 \neq l) \Rightarrow (l', l, l_0, G) \in \varepsilon$$
$$\wedge \, (\forall G'.\chi(l', \vec{l''}, l, G') \wedge G \# G') \Rightarrow (l', l, G') \in \varepsilon$$

$$\chi, \rho, l \vdash_A \mathbf{get}(\vec{b^\lambda}, G)@l' : \varepsilon \qquad \text{iff } \forall \vec{l''}. \, \rho(\vec{b^\lambda}, \vec{l''}) \wedge \chi(l', \vec{l''}, l, G) \,\wedge \qquad (8)$$
$$(\forall l_0. \, \chi(l', \vec{l''}, l_0, G) \wedge l_0 \neq l) \Rightarrow (l', l, l_0, G) \in \varepsilon$$
$$\wedge \, (\forall G'.\chi(l', \vec{l''}, l, G') \wedge G \# G') \Rightarrow (l', l, G') \in \varepsilon$$

$$\chi, \rho, l \vdash_A \mathbf{in}(\vec{b^\lambda}, G)@l' : \varepsilon \qquad \text{iff } \forall \vec{l''}. \, \rho(\vec{b^\lambda}, \vec{l''}) \,\wedge\, \chi(l', \vec{l''}, l, G) \wedge \qquad (9)$$
$$(\forall l_0. \, \chi(l', \vec{l''}, l_0, G) \wedge l_0 \neq l) \Rightarrow (l', l, l_0, G) \in \varepsilon$$
$$\wedge \, (\forall G'.\chi(l', \vec{l''}, l, G') \wedge G \# G') \Rightarrow (l', l, G') \in \varepsilon$$

$$\chi, \rho, l \vdash_A \mathbf{out}(\vec{b})@l' : \varepsilon \qquad \text{iff } \forall G, \vec{l''}. \, \chi(l', \vec{l''}, l, G) \Rightarrow \rho(\vec{b}, \vec{l''}) \qquad (10)$$

$$\chi, \rho, l \vdash_A \mathbf{noread}(\vec{b^\lambda}, G)@l' : \varepsilon \text{ iff } \text{true} \qquad (11)$$

$$\chi, \rho, l \vdash_A \mathbf{noget}(\vec{b^\lambda}, G)@l' : \varepsilon \text{ iff } \text{true} \qquad (12)$$

for **noread** and **noget** give true because the information we can abstract from them is everything, which is not relevant for us.

Example 7. Let's go back to the first case that the semantics could not capture. After reading the tuple of data $\vec{b}$ for G_1, l_P writes it in l_2, and l_P had already accessed to the data before: $l_P :: \mathbf{read}(\vec{b}, G_1)@l_1.\mathbf{out}(\vec{b})@l_2 \, \| \, l_1 :: \vec{d}, \mathrm{AC}$ that means:

$$\chi, \rho \vdash_N l_P :: \mathbf{read}(\vec{b}, G_1)@l_1.\mathbf{out}(\vec{b})@l_2 \, \| \, l_1 :: \vec{d}, \mathrm{AC} : \varepsilon.$$

It is transformed by using the judgments of Table 6 in:

$$\chi, \rho \vdash_N l_P :: \mathbf{read}(\vec{b}, G_1)@l_1.\mathbf{out}(\vec{b})@l_2 : \varepsilon_1 \,\wedge\, \chi, \rho \vdash_N l_1 :: \vec{d}, \mathrm{AC} : \varepsilon_2$$

where $\varepsilon_1 \cup \varepsilon_2 \subseteq \varepsilon$, and $\varepsilon_1, \varepsilon_2$ fresh. The first part is transformed in:

$$\chi, \rho, l_P \vdash_P \mathbf{read}(\vec{b}, G_1)@l_1 : \varepsilon_1 \,\wedge\, \chi, \rho, l_P \vdash_P \mathbf{out}(\vec{b})@l_2.$$

The part of the **read** action is transformed in:

$$\forall \overrightarrow{l''}.\ \rho(\overrightarrow{b},\overrightarrow{l''})\ \wedge\ \chi(l_1,\overrightarrow{l''},l_P,G_1)$$
$$\wedge\ (\forall l_0.\ \chi(l_1,\overrightarrow{l''},l_0,G_1)\wedge l_0 \neq l_P) \Rightarrow (l_1,l_P,l_0,G_1) \in \varepsilon_1$$
$$\wedge\ (\forall G'.\ \chi(l_1,\overrightarrow{l''},l_P,G')\wedge G_1\#G') \Rightarrow (l_1,l_P,G') \in \varepsilon_1$$

where, as l_P has accessed to the data for G_1 we have $\forall \overrightarrow{l''}.\ \rho(\overrightarrow{b},\overrightarrow{l''})\ \wedge$ $\chi(l_1,\overrightarrow{l''},l_P,G_1)$. The part of the **out** is transformed in: $\forall G,\overrightarrow{l''}.\ \chi(l_2,\overrightarrow{l''},l_P,G) \Rightarrow$ $\rho(\overrightarrow{b},\overrightarrow{l''})$. The remaining subnet is transformed in:

$$\forall G,l^*.\ (G:l^*) \in \text{AC}\ \wedge\ \not\exists \overrightarrow{l'}.\ \chi(l_1,\overrightarrow{l'},l^*,G) \Rightarrow (l_1,l^*,G) \in \varepsilon_2$$

and as we have $(G_1:l_P) \in \text{AC}$, then: $\exists \overrightarrow{l'}.\ \chi(l_1,\overrightarrow{l'},l_P,G_1)$.

In the second net, we have the requests of l_K to read the data in l_2 for G_1 and of l_P to read the data in l_2 for G', where $G_1\#G'$:

$$\chi,\rho \vdash_N l_K::\textbf{read}(\overrightarrow{b},G_1)@l_2\ ||\ l_P::\textbf{read}(\overrightarrow{b},G')@l_2 : \varepsilon^*$$

that is transformed in two subnets:

$$\chi,\rho \mid_N l_K::\textbf{read}(\overrightarrow{b},G_1)@l_2 : \varepsilon'\ \wedge \chi,\rho \vdash_N l_P::\textbf{read}(\overrightarrow{b},G')@l_2 : \varepsilon''$$

where $\varepsilon'\cup\varepsilon'' \subseteq \varepsilon^*$, and $\varepsilon',\varepsilon''$ fresh. The first subnet is transformed in: $\chi,\rho,l_K \vdash_P$ $\textbf{read}(\overrightarrow{b},G_1)@l_2 : \varepsilon'$

iff $\&\ \forall\ \overrightarrow{l'}.\ \rho(\overrightarrow{b},\overrightarrow{l'})\ \wedge\ \chi(l_2,\overrightarrow{l'},l_K,G_1)$
$\wedge\ (\forall\ l_0.\ \chi(l_2,\overrightarrow{l'},l_0,G_1)\wedge l_0 \neq l_K) \Rightarrow (l_2,l_K,l_0,G_1) \in \varepsilon'$
$\wedge\ (\forall\ G''.\ \chi(l_2,\overrightarrow{l'},l_K,G'')\wedge G_1\#G'') \Rightarrow (l_2,l_K,G'') \in \varepsilon'$.

We have from the **out** action that for all $G,\overrightarrow{l''}$ such that $\chi(l_2,\overrightarrow{l''},l_P,G) \Rightarrow$ $\rho(\overrightarrow{b},\overrightarrow{l''})$, and we also know that l_P had accessed the data in l_1: $\forall \overrightarrow{l''}.\ \rho(\overrightarrow{b},\overrightarrow{l''})$ $\wedge\ \chi(l_1,\overrightarrow{l''},l_P,G_1)$, so we have that $\chi(l_2,\overrightarrow{l''},l_P,G_1)$. Thus, an error occurs in this case because an agent that is not l_K has accessed to the data for G_1 and the transformation of the first subnet with the **read** action of l_K gives an error $(l_2,l_K,l_P,G_1) \in \varepsilon'$, and l_K cannot access the data in l_2 for goal G_1.

The second subnet is transformed in: $\chi,\rho,l_P \vdash_P \textbf{read}(\overrightarrow{b},G')@l_2 : \varepsilon''$ iff

$$\forall \overrightarrow{l'}.\ \rho(\overrightarrow{b},\overrightarrow{l'})\ \wedge\ \chi(l_2,\overrightarrow{l'},l_P,G')$$
$$\wedge\ (\forall l_0.\ \chi(l_2,\overrightarrow{l'},l_0,G')\wedge l_0 \neq l_P) \Rightarrow (l_2,l_P,l_0,G') \in \varepsilon''$$
$$\wedge\ (\forall G''.\ \chi(l_2,\overrightarrow{l'},l_P,G'')\wedge G'\#G'') \Rightarrow (l_2,l_P,G'') \in \varepsilon''.$$

From **out** we have that for all $G,\overrightarrow{l''}$ such that $\chi(l_2,\overrightarrow{l''},l_P,G) \Rightarrow \rho(\overrightarrow{b},\overrightarrow{l''})$, and we also know that l_P had accessed the data in l_1: $\forall \overrightarrow{l''}.\rho(\overrightarrow{b},\overrightarrow{l''})\ \wedge\ \chi(l_1,\overrightarrow{l''},l_P,G_1)$, so we know that $\chi(l_2,\overrightarrow{l''},l_P,G_1)$. Thus, we have an error because $G_1\#G'$ and the transformation of the second subnet with the **read** action of l_P for G' gives an error $(l_2,l_P,G') \in \varepsilon''$, and l_P cannot access the data in l_2 for goal G'. $\qquad\square$

Through our static analysis we can avoid the re-use of the same data set: by the same agent for different goals that are in conflict; and by different agents for the same goal even for indirect accesses. Our analysis is based on Flow Logic, thus we use the same techniques used in it [12].

Semantic correctness amounts to ensuring that the judgment $\chi, \rho \vdash_N N : \varepsilon$ correctly captures the behavior of a net N. A subject reduction result means that if we have an analysis result for N and N evolves into some net M, then the very same analysis result is also valid for M.

We can now establish the following results, and their proofs are in Appendix A.

Lemma 1. *If two nets are congruent between each other, $N_1 \equiv N_2$, then $\chi, \rho \vdash N_1 : \varepsilon$ if and only if $\chi, \rho \vdash N_2 : \varepsilon$.*

Lemma 2 (Substitution). *If $\chi, \rho, l \vdash_P P : \varepsilon$ then $\chi, \rho, l \vdash_P P\theta : \varepsilon$ where $\theta = match(\overrightarrow{b^\lambda}, \overrightarrow{d})$ and $\exists \overrightarrow{l_0}$ s.t. $\rho(\overrightarrow{b^\lambda}, \overrightarrow{l_0})$ and $\exists l', G$ s.t. $\chi(l', \overrightarrow{l_0}, l, G)$.*

Lemma 3 (Subject Reduction). *If $N_C \vdash N \to M$ and $\chi, \rho \vdash N : \varepsilon$, then $\chi, \rho \vdash M : \varepsilon$.*

3.2   Well-Behaved Processes

A net N is *statically well-behaved* if there exist χ, ρ s.t. $\chi, \rho \vdash_N N : \emptyset$, that means there is a valid analysis result for N, where the error component ε is empty.

A net N is *dynamically well-behaved* if whenever N evolves into a net that is structurally congruent to one of the forms: $l_s :: \mathbf{in}(\overrightarrow{b^\lambda}, G)@l_t.P \parallel l_t :: \overrightarrow{d}, AC$, or $l_s :: \mathbf{read}(\overrightarrow{b^\lambda}, G)@l_t.P \parallel l_t :: \overrightarrow{d}, AC$, or $l_s :: \mathbf{get}(\overrightarrow{b^\lambda}, G)@l_t.P \parallel l_t :: \overrightarrow{d}, AC$ with respect to a context net N_C, then for the first and second form holds:

$$match(\overrightarrow{b^\lambda}; \overrightarrow{d}) = \theta \;\Rightarrow\; (\forall l. \, (G : l) \in AC \Rightarrow l = l_s \wedge \\ \forall l, G'.(G' : l) \in AC \wedge G' \# G \Rightarrow l \neq l_s)$$

while for the third form holds:

$$match(\overrightarrow{b^\lambda}; \overrightarrow{d}) = \theta \Rightarrow (\not\exists l.(G : l) \in AC \wedge \forall l, G'.(G' : l) \in AC \wedge G' \# G \Rightarrow l \neq l_s).$$

The below theorem proves that our processes are well-behaved, and its proof is in Appendix A.

Theorem 1 (Adequacy for well-behaved nets). *If a net is statically well-behaved, then it is also dynamically well-behaved.*

4   Conclusion

The massive usage of Big Data has led to an increasing re-use of data, especially in the scientific community. In this paper, we propose an IT solution that models the coordination needed for data re-use. We introduce a real case from the research community of alleged mispractice of data re-use. The coordination language we introduce, ensures the correct and reliable re-use of data, and solves some of the trust issues of the scientists to share and re-use data. Indeed, our language does not permit the re-use of data sets, by different agents for the same goal, or by the same agent for similar goals. In our work we assume the scientist is sincere and does not lie about his goals. Our solution does not deal with insincere declarations, but it does deal with dishonest scientists that try to indirectly access the data. We develop a static analysis that ensures the correct re-use of data also during indirect accesses. Our analysis is a history-sensitive one that needs the history of data sets and processes. Our solution is a generic one and is very flexible. It is easily extendable to various types of conflicts and different scenarios.

As future work we plan to develop a linearity analysis for the processes and data sets. In this paper, we deal with goals and the conflict relation between them, where this relation is a binary one and is already given a priori. An interesting extension of our work is to introduce the conflictual sets of goals, and to use access control policies, like the Chinese Wall [5].

Acknowledgments. We are supported by IDEA4CPS (DNRF 86-10).

A   Appendix: Proofs

Proof (Lemma 1). The proof is by induction on how $N_1 \equiv N_2$ is obtained from Table 2.

There are three base cases, for $N_1 \equiv N_2$: (a) $N_1 := l :: P$ and $N_2 := l :: P||l :: 0$ (b) $N_1 : l :: P_1|P_2$ and $N_2 := l :: P_1||l :: P_2$ (c) $N := l :: *P$ and $N_2 := l :: P|*P$. We are going to show just the second case, the remaining cases are proved similarly.

The base case is when $N_1 := l :: P_1|P_2$ and $N_2 := l :: P_1||l :: P_2$, where we have to prove that if $N_1 \equiv N_2$, then $\chi, \rho \vdash_N l :: P_1|P_2 : \varepsilon \Leftrightarrow \chi, \rho \vdash_N l :: P_1||l :: P_2 : \varepsilon$. Let's prove the ($\Rightarrow$): If $\chi, \rho \vdash_N l :: P_1|P_2 : \varepsilon$, then $\chi, \rho \vdash_N l :: P_1||l :: P_2 : \varepsilon$. By applying Judgment[4] (2) to the left-hand side formula we have $\chi, \rho, l \vdash_P P_1|P_2 : \varepsilon$ and by applying (4) to it we have: $\chi, \rho, l \vdash_P P_1 : \varepsilon_1 \wedge \chi, \rho, l \vdash_P P_2 : \varepsilon_2 \wedge \varepsilon_1 \cup \varepsilon_2 \subseteq \varepsilon$. By applying (2) to the above formulas we have: $\chi, \rho \vdash_N l :: P_1 : \varepsilon_1 \wedge \chi, \rho \vdash_N l :: P_2 : \varepsilon_2 \wedge \varepsilon_1 \cup \varepsilon_2 \subseteq \varepsilon$ and by applying (1) we have: $\chi, \rho \vdash_N l :: P_1||l :: P_2 : \varepsilon$ that is what we need to prove.

Let's prove the ($\Leftarrow$): If $\chi, \rho \vdash_N l :: P_1||l :: P_2 : \varepsilon$, then $\chi, \rho \vdash_N l :: P_1|P_2 : \varepsilon$. By applying (1) we have: $\chi, \rho \vdash_N l :: P_1 : \varepsilon_1 \wedge \chi, \rho \vdash_N l :: P_2 : \varepsilon_2 \wedge \varepsilon_1 \cup \varepsilon_2 \subseteq \varepsilon$ where by (2) we have: $\chi, \rho, l \vdash_P P_1 : \varepsilon_1 \wedge \chi, \rho, l \vdash_P P_2 : \varepsilon_2 \wedge \varepsilon_1 \cup \varepsilon_2 \subseteq \varepsilon$. By applying (4) to it, we have: $\chi, \rho, l \vdash_P P_1|P_2 : \varepsilon$ and by applying (2) we get what we need to prove: $\chi, \rho \vdash l :: P_1|P_2 : \varepsilon$.

Our inductive hypothesis says: if $N_1 \equiv N_2$, then we have: $\chi, \rho \vdash N_1 : \varepsilon$ iff $\chi, \rho \vdash N_2 : \varepsilon$, where N_1 and N_2 are constructed as above.

---

[4] During our proofs we are going to refer to the judgments given in Table 6 just by giving their number.

Let's analyze the inductive step, where given $N_1 := N||N_1'$ and $N_2 := N||N_2'$, and $N_1 \equiv N_2$, then $\chi, \rho \vdash N||N_1' : \varepsilon \Leftrightarrow \chi, \rho \vdash N||N_2' : \varepsilon$, and we also have that $N_1' \equiv N_2'$, where N_1', N_2', N are nets constructed as described above.

Let's prove the $(\Rightarrow)$: If $\chi, \rho \vdash_N N||N_1' : \varepsilon$, then by applying (1) we have: $\chi, \rho \vdash_N N : \varepsilon_1 \wedge \chi, \rho \vdash_N N_1' : \varepsilon_2 \wedge \varepsilon_1 \cup \varepsilon_2 \subseteq \varepsilon$. Given $N_1' \equiv N_2'$ by the inductive hypothesis and the above result we have: $\chi, \rho \vdash_N N_1' : \varepsilon_2 \Leftrightarrow \chi, \rho \vdash_N N_2' : \varepsilon_2$ that transforms the previous formula in: $\chi, \rho \vdash_N N : \varepsilon_1 \wedge \chi, \rho \vdash_N N_2' : \varepsilon_2 \wedge \varepsilon_1 \cup \varepsilon_2 \subseteq \varepsilon$. Thus, by applying again (1) we have the formula that we want to prove: $\chi, \rho \vdash_N N||N_2' : \varepsilon$.

The proof for $(\Leftarrow)$: $\chi, \rho \vdash_N N||N_1' : \varepsilon \Leftarrow \chi, \rho \vdash_N N||N_2' : \varepsilon$ is done analogously.

Proof (Substitution Lemma 2). The proof is by structural induction on P. From the syntax of P we have that: $P ::= P_1|P_2 \mid *P \mid \sum_i a_i.P_i$.

Basic Step: the sum of the action prefixed processes is 0: if $\chi, \rho, l \vdash_P 0$, then $\chi, \rho, l \vdash_P 0\theta$.

Our inductive hypothesis says that if $\chi, \rho, l \vdash_P P : \varepsilon$, then $\chi, \rho, l \vdash_P P\theta : \varepsilon$. The first inductive step is when the processes is a non empty sum of action prefixed processes: $\chi, \rho, l \vdash_P \sum_i a_i.P_i : \varepsilon$ which by applying (6) becomes: $\forall i. \chi, \rho, l \vdash_A a_i : \varepsilon_i' \wedge \chi, \rho, l \vdash_P P_i : \varepsilon_i'' \wedge \varepsilon_i' \subseteq \varepsilon \wedge \varepsilon_i'' \subseteq \varepsilon$. It is sufficient to show that $\forall i$, given $\theta[d/x]$:

(1) if $x \notin bv(a_i)$, then $\chi, \rho, l \vdash a_i\theta : \varepsilon_i' \wedge \chi, \rho, l \vdash P_i\theta : \varepsilon_i''$
(2) if $x \in bv(a_i)$, then $\chi, \rho, l \vdash a_i\theta : \varepsilon_i' \wedge \chi, \rho, l \vdash P_i : \varepsilon_i''$.

The second part of the first condition follows from the inductive hypothesis, and the second part of the second condition is trivial. Below we prove the first part of both conditions, where a_i is an action. We prove it for the **read** action, the proofs for the other actions follow similarly. We have to prove that if $\chi, \rho, l \vdash_A$ **read**$(\overrightarrow{x}, G)@l'$, then $\chi, \rho, l \vdash_A$ **read**$(\overrightarrow{x}\theta, G)@l'$. Thus, we have to prove that:

$$\forall \overrightarrow{l''}, \rho(\overrightarrow{x}\theta, \overrightarrow{l''}) \wedge (\forall l_0. \chi(l', \overrightarrow{l''}, l_0, G) \Rightarrow l_0 = l) \wedge ((\forall l_0. \chi(l', \overrightarrow{l''}, l_0, G) \wedge l_0 \neq l) \Rightarrow$$
$$(l', l, l_0, G) \in \varepsilon) \wedge (\forall G'. \chi(l', \overrightarrow{l''}, l, G') \wedge G \# G') \Rightarrow (l', l, G') \in \varepsilon$$

since then $\chi, \rho, l \vdash_A$ **read**$(\overrightarrow{x}\theta, G)@l'$. In this case, if $x \neq y$ and $\theta[d/y]$, then $\rho(\overrightarrow{x}\theta, \overrightarrow{l''})$ is trivial. Otherwise, if $x = y$ and $\theta[d/y]$, then $\rho(\overrightarrow{x}[d/y], \overrightarrow{l''})$ it's always true by the definition of ρ. Thus, $\chi, \rho, l \vdash_A$ **read**$(\overrightarrow{x}\theta, G)@l'$ it true.

The remaining two cases of how P is constructed, are easily proved by using the Judgments of Table 6.

Proof (Subject Reduction Lemma 3). The proof is by induction on how $N \rightarrow M$ is obtained using the rules of Tables 4 and 5. As basic step we use the rules in Table 5. We show one case, for the **read** action, the others follow similarly. What we need to prove is given: $N_C \vdash l_s :: read(\overrightarrow{x}, G)@l_t.P||l_t :: \overrightarrow{d}, \text{AC} \rightarrow l_s :: P\theta||l_t :: \overrightarrow{d}, \text{AC} \cup \{(G : l_s)\}$ and $\chi, \rho \vdash l_s :: \textbf{read}(\overrightarrow{x}, G)@l_t.P||l_t :: \overrightarrow{d}, \text{AC} : \varepsilon$ then we can imply $\chi, \rho \vdash l_s :: P\theta||l_t :: \overrightarrow{d}, \text{AC} \cup \{(G : l_s)\} : \varepsilon$ assuming

$match(\overrightarrow{x}, d) = \theta \wedge \forall l.\ (G : l) \in AC \rightarrow l = l_s \wedge (\forall l, G'.\ (G' : l) \in AC \wedge G\#G' \Rightarrow l \neq l_s)$.

Given the formula $\chi, \rho \vdash l_s :: \mathbf{read}(\overrightarrow{x}, G)@l_t.P\|l_t :: \overrightarrow{d}, AC : \varepsilon$ then by applying (1) we have: $\chi, \rho \vdash l_s :: \mathbf{read}(\overrightarrow{x}, G)@l_t.P : \varepsilon_1 \wedge \chi, \rho \vdash l_t :: \overrightarrow{d}, AC : \varepsilon_2$ and $\varepsilon_1 \subseteq \varepsilon$, $\varepsilon_2 \subseteq \varepsilon$ where $\varepsilon_1, \varepsilon_2$ are fresh. By applying (2) and (6) to $\chi, \rho \vdash l_s :: \mathbf{read}(\overrightarrow{x}, G)@l_t.P : \varepsilon_1$, we have: $\chi, \rho, l_s \vdash_P \mathbf{read}(\overrightarrow{x}, G)@l_t : \varepsilon_3 \wedge \chi, \rho, l_s \vdash_P P : \varepsilon_4$ and $\varepsilon_3 \subseteq \varepsilon_1, \varepsilon_4 \subseteq \varepsilon_1$ where $\varepsilon_3, \varepsilon_4$ are fresh. From the Substitution Lemma 2 if $match(\overrightarrow{x}, \overrightarrow{d}) = \theta$, then we have that: $\chi, \rho, l_s \vdash \mathbf{read}(\overrightarrow{x}\theta, G)@l_t : \varepsilon_3 \wedge \chi, \rho, l_s \vdash P\theta : \varepsilon_4$ and by applying the Substitution Lemma 2 and (7) to the left-hand side we have that: $\forall \overrightarrow{l''}.\ \rho(\overrightarrow{x}\theta, \overrightarrow{l''}) \wedge (\forall l'.\chi(l_t, \overrightarrow{l''}, l', G) \Rightarrow l' = l_s) \wedge (\forall l'.\chi(l_t, \overrightarrow{l''}, l', G) \Rightarrow l' \neq l_s \Rightarrow (l_t, l_s, l', G) \in \varepsilon_3) \wedge (\forall G'.\chi(l_t, \overrightarrow{l''}, l_s, G') \wedge G\#G' \Rightarrow (l_t, l_s, G') \in \varepsilon_3)$. In case we don't have an error, we always have $l_t :: \overrightarrow{d}, AC \cup \{(G : l_s)\}$ from $\chi(l_t, \overrightarrow{l''}, l_s, G)$, and by using (2) and (1) we have: $\chi, \rho \vdash l_s :: P\theta\|l_t :: \overrightarrow{d}, AC \cup \{(G : l_s)\} : \varepsilon$.

Our inductive hypothesis says if $N_C \vdash N \rightarrow M$ and $\chi, \rho \vdash N : \varepsilon$, then $\chi, \rho \vdash M : \varepsilon$. Let's analyze now the inductive steps, that are taken from Table 4. By the first rule we have to prove that given $N_C \vdash N_1\|N_2 \rightarrow N_1'\|N_2$ and $\chi, \rho \vdash N_1\|N_2 : \varepsilon$, then $\chi, \rho \vdash N_1'\|N_2 : \varepsilon$, assuming also $N_C \cup \{N_2\} \vdash N_1 \rightarrow N_1'$. Given $\chi, \rho \vdash N_1\|N_2 : \varepsilon$, by using (1), we have $\chi, \rho \vdash N_1 : \varepsilon$ and $\chi, \rho \vdash N_2 : \varepsilon$. By the inductive hypothesis given $N_C \cup \{N_2\} \vdash N_1 \rightarrow N_1'$ and $\chi, \rho \vdash N_1 : \varepsilon$ we have: $\chi, \rho \vdash N_1' : \varepsilon$, where by using (1), we have: $\chi, \rho \vdash N_1'\|N_2 : \varepsilon$.

Let's analyze the second rule, where given $N_C \vdash N \rightarrow N'$ and $\chi, \rho \vdash N : \varepsilon$ we need to prove that $\chi, \rho \vdash N' : \varepsilon$, assuming also that $N \equiv M$, $N_C \vdash M \rightarrow M'$ and $M' \equiv N'$. Given $N \equiv M$ and $\chi, \rho \vdash N : \varepsilon$ from Lemma 1 we have $\chi, \rho \vdash M : \varepsilon$. We can apply the inductive hypothesis to the last result and $N_C \vdash M \rightarrow M'$, and we have $\chi, \rho \vdash M' : \varepsilon$. By Lemma 1 given $\chi, \rho \vdash M' : \varepsilon$ and $M' \equiv N'$ we have $\chi, \rho \vdash N' : \varepsilon$.

Proof (Theorem 1). The proof is by contradiction, so assume that $\chi, \rho \vdash_N : \varepsilon$ where $\varepsilon = \emptyset$ and that $N \rightarrow \cdots \rightarrow l_s :: \mathbf{in}(\overrightarrow{b^\lambda}, G)@l_t.P\|l_t :: \overrightarrow{d}, AC$ but this condition is not true: $(match(\overrightarrow{b^\lambda}, \overrightarrow{d}) = \theta \Rightarrow \forall l.(G : l) \in AC \Rightarrow l = l_s \wedge (\forall l, G'.\ (G' : l) \in AC \wedge G\#G' \Rightarrow l \neq l_s))$. From Lemma 3, as we have $\chi, \rho \vdash N : \emptyset$ and $N \rightarrow \cdots \rightarrow l_s :: \mathbf{in}(\overrightarrow{b^\lambda}, G)@l_t.P\|l_t :: \overrightarrow{d}, AC$, then $\chi, \rho \vdash l_s :: \mathbf{in}(\overrightarrow{b^\lambda}, G)@l_t.P\|l_t :: \overrightarrow{d}, AC : \emptyset$. That we can rewrite as: $\chi, \rho \vdash l_s :: \mathbf{in}(\overrightarrow{b^\lambda}, G)@l_t.P : \emptyset \wedge \chi, \rho \vdash l_t :: \overrightarrow{d}, AC : \emptyset$ and the left-hand side can be rewritten as: $\chi, \rho \vdash l_s :: \mathbf{in}(\overrightarrow{b^\lambda}, G)@l_t : \emptyset \wedge \chi, \rho \vdash l_s :: P : \emptyset$. For the left-hand side, as the condition is not true, we have $match(\overrightarrow{b^\lambda}, G) = \theta$ and that $(l_t, l_s, l, G) \in \varepsilon$ or $(l_t, l_s, G') \in \varepsilon$, which is not true as $\varepsilon = \emptyset$. We prove similarly for the other two cases.

References

1. Agha, G.A., Kim, W.: Actors: a unifying model for parallel and distributed computing. J. Syst. Architect. **45**(15), 1263–1277 (1999)
2. Arbab, F.: Reo: a channel-based coordination model for component composition. Math. Struct. Comp. Sci. **14**(3), 329–366 (2004)
3. Basu, A., Bozga, M., Sifakis, J.: Modeling heterogeneous real-time components in BIP. In: Proceedings of SEFM, pp. 3–12 (2006)
4. Bliudze, S., Sifakis, J.: The algebra of connectors-structuring interaction in BIP. IEEE Trans. Comput. **57**(10), 1315–1330 (2008)
5. Brewer, D.F.C., Nash, M.J.: The chinese wall security policy. In: Proceedings of IEEE Symposium on Security and Privacy, pp. 206–214 (1989)
6. Callaway, E.: Fraud investigation rocks danish university (2011). http://www.nature.com/news/2011/110107/full/news.2011.703.html
7. De Nicola, R., Ferrari, G.L., Pugliese, R.: KLAIM: a kernel language for agents interaction and mobility. IEEE Trans. Softw. Eng. **24**(5), 315–330 (1998)
8. Hankin, C., Nielson, F., Nielson, H.R.: Advice from belnap policies. In: Proceedings of IEEE Computer Security Foundations Symposium, pp. 234–247 (2009)
9. Hankin, C., Nielson, F., Nielson, H.R., Yang, F.: Advice for coordination. In: Lea, D., Zavattaro, G. (eds.) COORDINATION 2008. LNCS, vol. 5052, pp. 153–168. Springer, Heidelberg (2008)
10. Hartswood, M., Procter, R., Taylor, P., Blot, L., Anderson, S., Rouncefield, M., Slack, R.: Problems of data mobility and reuse in the provision of computer-based training for screening mammography. In: Human Factors in Computing Systems, pp. 909–918 (2012)
11. Lapadula, A., Pugliese, R., Tiezzi, F.: A calculus for orchestration of web services. In: De Nicola, R. (ed.) ESOP 2007. LNCS, vol. 4421, pp. 33–47. Springer, Heidelberg (2007)
12. Nielson, H.R., Nielson, F., Pilegaard, H.: Flow logic for process calculi. ACM Comput. Surv. **44**(1), 3:1–3:39 (2012)
13. Petković, M., Prandi, D., Zannone, N.: Purpose control: did you process the data for the intended purpose? In: Jonker, W., Petković, M. (eds.) SDM 2011. LNCS, vol. 6933, pp. 145–168. Springer, Heidelberg (2011)
14. Prandi, D., Quaglia, P., Zannone, N.: Formal analysis of BPMN via a translation into COWS. In: Lea, D., Zavattaro, G. (eds.) COORDINATION 2008. LNCS, vol. 5052, pp. 249–263. Springer, Heidelberg (2008)
15. Wallis, J.C., Rolando, E., Borgman, C.L.: If we share data, will anyone use them? data sharing and reuse in the long tail of science and technology. PLoS ONE **8**(7), e67332 (2013)

Towards Balancing Privacy and Efficiency: A Principal-Agent Model of Data-Centric Business

Christian Zimmermann$^{(\boxtimes)}$ and Claus-Georg Nolte

University of Freiburg, Freiburg im Breisgau, Germany
{zimmermann,nolte}@iig.uni-freiburg.de

Abstract. Personal data has emerged as a crucial asset of the digital economy. However, unregulated markets for personal data severely threaten consumers' privacy. Based upon a commodity-centric notion of privacy, this paper takes a principal-agent perspective on data-centric business. Specifically, this paper presents an economic model of the privacy problem in data-centric business, in that drawing from contract theory. Building upon a critical analysis of the model, this paper analyzes how regulatory and technological instruments could balance efficiency of markets for personal data and data-subjects' right to informational self-determination.

Keywords: Privacy economics · Privacy · Property rights · Accountability · Principal-agent model

1 Personal Data Markets and Privacy

In the information society, superior capacities to analyze data and superior data sets can constitute crucial competitive advantages for companies [30]. Among the different classes of data, especially personal data is, as the World Economic Forum states, a "critical source of innovation and value" [53]. The, now commonplace, metaphor of personal data as "the new oil" by European Commissioner Kuneva (as cited in [53]) further illustrates the crucial role that is attributed to personal data in the economy. Consequently, markets for personal data have emerged, which, however, are barely regulated [45]. In those markets data subjects participate as suppliers of personal data, in that often not knowing who collects, transfers and monetizes which data relating to them [41]. While markets with highly transparent data-subjects might be efficient (cf. [37]), not only economic factors have to be considered in the debate on markets for personal data. The human rights aspect of privacy has to be taken into account in order to find a balance between the economic efficiency of markets for personal data and data-subjects' right to informational self-determination [9].

   This paper analyzes from an economic perspective how such a balance can be achieved by technological and regulatory instruments, in that focusing on the

© Springer International Publishing Switzerland 2015
S. Foresti (Ed.): STM 2015, LNCS 9331, pp. 89–104, 2015.
DOI: 10.1007/978-3-319-24858-5_6

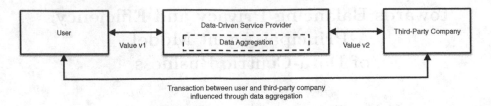

Fig. 1. Schematic representation of transactions in data-centric business (taken from [32])

"First Tier Relationship Space" [35] of markets for personal data, i.e., on the direct relation of primary data-controller and data-subject. In particular, this paper focuses on data-centric business as defined by Müller et al. [32] and the privacy problems inherent in this business model [32,41]. A simplified scheme of data-centric business is depicted in Fig. 1.

Data-centric service providers such as Google or Facebook provide (often free of charge) services to consumers and generate revenue by providing third companies with the ability to present targeted advertisements to theses consumers. Hence, data-centric businesses act as multi-sided platforms [17] that cater to users of their services on the one hand and to advertisers on the other hand. The collection of personal data and the generation of user profiles are at the core of data-centric business models, as these profiles build the foundation for delivering targeted advertisements. Hence, it is in data-centric businesses' interest to collect as much data relating to users as possible in order to be able to generate precise targeting profiles [34]. However, not only providers of data-centric services, but also their users benefit from profiling [19], e.g., through decreased transaction cost due to automatically personalized recommender systems [49]. However, extensive collection, analysis and usage of data relating to users affect and threaten their privacy [41,51]. In the context of data-centric business, this paper addresses the following research questions:

1. How can the relation of users and providers be modeled in economic terms?
2. Which leverage points for balancing economic efficiency and privacy can be identified and how can technological and regulatory instruments help in establishing such a balance?

This paper contributes as follows: In order to describe the privacy problems in data-centric business and subsequently be able to identify leverage points for balancing efficiency and privacy, this paper provides an economic model of the privacy trade-offs in data-centric business. The presented model builds upon a novel principal-agent perspective on data-centric business that is rooted in a commodity-centric notion of privacy. Building upon a critical analysis of the model, this paper analyzes how regulatory and technological instruments could balance efficiency of markets for personal data and data-subjects' right to informational self-determination.

The remainder of this paper is structured as follows: the next section provides an overview on related work. Section 3 presents our economic model of the privacy trade-offs in data-centric business. Section 4 presents an analysis of the model, illustrates regulatory and technological leverage points for balancing market efficiency and privacy and discusses instruments for this balancing. We conclude the paper and provide an outlook on future work in Sect. 5.

2   Related Work

The emergence of barely regulated markets for personal data and their threats to privacy have not gone unnoticed by academia. Scholars in the computer sciences, jurisprudence and IS are investigating legal and technological instruments to regulate such markets and to provide instruments for data subjects to exercise greater control over their personal data. Notable approaches towards organizing markets for personal data have been proposed by Laudon [27], Schwartz [42] or Novotny and Spiekermann [35].

Technological and legal instruments for addressing the privacy problems in markets for personal data have recently been discussed by Spiekermann and Novotny [45]. We build upon their commodity-centric notion of privacy, in that considering only usage rights for personal data tradable. Acquisti provides an economic model of privacy trade-offs in electronic commerce, in that focussing on data-subjects' decision process and arguing for models based on psychological distortions [2]. He does, however, not investigate the perspective of the data-controller and the structure of the market. Chellappa & Shivendu provide a model for game-theoretic analysis of property rights approaches towards privacy, in that, however, considering only monopolistic markets [12].

In contrast to existing work, the model provided in this paper takes a principal-agent perspective and focuses on the market structure in data-centric business.

3   Principal-Agent Model of the Privacy Problems in Data-Centric Business

Identification of leverage points for balancing efficiency of the market for personal data and data-subjects' privacy in data-centric business requires a model fit to describe the market, its agents' behavior and the market's power structure. Building upon a commodity-centric notion of privacy, we provide a principal-agent model of data-centric business in Sect. 3.2. However, we first elaborate on data-centric business and the assumptions underlying our model in the following.

3.1   Assumptions and Background

We base our model upon the following three assumptions, on which we elaborate further in the following.

1. Usage rights to personal data are transferable and tradable.
2. Providers and users act rational and have homogeneous utility functions within their constraints.
3. Users are privacy pragmatists that are willing to substitute privacy for functionality up to a certain degree.

Assumption 1: Among many others, Campell and Hanson or Davies argued that the growing economic importance of personal data is paralleled by a shift in public perception of personal data and a reconceptualization of privacy that moves it from the domain of civil rights to the domain of commodification [10,16]. That means that personal data increasingly is considered a tradable commodity that is separable from the individual [10,16]. In the wake of this shift in perception, property rights for personal data have increasingly been debated not only in jurisprudence, but also in IS and the computer sciences (cf. [6,15,28,39,40,42]). Recently, Purtova has shown that current European data protection regime "endorses the'property thinking' with regard to personal data" [40, p. 211] and that data-subjects' ownership claims to personal data are compatible with the principle of informational self-determination [40]. However, the human rights aspect of privacy excludes full propertization of personal data. In particular, ownership claims to it can not be alienated [6,42]. Our model does not build upon full propertization of personal data. Instead, we follow Spiekermann and Novotny and consider only usage rights to personal data transferable and tradable [45].

Assumption 2: For mathematical simplicity we assume that all agents within our model, providers as well as users, act rational under their constraints. Thus, an agent will perform any action that increases her expected utility and will avoid any action that has no positive expected utility for her. Moreover, also for easy modeling, we assume that users and providers have homogeneous utility functions. This allows for utilization of just one expected utility function for all users and just one for all providers within our model. Those assumptions are also common and necessary for the standard principal-agent model [50].

Assumption 3: Building upon Westin and Ackerman et al., we further put "pragmatic users" into the center of our investigation [1,52]. Pragmatic users are concerned about their privacy, i.e., the usage of data regarding them, but weigh their concerns against the benefits of disclosing data about themselves. This user model is supported by current research that shows that users are willing to engage in online transactions and disclose personal data in case the perceived benefits of doing so outweigh the cost, including the perceived cost of reduced privacy [3,20,21,34,44].

In data-centric business as defined above, users receive benefits from data-centric service providers' data aggregation and analysis, e.g. personalized search results. However, to be able to reap these benefits from data processing, users need to entrust data relating to them to a provider of a data-centric service, i.e., transfer usage rights to that data to the provider. Hence, given the above presented commodity-centric perspective on privacy, we consider the relation of users and providers of data-centric services a principal-agent relation [43]. In this principal-agent relation, users suffer severe information asymmetries [41], i.e., they are unable to fully comprehend which data a provider collects, how that data is aggregated, which data is inferred from collected data and how personal data is used by the provider. Thus, users face a problem of moral hazard [50], i.e., they face the risk that providers exercise transferred usage rights in ways users do not wish them to be used.

The classic approach towards describing and investigating solutions to moral hazard problems in principal-agent relations is provided by contract theory [50], upon which we build our investigation. However, the classic contract theory model can not be applied straight forward in the context of data-centric business. The classic model builds upon the idea that principal and agent negotiate a contract and the principal pays the agent a price that will incent the agent to follow strategies that benefit the principal rather than following strategies that maximize solely the agent's own benefit. In current data-centric business, the user (the principal) undoubtedly enters a contract with the provider (the agent) by agreeing to its terms of usage. Hence, currently, the user is unable to negotiate this contract and has to accept the conditions set by the provider.

Further, in data-centric business, the user transfers usage rights to personal data to the provider so that she can reap benefits from the provider's usage of the data. However, based on the contract, the user transfers more data and wider-reaching usage rights than necessary (and, possibly, desired by the user) for receiving the desired benefits and, hence, pays a price to the provider. This price is set by the provider and, thus, it does not incent the provider to act in the user's interest. In fact, regarding privacy, the price is set such as to maximize benefits for the provider. Although the user seldom is able to fully comprehend common privacy policies or terms of usage [31,33,34], we assume that the user expects the provider to be able and eager to collect more data than technologically necessary and to use the data for defined purposes (e.g. for advertising) that are beyond solely providing the desired service (see Assumption 2). Current research supports this assumptions and has shown that users engage in "privacy-seeking" behavior when using data-centric services [47].

3.2 Principal-Agent Model

Game theory addresses problems where the probability of a certain outcome is utterly unknown. In our approach, users face a decision under risk but not under complete uncertainty. While the probabilities can not necessarily be determined exactly, general outcome probabilities are rough deducible. For example, users can infer the probabilities for some extreme outcomes based on media reports about data leakage scandals or similar reported events. Hence, following the classic model [50], we represent a user's expected utility as a concave Neumann-Morgenstern function. This also allows us to consider different user types, for example, as in this paper, a risk-averse privacy pragmatic user. We formulate the user's expected utility as follows:

$$EU(a, s, x, r, z) := \pi(s, a) - (g(x, r, z) + z) \tag{1}$$

The user desires the data-centric service provider to perform action $\hat{a}$, i.e., provide the desired services and exercise the transferred usage rights solely to provide these services. Thereby $\hat{a}$ is part of a finite set of possible provider actions A. Depending on the random variable s and the action a chosen by the provider, the user receives the outcome function $\pi(s, a)$, with $s \in S, S = \{s_1, \ldots, s_n\}, p(s) \in [0, 1]$ being a random variable individually drawn for each user, accounting for the provider's ability to take action a (e.g., exercise usage rights for purposes undesired by the user). Hence, because the outcome $\pi(s, a)$ partly depends on chance the user is not able to fully compare it to the desired outcome $\pi(s, \hat{a})$.

Moreover, the user can not definitely determine which data and which usage rights are at minimum necessary to provide the desired services. For example, a user can not estimate which data and which usage of the data are necessary for receiving personalized search results. We represent the cost of disclosing this technologically at minimum necessary amount of data and transferring the resp. usage rights by $x_{min} > 0$. The user's at maximum desired cost of disclosing data and transferring usage rights is represented by $\hat{x}$. As described above, the user suspects the provider to collect more data than technologically necessary for providing the desired service and to use the transferred usage rights for purposes (specified in the terms of usage) beyond solely providing the desired services. For simplicity we do not consider illegal data usage by the provider. We represent the user's expected cost of data disclosure and transfer of usage rights by x with $x \geq x_{min} > 0$.

We take users' privacy-seeking behavior into account by representing the subjectively expected privacy-related overall cost of using data-centric services by $(g(x, r, z) + z)$ with $g(x, r, z) \geq x_{min}, z \in [0, 1]$. For simplicity and clarity, we neglect the cost of using the service per se, e.g., expenditure of time. In the construct $(g(x, r, z) + z)$, the variable $z \in [0, 1]$ represents the cost that a user incurs when engaging in privacy-seeking behavior, trying to reduce x by, e.g., the usage of Privacy-Enhancing Technologies (PET) [48] or by adjustment of privacy settings. In case the user does not engage in privacy-seeking behavior, then $z = 0$. In case the user engages in privacy-seeking behavior to the maximum extent technologically currently available, then $z = 1$. We assume that the user is aware of the fact that privacy-seeking behavior is not necessarily successful, i.e., does not necessarily decrease x (e.g., data might be inferred anyway and be usable for advertising). We represent this uncertainty by the random variable r individually drawn for each user, with $r \in R, R = \{r_1, \ldots, r_m\}, r \in [0, 1]$ and the probability $q(r) \in [0, 1]$. In this construct r represents the chance of success of a user's privacy-seeking behavior, with $r = 0$ meaning no success at all, i.e., $g(x, r, z) = x$. In case $r = 1$, success is depending on the invested z, i.e., $g(x, r, z) = \hat{x}$ (or $g(x, r, z) = x_{min}$ if $\hat{x} < x_{min}$) provided $z = 1$. In case $r = 1, z \in\ ]0, 1[$ then $g(x, r, z) \in\ ]x_{min}, x[$. We formulate a provider's expected utility from providing a user with data-centric services as follows:

$$EF(a, x, r, z) := f(h(x, r, z)) - c(a) \qquad (2)$$

The provider aims at receiving x (i.e., data relating to the users and the respective usage rights) and incurs the cost $c(a)$ of its action (providing the service and exercising usage rights to user's data), with $c(a) \geq 0$ and $c(a) = 0$ only for $a = 0$. The utility function $f(h(x, r, z))$ the provider expects depends on the expected effectiveness of users' privacy-seeking behavior, i.e., on r, z and x which we take into account by the outcome function $h(x, r, z)$. In any case, the provider receives at least $h(x, r, z) \geq x_{min}$. Given the high information asymmetries in data-centric business [41], currently, the provider is in the position to set the price in terms of transfer of data and usage rights, i.e., to set x as high as possible for profit maximization. Hence, the provider aims at establishing contract $x(\pi)$ that maximizes:

$$\sum_{i=1}^{n} p(s_i) * \sum_{j=1}^{m} q(r_j) * EF(a, g(x(\pi(s_i, a)), r_j, z), r_j, z) \qquad (3)$$

While the assumed pragmatic user is willing to trade-off privacy and benefits from using data-centric services, even a pragmatic user [1,52] is not willing to completely substitute privacy with functionality [34]. This means, that the assumed pragmatic user will refrain from using a specific data-centric service in case she expects the provider to collect data and to exercise data usage rights to an extent too far beyond the desired extent. In that case, $EU < U^0$ with U^0 being the user's expected utility from not using a service at all. Similar as in classic contract theory, we represent this constraint as follows:

$$\sum_{i=1}^{n} p(s_i) * \sum_{j=1}^{m} q(r_j) * EU(a, s_i, x, r_j, z) \geq U^0 \qquad (4)$$

As we assume non-monopolistic markets, users can choose from several providers of data-centric services, e.g., different online search engines, to get similar benefits. Thus, a privacy pragmatic user will only use a specific service if, besides the constraint formulated above, the following constraint holds:

$$\sum_{i=1}^{n} p(s_i) * \sum_{j=1}^{m} q(r_j) * EU(a, s_i, x, r_j, z) \geq \sum_{i=1}^{n} p(s_i) * \sum_{j=1}^{m} q(r_j) * EU(a', s_i, x', r_j, z)$$

$$(5)$$

Here a' and x' represent actions of a data-centric service provider's competitors and the data and data usage rights to be transferred for using their services. Hence, provided competitors exist, the provider can not completely neglect the assumed pragmatic user's concerns for privacy.

In the following, we discuss our model and illustrate possibilities to achieve a balance between privacy and efficiency by means of technological and regulatory instruments.

4   Towards Balancing Privacy and Efficiency

The presented model exhibits some limitations. First, in line with the majority of economic models, it builds upon the assumption of rational agents. Hence, while our model can be adapted to model privacy-affine or privacy-uninterested users by adapting U^0 or $g(\bullet)$, the model does not take into account psychological distortions [2]. Second, while our model covers the moral hazard problem on the user's side, it does not consider the inverse information asymmetry suffered by the provider with respect to the user's characteristics. Thus, while the model does account for the asymmetry regarding users' privacy-seeking behavior, it does not take into account possible misuse of services by the user, e.g., data crawling and reselling. Third, the model does also not consider illegal behavior by the provider (e.g., privacy policy violations or non-compliance with data protection regulation). Last, the positive network effects between users within the same service are only rudimentary covered by the outcome $\pi(s, a)$ but not explicitly included. Taking into account these limitations, we discuss possibilities to achieve a balance between privacy and efficiency by means of technological and regulatory instruments in the following.

In perfect competition with providers as price-takers [50], providers would be forced by competition to set x as low as possible so that they can just cover their marginal cost of the provided action a. Hence, if the minimal necessary data and usage rights x_{min} to perform action a suffice to cover the marginal costs of providing it to yet another user the x demanded by all providers would consequentially be x_{min} and an equilibrium would exist for $x = x_{min}$ with $a \geq a'$. However, current data-centric business is far from a state of perfect competition. The actual market situation indicates that each branch is dominated by one powerful provider (e.g. Google with 90 % market share for online search [46]) that is flanked by a few small competitors competing for the left-over market share. Hence, the current market situation resembles a monopolistic situation where the provider maximizes its revenue and therefore x with the only constraint to deliver a service with expected user utility equal to or greater the user's utility without any service: $EU \geq U_0$ (see Eq. 4). Thus, the dominant providers are currently in the position to establish contracts with their users, possibly but not necessarily in all cases, such as that $x > \hat{x} > x_{min}$ [47]. Hence, as long as $EU \geq U^0$ wit $x > \hat{x}$ there are few incentives for providers to establish contracts that are more "privacy-friendly", i.e., set $x = \hat{x}$ and $a = \hat{a}$. Three scenarios in the first relationship tier [35] to be investigated can be distinguished:

(S1) Privacy is not considered a competitive factor by users.
(S2) Privacy is perceived as a competitive factor by users but they are unable to determine providers' level of "privacy-friendliness".
(S3) Markets for data-centric services are currently monopolistic.
    (a) Users perceive privacy as worthy of protection.
    (b) User do not perceive privacy as worthy of protection.

It is obvious that these scenarios require different approaches towards balancing market efficiency and privacy. Further, it is to be investigated whether there is a need for privacy protection at all. Some scholars have argued that privacy protection generally decreases efficiency and general welfare [37]. While full transparency and full information might increase efficiency, the human rights aspect of privacy [9] excludes purely efficiency-focused approaches towards markets for personal data. Hence, regardless of which scenario currently exists, a balance between efficiency and privacy in data-centric business has to be established.

Table 1. Applicability of the high-level approaches in different scenarios

	Market-Centric	Regulation-Centric	User-Centric
	Privacy through market mechanisms, primarily driven by incentive-based approaches, possibly supported by technological instruments and/or regulatory instruments.	Privacy through regulatory instruments, focussing primarily on prohibition, possibly supported by technological instruments and/or market mechanisms.	Privacy through technological instruments, primarily driven by user demand, possibly supported by market mechanisms and/or regulatory instruments.
Scenario 1	-	X	-
Scenario 2	X	X	(X)
Scenario 3	-	X	(X)

Which instruments are suited for achieving such a balance depends on the market structure in data-centric business. In order to identify and discuss instruments for balancing privacy and efficiency we analyze the above provided scenarios in the following. We distinguish between three high-level approaches towards balancing privacy and efficiency: market-centric approaches, regulation-centric approaches and user-centric approaches. The differentiation criterion for these approaches is their primary instrument for balancing privacy and efficiency in data-centric business. Table 1 provides an overview over the approaches and their applicability in the above-described scenarios under the premise that privacy requires protection.

4.1 S1: Privacy is Not Considered a Competitive Factor by Users

In S1, purely market-centric approaches, i.e., regulatory laissez-faire or incentive-centered interventions, are not suited to foster increased privacy-friendliness in data-centric business as both providers and users have no self-motivated incentives to provide or demand respective services. The same holds true for user-centric approaches. If privacy is to be achieved in S1, only regulatory action and a (soft-)paternalistic regulatory regime can be applied. Our model does not aim at providing insight into the challenges of such an approach and we do not further consider S1 in this paper.

4.2   S3: Markets for Data-Centric Services Are Currently Monopolistic

In S3, market-centric approaches obviously are not suited to balance efficiency and privacy. In S3b, user-centric approaches are not well suited as users have no incentive to take action to protect their privacy. In S3a, at least users such as the pragmatic user of our model have incentives to expend $z > 0$ to protect their privacy. Provided privacy-seeking behavior is effective and users can determine its effectiveness, user-centric approaches can lead to increased privacy in S3a but only on an individual level when PET [48] are used on the users-side. However, purely user-centric approaches would not change the market structure and monopoly would continue. Hence, regulatory action to weaken or even break the monopoly and to enable and increase market competition would be necessary. Thus, if a balance between efficiency and privacy is to be achieved, only regulation-centric approaches are applicable in S3. Such approaches would need to convert S3 into S1 or S2 and subsequently perform regulatory action as described in Sects. 4.1 and 4.3, respectively, to achieve a balance between privacy and efficiency. Chellappa and Shivendu propose the introduction of property rights to personal information as a regulatory approach towards balancing efficiency and privacy in monopoly [12].

4.3   S2: Privacy is Perceived as a Competitive Factor by Users But They are Unable to Determine Providers' Level of "Privacy-Friendliness"

Scenario 2 exhibits characteristics that are partly similar to those of "lemon markets" which are deemed doomed to fail in the long run [4]. While users in S2 value privacy, they are unable to determine the privacy-friendliness of a provider ex ante and ex post entering a contract and, hence, providers have no incentive to compete on privacy and rather compete on functionality. Thus, in the long run, privacy-friendly providers would leave the market due to their lower profits caused by a lower x and the market would "fail" in the sense that no balance between privacy and efficiency could be achieved. In classic lemon markets as in data-centric business the problem is rooted in information asymmetry and power asymmetries [41]. Hence, in S2 classic instruments for reducing asymmetries of information and power seem best suited to achieve a balance between privacy and market efficiency. Because of the principal-agent relation in data-centric business and the human-rights aspect of privacy, however, further instruments as well as the suitability of classic instruments for reducing information and power asymmetries have to be investigated for the context at hand. In the following, we analyze and discuss technological and regulatory instruments for balancing privacy and efficiency in S2. Figure 2 provides an overview on the categories of analyzed instruments.

Signaling and screening are instruments for reducing information asymmetries ex ante establishment of a contract [29]. The informed party can utilize signaling instruments to signal to the uninformed party its characteristics in

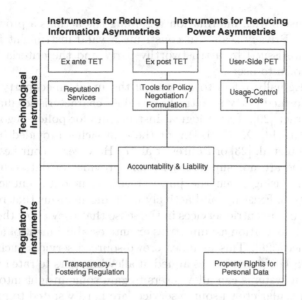

Fig. 2. Instruments for addressing the privacy problem in data-centric business

order to reduce the information asymmetry and convince the uninformed party to establish a contract with the signaling party instead of with another party. Signaling, however, can only be a successful mechanisms in case the uninformed party has good reason to trust in the signal, i.e., the cost of falsely signaling a characteristic while not exhibiting it has to be high, ideally exceeding the benefits of doing so. Screening can be seen as inverse signaling, i.e., screening instruments can be utilized by the uninformed party in order to reduce information asymmetries by actively trying to find out the informed party's characteristics. In the context of data-centric business, a provider of data-centric services has superior information regarding x_{min}, x and a, i.e., she is the informed party [41]. Signaling and screening are instruments for market-centric approaches towards balancing privacy and efficiency (see Table 1).

Drawing from the literature, we identify Transparency-Enhancing Technologies (TET) [22] that are applied before establishment of a contract [25] ("ex ante TET") as potential instruments for signaling in data-centric business. Ex ante TET comprise all TET that are applied before using a service and include tools for policy visualization (e.g., "PrivacyBird"[1]), privacy seals (e.g., the "European Privacy Seal"[2]) and other instruments for providing information regarding intended data collection and usage, i.e., information on x, a and, possibly, x_{min}. A variety of ex ante TET exist, however, their suitability regarding balancing privacy and efficiency in data-centric business is limited. While tools for policy visualization are able to signal intended data collection and usage, i.e., x, they

---

[1] http://www.privacybird.org.
[2] https://www.european-privacy-seal.eu.

do not provide users with information regarding the actions a provider actually performs, i.e., a. Privacy seals can constitute a valid instrument for signaling, provided they are issued by a trustworthy party and the criteria for awarding the seals are known to users.

Screening originally refers to actions of the uninformed party that aim at inducing the informed party to actively reveal its characteristics during negotiation of the contract [29]. Technological instruments for policy negotiation exist, e.g., P3P/APPEL [14], XACML [13] or the approaches provided by Pretschner et al. [38], Hanson et al. [23] or Bohrer et al. [7]. However, to our best knowledge, these mechanisms are not supported by any provider of data-centric services, which is not surprising given the power relations in data-centric business as described in Sect. 3. Existing, and actively used, mechanisms that resemble classic screening for data-centric services in the sense that they allow the uninformed party to reduce information asymmetries ex ante establishment of a contract are reputation services [26]. This includes crowd-sourced services such as "Web of Trust"[3] or "TOS;DR"[4] or services aimed at allowing users to rate other services. While reputation systems can allow users to gain some insight into a provider's behavior, in particular crowd-source services are hardly suited to provide meaningful information regarding x_{min}, x or a as other users (even if they already have established a contract with a specific provider) are unable to fully determine the provider's actions. In case the provider grants wide-ranging insight into x_{min}, x or a after establishment of a contract, however, crowd-sourced reputation services can constitute effective instruments for estimating x_{min}, x or a. However, to our best knowledge, no data-centric provider already does so (see below). Besides instruments to be applied ex ante establishment of a contract, instruments that can be applied to reduce asymmetries of information and power ex post have to be investigated. Further, some instruments, especially regulatory ones, exist that can not be categorized as ex ante or ex post instruments.

Users themselves can apply user-side PET [48] at cost z in order to reduce the information they disclose and a provider's power to exercise usage rights to data. Such PET include, among many other, tools for anonymity (e.g., "Tor"[5]) or obfuscation (e.g., "TrackMeNot" [24]). While user-side PET could also be seen as instruments for reducing information asymmetry we consider them instruments for elusion of power asymmetries. We do so, as data-minimization on the user-side does not help users to learn the hidden characteristics of the provider. While they do not allow users to estimate x_{min}, x or a, they can reduce the privacy-related cost of using data-centric services ex post establishing of a contract by reducing $h(x, r, z)$. Usage control tools, as presented in, e.g., [5,11], in combination with policy negotiation tools can also be applied to reduce power asymmetries (and information asymmetries in case policy negotiation can be used for screening) by giving users a means for setting rules for the exercise of usage rights by the provider, i.e., for influencing a.

---

[3] https://www.mywot.com.

[4] https://tosdr.org.

[5] https://www.torproject.org.

Ex post TET aim at providing users with insight into actual data collection and usage [25]. The most prominent class of ex post TET are so-called privacy dashboards. Depending on their functionality, they can be considered both instruments for reducing information asymmetry and instruments for reducing power asymmetries. While read-only ex post TET are instruments for reducing information asymmetry ex post establishment of the contract, interactive ex post TET are instruments for reduction of asymmetries of power and information [54]. While ex post TET, and privacy dashboards in particular, seem promising approaches towards balancing privacy and efficiency in data-centric business, current approaches as proposed in, e.g., [8,18] or the privacy dashboards provided by Google[6] or Acxiom[7] do not provide trustworthy information and, hence, are not well suited for balancing privacy and efficiency (cf. [54]).

Accountability-centric approaches are currently widely discussed as means towards balancing privacy and efficiency [36,55]. Privacy by accountability inherently requires a combination of technological and regulatory instruments [36,55]. Respective approaches towards privacy build upon audit in order to determine providers' adherence to data protection regulation and/or agreed-upon polices. A central concept within accountability-centric approaches towards privacy is liability, i.e., sanctioning of providers in case of noncompliance with regulation and agreed-upon policies. While accountability-centric approaches towards balancing privacy and efficiency are promising and increasingly investigated, no respective solution currently exists.

Regulatory action towards reducing information asymmetry is currently being taken, e.g., in the new GDPR. Regulatory instruments can set the legal frame such as to reduce information asymmetry ex ante and ex post establishment of contracts and can support both regulation-centric and market-centric approaches towards balancing privacy and efficiency. Another purely regulatory approach towards balancing privacy and efficiency is the assignment of property rights to personal data, which is currently widely debated in the fields of jurisprudence, IS and computer science (see Sect. 3).

5   Conclusion

In this paper, we provided a principal-agent model of the privacy problems and trade-offs in data-centric business, in that drawing from contract theory. Building upon an analysis of the model, we identified asymmetries of information and power as the primary leverage points for balancing efficiency and privacy in data-centric business. We analyzed and discussed the suitability of existing regulatory and technological instruments for reducing the identified asymmetries. We showed that, in non-monopolistic markets and provided that privacy is perceived as a competitive factor by users and providers, providers have the incentive to provide users with increased transparency and control regarding their personal

---

[6] https://myaccount.google.com.
[7] http://www.acxiom.com.

data. We also showed that regulatory pressure might be necessary to foster competition in data-centric business. Based upon our analysis, we conclude that a transparency-fostering regulatory regime in combination with trustworthy ex ante and ex post TET, respectively accountability mechanisms, seems best suited for achieving a more privacy-friendly balance of efficiency and privacy in data-centric business. Adopting a commodity-centric notion of privacy as described in Sect. 3 into law might further increase users' ability to exercise their right to informational self-determination without loss of the benefits of data-centric service. Currently, we are investigating requirements of accountability-oriented instruments for balancing privacy and efficiency in data-centric business. Among others, this includes the investigation of the suitability of privacy dashboards as instruments for accountability and the economic implications of such an approach.

References

1. Ackerman, M.S., Cranor, L.F., Reagle, J.: Privacy in e-Commerce: examining user scenarios and privacy preferences. In: Proceedings of EC 1999, pp. 1–8. ACM (1999)
2. Acquisti, A.: Privacy in electronic commerce and the economics of immediate gratification. In: Proceedings of EC 2004, pp. 21–29. ACM, New York (2004)
3. Acquisti, A., Gross, R.: Imagined communities: awareness, information sharing, and privacy on the facebook. In: Danezis, G., Golle, P. (eds.) PET 2006. LNCS, vol. 4258, pp. 36–58. Springer, Heidelberg (2006)
4. Akerlof, G.A.: The market for "Lemons": quality uncertainty and the market mechanism. Q. J. Econ. **84**(3), 488–500 (1970)
5. Ashley, P., Powers, C., Schunter, M.: From privacy promises to privacy management. In: Proceedings of NSPW 2002, pp. 43–50. ACM (2002)
6. Bergelson, V.: It's personal but is it mine? toward property rights in personal information. U.C. Davis Law Rev. **37**(2), 379–452 (2003)
7. Bohrer, K., Liu, X., Kesdogan, D., Schonberg, E., Singh, M., Spraragen, S.: Personal information management and distribution. In: Proceedings of ICECR-4 (2001)
8. Buchmann, J., Nebel, M., Rossnagel, A., Shirazi, F., Fhom, H.S., Waidner, M.: Personal information dashboard: putting the individual back in control. In: Digital Enlightenment Yearbook 2013, pp. 139–164. IOS Press (2013)
9. Bundesverfassungsgericht: BVerfG, Urteil v. 15. Dezember 1983, Az. 1 BvR 209, 269, 362, 420, 440, 484/83 (1983)
10. Campbell, J.E., Carlson, M.: Panopticon.com: online surveillance and the commodification of privacy. J. Broadcast. Electron. Media **46**(4), 586–606 (2002)
11. Mont, M.C., Pearson, S., Bramhall, P.: Towards accountable management of identity and privacy: sticky policies and enforceable tracing services. In: Proceedings of DEXA 2003, pp. 377–382. IEEE (2003)
12. Chellappa, R.K., Shivendu, S.: An economic model of privacy: a property rights approach to regulatory choices for online personalization. J. Manage. Inf. Syst. **24**(3), 193–225 (2007)
13. Cheng, V., Hung, P., Chiu, D.: Enabling web services policy negotiation with privacy preserved using XACML. In: Proceedings of HICSS 2007, pp. 33–33. IEEE (2007)

14. Cranor, L., Langheinrich, M., Marchiori, M.: A P3P Preference Exchange Language 1.0 (APPEL1.0) (2002). http://www.w3.org/TR/P3P-preferences/
15. Cuijpers, C.: A private law approach to privacy; mandatory law obliged? SCRIPT-ed **4**(4), 304–318 (2007)
16. Davies, S.G.: Re-engineering the right to privacy: how privacy has been transformed from a right to a commodity. In: Technology and privacy, pp. 143–165. MIT Press (1997)
17. Evans, D.S.: The economics of the online advertising industry. Rev. Netw. Econ. **7**(3), 1–33 (2008)
18. Fischer-Hübner, S., Hedbom, H., Wästlund, E.: Trust and assurance HCI. In: Camenisch, J., Fischer-Hübne, S., Rannenberg, K. (eds.) Privacy and Identity Management for Life, pp. 245–260. Springer, Heidelberg (2011)
19. Franke, N., Keinz, P., Steger, C.J.: Testing the value of customization: when do customers really prefer products tailored to their preferences? J. Mark. **73**, 103–121 (2009)
20. Fujitsu Res. Inst.: Personal data in the cloud: a global survey of consumer attitudes (2010). http://www.fujitsu.com/downloads/SOL/fai/reports/fujitsu_personal-data-in-the-cloud.pdf
21. Gross, R., Acquisti, A.: Information revelation and privacy in online social networks. In: Proceedings of WPES 2005, pp. 71–80. ACM (2005)
22. Hansen, M.: Marrying transparency tools with user-controlled identity management. In: Fischer-Hübner, S., Duquenoy, P., Zuccato, A., Martucci, L. (eds.) FIDIS 2007. IFIP Advances in Information and Communication Technology, vol. 262, pp. 199–220. Springer, Heidelberg (2008)
23. Hanson, C., Kagal, L., Berners-Lee, T., Sussman, G., Weitzner, D.: Data-purpose algebra: modeling data usage policies. In: Proceedings of POLICY 2007, pp. 173–177. IEEE (2007)
24. Howe, D.C., Nissenbaum, H.: TrackMeNot: resisting surveillance in web search. In: Lessons from the Identity Trail: Anonymity, Privacy, and Identity in a Networked Society, pp. 417–436. Oxford University Press (2009)
25. Janic, M., Wijbenga, J., Veugen, T.: Transparency enhancing tools (TETs): an overview. In: STAST 2013, pp. 18–25 (2013)
26. Josang, A., Ismail, R., Boyd, C.: A survey of trust and reputation systems for online service provision. Decis. Support Syst. **43**(2), 618–644 (2007)
27. Laudon, K.C.: Markets and privacy. Commun. ACM **39**(9), 92–104 (1996)
28. Lessig, L.: Privacy as property. Soc. Res. **69**(1), 247–269 (2002)
29. Mankiw, N.: Principles of Macroeconomics. Cengage Learning, Boston (2014)
30. McAfee, A., Brynjolfsson, E.: Big data: the management revolution. Harv. Bus. Rev. **90**(10), 60–68 (2012)
31. McDonald, A.M., Cranor, L.F.: Cost of reading privacy policies. J. Law Policy Inf. Soc. **4**, 543–568 (2008)
32. Müller, G., Flender, C., Peters, M.: Vertrauensinfrastruktur und Privatheit als ökonomische Fragestellung. In: Buchmann, J. (ed.) Internet Privacy. acatech STUDY, pp. 143–188. Springer, Heidelberg (2012)
33. Nissenbaum, H.: A contextual approach to privacy online. Daedalus **140**(4), 32–48 (2011)
34. Nolte, C.G.: Personal data as payment method in SNS and users' concerning price sensitivity - a survey. In: Business Information Systems Workshops. LNBIP, vol. 228. Springer (2015), to appear
35. Novotny, A., Spiekermann, S.: Personal information markets and privacy: a new model to solve the controversy. In: Proceedings of WI 2013, pp. 1635–1649 (2013)

36. Pearson, S., Charlesworth, A.: Accountability as a way forward for privacy protection in the cloud. In: Jaatun, M.G., Zhao, G., Rong, C. (eds.) Cloud Computing. LNCS, vol. 5931, pp. 131–144. Springer, Heidelberg (2009)

37. Posner, R.A.: The economics of privacy. Am. Econ. Rev. **71**(2), 405–409 (1981)

38. Pretschner, A., Hilty, M., Basin, D.: Distributed usage control. CACM **49**(9), 39–44 (2006)

39. Purtova, N.: Property rights in personal data: learning from the American discourse. Comput. Law Secur. Rev. **25**(6), 507–521 (2009)

40. Purtova, N.: Property rights in personal data: A European perspective. Ph.D. thesis, Universiteit van Tilburg, Tilburg (2011)

41. Schermer, B.W.: The limits of privacy in automated profiling and data mining. Comput. Law Secur. Rev. **27**(1), 45–52 (2011)

42. Schwartz, P.M.: Property, privacy, and personal data. Harv. Law Rev. **117**(7), 2056–2128 (2004)

43. Shapiro, S.P.: Agency theory. Ann. Rev. Soc. **31**, 263–284 (2005)

44. Spiekermann, S., Dickinson, I., Günther, O., Reynolds, D.: User agents in e-commerce environments: industry vs. consumer perspectives on data exchange. In: Eder, Johann, Missikoff, Michele (eds.) CAiSE 2003. LNCS, vol. 2681, pp. 696–710. Springer, Heidelberg (2003)

45. Spiekermann, S., Novotny, A.: A vision for global privacy bridges: technical and legal measures for international data markets. Comput. Law Secur. Rev. **31**(2), 181–200 (2015)

46. StatCounter: Worldwide market share of leading search engines from january 2010 to April 2015. http://www.statista.com/statistics/216573/worldwide-market-share-of-search-engines/

47. Stutzman, F., Gross, R., Acquisti, A.: Silent listeners: the evolution of privacy and disclosure on facebook. J. Priv. Confid. **4**(2), 7–41 (2013)

48. Van Blarkom, G., Borking, J., Olk, J. (eds.): Handbook of Privacy and Privacy-Enhancing Technologies. College bescherming persoonsgegevens, The Hague (2003)

49. Varian, H.R.: Economic aspects of personal privacy. In: Lehr, W.H., Pupillo, L.M. (eds.) Internet Policy and Economics, pp. 101–109. Springer, Heidelberg (2009)

50. Varian, H.R.: Intermediate Microeconomics: A Modern Approach, 8th edn. WW Norton & Company, New York (2010)

51. Weitzner, D.J.: Google, profiling, and privacy. IEEE Internet Comput. **11**(6), 95–97 (2007)

52. Westin, A., Harris Louis & Associates: Harris-Equifax Consumer Privacy Survey. Technical report, 1991. Conducted for Equifax Inc. 1,255 adults of the U.S. public. Technical report (1991)

53. World Economic Forum: Personal Data: The Emergence of a New Asset Class (2011). http://www3.weforum.org/docs/WEF_ITTC_PersonalDataNewAsset_Report_2011.pdf

54. Zimmermann, C., Accorsi, R., Müller, G.: Privacy dashboards: reconciling data-driven business models and privacy. In: Proceedings of ARES 2014, pp. 152–157. IEEE (2014)

55. Zimmermann, C., Cabinakova, J.: A conceptualization of accountability as a privacy principle. In: Business Information Systems Workshops. LNBIP, vol. 228. Springer (2015), to appear

Intrusion Detection and Software Vulnerabilities

The AC-Index: Fast Online Detection
of Correlated Alerts

Andrea Pugliese$^{(\boxtimes)}$, Antonino Rullo, and Antonio Piccolo

DIMES Department, University of Calabria, Rende, Italy
{apugliese,nrullo,piccolo}@dimes.unical.it

Abstract. We propose an indexing technique for alert correlation
that supports DFA-like patterns with user-defined correlation functions.
Our *AC-Index* supports (i) the retrieval of the top-k (possibly non-
contiguous) sub-sequences, ranked on the basis of an arbitrary user-
provided severity function, (ii) the concurrent retrieval of sub-sequences
that match any pattern in a given set, (iii) the retrieval of partial occurrences of the patterns, and (iv) the online processing of streaming logs.
The experimental results confirm that, although the supported model is
very expressive, the AC-Index is able to guarantee a very high efficiency
of the retrieval process.

1 Introduction

Intrusion Detection Systems (IDSs) usually generate logs whose tuples encode
timestamped security-related alerts that are recorded from a monitored system. In general, the *alert correlation* process transforms groups of such alerts
into *intrusion reports* of interest for the security expert. Alerts typically contain attributes like the type of event, the address of the source and destination
hosts, etc. These attributes are matched against known vulnerabilities, in order
to avoid reporting alerts with no actual associated risk (e.g., a Linux-oriented
attack blindly launched on a Windows machine). However, applying this approach alone can lead to missing relevant alerts that do not match any vulnerability (e.g., ICMP PINGs) but that can be part of a more complex multi-step attack.
Alerts must therefore also be correlated using the knowledge encoded in specific
structures (e.g. *attack graphs* [2]) that describe logical connections of interest
among correlated alerts. In *anomaly detection* systems [11,15,20,23,25,32], historical data is used to build profiles of the "normal" user behaviors, so that
sequences of actions that deviate from the profiles are classified as "anomalous".
Misuse detection systems [2,3,24,31,35] make instead use of sets of descriptions
of suspicious activities that are matched against the log in order to identify
ongoing activities.

In order to describe logical connections among alerts, *multi-step* and *fusion-
based* correlation techniques have been used in the past [29]. Multi-step correlation
[14,22,34] seeks to identify suspicious activities that consist of multiple "steps"
by modeling activities through attack graphs [2,18,28,36] or deterministic finite

© Springer International Publishing Switzerland 2015
S. Foresti (Ed.): STM 2015, LNCS 9331, pp. 107–122, 2015.
DOI: 10.1007/978-3-319-24858-5_7

automata (DFAs). Any activity that complies with a graph or a DFA description is considered suspicious. Fusion-based correlation [14, 17, 34] uses instead similarity functions that, when applied to the attributes of incoming alerts, establish whether they should be considered part of a same activity.

In this paper, we propose a technique whose objective is the fast retrieval of occurrences of given patterns in streams of events, where each event corresponds to a security alert. Our specifically-designed AC-Index supports a very expressive DFA-based model for the patterns and arbitrary correlation functions. More specifically, the overall framework provides the following main features:

- The general objective is that of retrieving the *top-k sub-sequences* of a log that match some given DFA-based pattern.
- The log is *streamed* into the system, so the retrieval of correlated alerts is performed in an *online* fashion.
- The ranking of the sub-sequences is done on the basis of user-provided *severity functions*.
- The retrieved sub-sequences can be constrained through user-provided *correlation functions* and *maximum durations*.
- The correlation and severity functions and the maximum durations are *pattern-specific* – moreover, the functions can be *arbitrary*, as we only mandate their polynomial-time computability.
- We *do not mandate any specific schema for the alerts*: we simply regard each alert as a relational tuple with a user-provided schema.
- We aim at managing *multiple patterns concurrently*.
- The retrieved sub-sequences can possibly be *non-contiguous*.
- The reports built can be based on *partial occurrences* of patterns, i.e., sub-sequences that have not yet reached their terminal stages in the DFAs.

Figure 1 shows the two patterns we will use as our running example throughout the paper. Edges are labeled with alert symbols and each stage is annotated with its associated severity value. The sequence {*access, service exploit, DoS*} represents a possible *Denial of Service* attack. A security expert may want to take security measures at a certain "depth" of this attack. To this end, the expert wants to receive a report every time a stage of the sequence is traversed. In other words, we must look at all sub-sequences of the log that match some prefix of any path in the pattern. Furthermore, in order to counter the intrusions more quickly, the expert may want to only look at the first k sub-sequences, based on their associated severity value – in the example, we assume that the severity of a sub-sequence only depends on the stage reached in the pattern. Moreover, the correlation function looks at the attributes of the alerts in order to decide which alerts are to be considered part of a same attack. Finally, for each pattern, only the sequences that fit in a time window of maximum length τ are considered.

The rest of the paper is organized as follows. In Sect. 2 we formalize the alert correlation problem targeted by our proposed AC-Index. In Sect. 3 we describe the AC-Index, which is then experimentally validated in Sect. 4. Finally, in Sects. 5 and 6 we discuss related works and outline our conclusions.

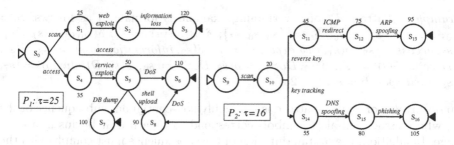

Fig. 1. Example patterns. Each stage is annotated with its associated severity value.

2 Preliminaries and Problem Formalization

In this section we introduce some preliminary notions and formalize the alert correlation problem targeted by our proposed index, which basically consists in finding the top-k sub-sequences of a log that represent an attack w.r.t. a given set of patterns.

We assume the existence of (i) a finite set $\mathcal{A}$ of *alert* symbols and (ii) w *attribute domains* $ATT_1, \ldots, ATT_w$. A *log* is a set $L - \{\ell_1, \ldots, \ell_n\}$ of tuples (each corresponding to an alert) of the form $\langle id, symbol, ts, att_1, \ldots, att_w \rangle$ where id is an identifier, $symbol \in \mathcal{A}$, $ts \in \mathbb{N}$ is a timestamp, and $\forall i \in [1, w]$, $att_i \in ATT_i$. We assume that $\forall i \in [1, n-1]$, $\ell_i.ts < \ell_{i+1}.ts$. Moreover, we denote component c of log tuple ℓ as $\ell.c$.

The notion of a pattern is formalized by the following definition.

Definition 1 (Pattern). *A pattern is a tuple* $P = \langle S, s_s, S_t, \delta, \tau \rangle$ *where:*

- *S is a set of stages;*
- *$s_s \in S$ is the start stage;*
- *$S_t \subseteq S$ is the set of terminal stages;*
- *$\delta : S \times \mathcal{A} \to S$ is the stage transition (partial) function;*[1]
- *$\tau \in \mathbb{N}$ is the maximum duration of an occurrence of P.*

We assume that $\forall s \in S_t, \forall sym \in \mathcal{A}$, $\delta(s, sym)$ is not defined, and that $\forall s \in S, \forall sym \in \mathcal{A}$, $\delta(s, sym) \neq s_s$.

In the following, when $\delta(s, sym) = s'$, we say that there is an edge from s to s' labeled with sym.

---

[1] Some past works assume aciclicity of the patterns because, in many practical cases, (i) the attacker's control over the network increases *monotonically*, i.e., the attacker need not relinquish resources already gained during the attack, and (ii) the "critical-ity" associated with a sequence of alerts does not change when the sequence contains a portion that is repeated multiple times as it matches a cycle in the pattern. In such cases, the overall sequence is equivalent to the one obtained after removing the portion matching the cycle. We do not make this assumption as it would reduce the expressiveness of the model and it is not required by the AC-Index.

Example 1. Pattern P_1 of our running example is formalized as follows: $S = \{s_0, \ldots, s_8\}$; $s_s = s_0$; $S_t = \{s_3, s_6, s_7\}$; $\delta(s_0, scan) = s_1$, $\delta(s_0, access) = s_4$, $\delta(s_1, access) = s_8$, $\delta(s_1, web\ exploit) = s_2$, $\delta(s_2, information\ loss) = s_3$, $\delta(s_4, service\ exploit) = s_5$, $\delta(s_5, DoS) = \delta(s_8, DoS) = s_6$, $\delta(s_5, DB\ dump) = s_7$, $\delta(s_5, shell\ upload) = s_8$; $\tau = 25$.

An occurrence of a given pattern is a possibly non-contiguous subsequence of the log whose associated alert symbols correspond to a path that begins in a start stage. In addition, the overall duration of the subsequence must comply with the maximum duration allowed by the pattern. The following definition formalizes this.

Definition 2 (Occurrence). *Given a pattern $P = \langle S, s_s, S_t, \delta, \tau \rangle$ and a log L, an occurrence of P in L is a set $O = \{\ell_1, \ldots, \ell_m\} \subseteq L$ such that (i) $\forall i \in [1, m-1]$, $\ell_i.ts < \ell_{i+1}.ts$; (ii) there exists a set $\{s_0, s_1, \ldots, s_m\} \subseteq S$ such that $s_s = s_0$ and $\forall i \in [1, m]$, $\delta(s_{i-1}, \ell_i.symbol) = s_i$; (iii) $\ell_m.ts - \ell_1.ts \leq \tau$.*

It should be observed that Definition 2 does not require an occurrence to reach a terminal stage. This feature gives security experts complete freedom in deciding whether or not a certain subsequence must be considered "critical" (i.e., with a high severity). Thus, any prefix of a complete path in the pattern can correspond to a critical subsequence the framework must take into account. Terminal stages are used to semantically represent the "final goal" of the attacker. Moreover, they help the retrieval algorithm as they signal that a subsequence can no longer be extended.

The following definition formalizes the way we characterize the severity of a subsequence and the attribute-based correlation among log tuples.

Definition 3 (Severity and Correlation Functions). *Given a pattern P and a log L, the severity w.r.t. P is a function $\sigma_P : 2^L \to \mathbb{N}$. Moreover, the correlation w.r.t. P is a function $\gamma_P : 2^L \to \{true, false\}$ such that $\gamma_P(X) = true$ for all subsets $X \subseteq L$ that, based on their attribute values, can be part of a same occurrence.*

We assume transitivity of function γ_P, that is, if $\gamma_P(X_1 \cup X_2) = true$ and $\gamma_P(X_2 \cup X_3) = true$, then $\gamma_P(X_1 \cup X_3) = true$. It should also be observed that it is natural to assume $\sigma_P(X) = 0$ when X is not an occurrence of P in L.

We are now ready to define the alert correlation problem we address.

Definition 4 (Alert Correlation Problem). *Given a set $\mathcal{P}$ of patterns, a log L, and a number $k \in \mathbb{N}$, the alert correlation problem consists in finding a set $\mathcal{O} = \{O_1, \ldots, O_k\}$ such that: (i) each O_i is an occurrence in L of a pattern $P_i \in \mathcal{P}$; (ii) $\forall i \in [1, k]$, $\gamma_{P_i}(O_i) = true$; (iii) $\forall i \in [1, k-1]$, $\sigma_{P_i}(O_i) \geq \sigma_{P_{i+1}}(O_{i+1})$; (iv) there do not exist a pattern $P \in \mathcal{P}$ and an occurrence $O \notin \mathcal{O}$ of P in L such that $\sigma_P(O) > \sigma_{P_k}(O_k)$.*

In Definition 4, the second condition states that all tuples in each occurrence $O_i \in \mathcal{O}$ must be correlated to one another; the third condition states that $\mathcal{O}$

contains occurrences in decreasing order of severity value; the fourth condition ensures that the occurrences in $\mathcal{O}$ are the ones with the top-k severity values. We do not assume that $\forall i, j$ with $i \neq j$, $P_i \neq P_j$ – in other words, set $\mathcal{O}$ can contain two different occurrences of the same pattern. It should be noted that if the security expert is only interested in contiguous occurrences (as the majority of existing approaches do), our proposed framework can be straighforwardly extended to post-process the retrieved occurreces and filter out non-contiguous ones.

Example 2. Returning to our running example, suppose we want to find the occurrences of the patterns in the log of Fig. 2 (top left). In this case, log tuples are of the form $\langle id, symbol, ts, sourceIP, targetIP \rangle$. We assume that γ_{P_1} and γ_{P_2} consider log tuples as correlated if their *sourceIP*s are equal and their *targetIP*s are in the same subnetwork w.r.t. the example network in Fig. 2 (top right). Moreover, σ_{P_1} and σ_{P_2} return the values in Fig. 1 if the *targetIP*s of the tuples are outside the firewall – values are doubled if the *targetIP*s are inside the firewall. The resulting sub-sequences are listed in Fig. 2 (bottom), ordered by severity value.

id	symbol	ts	sourceIP	targetIP
100	scan	12	160.57.91.110	110.80.70.120
101	reverse key	13	160.57.91.110	110.80.70.120
102	scan	14	130.10.71.151	120.15.62.140
103	buffer overflow	15	190.23.41.170	170.21.88.124
104	web exploit	16	130.10.71.151	120.15.62.141
105	SQL injection	24	190.23.41.170	170.21.88.124
106	information loss	26	190.23.41.170	170.21.88.124
107	ICMP redirect	28	160.57.91.110	110.80.70.122
108	ARP spoofing	29	160.57.91.110	110.80.70.129
109	DoS	32	190.23.41.170	170.21.88.124
110	information loss	35	130.10.71.151	120.15.62.146

Sub-sequence	Pattern	Severity	Duration
$O_1 = \{102, 104, 110\}$	P_1	240	21
$O_2 = \{102, 104\}$	P_1	80	2
$O_3 = \{100, 101, 107\}$	P_2	75	16
$O_4 = \{100, 101\}$	P_2	45	1
$O_5 = \{102\}$	P_1	50	0
$O_6 = \{100\}$	P_2	25	0
$O_7 = \{100\}$	P_1	20	0
$O_8 = \{100, 101, 107, 108\}$	P_2	0	17

Fig. 2. Example log (top left), network (top right), and sub-sequences (bottom).

Note that O_8 is not an occurrence of P_2 according to Definition 2, since its duration is 17 time units which is longer than the maximum duration of any occurrence of P_2 (that is, 16 time units). The set $\mathcal{O} = \{O_1, \dots, O_4\}$ is a solution for the alert correlation problem with $k = 4^2$. In fact, it satisfies all of

---

[2] Note that a security expert may want to discard O_2 and O_4 because they are prefixes of O_1 and O_3 respectively.

the conditions of Definition 4: (i) each O_i has an associated pattern P_i for which it is an occurrence in L; (ii) $\gamma_{P_1}(O_1) = \gamma_{P_2}(O_2) = \gamma_{P_3}(O_3) = \gamma_{P_4}(O_4) = true$; (iii) $\sigma_{P_1}(O_1) \geq \sigma_{P_1}(O_2) \geq \sigma_{P_2}(O_3) \geq \sigma_{P_2}(O_4)$; (iv) $\sigma_{P_1}(O_5) \leq \sigma_{P_2}(O_4)$ and $\sigma_{P_2}(O_6) \leq \sigma_{P_2}(O_4)$.

In the characterization of the complexity of the alert correlation problem we target, we make the realistic assumption that the computation of functions γ and σ can be performed in polynomial time. We therefore denote the complexity of computing such functions as $O(poly_{\gamma,\sigma}(x))$, that is a polynomial in the cardinality x of the set to which the functions are applied. The following result establishes the overall complexity of the problem.

Proposition 1. *The worst-case asymptotical time complexity of solving the alert correlation problem is* $\Omega\left(log\ k \cdot \sum_{P=\langle S,s_s,S_t,\delta,\tau\rangle \in \mathcal{P}}(\tau^{|S|} \cdot poly_{\gamma,\sigma}(\tau))\right)$.

To see why the above result is true, it suffices to observe the following. τ is the maximum cardinality of an occurrence of P, so $\tau^{|S|}$ is the maximum possible number of occurrences of P in L. It should be observed that the existence of a "local time window" where alerts can be "connected" is common to all the models that allow to constrain the length of the sub-sequences (see, e.g., [3]) – obviously, without such constraints, this term would become $|L|^{|S|}$. Moreover, $poly_{\gamma,\sigma}(\tau)$ represents the time needed to check the correlation among the tuples of an occurrence of P and to compute their severity. Finally, to extract the top-k occurrences, it suffices to maintain a priority queue of maximum size k while scanning the whole set of occurrences – this takes time $log\ k$ for each occurrence.

3   The AC-Index

In this section we describe our proposed AC-Index, whose objective is that of efficiently "tracking" the occurrences of a given set of patterns in a log. The index is updated as soon as a new log tuple enters the system, and it contains a priority queue whose content represents the top-k occurrences found so far in the log.

We denote the set of patterns as $\mathcal{P}$. Without loss of generality, we assume $\bigcap_{\langle S,s_s,S_t,\delta,\tau\rangle\in\mathcal{P}} S = \emptyset$. Moreover, we use $\mathcal{S}$ to denote the set $\bigcup_{\langle S,s_s,S_t,\delta,\tau\rangle\in\mathcal{P}} S$. Finally, given an alert symbol $sym \in \mathcal{A}$, we define $stages(sym) \subseteq \mathcal{S}$ as the set of non-terminal stages having an incoming edge labeled with sym — formally, $\forall s \in stages(sym), \exists\langle S, s_s, S_t, \delta, \tau\rangle \in \mathcal{P}$ such that $s \in S$, $s \neq s_s$, $s \notin S_t$, and $\exists s' \in S$ such that $\delta(s', sym) = s$.

Definition 5 (AC-Index). *Given a set $\mathcal{P}$ of patterns an a log L, an AC-Index $I_\mathcal{P}$ is a tuple $\langle Tables, MainTable, PQ\rangle$ where:*

- *Tables is a set containing a table $table(s)$ for each $s \in stages(sym)$ with $sym \in \mathcal{A}$. $table(s)$ contains rows of the form (PL, sev) where PL is a list of pointers to tuples in L, and $sev \in \mathbb{N}$ is the severity value corresponding to the set of tuples pointed by PL;*

- *MainTable is a table where each row is of the form (sym, Z), where $sym \in \mathcal{A}$ and Z is a set of pointers to tables $table(s)$;*
- *PQ is a priority queue containing pairs of the form (PL, sev) that are copies of table rows in tables(s). The size of PQ is bounded by k and the priority is the value of sev.*

In the AC-Index, a row $(PL = \{\ell_0^\uparrow, \ldots, \ell_m^\uparrow\}, sev) \in table(s)$ corresponds to an occurrence $O = \{\ell_0, \ldots, \ell_m\}$ in L of a pattern $P = \langle S, s_s, S_t, \delta, \tau \rangle \in \mathcal{P}$ with $sev = \sigma_P(O)$ and $\delta(s', \ell_m.symbol) = s$ for some $s' \in S$. Following the definition of set *stages*, no table is built for neither initial stages (because such stages cannot correspond to occurrences) nor terminal stages (because we do not need to store non-extendable occurrences). In *MainTable*, a row (sym, Z) encodes the fact that, for each table $tables(s)$ pointed by Z there exists a stage $s \in S$ with at least one ingoing edge labeled with sym. Finally, PQ always contains the k occurrences found so far with higher severity values. Moreover, if requested by the security expert, PQ can be configured in such a way that it will discard the occurrences that are prefixes of some occurrence of the same pattern. In our running example, O_2 and O_4 would be discarded since they are prefixes of O_1 and O_3, respectively.

Example 3. Figure 3 (left) shows the initial status of the AC-Index built over pattern $P_1 = \langle S, s_s, S_t, \delta, \tau \rangle$. At this stage, PQ and all $table(s)$ are empty. *MainTable* contains a number of rows equal to the number of distinct alert symbols labeling edges that end in non-terminal stages.

Figure 3 (right) shows the pseudo-code of the Insert algorithm that indexes a new log tuple ℓ_{new} with associated alert symbol $\ell_{new}.symbol$.

In the algorithm, Lines 6–9 deal with the case where s is a start stage, by creating a new occurrence. Specifically, it creates a new row table r and adds it to PQ and to $table(s')$, where s' is the stage reached from s by following the edge labeled with sym. Lines 11–20 check whether the new log tuple ℓ_{new} can be correlated with those in the existing occurrences. If it does (Lines 13–20), it is appended to such occurrences and the latter are added to PQ. Otherwise, i.e., if it does not fit in the time window τ, then the last log tuple of each occurrence that can not be extended is removed from its related table (Line 22). Observe that this implicitly corresponds to a pruning process that is applied during the construction of the index.

Example 4. Figure 4 shows the status of the AC-Index after indexing log tuples from 102 to 110 of our running example when considering pattern $P_1 = \langle S, s_s, S_t, \delta, \tau \rangle$ only. The indexing process can be divided into 3 distinct macro-steps:

1. The first processed log tuple is $\langle 102, scan, \ldots \rangle$. Since there exists a row $(scan, \{table(s_1)^\uparrow\})$ in *MainTable*, row $r_1 = (PL = [102^\uparrow], sev = 50)$ is added to $table(s_1)$ (50 is the severity value returned by σ_{P_1}). Then, a copy of r_1 is added to PQ. Log tuple $\langle 103, buffer\ overflow, \ldots \rangle$ is skipped because there are no rows in *MainTable* with $sym = buffer\ overflow$.

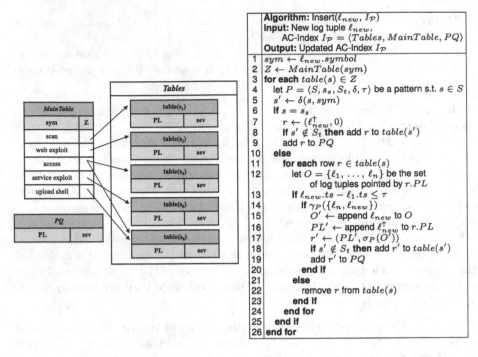

```
Algorithm: Insert(ℓ_new, I_P)
Input: New log tuple ℓ_new,
       AC-Index I_P = ⟨Tables, MainTable, PQ⟩
Output: Updated AC-Index I_P
1  sym ← ℓ_new.symbol
2  Z ← MainTable(sym)
3  for each table(s) ∈ Z
4     let P = ⟨S, s_s, S_t, δ, τ⟩ be a pattern s.t. s ∈ S
5     s' ← δ(s, sym)
6     If s = s_s
7        r ← (ℓ↑_new, 0)
8        If s' ∉ S_t then add r to table(s')
9        add r to PQ
10    else
11       for each row r ∈ table(s)
12          let O = {ℓ_1, ..., ℓ_n} be the set
                 of log tuples pointed by r.PL
13          If ℓ_new.ts − ℓ_1.ts ≤ τ
14             If γ_P({ℓ_n, ℓ_new})
15                O' ← append ℓ_new to O
16                PL' ← append ℓ↑_new to r.PL
17                r' ← (PL', σ_P(O'))
18                if s' ∉ S_t then add r' to table(s')
19                add r' to PQ
20             end if
21          else
22             remove r from table(s)
23          end if
24       end for
25    end if
26 end for
```

Fig. 3. Example initial index status (left) and Insert algorithm (right).

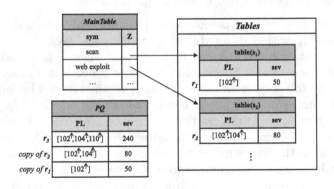

Fig. 4. Example index status after indexing log tuples from 102 to 110 of the log of Fig. 2 (top left).

2. Log tuple $\langle 104, web\ exploit, ...\rangle$ can be correlated with $\langle 102, scan, ...\rangle$, because $\delta_{P_1}(s_1, scan) = s_2$ and $\gamma_{P_1}(102, 104) = true$. Thus, row $r_2 = ([102^\uparrow, 104^\uparrow], 80)$ is added to $table(s_2)$ and PQ. Log tuples from 105 to 109 are skipped because none of them can be correlated with log tuples 102 or 104. As an example, tuple $\langle 106, information\ loss, ...\rangle$ cannot be linked to the occurrence $O=\{102,\ 104\}$ although $\delta_{P_1}(s_2, information\ loss) = s_3$, because

$\gamma_{P_1}(\{102, 104, 106\}) = false$ due the $IPAttacker$ attribute value, which is distinct from that of tuples 102 and 104.

3. Log tuple $\langle 110, \text{ information loss}, \ldots \rangle$ can be correlated with $\{102, 104\}$, because $\delta_{P_1}(s_2, \text{ information loss}) = s_3$ and $\gamma_{P_1}(\{104, 110\}) = true$. However, in this case, a new row $r_3 = ([102^\top, 104^\top, 110^\top], 240)$ is directly added to PQ because there does not exist $table(s_3)$ since s_3 is a terminal stage.

As the example shows, we only need to store occurrences in $Tables$ if they can be extended. In fact, when an occurrence ends in a terminal stage it is no longer extendable, so it can be directly stored in PQ – this is why the AC-Index does not contain any $table(s)$ with s being a terminal stage. The following result ensures that Algorithm Insert solves the alert correlation problem both correctly and optimally.

Proposition 2. *Given a log L, the execution of Algorithm Insert on all tuples in L terminates, and after the execution, the content of PQ represents the correct solution to the alert correlation problem. The worst-case asymptotical time complexity of Insert is $O\left(\log k \cdot \sum_{P = \langle S, s_s, S_t, \delta, \tau \rangle \in \mathcal{P}}(\tau^{|S|} \cdot poly_{\gamma, \sigma}(\tau))\right)$.*

4   Experimental Results

In this section we report on the experimental assessment we performed on our proposed AC-Index when applied to both real-world and synthetic patterns and logs. We implemented the whole framework in Java and run the experiments on an Intel Core i7-3770 K CPU clocked at 3.50 GHz, with 12 GB RAM, running Windows 8.

We ran three different rounds of experiments. In the first round, we used real-world patterns P_1 and P_2 of Fig. 1 and P_3 and P_4 of Fig. 5. In the second round, we used synthetic patterns P_5 and P_6 of Fig. 6, in order to outline the behavior of our framework when varying the "density" of the patterns (number of edges w.r.t. the number of vertices). In fact, much denser patterns usually yield a much bigger AC-Index as each log tuple can be attached to many more occurrences.

For the first and second round, we built synthetic logs consisting of 300 K tuples. Each log was built by combining a set of sub-logs, each of which is a sequence of alert symbols that can represent an occurrence of a given pattern. Specifically, a log combines several sub-logs $\{L_1, \ldots, L_n\}$ where each L_i is built by considering a path from an initial to a terminal stage in a pattern. These sub-logs were built and combined under six different *log generation modes*, each corresponding to a possible real-world scenario:

1. each sub-log only contains alert symbols in its corresponding pattern, and the sub-logs are concatenated;
2. same as mode 1, except that some alert symbols are *replaced* with "noise", i.e. with symbols not present in the corrisponding pattern, with a certain frequency;

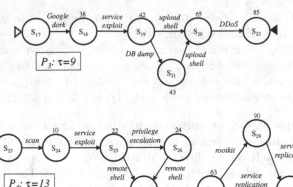

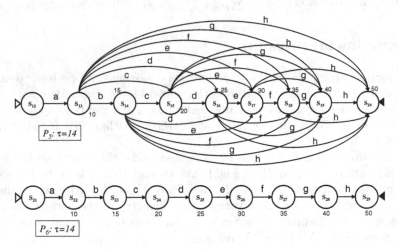

Fig. 5. Real-world patterns P_3 and P_4.

Fig. 6. Synthetic patterns P_5 and P_6.

3. same as mode 1, except that noise is *inserted* in the sequence, i.e., it is added between alert symbols which are present in the pattern;
4. same as mode 1, except that a certain percentage of each L_i partially overlaps with L_{i+1};
5. same as mode 2, but with partial overlap as in mode 4;
6. same as mode 3, but with partial overlap as in mode 4.

We performed 14 runs for each of the first and second round. The log generation mode, noise frequency, and overlap percentage used are reported in Fig. 7. For each run indicated in the figure, the values of the other parameters were set to the defaults (in bold) – for instance, run 3 was performed with noise frequency

Log generation mode	Noise frequency	Overlap percentage
1 (run 1)	1/10 (run 7)	20% (run 12)
2 (run 2)	2/10 (run 8)	30% (run 13)
3 (run 3)	**3/10** (run 9)	**40%** (run 14)
4 (run 4)	4/10 (run 10)	50% (run 15)
5 (run 5)	5/10 (run 11)	60% (run 16)
6 (run 6)		

Fig. 7. Parameter values used for each experimental run.

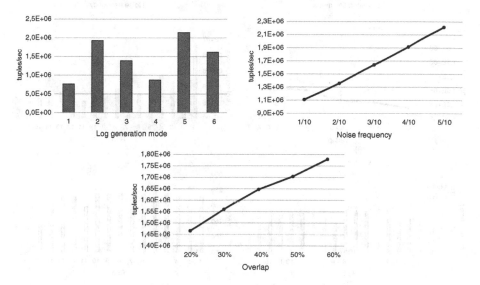

Fig. 8. Tuple rates in the first round of experiments.

3/10 and overlap percentage 40 %.[3] We assumed worst-case behavior of function γ, i.e., it always returns *true*. We also performed experiments with much larger logs (1M tuples) – interestingly, the performance we obtained in terms of tuples processed per second was 5.1 % worse at most.

Finally, in the third round, we used a 112 K-tuple log produced by running SNORT [27] on the second, fourth, and fifth week of inside traffic from the *1999 DARPA intrusion detection evaluation dataset* [16] and manually extracted 14 patterns from it. In this round, function γ was set to return *true* when the alerts shared the same destination IP address, and we fixed $\tau = 10$.

Figure 8 reports the results of the first round. In particular, Fig. 8 (top left) shows the number of log tuples processed per second when varying the log generation mode (runs 1–6), Fig. 8 (top right) shows the variation with respect to noise frequency (runs 7–11), and Fig. 8 (bottom) the variation with respect to overlap percentage (runs 12–16).

---

[3] For simplicity of presentation, the run with all parameters set to default values is reported as three separate runs (6, 9, and 14) in Fig. 7.

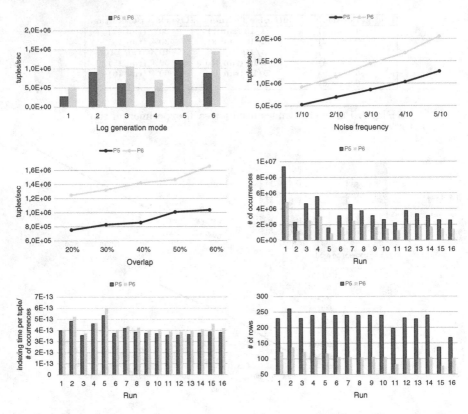

Fig. 9. Tuple rates (top and center left), number of occurrences (center right), normalized indexing time per tuple (bottom left), and maximum size of the AC-Index (bottom right) in the second round of experiments.

The results confirm our expectations and show extremely good overall performances. As expected, the presence of noise in the log or overlap between consecutive instances reduces the overall number of occurrences, thus improving performances. Moreover, when noise appears *instead of* alert symbols of actual interest (which we believe is an even more realistic case), we obtain better results than when noise appears *between* such symbols. Generally, the number of tuples processed per second is extremely high – it is consistently higher than 765 K, and around 1.4 M on average. In both Fig. 8 (top right) and Fig. 8 (bottom) the trend is basically linear in the frequency of noise and percentage of overlap – in these experiments, the average tuple rate is around 1.6 M tuples/sec.

Figure 9 shows the results obtained in the second round, which again appear very satisfactory. We can notice in Fig. 9 (top left) that the performance loss is always around 40 % when moving from a sparse pattern (P_6) to a much denser one (P_5). The tuple rate never dropped below 260 K tuples/sec, and it was around 700 K tuples/sec on average. In the experiments where we fixed the log generation mode to 6 and varied noise frequency and overlap percentage (top right and center left of the figure) the performance loss was always around 60 %. It should be observed that the number of paths in P_5 is 64 times that of P_6. Thus, the relationship between the number of paths and the tuple rates is much less than linear.

For the second round, we also measured the number of occurrences and the indexing time per tuple normalized by the number of occurrences. As expected (Fig. 9 (center right)), the number of occurrences is lower when using P_6. Interestingly, the normalized indexing time (bottom left) shows very small variations with respect to the specific configuration used (8 % on average). Finally, the maximum size of the AC-Index (bottom right) using P_5 is much larger – the difference was around 60 % on average (again, showing a sub-linear relationship with the number of paths in the patterns). Moreover, in this case the size of the AC-Index shows very small variations with respect to the configuration used.

Finally, Fig. 10 shows the results of the third round of experiments, when varying the number of patterns considered. Here, the tuple rate (top left) is consistently higher than 140 K tuples/sec, and around 410 K tuples/sec on average – again, it appears closely dependent on the actual number of occurrences in the log (top right). Interestingly, the normalized indexing time (bottom left) shows relatively small variations even with respect to the number of patterns used. As expected, the maximum size of the AC-Index (bottom right) is larger when indexing for more patterns – however, its size is always kept under 140 rows.

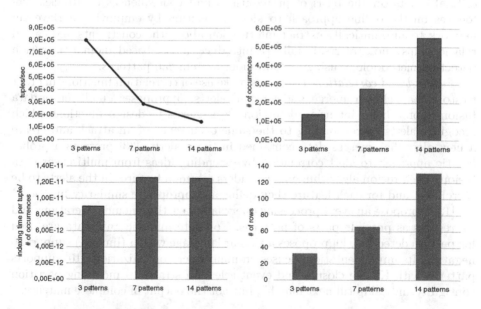

Fig. 10. Tuple rates (top left), number of occurrences (top right), normalized indexing time per tuple (bottom left), and maximum size of the AC-Index (bottom right) in the third round of experiments.

5   Related Work

A number of interesting graph-based alert correlation frameworks has been proposed in the past. Attack graphs and finite automata have often been used for this purpose. [19] proposed a technique for identifying malicious execution traces with automatically-learned finite automata. [30] created an automaton-based approach for detecting anomalous program behaviors. Each node in the DFA represents a state in the program under inspection which the algorithm utilizes to learn "normal" data and perform detection. [13] proposes to increase the accuracy of the N-gram learning algorithm by using a DFA representation for intrusion detection via system call traces. In [4] a technique is presented to automatically produce candidate interpretations of detected failures from anomalies identified by detection techniques that use inferred DFAs to represent the expected behavior of software systems. [6] proposes an approach for the real-time detection of denial of service attacks using time-dependent DFAs. [28] proposes a correlation algorithm based on attack graphs that is capable of detecting multiple attack scenarios for forensic analysis. In [36] attack graphs are used for correlating, hypothesizing, and predicting intrusion alerts. [18] proposes to represent groups of alerts with graph structures, along with a method that automatically identifies frequent groups of alerts and summarizes them into a suspicious sequence of activity. [2,21] construct attack scenarios that correlate critical events on the basis of prerequisites and consequences of attacks. [26] focuses on the online approach to alert correlation by employing a Bayesian network to automatically extract information about the constraints and causal relationships among alerts. Finally, [7] introduces a host-based anomaly intrusion detection methodology using discontinuous system call patterns.

Fusion-based correlation techniques make use of correlation functions in order to store, map, cluster, merge, and correlate alerts. [5] proposes a multisensor data fusion approach for intrusion detection. [8] suggests to design functions which recognize alerts corresponding to the same occurrence of an attack and create a new alert that merges data contained in those alerts. [33] presents a probabilistic approach to alert correlation by extending ideas from multisensor data fusion. Their fusion algorithm only considers common features in the alerts to be correlated, and for each feature they define an appropriate similarity function.

[1,12] propose an event processing query language that includes iterations and aggregates as possible parts of patterns. Non-deterministic automata are used for pattern detection. [9] proposes a similar language with a (limited) support to negation. Its implementation focuses on multi-query optimization. [10] supports patterns with Kleene closure and event selection strategies including partition contiguity and "skip till next match", but not the output of complete matches.

6   Conclusions

In this paper we proposed an indexing technique for alert correlation that supports DFA-like patterns and user-provided correlation functions and provides very fast retrieval of occurrences of the patterns. The experimental results have proven that, although the supported model is very expressive, the framework is able to guarantee a very high efficiency of the retrieval process. It is capable of processing logs that enter the system at extremely large rates – orders of magnitude of 100 K–1 M tuples/sec are definitely sufficient for fully covering a wide range of real-world applications. Moreover, the framework scales well w.r.t. the amount of noise in the log, the overlap between consecutive occurrences, and the number of occurrences retrieved.

Acknowledgements. This work has been partially supported by the "Technological District on Cyber Security" PON Project (grant n. PON03PE_00032_2), funded by the Italian Ministry of University and Research.

References

1. Agrawal, J., Diao, Y., Gyllstrom, D., Immerman, N.: Efficient pattern matching over event streams. In: SIGMOD (2008)
2. Albanese, M., Jajodia, S., Pugliese, A., Subrahmanian, V.S.: Scalable analysis of attack scenarios. In: Atluri, V., Diaz, C. (eds.) ESORICS 2011. LNCS, vol. 6879, pp. 416–433. Springer, Heidelberg (2011)
3. Albanese, M., Pugliese, A., Subrahmanian, V.S.: Fast activity detection: Indexing for temporal stochastic automaton-based activity models. IEEE Trans. Knowl. Data Eng. **25**(2), 360–373 (2013)
4. Babenko, A., Mariani, L., Pastore, F.: Ava: automated interpretation of dynamically detected anomalies. In: ISSTA (2009)
5. Bass, T.: Intrusion detection systems and multisensor data fusion. Commun. ACM **43**(4), 99–105 (2000)
6. Branch, J., Bivens, A., Lee, T.K.: Denial of service intrusion detection using time dependent deterministic finite automata. In: Graduate Research Conference (2002)
7. Creech, G., Hu, J.: A semantic approach to host-based intrusion detection systems using contiguousand discontiguous system call patterns. IEEE Trans. Comput. **63**(4), 807–819 (2014)
8. Cuppens, F., Miege, A.: Alert correlation in a cooperative intrusion detection framework. In: S&P (2002)
9. Demers, A., Gehrke, J., Hong, M., Riedewald, M., White, W.: Towards expressive publish/subscribe systems. In: Ioannidis, Y., Scholl, M.H., Schmidt, J.W., Matthes, F., Hatzopoulos, M., Böhm, K., Kemper, A., Grust, T., Böhm, C. (eds.) EDBT 2006. LNCS, vol. 3896, pp. 627–644. Springer, Heidelberg (2006)
10. Demers, A.J., Gehrke, J., Panda, B., Riedewald, M., Sharma, V., White, W.M.: Cayuga: a general purpose event monitoring system. In: CIDR (2007)
11. Garcia-Teodoro, P., Díaz-Verdejo, J.E., Maciá-Fernández, G., Vázquez, E.: Anomaly-based network intrusion detection: techniques, systems and challenges. Comput. Secur. **28**(1–2), 18–28 (2009)
12. Gyllstrom, D., Agrawal, J., Diao, Y., Immerman, N.: On supporting kleene closure over event streams. In: ICDE (2008)
13. Kosoresow, A.P., Hofmeyr, S.A.: Intrusion detection via system call traces. IEEE Softw. **14**(5), 35–42 (1997)
14. Kruegel, C., Valeur, F., Vigna, G.: Intrusion Detection and Correlation - Challenges and Solutions. Advances in Information Security. Springer, New York (2005)

15. Kumar, S., Spafford, E.H.: A pattern matching model for misuse intrusion detection. In: National Computer Security Conference (1994)
16. Lippmann, R., Haines, J.W., Fried, D.J., Korba, J., Das, K.: The 1999 DARPA off-line intrusion detection evaluation. Comp. Netw. **34**(4), 579–595 (2000)
17. Liu, J., Li, R., Liu, Y., Zhang, Z.: Multi-sensor data fusion based on correlation function and fuzzy integration function. Syst. Eng. Electron. **28**(7), 1006–1009 (2006)
18. Mao, C.H., Pao, H.K., Faloutsos, C., Lee, H.M.: Sbad: Sequence based attack detection via sequence comparison. In: PSDML (2010)
19. Michael, C., Ghosh, A.: Using finite automata to mine execution data for intrusion detection: a preliminary report. In: Debar, H., Mé, L., Wu, S.F. (eds.) RAID 2000. LNCS, vol. 1907, p. 66. Springer, Heidelberg (2000)
20. Molinaro, C., Moscato, V., Picariello, A., Pugliese, A., Rullo, A., Subrahmanian, V.S.: Padua: parallel architecture to detect unexplained activities. ACM Trans. Internet Techn. **14**(1), 3 (2014)
21. Ning, P., Cui, Y., Reeves, D.S., Xu, D.: Techniques and tools for analyzing intrusion alerts. ACM Trans. Inf. Syst. Secur. **7**(2), 274–318 (2004)
22. Ou, X., Govindavajhala, S., Appel, A.W.: Mulval: a logic-based network security analyzer. In: USENIX (2005)
23. Patcha, A., Park, J.M.: An overview of anomaly detection techniques: existing solutions and latest technological trends. Comp. Netw. **51**(12), 3448–3470 (2007)
24. Paxson, V.: Bro: a system for detecting network intruders in real-time. Comp. Netw. **31**(23–24), 2435–2463 (1999)
25. Piciarelli, C., Micheloni, C., Foresti, G.L.: Trajectory-based anomalous event detection. IEEE Trans. Circuits Syst. Video Techn. **18**(11), 1544–1554 (2008)
26. Ren, H., Stakhanova, N., Ghorbani, A.A.: An online adaptive approach to alert correlation. In: Kreibich, C., Jahnke, M. (eds.) DIMVA 2010. LNCS, vol. 6201, pp. 153–172. Springer, Heidelberg (2010)
27. Roesch, M.: Snort: Lightweight intrusion detection for networks. In: LISA (1999)
28. Roschke, S., Cheng, F., Meinel, C.: A new alert correlation algorithm based on attack graph. In: Herrero, Á., Corchado, E. (eds.) CISIS 2011. LNCS, vol. 6694, pp. 58–67. Springer, Heidelberg (2011)
29. Sadoddin, R., Ghorbani, A.: Alert correlation survey: framework and techniques. In: PST (2006)
30. Sekar, R., Bendre, M., Dhurjati, D., Bollineni, P.: A fast automaton-based method for detecting anomalous program behaviors. In: S&P (2001)
31. Sheikhan, M., Jadidi, Z.: Misuse detection using hybrid of association rule mining and connectionist modeling. World Appl. Sci. J. **7**, 31–37 (2009)
32. Shon, T., Moon, J.: A hybrid machine learning approach to network anomaly detection. Inf. Sci. **177**(18), 3799–3821 (2007)
33. Valdes, A., Skinner, K.: Probabilistic alert correlation. In: Lee, W., Mé, L., Wespi, A. (eds.) RAID 2001. LNCS, vol. 2212, p. 54. Springer, Heidelberg (2001)
34. Valeur, F., Vigna, G., Krügel, C., Kemmerer, R.A.: A comprehensive approach to intrusion detection alert correlation. IEEE Trans. Dependable Sec. Comput. **1**(3), 146–169 (2004)
35. Vigna, G., Kemmerer, R.A.: Netstat: A network-based intrusion detection system. J. Comput. Secur. **7**(1), 37–71 (1999)
36. Wang, L., Liu, A., Jajodia, S.: Using attack graphs for correlating, hypothesizing, and predicting intrusion alerts. Comput. Commun. **29**(15), 2917–2933 (2006)

Intrusion Detection System for Applications Using Linux Containers

Amr S. Abed[1]([✉]), Charles Clancy[2], and David S. Levy[3]

[1] Department of Electrical & Computer Engineering,
Virginia Tech, Blacksburg, VA, USA
amrabed@vt.edu
[2] Hume Center for National Security & Technology,
Virginia Tech, Arlington, VA, USA
tcc@vt.edu
[3] The MITRE Corporation, Annapolis Junction, MD, USA
dslevy@mitre.org

Abstract. Linux containers are gaining increasing traction in both individual and industrial use, and as these containers get integrated into mission-critical systems, real-time detection of malicious cyber attacks becomes a critical operational requirement. This paper introduces a real-time host-based intrusion detection system that can be used to passively detect malfeasance against applications within Linux containers running in a standalone or in a cloud multi-tenancy environment. The demonstrated intrusion detection system uses bags of system calls monitored from the host kernel for learning the behavior of an application running within a Linux container and determining anomalous container behavior. Performance of the approach using a database application was measured and results are discussed.

Keywords: Intrusion detection · Anomaly detection · System call monitoring · Container security · Security in cloud computing

1 Introduction

Linux containers, such as Docker [13] and LXC [9], rely on the kernel namespaces and control groups (cgroups) for isolating the application running within the container. They provide a significantly more efficient alternative to virtual machines, since only the application and its dependencies need to be included in the container, and not the kernel and its processes. With the use of control groups and security profiles applied to containers, attack surface can be minimized [17]. However, attacks on mission-critical applications running within the container can still occur, and can represent an attack vector to the host kernel itself [17]. As a result, understanding when the container has been compromised is of key interest, yet little research has been conducted in this area.

Indeed, Linux containers are typically used to run applications in a multi-tenancy cloud environments, where they share the same host kernel with other

© Springer International Publishing Switzerland 2015
S. Foresti (Ed.): STM 2015, LNCS 9331, pp. 123–135, 2015.
DOI: 10.1007/978-3-319-24858-5_8

containers. In a multi-tenancy environment, the service provider is entitled by contractual means to monitor the behavior of containers running on the host kernel to provide safe environment for all hosted containers, and to protect the host kernel itself from the attack of a malicious container. However, providing information about the nature of the application running in the container, or altering the container for monitoring purposes is usually undesirable, and more often impermissible, especially when critical applications are running inside the container. Such constraints mandate the use of a host-based intrusion detection system (HIDS) that does not interfere with the container structure or application.

One source of attack originates from outside the host attacking the host kernel and/or the guest containers. Another source of attack comes from another containers residing on the same host and attacking neighboring containers. A third class of attack is when a container attacks the host kernel. To target these attacks, we propose a HIDS that monitors system calls between the container processes and the host kernel for malfeasance detection.

Utilizing system call traces for anomaly detection has been previously applied at the process level [7, 8, 11, 14], and has shown promising results when extended to the granularity of virtual machines (VMs) [1, 2, 15]. It has also been used to detect anomalies in Android applications by monitoring actions (aka system calls) included in their Android intents [3].

There are two basic approaches to anomaly detection using system calls; sequence-based approach and frequency-based approach. The former approach keeps track of system call sequences in a database of normal behavior. The latter drops the order of the system calls while keeping the frequency of occurrence of each distinct system call. By not storing order information of the system call sequence, frequency-based techniques requires much less storage space while providing better performance and accuracy [8].

Bag of system calls (BoSC) [8] is a frequency-based approach that has been used as VM-based anomaly detectors in the past, and has been found to be a good performer [1, 2, 15]. Particular advantages associated with the use of bags of systems calls, as opposed to sequences of system calls, are that it is computationally manageable [1] and does not require limiting the application programming interfaces [15].

This paper serves to propose a real-time HIDS that can be used to passively detect anomalies of container behavior by using a technique similar to the one described in [1]. We show that a frequency-based technique is sufficient for detecting abnormality in container behavior. The proposed system does not require any prior knowledge of the nature of the application inside the container, neither does it require any alteration to the container nor the host kernel, which makes it the first system to introduce opaque anomaly detection in containers, to the best of our knowledge.

The rest of this paper is organized as follows. Section 2 gives a brief summary of related work. Section 3 provides an overview of the proposed system. Section 4 discusses the system evaluation. Section 5 concludes with summary and future work.

2   Related Work

The *Bag of System Calls* (BoSC) technique is a frequency-based anomaly detection technique, that was first introduced by Kang et al. in 2005 [8]. In their paper, Kang et al. define the bag of system call as an ordered list $< c_1, c_2, \ldots, c_n >$, where n is the total number of distinct system calls, and c_i is the number of occurrences of the system call, s_i, in the given input sequence. By applying different machine learning techniques, such as 1-class Naïve Bayes classification and 2-means clustering, to the BoSC representation of two publicly-available system-call datasets, namely the University of New Mexico (UNM) dataset and the MIT Lincoln Lab dataset, they were able to show that the BoSC has better performance and accuracy compared to STIDE [7], one of the most famous and most popular sequence-based approaches.

The *Sequence Time-Delay Embedding* (STIDE) technique, introduced by Forrest and Longstaff [7], defines normal behavior using a database of short sequences, each of size k. For building the database, they slide a window of size $k + 1$ over the trace of system calls, and store the sequences of system calls. Although STIDE is a simple and efficient technique, it can be seen that by keeping the order information of the calls, the size of the database can grow linearly with the number of system calls in the trace. Some improvements to the STIDE technique were introduced in [11,19].

Another famous sequence-based intrusion detection technique is the one introduced in [12]. The technique uses sliding windows (regions) of size $2l + 1$, with a sliding step of l, and relies on the RIPPER rule-induction application [5] to classify sequences of system calls into normal and abnormal regions. If the percentage of abnormal regions exceeds certain threshold, the trace is declared intrusive.

A number of intrusion detection systems used sequences of system calls to train a Hidden Markov Model (HMM) classifier [4,10,18–20]. However, each system differs in the technique used for raising anomaly signal. Wang et al. [18], for example, raise anomaly signal when the probability of the whole sequence is below certain threshold. Warrender et al. [19], on the other hand, declares a sequence as anomalous when the probability of one system call within a sequence is below the threshold. Cho and Park [4] used HMM for modeling normal root privilege operations only. Hoang et al. [10] introduced a multi-layer detection technique that combines both outcomes from applying the Sliding Window approach and the HMM approach.

Warrender et al. compared STIDE, RIPPER, and HMM-based methods in [19]. They concluded that all methods performed adequately, while HMM gave the best accuracy on average. However, it required higher computational resources and storage space, since it makes multiple passes through the training data, and stores significant amount of intermediate data, which is computationally expensive, especially for large traces.

The *Kernel State Modeling* (KSM) technique represents traces of system calls as states of Kernel modules [14]. The technique observes three critical states, namely Kernel (KL), Memory Management (MM), and File System (FS) states.

The technique then detects anomaly by calculating the probability of occurrences of the three observed states in each trace of system calls, and comparing the calculated probabilities against the probabilities of normal traces. Applied to Linux-based programs of the UNM dataset, the KSM technique shows higher detection rates and lower false positive rates, compared to STIDE and HMM-based techniques.

Alarifi and Wolthusen used system calls for implementing a HIDS for virtual machines residing in a multi-tenancy Infrastructure-as-a-service (IaaS) environment. They dealt with the VM as a single process, despite the numerous processes running inside it, and monitored system calls between the VM and the host operating system [1, 2].

In [1], they used the BoSC technique in combination with the sliding window technique for anomaly detection. In their technique, they read the input trace epoch by epoch. For each epoch, a sliding window of size k moves over the system calls of each epoch, adding bags of system calls to the normal behavior database. The normal behavior database holds frequencies of bags of system calls. After building the normal-behavior database, i.e. training their classifier, an epoch is declared anomalous if the change in BoSC frequencies during that epoch exceeds certain threshold. For a sliding window of size 10, their technique gave 100 % accuracy, with 100 % detection rate, and 0 % false positive rate.

In [2], Alarifi and Wolthusen applied HMM for learning sequences of system calls for short-lived virtual machines. They based their decision on the conclusion from [19] that "HMM almost always provides a high detection rate and a low minimum false positives but with high computational demand". Their HMM-based technique gave lower detection rates, yet required lower number of training samples. By using 780, 000 system calls for training, the resulting detection rate was 97 %.

In their work, Chen et al. [3] applied HMM for recognizing malicious Android applications by monitoring actions (system calls) in Android intents issued by the application. They concluded that their technique, while capable of detecting malicious Android applications at runtime, did not have high performance, which they ascribed to not having enough Intent messages to further train the classifier.

3   Real-Time Intrusion Detection

In this paper, we propose a HIDS that uses a technique similar to the one described in [1] to be applied to Linux containers. The technique combines the sliding window technique [7] with the bag of system calls technique [8]. The technique ignores the order of system calls, and only keeps track of the frequencies of the system calls in the current window. As described in Sect. 1, the system works in real time, i.e. it learns behavior of the container and detects anomaly at runtime. It also works in opaque mode, i.e. it does not require any prior knowledge about the nature of the container nor the enclosed application. Figure 1 gives an overview of the system architecture and data flow as described below.

Our system employs a background service running on the host kernel to monitor system calls between any Docker containers and the host Kernel.

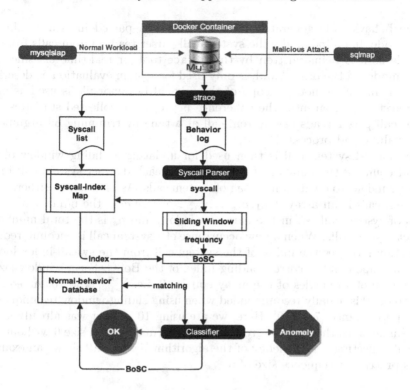

Fig. 1. Real-time intrusion detection system

Starting a new container on the host kernel triggers the service, which uses the Linux `strace` tool to trace all system calls issued by the container to the host kernel. The `strace` tool reports system calls with their originating process ID, arguments, and return values.

In addition, `strace` is also used to generate a syscall-list file that holds a preassembled list of distinct system calls sorted by the number of occurrences. The list is collected from a container running the same application under no attack. The syscall-list file is used to create a syscall-index lookup table. Table 1 shows sample entries of a typical syscall-index lookup table.

Table 1. Syscall-index lookup table

Syscall	Index
Select	4
Access	12
Iseek	22
Other	40

The behavior file generated by `strace` is then parsed in either online or offline mode. In online mode, the system-call parser reads system calls from the same file as it is being written by the `strace` tool for real-time classification. Offline mode, on the other hand, is only used for system evaluation as described in Sect. 4. In offline mode, a copy of the original behavior file is used as input to the system to guarantee the coherence between the collected statistics. The system call parser reads one system call at a time by trimming off arguments, return values, and process IDs.

The parsed system call is then used for updating a sliding window of size 10, and counting the number of occurrences of each distinct system call in the current window, to create a new bag of system calls. As mentioned earlier, a bag of system calls is an array $< c_1, c_2, \ldots, c_{n_s} >$ where c_i is the number of occurrences of system call, s_i, in the current window, and n_s is the total number of distinct system calls. When a new occurrence of a system call is encountered, the application retrieves the index of the system call from the syscall-index lookup table, and updates the corresponding index of the BoSC. For a window size of 10, the sum of all entries of the array equals 10, i.e. $\sum_{i=1}^{n_s} c_i = 10$. A sequence size of 6 or 10 is usually recommended when using sliding-window techniques for better performance [7,11,19]. Here, we are using 10 since it was already shown for a similar work that size 10 gives better performance than size 6 without dramatically affecting the efficiency of the algorithm [1]. Table 2 shows an example of this process for sequence size of 6.

Table 2. Example of system call parsing

Syscall	Index	Sliding window	BoSC
pwrite	6	[futex, futex, sendto, futex, sendto, pwrite]	[2, 0, 3, 0, 0, 0, **1**, 0, ..., 0]
sendto	0	[futex, sendto, futex, sendto, pwrite, sendto]	[**3**, 0, **2**, 0, 0, 0, 1, 0, ..., 0]
futex	2	[sendto, futex, sendto, pwrite, sendto, futex]	[3, 0, **2**, 0, 0, 0, 1, 0, ..., 0]
sendto	0	[futex, sendto, pwrite, sendto, futex, sendto]	[**3**, 0, 2, 0, 0, 0, 1, 0, ..., 0]

The created BoSC is then passed to classifier, which works in one of two modes; training mode and detection mode. For training mode, the classifier simply adds the new BoSC to the normal-behavior database. If the current BoSC already exists in the normal-behavior database, its frequency is incremented by 1. Otherwise, the new BoSC is added to the database with initial frequency of 1. The normal-behavior database is considered stable once all expected normal-behavior patterns are applied to the container. Table 3 shows sample entries of a normal-behavior database.

For detection mode, the system reads the behavior file epoch by epoch. For each epoch, a sliding window is similarly used to check if the current BoSC is present in the database of normal behavior database. If a BoSC is not present in the database, a mismatch is declared. The trace is declared anomalous if the number of mismatches within one epoch exceeds a certain threshold.

Table 3. Normal behavior database

BoSC	Frequency
0, 1, 0, 2, 0, 0, 0, 0, 1, 0, 3, 0, 1, 0, 0, 0, 1, 0, 0, 1	15
0, 1, 0, 1, 0, 0, 1, 0, 1, 0, 3, 0, 0, 0, 0, 0, 1, 1, 0, 1	8
0, 1, 0, 2, 0, 0, 5, 0, 0, 0, 0, 0, 0, 0, 0, 0, 1, 0, 0, 1	2
0, 1, 0, 2, 0, 2, 0, 0, 1, 0, 2, 0, 0, 0, 0, 0, 1, 0, 0, 1	1

Furthermore, a continuous training is applied during detection mode to further improve the false positive rate of the system. The bags of system calls seen during the current epoch are stored in a temporary current-epoch-change database rather than being added directly to the normal-behavior database. At the end of each epoch, if no anomaly signal was raised during the current epoch, the entries of the current-epoch-change database are committed to the normal-behavior database, to be included in classification for future epochs.

4   System Evaluation

4.1   Environment Setup

For our experiments, we are using a Docker container running on a Ubuntu Server 14.04 host operating system. The docker image we used for creating the container is the official `mysql` Docker image, which is basically a Docker image with MySQL 5.6 installed on a Debian operating system.

On container start, the container automatically creates a default database, adds users defined by the environment variables passed to the container, and then starts listening for connections. Docker maps the MySQL port from the container to some custom port on the host.

Since there is no dataset available that contains system calls collected from containers, we needed to create our own datasets for both normal and anomalous behavior. For that, we created a container from the `mysql` Docker image. A normal-behavior work load was initially applied to the container, before it got "attacked" using a penetration testing tool. More details about generating datasets are given in Sects. 4.2 and 4.3.

4.2   Generating Normal Workload

For generating normal-behavior dataset, we used `mysqlslap` [16]; a program that emulates client load for a MySQL server. The tool has command-line options that allow the user to select the level of concurrency, and the number of iterations to run the load test. In addition, it gives the user the option to customize the created database, e.g. by specifying the number of `varcher` and/or `int` columns to use when creating the database. Moreover, the user can select the number of insertions and queries to perform on the database.

Table 4. Parameters used for automatic load generation

Parameter	Value
Number of generated `varchar` columns	4
Number of generated `int` columns	3
Number of simulated clients	50
Number of load-test iterations	5
Number of unique insertion statements	100
Total number of insertions per thread	1000
Number of unique query statements	100
Total number of queries per thread	1000

The tool runs on the host kernel, and communicates with the MySQL server running on the container. The values we used for generating the normal-behavior workload are shown in Table 4.

Additionally, we used the SQL dump file of a real-life database to create schemas, tables, views, and to add entries to the tables, on the MySQL server of the container.

4.3 Simulating Malicious Behavior

To simulate an attack on the container, we used `sqlmap` [6]; an automatic SQL injection tool normally used for penetration testing purposes. In our experiment, we are using it to generate malicious-behavior dataset by attacking the MySQL database created on the container. Similarly, the `sqlmap` tool runs on the host kernel, and communicates with the attacked database through the Docker proxy.

We applied the following attacks on the container:

- Denial-of-Service (DoS) Attack: Using wild cards to slow down database. The attack generated an average of 37 mismatches
- Operating system takeover attempt: Attempt to run cat /etc/passwd shell command (failed). Generated 279 mismatches
- File-system access: Copy /etc/passwd to local machine. Generated 182 mismatches
- Brute-force attack: We used the `--all` option of `sqlmap` to retrieve all info about the database management system (DBMS), including users, roles, schemas, passwords, tables, columns, and number of entries. The attack was strong enough to generate around 42,000 mismatches.

4.4 Collecting Container-Behavior Data

A background service, running on the host kernel, automatically detects any newly started Docker container, and traces system calls of the new container using the Linux `strace` tool.

The service relies on the Docker command events to signal the service whenever a new container is started on the host kernel. Upon detection of the new container, the service starts to trace all processes running, on container start, within the control group (cgroup) of the container. The list of processes is retrieved from the tasks file located at /sys/fs/cgroup/devices/docker/$CID/tasks, where $CID is the long ID of the new container. The service also traces any forked child processes by using the -F option of the strace tool.

To separate the normal behavior from the malicious behavior of the container for testing purposes, an indicator signal is injected into the behavior file before and after each attack, to be recognized by the classifier.

4.5 Training Classifier

We have implemented the classification system described in Fig. 1 in a Java application that uses the technique described in Sect. 3.

The application starts by building a syscall-index hash map from the syscall-list file. The hash map stores distinct system calls as the key, and a corresponding index as the value. A system call that appears in the whole trace less than the total number of distinct system calls is stored in the map as "other". Using "other" for relatively rarely-used system calls saves space, memory, and computation time, as described in [1]. By using a hash map, looking up the index of a system call is an $O(1)$ operation.

The system call parser then reads one system call at a time from the behavior log file, and updates the normal-behavior database. The normal-behavior database is another hash map with the BoSC as the key and the frequency of the bag as the value. If the current bag already exists in the database, the frequency value is incremented. Otherwise, a new entry is added to the database. Again, by using a hash map for implementing the database, the time complexity for updating the database is $O(1)$.

As described in Sect. 3, the application uses the sliding window technique to read sequences of system calls from the trace file, with each sequence is of size 10. A bag of system calls is then created by counting the frequency of each distinct system call within the current window. The created bag of system calls is a frequency array of size n_s, where n_s is the number of distinct system calls. When a new occurrence of a system call is encountered, the application retrieves the index of the system call from the syscall-index hash map, and the corresponding index of the frequency array is updated. The new BoSC is then added to the normal-behavior database.

4.6 Classifier Evaluation

The generated normal-behavior database is then applied to the rest of the behavior file epoch by epoch for anomaly detection. For each epoch, the sliding window technique is similarly used to create BoSCs. The BoSCs noticed during the current epoch are added to temporary database. A mismatch is declared whenever a BoSC is not present in the database. If the number of mismatches exceeds a certain threshold, T_d, within one epoch, an anomaly signal is raised. Otherwise, the entries of the temporary database are committed to the normal-behavior database for future epochs.

For evaluation purposes, the system-call parser recognizes the start-of-attack and end-of-attack signals injected during the data collection phase to mark the epochs involved in the attack as malicious. This information is used to accurately and automatically calculate the true positive rate (TPR) and false positive rate (FPR) metrics, defined as follows:

$$TPR = N_{tp}/N_{malicious} \qquad (1)$$

$$FPR = N_{fp}/N_{normal} \qquad (2)$$

where N_{normal} and $N_{malicious}$ are the total number of normal and malicious sequences, respectively, and N_{tp} and N_{fp} are the number of true positives and false positives, respectively.

To evaluate the system accuracy with respect to different system parameters, we applied the classifier to the same input behavior file while varying the following test parameters:

- Epoch Size (S): The total number of system calls in one epoch. For our experiment, we used epoch size between 1000 and 10,000 with step of 500.
- Detection Threshold (T_d): The number of detected mismatches per epoch before raising an anomaly signal. We used values between 10 to 100 with a step of 10 for each epoch size listed above.

4.7   Evaluation Results

We applied the proposed system to a trace of $3,804,000$ system calls, of which the classifier used $875,000$ system calls for training. The number of distinct system calls (n_s) was 40, and the size of the normal behavior database was around $17\,k$ BoSCs.

The malicious data created a strong anomaly signal with an average of 695 mismatches per epoch, as compared to an average of 33 mismatches per epoch for normal data. For $S = 1000$ and $T_d = 10S$, the TPR is 100 % and the FPR is 2 %. Figure 2 shows the TPR and FPR of the system for different epoch sizes at the same detection threshold of 10. It can be seen that the lower the epoch size, the lower the FPR.

As shown in Fig. 3, the detection threshold highly affects the detection rate of the system especially when short-lived attacks are introduced to the container.

4.8   Complexity Analysis

By using hash map for the index map and the database, the time complexity for looking up an index for a given system call, and for updating the database with a new BoSC, are both $O(1)$ operations. The time complexity for comparing the database before and after an epoch k, and computing the similarity metric,

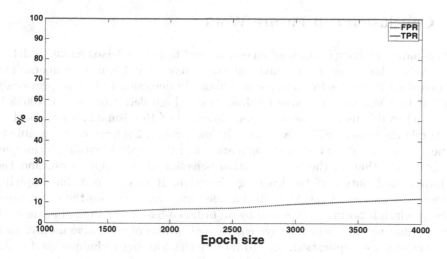

Fig. 2. Effect of changing epoch size on system accuracy

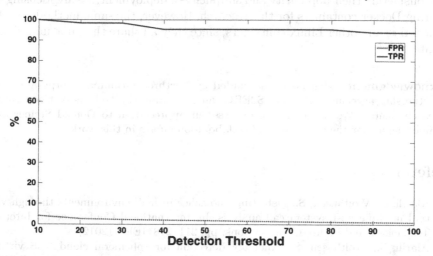

Fig. 3. Effect of changing detection threshold on system accuracy

is $O(n_k)$, where n_k is the size of the database after epoch k. Hence, it can be seen that the algorithm used is linear in the size of the input trace. The time complexity of running an epoch of size S is $O(S + n_k)$.

The algorithm only uses storage for the index map and the database. The index map holds $<$ String, Integer $>$ pairs. Assuming the average size of the system-call hash to be 8 characters, the total size of an index map of size n_s is $16n_s$ bytes (Typically $n_s < 50$). The database stores array of bytes (a string) of size n_s as the key, and an integer as the value. For a normal-behavior database of size n_k, the total size of the database is $(n_s + 8)n_k$ bytes.

5   Conclusion and Future Work

In this paper, we have introduced an opaque real-time host-based intrusion detection system for detecting anomaly in the behavior of Linux containers. The proposed HIDS used a frequency-based anomaly detection technique previously applied to VMs. We were able to show that a high detection rate of 100 % is easily achievable using a low detection threshold of 10 mismatches per epoch.

While the noticed FPR was relatively low (around 2 %), we were not able to achieve a zero FPR for the used application and the applied learning technique. We attribute that to the non-repetitive behavior of the application, and the memory-based nature of the learning algorithm. It was noticed that applying the same workload to the MySQL database may not generate the exact same BoSCs, which is normally expected by an instance-based technique. Future work is to be directed to testing the system to applications of repetitive nature, such as a map-reduce application, and to modify the learning technique used to be more adaptive to slight changes of the BoSCs generated.

Considering their popularity and simplicity of deployment, we are focusing on securing Docker containers for this research. However, the same methods can be extended to any other Linux containers, since they all share the same underlying architecture.

Acknowledgment. This work was funded by Northrop Grumman Corporation via a partnership agreement through S2ERC; an NSF Industry/University Cooperative Research Center. We would like to express our appreciation to Donald Steiner and Joshua Shapiro for their support and collaboration efforts in this work

References

1. Alarifi, S., Wolthusen, S.: Detecting anomalies in IaaS environments through virtual machine host system call analysis. In: International Conference for Internet Technology and Secured Transactions, pp. 211–218. IEEE (2012)
2. Alarifi, S., Wolthusen, S.: Anomaly detection for ephemeral cloud IaaS virtual machines. In: Lopez, J., Huang, X., Sandhu, R. (eds.) NSS 2013. LNCS, vol. 7873, pp. 321–335. Springer, Heidelberg (2013)
3. Chen, Y., Ghorbanzadeh, M., Ma, K., Clancy, C., McGwier, R.: A hidden markov model detection of malicious android applications at runtime. In: 2014 23rd Wireless and Optical Communication Conference (WOCC), pp. 1–6, May 2014
4. Cho, S.B., Park, H.J.: Efficient anomaly detection by modeling privilege flows using hidden markov model. Comput. Secur. **22**(1), 45–55 (2003)
5. Cohen, W.W.: Fast effective rule induction. In: Proceedings of the Twelfth International Conference on Machine Learning, Lake Tahoe, California (1995)
6. Damele, B., Stampar, M.: sqlmap: Automatic SQL injection and database takeover tool (2015). http://sqlmap.org
7. Forrest, S., Hofmeyr, S., Somayaji, A., Longstaff, T.: A sense of self for unix processes. In: Proceedings of the 1996 IEEE Symposium on Security and Privacy, pp. 120–128, May 1996

8. Fuller, D., Honavar, V.: Learning classifiers for misuse and anomaly detection using a bag of system calls representation. In: Proceedings of the Sixth Annual IEEE Systems, Man and Cybernetics (SMC) Information Assurance Workshop, pp. 118–125. IEEE (2005)

9. Helsley, M.: LXC: Linux container tools. IBM developerWorks Technical Library (2009)

10. Hoang, X.D., Hu, J., Bertok, P.: A multi-layer model for anomaly intrusion detection using program sequences of system calls. In: Proceedings of the 11th IEEE International Conference on Networks, pp. 531–536 (2003)

11. Hofmeyr, S., Forrest, S., Somayaji, A.: Intrusion detection using sequences of system calls. J. Comput. Secur. 6(3), 151–180 (1998)

12. Lee, W., Stolfo, S.J.: Data mining approaches for intrusion detection. In: Usenix Security (1998)

13. Merkel, D.: Docker: lightweight linux containers for consistent development and deployment. Linux J. 2014(239), 2 (2014)

14. Murtaza, S.S., Khreich, W., Hamou-Lhadj, A., Couture, M.: A host-based anomaly detection approach by representing system calls as states of kernel modules. In: 2013 IEEE 24th International Symposium onSoftware Reliability Engineering (ISSRE), pp. 431–440. IEEE (2013)

15. Mutz, D., Valeur, F., Vigna, G., Kruegel, C.: Anomalous system call detection. ACM Trans. Inf. Syst. Secur. (TISSEC) 9(1), 61–93 (2006)

16. Oracle Corporation: mysqlslap - Load Emulation Client (2015). http://dev.mysql.com/doc/refman/5.6/en/mysqlslap.html

17. Petazzoni, J.: Containers & Docker: How Secure Are They? (2013). http://blog.docker.com/2013/08/containers-docker-how-secure-are-they

18. Wang, W., Guan, X.H., Zhang, X.L.: Modeling program behaviors by hidden markov models for intrusion detection. In: Proceedings of 2004 International Conference on Machine Learning and Cybernetics, vol. 5, pp. 2830–2835. IEEE (2004)

19. Warrender, C., Forrest, S., Pearlmutter, B.: Detecting intrusions using system calls: alternative data models. In: Proceedings of the 1999 IEEE Symposium on Security and Privacy, pp. 133–145 (1999)

20. Yeung, D.Y., Ding, Y.: Host-based intrusion detection using dynamic and static behavioral models. Pattern Recogn. 36(1), 229–243 (2003)

SUDUTA: Script UAF Detection Using Taint Analysis

John Galea[✉] and Mark Vella

PEST Research Lab, University of Malta, Msida, Malta
{john.galea.10,mark.vella}@um.edu.mt

Abstract. Use-after-free (UAF) vulnerabilities are caused by the use of dangling pointers. Their exploitation inside script engine-hosting applications, e.g. web browsers, can even bypass state-of-the-art countermeasures. This work proposes SUDUTA (**S**cript **UAF D**etection **U**sing **T**aint **A**nalysis), which aims at facilitating the diagnosis of UAF bugs during vulnerability analysis and improves an existent promising technique based on dynamic taint tracking. Firstly, precise taint analysis rules are presented in this work to clearly specify how SUDUTA manages the taint state. Moreover, it shifts its analysis to on-line, enabling instrumentation code to gain access to the program state of the application. Lastly, it handles the presence of custom memory allocators that are typically utilised in script-hosting applications. Results obtained using a benchmark dataset and vulnerable applications validate these three improvements.

Keywords: Use-after-free · Vulnerability analysis · Taint analysis

1 Introduction

Use-After-Free (UAF) vulnerabilities are memory corruption bugs that pose a serious software security threat. They are caused by the use of dangling pointers, and are particularly targeted inside client-side applications that host script-engines and expose host-application objects to scripts, e.g. web browsers and PDF viewers. Their exploitation can even break state-of-the-art operating system mitigations [11], and result in hijacking control-flow and leaking sensitive information. In just the first three months of 2015, the count of publicly disclosed UAF bugs in script-hosting applications was already up to 20[1]. It is crucial that UAF bugs are found by security researchers before hackers start exploiting them, yet their detection still relies on a predominantly manual procedure during vulnerability analysis. Typically, application binaries are first tested using random inputs, with the intent of crashing the application and discovering potential bugs in an automated manner (fuzzing). Once a crash occurs, manual diagnosis is then carried out by an analyst, utilising assembly debuggers, so that the source of the

---

The work disclosed is partially funded by the Master it! Scholarship Scheme (Malta).

[1] https://cve.mitre.org.

S. Foresti (Ed.): STM 2015, LNCS 9331, pp. 136–151, 2015.
DOI: 10.1007/978-3-319-24858-5_9

bug can be identified and its exploitation assessed [7]. Tools such as *PageHeap*[2] can be of aid in forcing crashes as close as possible to the bug location, but still do not eliminate manual analysis. Source code-level vulnerability scanning presents an automated option, however, analysing script-hosting applications involves the consideration of a multitude of combinations of code-block executions related to the many ways host application objects can be manipulated by scripts. Consequently, scalability issues arise when such an approach is adopted.

Alternatively, dynamic code analysis can be employed. Similar to fuzzing, it operates upon the executing binary file, with the difference that it aims to automate the detection and diagnosis of UAF vulnerabilities. One promising technique that is set in this direction has been implemented in a tool called Undangle [4]. It follows the fuzzing step by carrying out program information flow analysis of recorded execution traces. Specifically, Undangle carries out dynamic taint analysis [10], where only the 'tainted' flows of interest are marked and analysed, which in this case include the creation, propagation, deletion and dereferencing of pointer data. UAF bugs are immediately detected whenever dangling pointers are dereferenced or not properly cleared. The strength of this approach lies in the fact that UAF bug detection is tackled at its root cause. However, various possibilities for improvement exist. Firstly, the rules that specify taint analysis are ambiguously defined by using natural language, thus hindering both its understandability and reproducibility. Secondly, analysis is performed on instruction traces during a subsequent 'off-line' step, and loses access to the program state. Since some of the taint analysis rules, as well as for report generation, require access to program state, Undangle resorts to instruction emulation. This is more of an indirect solution rather than an appropriate one. Finally, a third limitation entails that all memory management functions, from which most pointer data is introduced, need to be manually defined. Taking into account that many script-hosting applications make use of custom memory allocators for their script engines [2], this limitation complicates UAF detection.

This work builds upon the technique underlying Undangle, aiming to improve both its reproducibility and effective use in the context of script-hosting applications by addressing its limitations. In this work, we propose SUDUTA (**S**cript **UAF D**etection **U**sing **T**aint **A**nalysis), which uses taint analysis rules that precisely specify how every x86 instruction updates the program's taint state. It manages the large size of this instruction-set by grouping instructions into equivalent classes. SUDUTA uses Just-In-Time (JIT) binary modification to weave in the code that implements the taint analysis rules directly with the application's execution trace, thus providing access to the program state. This analysis technique is the 'on-line' alternative to Undangle's off-line approach. Additionally, SUDUTA integrates a set of existing heuristics for memory management function identification in order to handle applications with custom memory allocators. Results obtained by experimenting with a benchmark dataset and vulnerable

---

[2] https://msdn.microsoft.com/en-us/library/windows/hardware/ff549561(v=vs.85).aspx.

applications show that SUDUTA is an effective UAF detector, and validates the taint analysis rules and its custom memory allocator handling capability. Avenues for optimizing analysis time are also identified.

This work is organized as follows: Sect. 2 expands further on UAF vulnerabilities, Undangle and taint analysis. Section 3 presents SUDUTA, and experimentation and comparison to existing work are detailed in Sects. 4 and 5 respectively. Lastly, Sect. 6 concludes this work.

2   Background

2.1   UAF Vulnerabilities

The control-flow graph (CFG), shown in Fig. 1a, illustrates an example of a simple UAF vulnerability that does not involve a script engine. The erroneous execution sequence takes the path *1b* → *2*, since the dangling pointer p is used to access the **field** data of the previously freed memory object. Clearly, similar UAF bugs are trivial to detect via static code analysis, e.g. [6]. However, their complexity pales in comparison with the erroneous sequences involved in script-hosting applications.

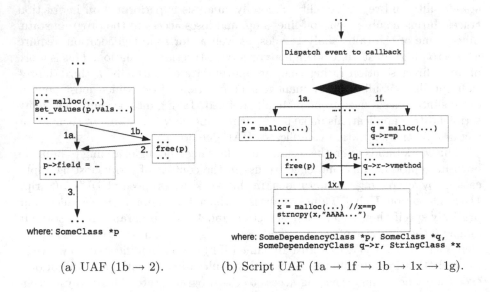

(a) UAF (1b → 2).   (b) Script UAF (1a → 1f → 1b → 1x → 1g).

Fig. 1. Increased complexity of UAF bugs in script-hosting applications.

In the context of web browsers, such applications have their code arranged in a series of callback functions that are invoked as a result of parsing HTML and JavaScript statements. In turn, these functions manipulate host-application objects, e.g. the DOM tree. Consequently, the execution sequence that triggers an exploitable bug can be quite convoluted, as seen in the CFG shown in Fig. 1b.

The execution of the script-controlled callback sequence *1a* → *1f* results in a memory region being referenced in separate parts of code by the two pointers p and q->r. On the execution of *1b*, this memory region is freed, and q->r becomes a dangling pointer. Furthermore, the execution of *1x* results in a third pointer, x, that also references the same region, and has been reused to serve for a new allocation request through `malloc`. Moreover, `strncpy` overwrites the original content that was an object structure for p, resulting in the corruption of its virtual function table (vtable) pointer. The block that is reached via *1g* is comprised of the *use* part of the bug, and enables control-flow hijacking when the q->r->vmethod virtual method is called through the corrupted vtable pointer that is overwritten with an attacker-controlled value. The root cause of the vulnerability is the dangling pointer creation in the block reached by *1b*. This could have been avoided through correct reference counting, where the memory region is freed only if its reference count reaches 0. However, in such complex scenarios where the same memory object is referenced from disparate code locations, reference counts become increasingly difficult to track correctly. Furthermore, the possibility of executing call-back handling code blocks in various combinations could place UAF detection beyond the reach of static code analysis. In fact, the second scenario is more complex than that shown in Fig. 1a.

2.2   Undangle

The UAF detection method implemented by Undangle [4] is the basis of our work. It detects UAF vulnerabilities by performing dynamic taint analysis [10], a technique which revolves around inspecting data flows of interest. In particular, Undangle is concerned with data flows that create, propagate, dangle, and dereference pointers. Overall, Undangle is a two-step approach. It firstly generates execution traces of the program under analysis from fuzzed inputs, and then proceeds by examining these traces in an off-line fashion. During this second step, Undangle analyses each trace instruction and marks, or *taints*, registers and memory locations that store pointer data. For each tainted location, a taint label stores its 'dangling' status that is maintained through memory management function tracking. Taint propagation occurs when pointer values are copied to other locations or used to derive other pointers via pointer arithmetic. As a result, these new pointers are associated with the same taint information that is linked to their sources. Since Undangle operates off-line, it has to perform instruction emulation to calculate the values of these new pointers. Additionally, a pointer is untainted and no longer analysed when it is overwritten with an untainted value, e.g. `NULL`. Whenever a register/memory address operand is dereferenced, Undangle firstly checks its taint label, and if it is a dangling pointer, a detailed report that includes the bug's location(s) is produced. Undangle uses two maps to store the program's taint state, namely, the *forward map* which links pointers to their corresponding taint labels, and the *reverse map* which associates the start location of a memory object with all the pointers that refer to it. The purpose of the reverse map is to link together all the dispersed pointers associated with the same UAF bug.

The example in Listing 1.1 demonstrates how Undangle tracks taint information and detects UAF bugs. Line 4 is a `ret` instruction that concludes a memory allocation function, which would just have stored a pointer to the allocated region in register `eax` (line 3). As a result `eax` is tainted, indicating that it stores pointer data. Taint propagation occurs in line 6 as the value stored in `eax` is copied to `edi`. This means that `edi` is now also marked as a pointer. At the stage where this region is deallocated by passing this same pointer value to a deallocation routine (lines 8–11), all pointers referring to this region will have their taint status updated to 'dangling'. Assuming `edi` still points to this region, its status would be set to 'dangling' and an alert is raised as soon as it is dereferenced in line 13. By taking an on-line approach, calculating new pointer values, such as that computed in line 15, is done automatically by the processor, and are readily accessible from the program state. However, this does not apply to Undangle's off-line approach, which requires performing instruction emulation to derive pointers and obtain their values.

Listing 1.1. An execution trace under analysis

```
1  call <alloc_function>
2  ...
3  mov eax <@start_of_allocation>
4  ret // Return from alloc function call
5  ...
6  mov edi , eax
7  ...
8  push edi
9  call <dealloc_function>
10 ...
11 ret // Return from dealloc function call
12 ...
13 mov ebx, dword ptr[edi]
14 ...
15 add edi , 07
```

Undangle relies on the analyst to provide information related to memory management functions, which as seen in the previous example, their correct identification is important in detecting UAF bugs. Whilst the functions provided by operating systems (e.g. Window's `VirtuallAlloc()` etc.) or standard run-times (e.g. C's `malloc` etc.) can be easily identified via available documentation, many script-hosting applications employ custom memory allocators to improve performance. Internally, custom memory allocators work by requesting large pools of memory through general purpose allocators, and subsequently use custom functions to manage these buffers in order to handle memory allocation requests [5]. As shown in Fig. 2, if the analyst is unaware of the utilisation of undocumented custom memory allocators and Undangle solely monitors general purpose functions, only the allocation of the larger memory pools would be observed, and not their subdivisions into smaller allocations. Consequently, pointers referring to objects managed by custom memory allocators would not be analysed correctly due to a mismatch in the allocation status between the pool/custom allocator levels (zones A-B and C-D in Fig. 2), thus opening the door to false negatives.

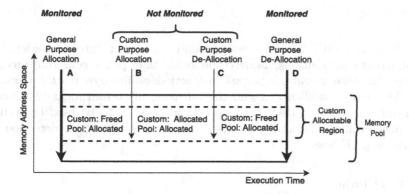

Fig. 2. Pool/custom allocator memory allocation status mismatches

2.3 Formalizing Taint Policy Rules

Another issue with the technique used for Undangle is that the taint analysis rules are only informally described. This aspect lead to replication difficulties due to its ambiguity, and we found the necessity for a notation that precisely defines the taint transitions with respect to the program's own state transitions. Existing notation, previously used to define the taint operation semantics for an intermediate representation language (lifted from assembly) also in a dynamic code analysis setting [10], acts as a basis for this work. However, in our case, we do not lift assembly to an intermediate representation as we define taint rules directly over machine instructions and the machine's context (CPU registers and the virtual memory address space) using the following format:

General Taint Policy Rule:

$$\frac{\text{computation}}{\langle\text{machine context}\rangle\langle\text{taint state}\rangle\text{instruction} \rightsquigarrow \langle\text{taint state'}\rangle}$$

Rules are read from bottom to top and left to right. The bottom-left part of the rule identifies the applicable instruction. Upon an instruction match, the computation defined in the top part of the rule updates the current *taint state* (bottom-left) to the new *taint state'* (bottom-right) as part of a taint state transition ($\rightsquigarrow$). While the machine context (the program state) maps each register/memory address to a q/dword value, its taint state maps each register/memory address to a taint label, specifying whether it is un/tainted. Computation of the new taint state may require values from the current machine context (bottom-left), as in the case of an effective memory operand, e.g. `0x120000[ebp + esi*4]`. During taint analysis, for each instruction in the trace (except those that implement memory management functions), pattern matching is carried out with the rules in order to update the program's taint state. Fundamentally, the rule-set must completely cover the relevant instruction-set, as otherwise the program's taint state would only be partially defined.

3 SUDUTA

We now describe SUDUTA, focusing mainly on how it extends Undangle in relation to our contributions, namely: the formal taint policy rules that precisely describe taint state transitions per x86 instruction; on-line dynamic taint analysis using JIT binary modification; and the provision of custom memory allocator monitoring for accurate UAF detection. It is intended to be used by security researchers during vulnerability analysis in order to facilitate the detection and diagnosis of UAF bugs.

3.1 Taint Policy

SUDUTA keeps track of the program taint state by accessing the machine context, and maintaining taint labels and the forward/reverse maps. The machine context access function ($\triangle$) maps register/memory locations (domain M) to their value (range V). The forward map τ maps register/memory locations (domain M) to taint labels if any (range $T \cup \varepsilon$), whilst the reverse map π associates root addresses (domain V) to a list of all registers/locations storing a pointer to that memory region (range $[M]$).

$$\triangle : M \longrightarrow V$$
$$\tau : M \longrightarrow T \cup \varepsilon$$
$$\pi : V \longrightarrow [M]$$

where: type M: {memory_addresses} $\cup$ {registers},
          type V: q/dword, type T: {TaintLabel}

Specifically the taint label structure is defined as:

```
type: struct TaintLabel = {
    state:          LIVE | DANGLING;
    dangling_pc:    V;
    root:           V;
}
```

It identifies whether a pointer is in a live (pointing to an allocated region) or dangling (pointing to a freed region) state, the value of the program counter (pc) when it turned dangling, and its root address (the start address of the memory buffer it points to as returned by a call to a memory allocation function). Updating the image y of x within a map is denoted by $map[x \leftarrow y]$. Whenever the elements of a map's range are lists, appending or removing values to/from the lists are denoted respectively by $map[x \hookleftarrow y]$ and $map[x \hookrightarrow y]$.

For each traced instruction, SUDUTA updates the taint state based on the instruction and its operands. In the case of x86, an operand can be either a register e.g. eax, a memory location e.g. [0x12000], or an immediate i.e. a constant value. Taint labels are only associated with registers and memory locations, and immediate operands are not applicable. Accessing the taint labels for memory operands can become complicated when expressed in terms of register values, e.g. 0x12000[ebp+esi*4]. In such cases, getting the required taint label firstly requires accessing the register values and evaluating the resultant address. Therefore, access is needed to both the machine context and the taint state, which are available through $\triangle$ and τ respectively. The operation of evaluating an operand *opnd* into its location m and accessing its taint label t within the current machine context/taint state, is expressed as: $\triangle, \tau \vdash opnd \Downarrow \langle m, t \rangle$. Note, in the case of a register or a fixed memory location operand, evaluation is not necessary.

Rules are specified over instruction equivalence classes, grouped by instructions that trigger the same state transition as shown in Listing 1.2. Operands that serve both as source and destination operands are either represented as separate *src/dst* arguments, or as a combined single *srcdst* argument, depending on their suitability with regards to their applicable taint rules.

Listing 1.2. Instruction groupings used by taint policy rules.

```
⊙(call_addr, v, ret) ::=  call
where:
– call_addr is an entry point to an allocation function
– v is the returned value pointing to the start of the
    allocated memory
– ret the register/location storing v
⊘(call_addr, v) ::=  call
where:
– call_addr is an entry point to a deallocation function
– v points to the memory to be freed
◁(dst, src) ::= mov | movs | rep_movs | push | pop
⊗(srcdst₁, srcdst₂) ::= xchg
◊(dst, src₁, src₂) ::= add | sub | lea
where:
– result is not an overflow/underflow
– src₂s value is a not a memory address
– in the case of lea: src₁ is the base or index register
□ ::= inc | dec | nop | cmp | test
○(dst₁,..,dstₙ,src₁,..,srcₖ) ::= all else
```

Rule 1 is a taint introduction rule where the invocation of a memory allocation function constitutes a taint source. When encountering a $\odot(call\_addr, v, ret)$ type of instruction, the register/location m_1 that stores the returned heap pointer is evaluated using $\triangle, \tau \vdash ret \Downarrow \langle m_1, t_1 \rangle$, and its taint label t_1, if existent, is also retrieved. If this location contained pointer data, i.e. it has an associated taint label, the overwrite by the return value v implies that all prior taint-related information needs to be cleared from the taint state, and then updated with the new taint information. This entails firstly removing the existing reverse map entry $(\pi'' = \pi[t_1.root \hookrightarrow m_1])$, and then creating a new taint label, indicating that this location is a live pointer to root address v ($t_{live} = \langle \text{LIVE, NULL, } v \rangle$). This taint label is used to overwrite the existing label or create a new entry in the forward map $(\tau' = \tau[m_1 \leftarrow t_{live}])$, as well as add/update the reverse map entry associated with v ($\pi' = \pi''[t_2.root \hookleftarrow m_1]$).

Rule 1 - Live pointer introduction:

$$\frac{\Delta, \tau \vdash ret \Downarrow \langle m_1, t_1 \rangle, \; \pi'' = \pi[t_1.root \hookrightarrow m_1], \; t_{live} = \langle LIVE, NULL, v \rangle, \; \tau' = \tau[m_1 \leftarrow t_{live}], \; \pi' = \pi''[v \leftarrow m_1]}{\Delta, \tau, \pi, \odot(call\_addr, v, ret) \rightsquigarrow \tau', \pi'}$$

Rules 2–4 follow a similar structure to Rule 1. However, they do not create any new taint labels but associate existing ones with new registers/locations. On the other hand, instructions related to Rule 5 do not update the taint state, whilst Rule 6 is concerned with untainting registers/locations. The latter also covers instances where arithmetic operations result in overflow/underflows or any other kind of invalid pointer values.

Rule 2 - Move propagation:

$$\frac{\Delta, \tau \vdash dst \Downarrow \langle m_1, t_1 \rangle, \; \pi'' = \pi[t_1.root \hookrightarrow m_1], \; \Delta, \tau \vdash src \Downarrow \langle m_2, t_2 \rangle, \; \tau' = \tau[m_1 \leftarrow t_2], \; \pi' = \pi''[t_2.root \leftarrow m_1]}{\Delta, \tau, \pi, \triangleleft(dst, src) \rightsquigarrow \tau', \pi'}$$

Rule 3 - Pointer arithmetic propagation:

$$\frac{\Delta, \tau \vdash dst \Downarrow \langle m_1, t_1 \rangle, \; \pi'' = \pi[t_1.root \hookrightarrow m_1], \; \Delta, \tau \vdash src_1 \Downarrow \langle m_2, t_2 \rangle, \; \tau' = \tau[m_1 \leftarrow t_2], \; \pi' = \pi''[t_2.root \leftarrow m_1]}{\Delta, \tau, \pi, \Diamond(dst, src_1, src_2) \rightsquigarrow \tau', \pi'}$$

Rule 4 - Exchange propagation:

$$\frac{\Delta, \tau \vdash srcdst_1 \Downarrow \langle m_1, t_1 \rangle, \; \Delta, \tau \vdash srcdst_2 \Downarrow \langle m_2, t_2 \rangle, \; \tau' = \tau[m_1 \leftarrow t_2, m_2 \leftarrow t_1], \; \pi' = \pi[t_2.root \hookrightarrow m_2, t_2.root \leftarrow m_1, t_1.root \hookrightarrow m_1, t_1.root \leftarrow m_2]}{\Delta, \tau, \pi, \otimes(srcdst_1, srcdst_2) \rightsquigarrow \tau', \pi'}$$

Rule 5 - No operation propagation:

$$\frac{\tau' = \tau, \; \pi' = \pi}{\Delta, \tau, \pi, \square \rightsquigarrow \tau', \pi'}$$

Rule 6 - Untaint:

$$\frac{\Delta, \tau \vdash dst_1..dst_n \Downarrow \langle m_1, t_1 \rangle..\langle m_n, t_n \rangle, \; \tau' = \tau[m_1 \leftarrow \varepsilon]..\tau[m_n \leftarrow \varepsilon], \; \pi' = \pi[t_1.root \hookrightarrow m_1]..\pi[t_n.root \hookrightarrow m_n]}{\Delta, \tau, \pi, \circ(dst_1..dst_n, src_1..src_k) \rightsquigarrow \tau', \pi'}$$

Rule 7 relates to dangling pointer creation, which occurs whenever a deallocation function is called. In such cases, all pointers referring to the deallocated memory region starting at v (retrieved through $\pi(v)$) are assigned to the taint label $t_{dangling}$, that associates the register/locations with a dangling state, and records the responsible code location ($\Delta(pc)$).

Rule 7 - Dangling pointer creation:

$$\frac{t_{dangling} = \langle DANGLING, \Delta(pc), v \rangle, \; \pi(v) = [m_1, .., m_n], \; \tau' = \tau[m_1 \leftarrow t_{dangling}]..\tau[m_n \leftarrow t_{dangling}], \; \pi' = \pi}{\Delta, \tau, \pi \oslash(call\_addr, v) \rightsquigarrow \tau', \pi'}$$

UAF Detection. Having specified, via formal taint rules, how taint state is maintained, we now move on by explaining how SUDUTA detects UAF vulnerabilities (i.e. dereferences of dangling pointers). For every instruction monitored, SUDUTA calls the UAF_Check function, which, at a high-level, is described in algorithm 1. At the machine code level, pointer dereferences occur as memory operands that are computed out of register values, termed 'effective'. The operand could simply constitute a single register e.g. [ebx], or could consist of more components e.g. [ebx +esi*4]. Importantly, the fact that ebx contains pointer data implies that both these example are cases of pointer dereferencing. More specifically, if ebx is pointing to the start of an allocated buffer on the heap, [ebx] retrieves the first value in this region, whilst [ebx +esi*4] obtains a value from an offset, e.g. as in the case of accessing a value from an array. Therefore, this function involves accessing and retrieving the taint labels for all individual registers inside source and destination operands. It assumes the existence of a function Get_Regs_From_Effective that returns all registers of an effective operand. An alert is raised if any of them are in a dangling state.

Algorithm 1. The UAF_Check function

Input: $\triangle$, τ, π, *inst*
Result: Raises an alert if an UAF vulnerability is detected
1 effective_oprnd_list = Get_All_Effective_Oprnds(inst);
2 **for** *all oprnd* $\in$ *effective_oprnd_list* **do**
3 $\quad$ reg_list = Get_Regs_From_Effective(opnd);
4 $\quad$ **for** *all reg* $\in$ *reg_list* **do**
5 $\quad\quad$ **if** $\tau(reg) == \langle DANGLING, *, * \rangle$ **then**
6 $\quad\quad\quad$ Raise_Alert($\triangle$, τ, π, *inst*);
7 $\quad\quad$ **end**
8 $\quad$ **end**
9 **end**

3.2   On-line Dynamic Taint Analysis

SUDUTA achieves its on-line taint analysis capabilities by carrying out Just-In-Time (JIT) binary modification of the analysed application. As shown in Fig. 3, instead of immediately executing application code, it is firstly copied, per-code block, into an intermediary code cache on the fly. Essentially, the cache provides the means to modify code at an individual instruction granularity. Specifically, SUDUTA inserts a number of 'transparent' calls prior to trace instructions, and thus they do not interfere with the state of the analysed application. This approach requires that CPU registers are duly saved and restored before/after these calls. Also, the code to which control flow is transferred, as well as the code driving the code-cache mechanism, must not interfere with the application's data. These calls invoke functions that encode SUDUTA's taint policy and that

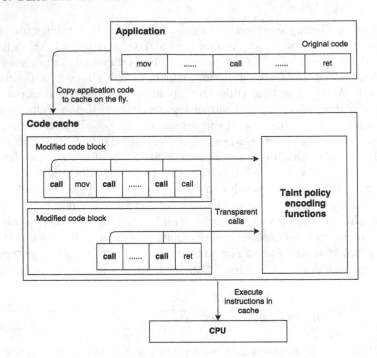

Fig. 3. On-line dynamic taint analysis using JIT binary modification.

have access to the entire machine context, enabling on-line dynamic taint analysis. The encoding functions also keep track of separate machine contexts per application thread. This is only necessary for CPU registers, since taint labels for memory locations are not thread-specific. Finally, each individual code block is executed only after binary modification is complete.

Additional noteworthy aspects of SUDUTA concern user/kernel-mode switching, optimized untainting, and selective module tracing. Since such applications do not usually comprise kernel-level components, on-line taint analysis is optimized by restricting traces to user-mode instructions. Essentially, kernel-mode instructions are ignored and instruction tracing resumes with the first user-mode instruction following a system call. However, this approach introduces intricate situations where kernel code updates the application's memory, and untaint should occur in event that a pointer's value is overwritten. SUDUTA takes the approach of keeping shadow values for all tainted locations, which are consulted prior to pointer propagation, dangling pointer creation and pointer dereference checks. When a current value does not match its corresponding shadow value, the untaint rule (Rule 6) is instead applied. The same method is in fact utilized as a general optimization strategy for untainting. Considering the large number of instructions applicable to this rule, the optimisation saves on the number of control flow transfers to its encoding function by performing untaint in the other rule-encoding functions when they detect a value/shadow value mismatch.

One final optimization involves selective module tracing. Similar to switching off tracing for kernel-mode code, it might be desirable that analysis is also switched off whenever execution control is transferred to loaded libraries that are not of interest. For example, in the case of a web browser, a system library that handles GUI window management and that excludes any form of memory management, is neither expected to contain an application-specific UAF bug nor affect the detection of UAF bugs inside prominent modules. Similarly, libraries that do not contain script/DOM-related code may be considered low priority and their exclusion might speed-up analysis time. Pointer modifications performed by the excluded modules are handled via the aforementioned optimized implementation of the untaint rule.

3.3 Custom Memory Allocator Monitoring

SUDUTA aims to maximize UAF detection by identifying undocumented custom memory allocators in a preliminary stage. It makes use of existing heuristics [5] that capture the typical characteristics of memory management functions. They are particularly suitable since they are independent of the data structures used for memory pool management. SUDUTA implements the heuristics in a filter-based approach, where all executed functions, except for provided memory management functions, are initially considered as candidates. Those that do not adhere to the heuristic-based filters are progressively removed. The memory allocation heuristics are: *(H1)* The function should return a heap pointer, *(H2)* Returned heap pointers should be used to firstly initialise memory before they are used for reading, and *(H3)* The function should not return the same heap address twice unless previously freed. The memory deallocation heuristics are: *(H4)* The function should take as a parameter a memory address previously returned by an allocation function, *(H5)* The function should reference a common memory address region shared with custom allocation functions, which is used for memory pool meta-data, and *(H6)* A freed region can be re-allocated again by custom allocation functions. Although no heuristics specific for memory re-allocation functions have yet been integrated into SUDUTA, their allocation and deallocation sub-components may still be detected by these heuristics.

4   Evaluation

SUDUTA was evaluated using a 32-bit prototype that uses DynamoRIO[3] [3] to implement JIT binary modification and program memory analysis. It consists of 5,657 lines of C code. Experimentation focused on validating its UAF detection capabilities based on taint analysis in an on-line setting, along with its support of monitoring custom memory allocators. Finally, SUDUTA's practicality in terms of analysis time was also explored. All experiments were carried out on a guest OS running Windows XP SP3, with an Intel Core i7 3.2 GHz Quad Core Processor. The reason for choosing this OS was due to availability of working exploits.

---

[3] http://www.dynamorio.org/.

Validating UAF detection capabilities. SUDUTA's detection capabilities were firstly validated using the Juliet for C\C++ v1.2 vulnerability benchmark test suite. All 459 UAF bugs were detected by SUDUTA without generating any false positives. Moreover, SUDUTA generated no false positives when it analysed the 459 benign test cases in the same test suite. Once basic UAF detection capabilities were confirmed, focus was shifted to script-hosting applications that contain known exploitable UAF vulnerabilities.

We chose three case studies, on the basis of a working exploit and a technical analysis report being available, which allowed us to verify whether the vulnerabilities reported by SUDUTA corresponded to the actual bugs. These were: Internet Explorer 6.0.2900 (CVE-2010-0249), Firefox 3.5.1 (CVE-2011-0073), and MS Excel 2003 (OSVDB-76840). Due to the size of the applications, we made use of SUDUTA's selective module tracing feature to focus on the priority modules that contain callback functions invoked by script engines, as per example shown in Fig. 1b, namely: `mshtml.dll` (IE), `xul.dll` (Firefox), and `vbe6.dll` (Excel). During the first vulnerability analysis, the *Bf3* browser fuzzer[4] was utilised for input generation. However, the fuzzer was not capable of triggering the execution paths affected by the UAF bugs. Therefore, we resorted to using their exploits[5]. Table 1 shows the results obtained. Each exploit was executed twice with the identification and monitoring of customer memory allocators enabled/disabled.

SUDUTA fails to identify the vulnerability in IE 6 without monitoring custom allocators, but is successful when this feature is turned on. This outcome demonstrates the importance of monitoring custom allocators when analysing script-hosting application. In fact, we confirmed through the `mshtml.dll`'s symbol file that this library uses the undocumented custom `MemAllocClear` and `MemFree` functions. This contrasts with Excel's case where monitoring the operating system's `HeapAlloc` and `HeapFree` suffices. In all cases, SUDUTA returned no false positives. Firefox's case was problematic since after 14 h, analysis was still running without having yet detected any vulnerabilities. The cause for this long analysis time was not immediately clear. However, `xul.dll`'s larger size

Table 1. Vulnerability detection results.

ID	Application	Custom allocator monitor	Detected?
CVE-2010-0249	Internet Explorer 6	Disabled	No
		Enabled	Yes
OSVDB-76840	MS Excel 2003	Disable	Yes
		Enabled	Yes
CVE-2011-0073	Firefox 3.5.1	Disabled	No
		Enabled	No

---

[4] http://www.aldeid.com/wiki/Bf3.
[5] Retrieved from Exploit-DB: https://www.exploit-db.com/.

Table 2. Performance results with respect to analysis time.

ID	Optimised?	Analysis time	Speed-up	Detected?
CVE-2010-0249	No	39.3 s	x0	Yes
	Yes	24.7 s	x1.6	Yes
OSVDB-76840	No	24.5 s	x0	Yes
	Yes	14.8s	x1.6	Yes
CVE-2011-0073	No	~ 14 h	x0	No
	Yes	1,868.2 s	~ x27.0	Yes

(x3.51 the size of `mshtml.dll`) pointed towards a trace size issue. This indication forced us to seek possibilities of optimization, which are presented as part of the following discussion on performance results.

Performance. The major bottleneck to analysis time is caused by the fine grained examination of instructions as described by SUDUTA's taint policy. The need to check pointer dereferences at every instruction is particularly expensive. Consequently, an optimisation is adopted that trades off pointer-tracking precision for performance by inspecting a smaller restricted group of instructions, with the aim of reducing analysis time. More specifically, the optimisation only examines the ◁ instruction group and the `lea` instruction in order to propagate taint. Furthermore, instead of considering all instructions, the optimisation solely checks dereferences of dangling pointers operated by `mov` instructions. Consequently, instructions including `add`, `sub`, `inc`, `dec` and `xchg` are not monitored. We base this optimisation on our assumption that host application objects, exposed to scripts, are accessed by utilising the root address, without performing pointer arithmetic. However, this assumption holds in cases where memory objects are not stored contiguously inside an array. Table 2 shows performance results obtained, comparing SUDUTA with its optimised version.

The optimised version of SUDUTA managed to significantly reduce the analysis time. Despite the imprecision incurred due to the monitoring of less instructions, it still detected the vulnerabilities in all applications. No false positives were produced by SUDUTA. With regards to Firefox, the optimised version speeded up analysis by a factor of 27, which resulted in reasonable time to carry out analysis in full and identify the vulnerability. Moreover, the optimised version also detected all UAF bugs present in the Juliet benchmark database, without generating any false positives. In general, SUDUTA's automated procedure lessens the manual effort required to diagnose and remove UAF vulnerabilities.

5   Related Work

Like SUDUTA, several proposed techniques detect UAF vulnerabilities with the overall aim of facilitating vulnerability analysis. Some [6,13] take a static approach but face difficult scalability challenges, such as conducting accurate point-to analysis, that make them only suitable to analyse small programs. Other techniques tackle the problem dynamically. Conventional memory debugging tools (e.g. Dr. Memory[6]) detect UAF bugs by checking whether dereferenced pointers access memory marked as live, but are ineffective when a used dangling pointer refers to re-allocated memory. Rather than taking a memory-centric approach, SUDUTA adopts a pointer-centric approach and thus avoids this concern.

Instead of detecting UAF vulnerabilities as part of a debugging effort, other works [9,12] focus on inserting dynamic checks during compilation, with the purpose of hardening applications for deployment. They are concerned with minimising overheads, particularly due to their requirement to perform potentially expensive checks upon all pointer dereferences. Recent works [8,14] avoid this bottleneck by nullifying all dangling pointers immediately after the deallocation of their referenced object. Other techniques such as hardened memory allocators [1] or process address spaces (e.g. EMET[7]) aim at mitigating exploits, regardless of the type of vulnerabilities leveraged.

6   Conclusion

UAF vulnerabilities stem from the incorrect dereference of dangling pointers and pose a threat to the security of script-hosting applications. Vulnerability analysts attempt to manually diagnose security holes, and this requires significant effort. Consequently, a need exists for automated tools that facilitate analysis in order to be competitive against adversaries.

In this work, we propose SUDUTA, which builds upon Undangle to address several limitations. Firstly, SUDUTA shifts analysis to on-line, so that program state can be accessed. Moreover, its specification is also defined as a formal taint policy, thus rendering the technique easier to understand and replicate. SUDUTA improves further by also identifying undocumented custom memory allocators automatically, in order to increase detection coverage. Experimentation results validate the approach, particularly the precise taint policy, since UAF vulnerabilities found in benchmark test cases and real-world script-hosting applications were successfully detected. Through the identification of custom memory allocators, SUDUTA manages to detect the vulnerability in IE 6 only when monitoring undocumented memory management functions. Furthermore, trading off pointer-tracking precision for performance improved analysis time greatly, with an average speed-up of x10.1, without producing any false negatives. Results also highlight the need for a smart fuzzing approach. Future work entails designing and integrating an improved fuzzer, where test case generation is based on exploit patterns rather than only grammatically correct syntax. Additionally, upgrading SUDUTA to support 64-bit applications would enable a larger scale evaluation.

---

[6] http://www.drmemory.org/.
[7] https://support.microsoft.com/en-us/kb/2458544.

References

1. Akritidis, P.: Cling: a memory allocator to mitigate dangling pointers. In: Proceedings of the 19th USENIX Conference on Security, USENIX Security 2010, p. 12. USENIX Association, Berkeley (2010)
2. Argyroudis, P., Karamitas, C.: Exploiting the Jemalloc Memory Allocator: Owning Firefox's Heap. Blackhat USA (2012)
3. Bruening, D., Zhao, Q., Amarasinghe, S.: Transparent dynamic instrumentation. In: Proceedings of the 8th ACM SIGPLAN/SIGOPS Conference on Virtual Execution Environments, VEE 2012, pp. 133–144. ACM, New York (2012)
4. Caballero, J., Grieco, G., Marron, M., Nappa, A.: Undangle: early detection of dangling pointers in use-after-free and double-free vulnerabilities. In: Heimdahl, M.P.E., Su, Z. (eds.) ISSTA, pp. 133–143. ACM (2012)
5. Chen, X., Slowinska, A., Bos, H.: Who allocated my memory? detecting custom memory allocators in C binaries. In: 2013 20th Working Conference on Reverse Engineering (WCRE), pp. 22–31 (2013)
6. Josselin, F., Laurent, M., Marie-Laure, P.: Statically detecting use after free on binary code. In: GreHack, pp. 61–71 (2013)
7. Kratzer, J.: Root cause analysis Memory Corruption Vulnerabilities. https://www.corelan.be/index.php/2013/02/26/root-cause-analysis-memory-corruption-vulnerabilities/. Accessed 15 June 2015
8. Lee, B., Song, C., Jang, Y., Wang, T., Kim, T., Lu, L., Lee, W.: Preventing use-after-free with dangling pointers nullification. In: Proceedings of the 2015 Annual Network and Distributed System Security Symposium (2015)
9. Nagarakatte, S., Zhao, J., Martin, M.M.K., Zdancewic, S.: CETS: compiler enforced temporal safety for C. In: Vitek, J., Lea, D. (eds.) ISMM, pp. 31–40. ACM (2010)
10. Schwartz, E.J., Avgerinos, T., Brumley, D.: All you ever wanted to know about dynamic taint analysis and forward symbolic execution (but might have been afraid to ask). In: Proceedings of the 2010 IEEE Symposium on Security and Privacy, SP 2010, pp. 317–331. IEEE Computer Society, Washington, DC (2010)
11. Snow, K.Z., Monrose, F., Davi, L., Dmitrienko, A., Liebchen, C., Sadeghi, A.R.: Just-in-time code reuse: on the effectiveness of fine-grained address space layout randomization. In: Proceedings of the 2013 IEEE Symposium on Security and Privacy, SP 2013, pp. 574–588. IEEE Computer Society, Washington, DC (2013)
12. Xu, W., DuVarney, D.C., Sekar, R.: An efficient and backwards-compatible transformation to ensure memory safety of C programs. ACM SIGSOFT Softw. Eng. Notes **29**(6), 117–126 (2004)
13. Ye, J., Zhang, C., Han, X.: POSTER: UAFChecker: scalable static detection of use-after-free vulnerabilities. In: Proceedings of the 2014 ACM SIGSAC Conference on Computer and Communications Security, CCS 2014, pp. 1529–1531. ACM, New York (2014)
14. Younan, Y.: Freesentry: Protecting against use-after-free vulnerabilities due to dangling pointers (2015)

Cryptographic Protocols

Two-Factor Authentication
for the Bitcoin Protocol

Christopher Mann and Daniel Loebenberger[✉]

B-IT, University of Bonn, Bonn, Germany
daniel@bit.uni-bonn.de

Abstract. We show how to realize two-factor authentication for a Bitcoin wallet. To do so, we explain how to employ an ECDSA adaption of the two-party signature protocol by MacKenzie and Reiter (2004) in the context of Bitcoin and present a prototypic implementation of a Bitcoin wallet that offers both: two-factor authentication and verification over a separate channel. Since we use a smart phone as the second authentication factor, our solution can be used with hardware already available to most users and the user experience is quite similar to the existing online banking authentication methods.

1 Introduction

Bitcoin (BTC) is a cryptographic currency proposed by Satoshi Nakamoto (2008) in the legendary email to the Cryptography Mailing list at metzdowd.com. One of the most important features of Bitcoin is that it is completely peer-to-peer, i.e. it does not rely on a trusted authority (the bank) which ensures that the two central requirements of any electronic cash system are met: Only the owner can spend money and it is impossible to spend money twice. In Bitcoin, these two features are realized with a common transaction history, the Bitcoin *block-chain*, known to all users. Each of the transactions in the chain contains the address to which some Bitcoins should be payed, the address from which the Bitcoins should be withdrawn and the amount. Both addresses are directly derived from the public key of the corresponding ECDSA key pairs of the recipient and the sender, respectively. The whole transaction is then signed using the ECDSA private key of the sender. We describe the details in Sect. 2. Since any user might have multiple addresses, its *wallet* consists of several key-pairs and is typically stored on the owner's device or within some online service.

Thus, from a thieves' perspective, the only thing one has to do in order to steal some Bitcoins, is to get hands on the corresponding wallet, just like in real life. Indeed, Lipovsky (2013) describe an online banking trojan that also steals Bitcoin wallets.

A common approach to complicate this is the use of two-factor authentication. This means that the wallet stored on a device does *not* contain the private keys but just shares of them. The other shares are stored on an independent device (such as a smart phone). Now, any transaction can only be signed with

© Springer International Publishing Switzerland 2015
S. Foresti (Ed.): STM 2015, LNCS 9331, pp. 155–171, 2015.
DOI: 10.1007/978-3-319-24858-5_10

the help of *both* shares of the private key. During the signing process, it has to be ensured that at no point in time the full private key is present on either of the devices.

There was already considerable effort to realize two-factor authentication for Bitcoin wallets. First of all, it is in principle possible to use Bitcoin's build-in functionality for threshold signatures. This has, however, three major disadvantages: First of all, it would be visible in the block-chain that multi-factor authentication is used. Second, the size of the transaction increases, which leads to higher transaction fees. Last but not least, there are Bitcoin clients around which do not work properly with the threshold-signature extension.

Goldfeder et al. (2014) tried to employ threshold signatures proposed by Ibrahim et al. (2003). However, as the authors pointed out there, it is quite difficult to use these kind of signatures for two-factor authentication, since the restrictions on the threshold are quite delicate to handle. In their blog post, they compare different threshold signatures with respect to their applicability to Bitcoin wallets. However, their reasoning remains quite high-level.

In this article, we show how to actually realize two-factor authentication for a Bitcoin wallet employing the two-party ECDSA signature protocol adapted from MacKenzie and Reiter (2004). We also present a prototypic implementation of a Bitcoin wallet that offers both: two-factor authentication and verification over a separate channel. Since we use a smart phone as the second authentication factor, our solution can be used with hardware already available to most users and the user experience is quite similar to the existing online banking authentication methods. Our source code is liberally licensed and can be found on GitHub, see Mann (2014). We also got in contact with the developers of the Java Bitcoin library. Indeed, there was lively discussion on the Bitcoin mailing list, when they got aware of our prototype. For details, see Hearn (2014).

Very recently, we got aware of the work of Goldfeder et al. (2015), where the authors present an extended version of the MacKenzie and Reiter scheme which allows t-party threshold signatures. This is a very nice idea in the context of Bitcoin and it would be very interesting to see their extended scheme running. Unfortunately, their prototype currently only implements the plain MacKenzie and Reiter scheme. Furthermore, we observed that in contrast to our implementation their desktop wallet serves as a trusted dealer during initialization. On a compromised computer this is a clear security problem. We addressed this issue here. For details, see Mann (2015).

2   Bitcoin Protocol

We will now describe some of the technical details of the Bitcoin protocol as described by Nakamoto (2008). In difference to other e-cash schemes such as the one proposed by Chaum et al. (1990) and many others, Bitcoin was designed to be completely decentralized. The Bitcoin network consists of a large number of independent nodes which verify incoming transactions independently of each other. These nodes use a synchronization protocol which is based on a proof-of-work similar to the hashcash system described in Back (2002). With the help of this protocol, the nodes agree on a common transaction history, which is called the Bitcoin *block chain*, see Fig. 1. A Bitcoin transaction contains the address to which the Bitcoins should be payed, the address from which the Bitcoins should be withdrawn and the amount. Furthermore, the transaction contains a digital signature, which authorizes the transaction, and the public key needed to verify the signature. Bitcoin uses the ECDSA signature scheme, specified by the Accredited Standards Committee X9 (2005) on the elliptic curve `secp256k1` as defined by Certicom Research (2000). All Bitcoin transactions must be correctly signed by the spender. In order to bind Bitcoin addresses and the public keys, the Bitcoin address of a user is directly derived from the user's public key by applying a cryptographic hash function to it.

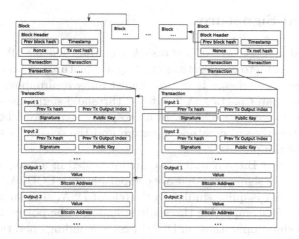

Fig. 1. Simplified view of the Bitcoin blockchain.

Any Bitcoin transaction actually consists of one or more inputs and outputs. Each output specifies a target address and an amount of Bitcoins to be transferred to this target address. Every input contains the hash of a preceding transaction and an index. Both values together unambiguously identify an output of a preceding transaction. All the Bitcoins from this referenced output are spent by the current transaction. Consequently, every transaction output is only used a single time as an input and is completely spent at this time. This increases the efficiency of the network nodes as these only need to keep track of the unspent outputs instead of all transactions having an impact on the balance of the user's address. Furthermore, any input contains a signature and a public key which must fit the address given in the output referenced by this input. In consequence, if multiple inputs are used, multiple signatures of the transaction must be created, one for each input.

Clearly, the sum of the Bitcoins from all inputs must be greater or equal than the sum of the Bitcoins spent by the outputs. If the sum of the inputs is greater, this is not a problem. Any unused Bitcoins are transferred as a fee to the miner of the block containing this transaction and increase the miner's revenue.

Therefore, this will increase the priority of the transaction as the miners will have an incentive to include it into a block.

For ease of exposition, we omitted the fact that Bitcoin uses a scripting language for transactions: In reality, a transaction does not really include a target address or a signature and a public key, but scripts which contains these as constants. Currently, only a very limited subset of the scripting functionality is actively used in the Bitcoin network and there are plans to restrict the scripting functionality even further to solve the problem of transaction malleability, see Wuille (2014). Bitcoin transactions are currently malleable, which means that certain bytes in a transaction can be changed without invalidating the ECDSA signatures.

3   Threshold Signatures

For a polynomial p, a $p(t)$-*out-of-u threshold signature scheme* allows $p(t)$ members out of a group of u to cooperate in creating a signature for a certain message. At the same time, the scheme is secure against an eavesdropping attacker who compromises less than t parties. A 2-out-of-2 threshold signature scheme is also called a *two-party signature scheme*. In a two-party signature scheme, two parties must work together to create a signature and the scheme is secure against attacks by one of the parties.

For our two-factor Bitcoin wallet, we are interested in a two-party signature scheme which creates signatures that are compatible with ECDSA. The signature algorithm of ECDSA is quite similar to the one of DSA, standardized by NIST (2013). Thus, a DSA-compatible threshold scheme can be ported to ECDSA by replacing the modular operations in DSA by corresponding operations on elliptic curves. Of course, while doing so, the operations in the exponent groups have to be replaced accordingly.

We have searched for threshold signature schemes for both DSA and ECDSA. Several secure and efficient threshold signature schemes exist for modified versions of the ElGamal signature scheme, see for example Harn (1994). Compatibility with DSA or ECDSA on the other hand is harder to achieve, as the signature algorithm requires the inversion of a secret value and the multiplication of two secret values.

Most threshold signature schemes use polynomial shares similar to Shamir (1979) secret sharing, but the multiplication of polynomial shares does not work well as the multiplication of two polynomials increases the degree of the resulting polynomial. There are several threshold schemes for DSA available, see for example Langford (1995), Gennaro et al. (1996), Wang and Hwang (1997). For ECDSA, Ibrahim et al. (2003) presents a $(2t - 1)$-out-of-u threshold signature scheme. In Goldfeder et al. (2014), this scheme is applied to secure Bitcoin wallets. However, as the authors point out, it is difficult to respect the restrictions on the threshold value in the scheme, rendering it somewhat unsuitable for two-factor authentication. More precisely, it was erroneously assumed that one could further improve the protocol to $(t + 1)$-out-of-u by applying the degree reduction protocol from Ben-Or et al. (1988) to circumvent the degree doubling caused by the multiplication of two secret sharing polynomials. Unfortunately, the protocol requires $2t + 1 \geq 3$ cooperating parties with secret shares to reduce the polynomial.

In MacKenzie and Reiter (2004), a two-party signature scheme for DSA with a different approach is presented. Instead of working with polynomial shares, the authors use a homomorphic cipher such as the Paillier (1999) cryptosystem. This allows one party to operate with cipher texts of another party's secrets without ever learning about these secrets. In difference to the other threshold signature schemes, this one works for only two parties. As we need a two-party signature scheme for ECDSA to implement our two-factor wallet, we decided to port their scheme to ECDSA. Also Goldfeder et al. (2014) came to the same conclusion: In the blog post related to their article they note that the scheme by MacKenzie and Reiter seems to be "close to ideal". They later describe in Goldfeder et al. (2015) a t-out-of-n extension for the MacKenzie and Reiter scheme which uses a threshold version of the Paillier crypto system.

3.1   Two-Party ECDSA

We now give a short overview of two-party signatures as described by MacKenzie and Reiter (2004) in the context of ECDSA. For more details, see Mann (2015). For the setup, one fixes a cryptographic hash function h (in our case we use SHA-256, see NIST (2012) and a particular set of elliptic curve domain parameters: A prime power $q \in \mathbb{N}_{\geq 2}$ denoting the size of the base field, the elliptic curve parameters $a, b \in \mathbb{F}_q$ defining the elliptic curve $E\colon y^2 = x^3 + ax + b$, a (finite) base-point $G \in E$ of prime order $n \in \mathbb{N}$, and a cofactor $h = \#E/n \in \mathbb{N}$. An $ECDSA$ key-pair is a pair $(d, Q) \in \mathbb{Z}_n^\times \times E$, where d was pseudorandomly generated and $Q = dG$ on the elliptic curve E. In the case of Bitcoin, q is a large prime, $a = 0$, $b = 7$ and the cofactor is $h = 1$, see Certicom Research (2000). In order to sign a message $m \in \{0,1\}^*$ in ECDSA, Alice selects pseudorandomly a non-zero integer $k \in \mathbb{Z}_n^\times$ and computes kG. The process is repeated as long as the x-coordinate $r = \mathrm{coord}_x(kG) \mod n = 0$. Now, Alice computes $s = k^{-1}(\mathrm{h}(m) + rd)$. If $s = 0$, the process is repeated using a new ephemeral key $k \in \mathbb{Z}_n^\times$.

The two-party signature scheme by MacKenzie and Reiter (2004) consists of three different phases for jointly signing a message $m \in \{0,1\}^*$.

Initialization. In this phase, Alice and Bob agree on a common ECDSA public key Q which is used to verify the cooperatively created signatures. Therefore, Alice and Bob choose private key shares $d_A, d_B \in \mathbb{Z}_n^\times$ pseudorandomly. Afterwards, they exchange the corresponding public keys $Q_A = d_A G$ and $Q_B = d_B G$. Both sides now compute the common public key as $Q = d_A Q_B = d_A d_B G$ and $Q = d_B Q_A = d_B d_A G$ respectively. As the scalar multiplication on elliptic curves is commutative, both sides now hold the same common public key Q. Essentially, they perform a Diffie-Hellman key exchange. We can define the fictive private key $d = d_A d_B$ which is the private key corresponding to the public key Q. Note that none of the two parties ever hold the full private key d nor are they able to compute it. Finally, Alice and Bob generate key pairs $(\text{sk}_A, \text{pk}_A)$ and $(\text{sk}_B, \text{pk}_B)$ respectively, for a homomorphic public key encryption scheme, such as the Paillier (1999) cryptosystem, and distribute the public key to the other party.

Constructing an Ephemeral Key. In the second phase, a shared ephemeral secret $k = k_A k_B \in \mathbb{Z}_n^\times$ is generated together with the corresponding public key $R = kG \in E$. Alice and Bob also compute the public keys corresponding to their shares of the ephemeral secret as $R_A = k_A G$ and $R_B = k_B G \in E$. Furthermore, Alice commits to the two values k_A^{-1} and $k_A^{-1} d_A$ in $\mathbb{Z}_n^\times$ by sending the corresponding encryptions under pk_A to Bob.

Form the Signature. In the final phase, Bob uses the two commitments together with the homomorphic property of the encryption scheme to finally compute the second part of the ECDSA signature s.

In Fig. 2, the full two-party ECDSA signature protocol is given. For details on the analysis and the security of this protocol see MacKenzie and Reiter (2004).

For the protocol to be secure, it is necessary to prove to the other side several facts using non-interactive zero-knowledge proofs, see Blum et al. (1988), which

Alice (d_A, Q_A, sk_A)   **Bob (d_B, Q_B, sk_B)**

$k_A \xleftarrow{R} \mathbb{Z}_n^\times$

$z_A \leftarrow k_A^{-1}$

$\alpha_A \leftarrow \text{Enc}_{\text{pk}_A}(z_A)$

$\beta \leftarrow \text{Enc}_{\text{pk}_A}(d_A z_A) \qquad \xrightarrow{\ m, \alpha_A, \beta\ } \text{check } \alpha_A, \beta \in \mathcal{C}_{\text{pk}_A}$

$\qquad\qquad\qquad\qquad\qquad\qquad\qquad k_B \xleftarrow{R} \mathbb{Z}_n^\times$

check $R_B \in \langle G \rangle \qquad\qquad \xleftarrow{\ R_B\ } R_B \leftarrow k_B G$

$R \leftarrow k_A R_B$

$\pi_A \leftarrow \text{zkp}_A(R_B, R, \alpha_A, \beta) \quad \xrightarrow{\ R, \pi_A\ } \text{check } R \in \langle G \rangle, \pi_A$

$\qquad\qquad\qquad\qquad\qquad\qquad\qquad r \leftarrow \text{coord}_\text{x}(R) \bmod n$

$\qquad\qquad\qquad\qquad\qquad\qquad\qquad z_B \leftarrow k_B^{-1}$

$\qquad\qquad\qquad\qquad\qquad\qquad\qquad c \xleftarrow{R} \mathbb{Z}_{n^5}$

$\qquad\qquad\qquad\qquad\qquad\qquad\qquad \sigma \leftarrow ((\alpha_A \times_{\text{pk}_A} \text{h}(m)) \times_{\text{pk}_A} z_B)$

$\qquad\qquad\qquad\qquad\qquad\qquad\qquad\qquad +_{\text{pk}_A} ((\beta \times_{\text{pk}_A} r) \times_{\text{pk}_A} d_B z_B)$

$\qquad\qquad\qquad\qquad\qquad\qquad\qquad\qquad +_{\text{pk}_A} \text{Enc}_{\text{pk}_A}(c \cdot n)$

$\qquad\qquad\qquad\qquad\qquad\qquad\qquad \alpha_B \leftarrow \text{Enc}_{\text{pk}_B}(z_B)$

check $\sigma \in \mathcal{C}_{\text{pk}_A}$, check $\alpha_B \in \mathcal{C}_{\text{pk}_B}, \pi_B \xleftarrow{\ \sigma, \alpha_B, \pi_B\ } \pi_B \leftarrow \text{zkp}_B(m, r, R_B, \alpha_A, \alpha_B, \beta, \sigma)$

$s \leftarrow \text{Dec}_{\text{sk}_A}(\sigma) \bmod n$

$r \leftarrow \text{coord}_\text{x}(R) \bmod n$

publish (r, s)

Fig. 2. Generating a two-party ECDSA signature using the modified MacKenzie and Reiter (2004) protocol.

we will denote by zkp. Also, there is frequent use of the (additively) homomorphic property of the underlying cipher. For any key pair (sk, pk), let $\mathcal{M}_{pk} \subset \mathbb{Z}$ be the message space and $\mathcal{C}_{pk}$ be the ciphertext space. The homomorphic property of the cipher gives raise to an operation

$$+_{pk}: \quad \begin{array}{c} \mathcal{C}_{pk} \times \mathcal{C}_{pk} \longrightarrow \mathcal{C}_{pk}, \\ (\text{Enc}_{pk}(m_1), \text{Enc}_{pk}(m_2)) \longmapsto \text{Enc}_{pk}(m_1 + m_2) \end{array}.$$

We stress that the encryption function Enc_{pk} is randomized such that in the above expression $\text{Enc}_{pk}(m_1 + m_2)$ denotes *one valid* encryption of the addition of the messages m_1 and m_2. Applying the function $+_{pk}$ repeatedly defines the function

$$\times_{pk}: \quad \begin{array}{c} \mathcal{C}_{pk} \times \mathbb{N} \longrightarrow \mathcal{C}_{pk}, \\ (\text{Enc}_{pk}(m_1), m_2) \longmapsto \text{Enc}_{pk}(m_1 \cdot m_2) \end{array}.$$

The protocol uses two zero-knowledge proofs to ensure correct execution of the protocol. The first proof π_A, constructed by Alice, proves to Bob the existence of values $x, y \in \left[-n^3, n^3\right]$, such that $xR = R_B, (y/x)\,G = Q_A$ and

$$\text{Dec}_{sk_A}(\alpha_A) \equiv_n x,$$
$$\text{Dec}_{sk_A}(\beta) \equiv_n y.$$

In other words, Alice proves to Bob that she has properly executed the previous steps in the protocol. The second zero-knowledge proof π_B is used on the other side by Bob to prove to Alice that he has also executed the necessary steps in the protocol and that the operations he performed fit to the operations Alice performed. Specifically, he proves that there are values $x, y \in \left[-n^3, n^3\right], z \in \left[-n^7, n^7\right]$, such that $xR_B = G, (y/x)\,G = Q_B$ and

$$\text{Dec}_{sk_B}(\alpha_B) \equiv_n x,$$

$$\text{Dec}_{sk_A}(\sigma) = \text{Dec}_{sk_A}\Big(((\alpha_A \times_{pk_A} h(m)) \times_{pk_A} x) +_{pk_A} ((\beta \times_{pk_A} r) \times_{pk_A} y)\Big) + zn.$$

It seems counterintuitive, that Bob can argue about decryptions of cipher texts which were encrypted with Alice's public key pk_A. One would expect that this requires knowledge of Alice's secret key sk_A. But Bob is arguing about homomorphic operations with the cipher texts, which are deterministic for him, as he also knows the randomization term zn. In the zero knowledge proof, he can encode the equality of the two decryptions as equality of two related cipher texts, which Bob can prove without any problems.

We finish with an illustration of the correctness of the modified two-party signature scheme:

$$s = \text{Dec}_{sk_A}(\sigma)$$

$$= \text{Dec}_{sk_A}\Big(((\alpha_A \times_{pk_A} h(m)) \times_{pk_A} z_B)$$

$$+_{pk_A} ((\beta \times_{pk_A} r) \times_{pk_A} d_B z_B) +_{pk_A} \text{Enc}_{pk_A}(c \cdot n)\Big)$$

$$= \text{Dec}_{sk_A}\Big(((\text{Enc}_{pk_A}(z_A) \times_{pk_A} h(m)) \times_{pk_A} z_B)$$

$$+_{\mathrm{pk}_A}\left(\left(\mathrm{Enc}_{\mathrm{pk}_A}\left(d_A z_A\right) \times_{\mathrm{pk}_A} r\right) \times_{\mathrm{pk}_A} d_B z_B\right) +_{\mathrm{pk}_A} \mathrm{Enc}_{\mathrm{pk}_A}\left(c \cdot n\right)\right)$$

$$=z_A \mathrm{h}\left(m\right) z_B + d_A z_A r d_B z_B + c \cdot n = k_A^{-1} k_B^{-1}\left(\mathrm{h}\left(m\right) + rd\right)$$

$$=k^{-1}\left(\mathrm{h}\left(m\right) + rd\right)$$

Thus, the modified two-party MacKenzie and Reiter signature is indeed a valid ECDSA signature under the private key $d = d_A d_B \in \mathbb{Z}_n^\times$ and the shared ephemeral secret $k = k_A k_B \in \mathbb{Z}_n^\times$.

Parameter Choices for Bitcoin. In Fig. 3, the parameters sizes required for the two-factor Bitcoin wallet are given. The parameter sizes were chosen based on the established recommendations for key sizes. ECDSA with the curve secp256k1, as used in the Bitcoin protocol, uses 256 bit keys. This corresponds to 128 bits of security. To achieve 128 bits of security with RSA, a 2048 bit modulus is required according to ANSSI (2014). Note that others are more pessimistic: NIST (Barker et al. 2012) recommends at least 3072 bit moduli. On the other hand, there is also an implicit lower bound for the moduli sizes by the protocol itself, since some of the above mentioned arguments only work when the used parameter sizes are large enough. We decided to use 2560 bit RSA moduli for the Paillier crypto system (the smallest multiple of 256 above 2304) which is a good compromise between the different recommendations and also offers acceptable performance on the smart phone.

	n	$\mathbf{N}_A$	$\mathbf{N}_B$
required by ANSSI (2014)	256	2048	2048
required for MacKenzie & Reiter (2004)	256	> 2304	> 1536

Fig. 3. Required parameter sizes for ECDSA as used in Bitcoin parameter sizes chosen for the prototype: 2560 bit for $\mathbf{N}_A$ and $\mathbf{N}_B$.

It should be stressed, that we are only talking about short term security. The Paillier crypto system is only used to encrypt private keys and ephemeral secrets for the ECDSA signature scheme, which uses 256 bit keys. The security can be easily increased later to the level provided by 256 bit ECDSA by increasing the RSA modulo size beyond 3072 bit and transferring all Bitcoins to new addresses with new ECDSA key pairs, which were not yet used in the two-party ECDSA signature protocol. Increasing the level of security any further is not possible as the used elliptic curve secp256k1 is fixed in the Bitcoin protocol.

3.2   Threshold Signature Support in Bitcoin

As part of the scripting functionality, Bitcoin supports t-out-of-u threshold signatures. Instead of only a single signature, a user must provide t signatures to spend a transaction output. Each of the t signatures must verify under one of the u public keys. Bitcoin's threshold signature support has been used by Bitpay Inc. (2014) to implement a web application that offers shared control of Bitcoin addresses.

In the standard single signature case, Bitcoins are sent to a Bitcoin address which is directly derived from a public key. The payee can spend the received Bitcoins by providing a transaction with a signature that verifies under the public key. In the threshold signature case, the payer must specify a list of u public keys instead of a single one. The payee can spend the received Bitcoins by providing a transaction with t signatures where each of the signatures verifies under one of the u public keys.

As a list of public keys is now used to identify the payee instead of a single one, no Bitcoin address can be derived any more. Thus, the payer must not only know a short Bitcoin address but the whole list of u public keys to send Bitcoins to the payee. This is very inconvenient for the payer. A further Bitcoin feature called Pay-to-script-hash (P2SH) solves this problem by adding another indirection: Instead of specifying the whole list of public keys, the payer only specifies the hash value of a Bitcoin script, which contains the list of public keys. The script is hashed with the same function that is used to hash the public keys. Therefore, it is possible to derive a Bitcoin address from the script. When spending the Bitcoins, the payee must not only provide the t signatures, but also a Bitcoin script that fits the hash value specified by the payer. The signatures in the spending transaction are then verified against the public keys in the script.

The combination of both features provides a threshold signature support that is as convenient for the payer as the single signature version of Bitcoin. Nevertheless, this variant of threshold signatures for Bitcoin has several disadvantages that are also mentioned by Goldfeder et al. (2014): First, it is visible in the public block chain that threshold signatures are used. Second, the spending transaction becomes much larger as it contains the t signatures and the script with the list of the u public keys. Signatures and public keys are responsible for most of the data in a transaction. Consequently, having several of them increases the size of the transaction significantly and can increase the transaction fees as these depend on the size of the transaction. Last but not least, there are Bitcoin clients around which do not work properly with the threshold-signature extension. The use of threshold signatures compatible with ECDSA as discussed in the previous section circumvents these kinds of problems.

4   Two-Factor Bitcoin Wallets

As mentioned in Lipovsky (2013), a first Bitcoin stealing online banking trojan has already been discovered in the wild. When Bitcoin is used by a wider public, attackers might come up with more sophisticated attacks inspired by the attacks on European online banking systems. Therefore, it makes sense to analyze such attacks and to consider the existing counter measures when designing a Bitcoin wallet.

In Sancho et al. (2014), a common attack on online banking is described. First, the user's computer is compromised by a trojan, which modifies the victim's DNS resolver and installs an additional attacker controlled certification authority on the system. Consequently, the trojan can now become a Man-in-the-middle between the user and the bank. After the user successfully logged in, the attacker displays a warning to trick the user into installing a malicious app on his phone, which finally allows the attacker to intercept incoming session tokens and transaction numbers. It is important to note that the phone is compromised by tricking the user into installing the spyware app and not by exploiting vulnerabilities in the phone's software.

To complicate such attacks as far as possible, state-of-the-art online banking systems offer both two-factor authentication and verification over a separate channel. In the commonly used SMS TAN system, the user creates a bank transaction on his computer and then needs to enter a TAN to confirm the transaction. The user receives this TAN via SMS from his bank. The SMS does not only contain the TAN but also the transaction details again and the user can verify them. A compromised computer cannot modify the information in the SMS which allows the user to detect any modifications done to the transaction by an online banking trojan.

With our Bitcoin wallet, we also provide both two-factor authentication and verification over a separate channel to Bitcoin users. We thus offer users a similar level of security for Bitcoin as they currently have in online banking.

As mentioned before, a Bitcoin address is directly derived from an ECDSA public key and anyone having access to the corresponding private key can spend all Bitcoins stored in this address. Therefore, the only secure way to implement two-factor authentication is to share the private key and to create transaction signatures with a two-party signature protocol. Any other solution would require to store the private key at one place. This place then becomes a single point of failure. Several Bitcoin service providers offer SMS TAN or one-time-password two-factor authentication, but in these cases the service provider stores the private key and becomes a single point of failure. Bitcoin service providers are hardly regulated at the moment and the when considering the bankruptcy of Mt. Gox, it is clear that leaving the security to the service provider is too risky.

For our Bitcoin wallet, we use the modified version of the two-party signature protocol by MacKenzie and Reiter (2004) as described in Sect. 3.1. This allows us to share the private key belonging to a Bitcoin address between two different devices and transactions can be signed without ever recombining the private key.

4.1   Description of the Prototype

Our two-factor wallet consists of a desktop wallet in form of a Java graphical user interface, and a phone counterpart that is realized as an Android application. Only the desktop application is a full Bitcoin wallet, which stores and processes all incoming transactions relevant to the user. Consequently, only the desktop wallet can display the transaction history and the current balance. The phone wallet is only required when signing a new transaction. It does not need to connect to the Bitcoin network at all, which makes the implementation much more lightweight. For further details on the design and the structure of the prototype as well as the full source code, see Mann (2014; 2015). Especially, we describe there the pairing protocol used by the prototype to initialize a wallet without using a trusted party.

In Fig. 4, the dataflow when signing a transaction is displayed. When a user wants to send Bitcoins to another person, he starts by creating a Bitcoin transaction with the desktop wallet ①. When the transaction is ready for signing, the desktop wallet displays a QR-Code which contains the IP address of the desktop wallet and the public key for a TLS connection. The desktop ad-hoc generates the key pair and a corresponding server certificate for the TLS connection. We did not use a pre-shared key, as this is not supported by most TLS stacks. Note that the TLS connection has only been added as an additional line of defense and for privacy reasons. The protocol by MacKenzie and Reiter is also secure when the phone and the desktop communicate in clear text.

The user now opens the smart phone wallet and scans the QR Code with the phone's camera ②. The smart phone wallet connects to the desktop wallet via the IP address specified in the QR code. The phone wallet establishes a TLS connection with the desktop wallet ③. During the connection setup, the phone wallet verifies that the public key from the desktop's certificate matches the public key in the QR code. This prevents any man-in-the-middle attacks.

Over the secured connection, the phone wallet requests the transaction to sign from the desktop wallet ④ and after receiving it from the desktop ⑤ displays it on the phone's screen ⑥. The user now has the possibility to review the transaction again to make sure that is has not been modified by a compromised desktop wallet.

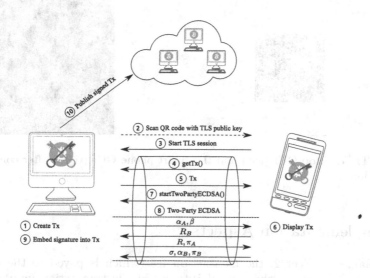

Fig. 4. The desktop and the smart phone GUI after completing a transaction.

When the user confirms the transaction on the phone, the phone wallet asks the desktop wallet to start the two-party signature protocol ⑦. The two wallets then exchange the messages required for the two-party signature protocol over the TLS connection ⑧.

At the end, the desktop wallet holds the correct ECDSA signature for the transaction. It can now embed the signature into the transaction ⑨. Afterwards, the desktop wallet publishes the now correctly signed transaction to the Bitcoin network ⑩. Figure 5 shows the desktop and the phone wallet after successfully completing the two-party ECDSA protocol in ⑧.

We currently assume that the desktop and the phone wallet are located in the same, most likely wireless, local area network. Over the IP connection, the two wallets then establish a TLS channel as described above. Afterwards, the wallets exchange messages with the help of the Apache Avro serialization protocol over the TLS channel. To further reduce the attack surface, the two wallets could be connected via Bluetooth by using the Bluetooth network encapsulation protocol (BNEP) which allows to establish IP connections over Bluetooth. This only allows connections between previously paired devices. Therefore, attacks would become much harder as an attacker could not directly connect to the desktop wallet any more.

Fig. 5. The desktop GUI (left) and the smart phone GUI (right) after completing a transaction.

5   Implementation Aspects

As explained in Sect. 2, the transaction fee (which is payed to the miner) is the difference between the sum of Bitcoins in the transaction inputs and the sum of Bitcoins in the transaction outputs. The inputs actually only reference the outputs of preceding transactions. Consequently, to correctly compute the fee, one needs access to the preceding transactions. In our case, the phone must compute the overpay, which is the fee, itself. Otherwise, the desktop can create a transaction which only contains benign outputs, but spends far too large inputs. The result would be a large fee for the miner and a financial damage for the user.

Implementing full Bitcoin network access is possible as wallet software exists for Android, but would make the phone wallet much more complex. Instead, in our solution, the phone does not only request the transaction to sign from the desktop, but also all transactions that are referenced in the inputs of the transaction to sign. The phone verifies that the hash values of the provided transactions fit the hash values in the transaction inputs. Now the phone can be sure that it has the correct transactions and can use the information from these to compute the overpay in the transaction to sign.

5.1 Runtime Analysis

In general, protocols that use zero-knowledge proofs tend to be quite slow. Therefore, we have benchmarked two different prototypes: one prototype using the two-party signature protocol from Sect. 3.1 and a second one using Bitcoin's built-in threshold signature support as described in Sect. 3.2. The benchmarks were performed on a core-i5-2520M notebook running Ubuntu 14.04 with Open-JDK, and a Nexus 4 smart phone running Android 4.4.4.

During the benchmark, the execution time of each prototype has been measured for transactions which have one, two or three inputs. The execution time measured is the time taken by a complete protocol run between the computer and the phone. The results in Fig. 6 show that the prototype using the two-party signature protocol achieves acceptable runtime, even though Bitcoin's built-in functionality is considerably faster. On the other hand, when using online banking with SMS TAN the user has to wait at least several seconds for the SMS. Our execution time is therefore well within the user's expectations.

	1 input	2 inputs	3 inputs
Section 3.1	3.8s	7.4s	11.1s
Section 3.2	0.22s	0.18s	0.25s

	1 input	2 inputs	3 inputs
Section 3.1	257 bytes	438 bytes	619 bytes
Section 3.2	370 bytes	696 bytes	1022 bytes

Fig. 6. Left: Protocol runtime. Right: Final size of signed transaction.

As mentioned in Sect. 3.2, Bitcoin's built-in threshold signature support has the disadvantage of increasing the transaction size significantly. We have verified this by recording the size of the resulting transaction during a benchmark. The result in Fig. 6 shows that the transaction size increases by at least 40 % when using Bitcoin's threshold signatures.

It should be noted that a transaction with only three inputs is already larger than 1000 bytes. Furthermore, larger transactions require a larger transaction fee and have a lower priority to be added to a new block. The priority can be increased by adding an additional fee. Consequently, the solution using Bitcoin's built-in threshold signature support comes with financial costs for the user. In contrast, our solution is transparent to the Bitcoin network and does not influence any fees.

6   Future Work

As our implementation is only a prototype, there is still some work to do. Besides a thorough code review, we identified the following aspects for future work:

Execution Time. Our prototype already achieves an acceptable execution time when signing a Bitcoin transaction, but there is still some place for improvements. Analyzing the prototype carefully, we found that most of the execution time is used by modular arithmetic on large integers. To reduce it, one could employ more efficient methods for integer multiplication, see for example Karatsuba and Ofman (1963) or Schönhage and Strassen (1971).

Random Numbers. Several versions of Android were shipped with a broken default pseudorandom generator that has not been correctly seeded on start up. This allowed an attacker to recover its state, see Kim et al. (2013), and lead to Android Bitcoin wallets which generated predictable private keys as described in Klyubin (2013). In a future version of our wallet this should be taken into account.

Integer Commitment. The zero knowledge proofs make use of the integer commitment scheme by Fujisaki and Okamoto (1997), which requires a RSA modulus to consist of two safe primes. We have implemented the prime sieve idea from Wiener (2003) and achieved a great speedup compared to our first trivial implementation, but on the phone the generation of a safe prime with 2048 bit still takes several minutes. In Damgard and Fujisaki (2002), a generalization of the commitment scheme is presented, where the requirement of safe primes has been relaxed to strong primes, which can be generated more easily, see Gathen and Shparlinski (2013). It would be nice to implement this.

7   Conclusion

We have shown that one can use the two-party ECDSA signature protocol adapted from MacKenzie and Reiter (2004) to realize two-factor authentication for a Bitcoin wallet. As far as we know, we were able to implement the first fully functional prototype compatible with the Bitcoin production network.

Acknowledgements. We would like to thank Michael Nüsken for various useful comments and Mike Hearn for greatly improving the performance of a first version of the prototype by suggesting a bouncy castle version with optimized arithmetic on the curve secp256k1. This work was funded by the B-IT foundation and the state of North Rhine-Westphalia.

References

Accredited Standards Committee X9: ANSI X9.62, public key cryptography for the financial services industry: the elliptic curve digital signature standard (ECDSA). Technical report, American National Standards Institute, American Bankers Association (2005)

ANSSI: Mécanismes cryptographiques - Règles et recommandations concernant le choix et le dimensionnement des mécanismes cryptographiques, Rev. 2.03. Agence nationale de la sécurité des systèmes dinformation (2014). http://www.ssi.gouv.fr/uploads/2015/01/RGS_v-2-0_B1.pdf

Back, A.: Hashcash - a denial of service counter-measure. Technical report (2002). http://www.hashcash.org/papers/hashcash.pdf

Barker, E., Barker, W., Burr, W., Polk, W., Smid, M.: NIST Special Publication 800-57 - Recommendation for Key Management - Part 1: General (Revision 3). National Institute of Standards and Technology (2012). http://csrc.nist.gov/publications/nistpubs/800-57/sp800-57_part1_rev3_general.pdf

Ben-Or, M., Goldwasser, S., Widgerson, A.: Completeness theorems for non-cryptographic fault-tolerant distributed computation. In: STOC 1988: Proceedings of the Twentieth Annual ACM Symposium on Theory of Computing, pp. 1–10. ACM, New York (1988). ISBN 0-89791-264-0, http://dx.doi.org/10.1145/62212.62213

Bitpay Inc.: Copay: A secure Bitcoin wallet for friends and companies (2014). www.copay.io

Blum, M., Feldman, P., Micali, S.: Proving security against chosen cyphertext attacks. In: Goldwasser, S. (ed.) CRYPTO 1988. LNCS, vol. 403, pp. 256–268. Springer, Heidelberg (1990)

Certicom Research: SEC 2: recommended elliptic curve domain parameters. Technical report, Certicom Corporation (2000)

Chaum, D., Fiat, A., Naor, M.: Untraceable electronic cash. In: Goldwasser, S. (ed.) CRYPTO 1988. LNCS, vol. 403, pp. 319–327. Springer, Heidelberg (1990). http://dx.doi.org/10.1007/0-387-34799-2_25

Damgård, I.B., Fujisaki, E.: A statistically-hiding integer commitment scheme based on groups with hidden order. In: Zheng, Y. (ed.) ASIACRYPT 2002. LNCS, vol. 2501, pp. 125–142. Springer, Heidelberg (2002). http://dx.doi.org/10.1007/3-540-36178-2_8

Fujisaki, E., Okamoto, T.: Statistical zero knowledge protocols to prove modular polynomial relations. In: Kaliski Jr, B.S. (ed.) CRYPTO 1997. LNCS, vol. 1294, pp. 16–30. Springer, Heidelberg (1997). http://dx.doi.org/10.1007/BFb0052225

von zur Gathen, J., Shparlinski, I.: Generating safe primes. J. Math. Cryptol. **7**(4), 333–365 (2013). ISSN 1862-2984 (Online) 1862-2976 (Print)), http://dx.doi.org/10.1515/jmc-2013-5011

Gennaro, R., Jarecki, S., Krawczyk, H., Rabin, T.: Robust threshold DSS signatures. In: Maurer, U.M. (ed.) EUROCRYPT 1996. LNCS, vol. 1070, pp. 354–371. Springer, Heidelberg (1996). http://dx.doi.org/10.1007/3-540-68339-9_31

Goldfeder, S., Bonneau, J., Felten, E.W., Kroll, J.A., Narayanan, A.: Securing Bitcoin wallets via threshold signatures (2014). http://www.cs.princeton.edu/~stevenag/bitcoin_threshold_signatures.pdf. Preprint

Goldfeder, S., Gennaro, R., Kalodner, H., Bonneau, J., Kroll, J.A., Felten, E.W., Narayanan, Λ.: Securing Bitcoin wallets via a new DSA/ECDSA threshold signature scheme (2015). http://www.cs.princeton.edu/~stevenag/threshold_sigs.pdf. Preprint

Harn, L.: Group-oriented (t, n) threshold digital signature scheme and digital multisignature. IEE Proc. Comput. Digital Techniques 141(5), 307–313 (1994). http://dx.doi.org/10.1049/ip-cdt:19941293

Hearn, M.: Update on mobile 2-factor wallets (2014). Bitcoin Mailing list at http://sourceforge.net, http://sourceforge.net/p/bitcoin/mailman/message/33017648/

Ibrahim, M.H., Ali, I.A., Ibrahim, I.I., El-sawi, A.H.: A robust threshold elliptic curve digital signature providing a new verifiable secret sharing scheme. In: MWCAS03, vol. 1, pp. 276–280. IEEE Computer Society, Cairo (2003). ISBN 0-7803-8294-3, ISSN 1548-3746, http://dx.doi.org/10.1109/MWSCAS.2003.1562272

Karatsuba, A., Ofman, Y.: Multiplication of multidigit numbers on automata. Sov. Phys. Doklady 7(7), 595–596 (1963). Translated from Doklady Akademii Nauk SSSR, vol. 145, No. 2, pp. 293–294, July 1962

Kim, S.H., Han, D., Lee, D.H.: Predictability of android openSSL's pseudo random number generator. In: Proceedings of the 2013 ACM SIGSAC Conference on Computer & Communications Security, pp. 659–668. ACM, New York (2013). ISBN: 978-1-4503-2477-9, http://dx.doi.org/10.1145/2508859.2516706

Klyubin, A.: Some SecureRandom Thoughts (2013). http://android-developers.blogspot.de/2013/08/some-securerandom-thoughts.html

Langford, S.K.: Threshold DSS signatures without a trusted party. In: Coppersmith, D. (ed.) CRYPTO 1995. LNCS, vol. 963, pp. 397–409. Springer, Heidelberg (1995). http://dx.doi.org/10.1007/3-540-44750-4_32

Lipovsky, R.: New Hesperbot targets: Germany and Australia (2013). http://www.welivesecurity.com/2013/12/10/new-hesperbot-targets-germany-and-australia/

MacKenzie, P., Reiter, M.K.: Two-party generation of DSA signatures. Int. J. Inf. Secur. 2(3–4), 218–239 (2004). http://dx.doi.org/10.1007/s10207-004-0041-0

Christopher Mann (2014). A prototypic implementation of a two-factor Bitcoin wallet: Source code. GitHub. https://github.com/ChristopherMann/2FactorWallet

Mann, C.: Two-factor authentication for the Bitcoin protocol. Master thesis, Mathematisch-Naturwissenschaftliche Fakultät der Rheinischen Friedrich-Wilhelms-Universität Bonn (2015). https://github.com/ChristopherMann/2FactorWallet/raw/master/BitcoinTwoFactorAuth.pdf

Nakamoto, S.: Bitcoin: A Peer-to-Peer Electronic Cash System. Cryptography Mailing list at metzdowd.com, 9 pages (2008). https://bitcoin.org/bitcoin.pdf

NIST: Federal Information Processing Standards Publication 180–4 - Secure Hash Standard. National Institute of Standards and Technology (2012). http://csrc.nist.gov/publications/fips/fips180-4/fips-180-4.pdf

NIST: FIPS 186-4: digital signature standard (DSS).Technical report, Information Technology Laboratory, NationalInstitute of Standards and Technology (2013)

Paillier, P.: Public-key cryptosystems based on composite degree residuosity classes. In: Stern, J. (ed.) EUROCRYPT 1999. LNCS, vol. 1592, pp. 223–238. Springer, Heidelberg (1999). http://dx.doi.org/10.1007/3-540-48910-X_16

Sancho, D., Hacquebord, F., Link, R.: Finding holes operation emmental. Technical report, Trend Micro Incorporated (2014). http://housecall.trendmicro.com/cloud-content/us/pdfs/security-intelligence/white-papers/wp-finding-holes-operation-emmental.pdf

Schönhage, A., Strassen, V.: Schnelle Multiplikation großer Zahlen. Computing 7, 281–292 (1971)

Shamir, A.: How to share a secret. Commun. ACM 22(11), 612–613 (1979)

Wang, C.-H., Hwang, T.: (t+1, n) threshold and generalized DSS signatures without a trusted party. In: Proceedings of the 13th Annual Computer Security Applications Conference (ACSAC 1997), pp. 221–226. IEEE (1997). ISBN: 0-8186-8274-4, http://dx.doi.org/10.1109/CSAC.1997.646193

Wiener, M.J.: Safe prime generation with a combined sieve. Cryptology ePrint Archive 2003/186 (2003). http://eprint.iacr.org/2003/186

Wuille, P.: Dealing with malleability. Technical report, Bitcoin Project (2014). https://github.com/bitcoin/bips/blob/master/bip-0062.mediawiki

Private Proximity Testing on Steroids:
An NTRU-based Protocol

Constantinos Patsakis[1]([✉]), Panayiotis Kotzanikolaou[1], and Mélanie Bouroche[2]

[1] Department of Informatics, University of Piraeus, Piraeus, Greece
{kpatsak,pkotzani}@unipi.gr
[2] Distributed Systems Group, School of Computer Science and Statistics,
Trinity College, Dublin, Ireland
melanie.bouroche@scss.tcd.ie

Abstract. Nowadays, most smartphones come pre-equipped with location (GPS) sensing capabilities, allowing developers to create a wide variety of location-aware applications and services. While location awareness provides novel features and functionality, it opens the door to many privacy nightmares. In many occasions, however, users do not need to share their actual location, but to determine whether they are in proximity to others, which is practically one bit of information. Private proximity protocols allow this functionality without any further information leakage. In this work we introduce a novel protocol which is far more efficient than the current state of the art and bases its security on lattice-based cryptography.

Keywords: Location privacy · Cryptographic protocols · Private equality testing · Location services

1 Introduction

Private equality testing is a very well-known problem in cryptography. In general, it involves two entities, Alice and Bob that want to reveal only a single bit of information: whether they have the same value or not. One solution to the problem is using Diffie-Hellman as proposed by Huberman, Franklin and Hogg [16]. A problem which is very close to private equality testing is *private proximity testing*. Again, we have Alice and Bob that want to reveal only a single bit of information, which now is whether they are in proximity or not. The twist here is that Alice and Bob may not have the same value (location), but they are "close". Notably, in this case we have an additional restriction: location is a low entropy source as the possible values are of the scale of 2^{32}, therefore one could easily brute force it. Narayanan et al. [23] with an ingenious encoding managed to reduce the problem of private proximity testing to private equality testing.

Lattices are being studied for decades and several problems in their theory, such as the shortest and closest lattice vector (SVP and CVP) have been proven to be extremely hard to solve. This has led to the development of several public key encryption schemes based on these problems. However, in the past few

© Springer International Publishing Switzerland 2015
S. Foresti (Ed.): STM 2015, LNCS 9331, pp. 172–184, 2015.
DOI: 10.1007/978-3-319-24858-5_11

years the interest in these schemes has greatly increased as they provide many interesting features in terms of security and applications. For instance, while the widely used public key algorithms such as RSA and ElGamal could be broken with quantum algorithms, lattice-based encryption algorithms seem to be immune to such attacks making them a good candidate for the post-quantum era of cryptography.

Moreover, lattices have very interesting algebraic features that can be exploited to develop fully homomorphic encryption (FHE) [8,20]. Nevertheless, most of the lattice-based encryption schemes provide only somewhat homomorphic encryption. While FHE supports arbitrary number of operations, somewhat homomorphic encryption support only a limited number of operations.

In this work we exploit the properties of NTRU, a well-known lattice-based algorithm to introduce a novel 2-party private protocol which is used for private equality matching and then tested for private proximity testing. The main advantages of the proposed protocol are the following:

1. It outperforms the current state of the art by a factor of around 20x, depending on the security level. The reason why the protocol is far more efficient than its peers is that it uses more lightweight computations, e.g. instead of performing calculations over large finite fields, the computations are performed over small polynomial rings.
2. In terms of security, NTRU is considered the best alternative for the post-quantum era [31] as its security does not seem to be significantly decreased by quantum algorithms [7].
3. Apart from private proximity testing, the protocol can be used for private equality testing.

The rest of this work is organized as follows. The next section provides an overview of the related work and in Sect. 3 we introduce the protocol and discuss its security. Section 4 presents some experimental results and a comparison of the proposed protocol with the one of Narayanan et al. Finally, the article concludes with some notes for future work.

2   Related Work

2.1   NTRU

NTRU is a secure and extremely fast public key encryption algorithm developed in the mid 90s, and its security is based on lattices. In fact it is so efficient that it can be even compared with symmetric ciphers [10]. The original algorithm, introduced by Hoffstein, Pipher and Silverman [13] works as follows. Firstly, we select some parameters N, p and q which are publicly known and determine the security of the NTRU instance. N is a prime, used to determine the degree of the polynomials that we are going to use, so every polynomial is reduced modulo $x^N - 1$. In NTRU we use two moduli numbers one "large" (q); currently q is set to 2048, and one "small" (p), which typically is equal to 3. Generally, all NTRU operations are $\mathbb{Z}_q[x]/(x^N - 1)$, while some of them are made in $\mathbb{Z}_p[x]/(x^N - 1)$.

To generate the secret/public key pair, we select two random polynomials f and g with small coefficients, that is -1, 0 and 1. However, for f we additionally require that it is invertible in $\mathbb{Z}_q[x]/(x^N - 1)$ and in $\mathbb{Z}_p[x]/(x^N - 1)$, so we denote these inverses f_q and f_p respectively. The public key h is defined as $h = pgf_q$, while f and f_p consist the private key. To encrypt a message m, we map m to a polynomial with small coefficients and pick a random "small" polynomial r, and send the message $c = hr + m \in \mathbb{Z}_q[x]/(x^N - 1)$. To decrypt c, the recipient multiplies it with f and rearranges the coefficients to reside within $[-q/2, q/2]$ and reduces it modulo p. Finally, we multiply the result with f_p.

To make NTRU work, the amount of 1s, 0s and -1s in f, g, m and r need to be specific to allow message decryption. A message can be decrypted only if the following inequality holds:

$$\|f * m + p * r * g\|_\infty \leq q$$

If this is not the case, then the result will be a random polynomial.

Due to a number of attacks, the original parameters of NTRU have been updated [11] and the algorithm and its parameters have been standardized in both IEEE 1363.1 and X9.98. A comparison of NTRU parameters with RSA and elliptic curves is illustrated in Table 1. While there are many variants of the algorithm such as [2,6,24], of specific interest are the recent variant of Stehlé and Steinfeld [39] which makes it even more secure[1], using Regev's learning with error approach [35], and the variant of Lopez et al. [20] which builds on top of NTRU to create a FHE scheme.

Table 1. Parameters for the most popular security levels (in bits). For RSA and elliptic curves, the numbers denote the length (in bits) of the underlying modulo field according to NIST (https://www.nsa.gov/business/programs/elliptic_curve.shtml). For NTRU, the numbers are precise and recommended by SecurityInnovation [12].

Security level	RSA	Elliptic curves	NTRU			
			p	q	n	Public key (bits)
128	3072	256	3	2048	439	4829
192	7680	384	3	2048	593	6523
256	15360	521	3	2048	743	8173

2.2 Private Proximity Testing

In private proximity testing, Alice and Bob want to check whether they are in proximity, without disclosing their whereabouts. These protocols are gaining

---

[1] In this variant, NTRU becomes CPA-secure in the standard model, under the assumed quantum hardness of standard worst-case problems over ideal lattices.

more importance due to the wide adoption of location awareness from Online Social Networks which notify users of friends that are close. The feeling of closeness and the hope that one could find the other half just around the corner is also exploited by mobile dating applications. However, as it has been shown, this exposes users to many threats [29,30,34].

The protocols in the literature can be categorized in three overlapping categories. The first categorization is made according to who makes the testing. For instance, if Alice and Bob outsource the testing to Trudy, a trusted third party, then we have the so called *asynchronous* protocols. Note that in these protocols while Alice and Bob trust Trudy in that she will make the proper computations and that she will not collude with either, they are not willing to provide her with their locations. On the contrary, Alice and Bob will only provide Trudy with an encrypted version of their locations. However, if Alice and Bob want to perform the tests on their own without another entity, we have the so-called *synchronous*. Clearly, in the first case only the initiator needs to be online, while in the latter both need to be online. We consider privacy preserving data dissemination techniques beyond the scope of this work, nevertheless, the interested reader may refer to [40] for an overview of such methods related to location privacy.

Depending on the nature of the exchanged data, we can have further categorization. Most protocols will use the GPS location of the users, or more precisely their position on a grid, allowing users to report fake locations. To counter this issue, Zheng et al. [41] as well as Lin et al. [19] have recently provided efficient solutions. Both these protocols gather "environmental" data such as GPS and WiFi signals which are known only to users who are in a specific area at a given time to derive some "fingerprints". These fingerprints are then sent to the other user to perform a private check to determine whether they are within proximity.

Finally, one could categorize the private proximity protocols depending on the underlying cryptographic primitive. For instance, there are protocols which are based on symmetric algorithms, grid transformation keys, while others are based on homomorphic encryption or specific hard mathematical problems.

An overview of the categorization of current state of the art algorithms in private proximity testing is illustrated in Fig. 1.

2.3   The Protocol of Narayanan et al.

Narayanan et al. in [23] make a significant contribution in private proximity testing. As already discussed, they introduced a new grid system with three overlapping grids which reduces the problem of private proximity testing to private equality testing. From the protocols that they introduced in their work, of specific interest is the synchronous protocol which is based on an elliptic curve variant of ElGamal.

Let g a generator of the group G, x Alice's private key and let $h = g^x$. For efficiency, we may use as G the additive group of an elliptic curve over a finite field. Moreover, we assume that Alice is located at ℓ_A, Bob at ℓ_B. Alice's public key is (E, g, h); where E denotes the elliptic curve she uses, and x is her private key. The steps of the protocol are the following:

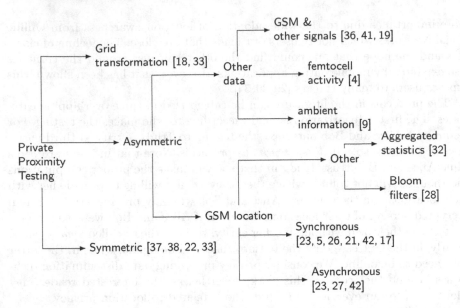

Fig. 1. Categorization of current state of the art protocols in private proximity testing.

Firstly, Alice encrypts ℓ_A with her public key and sends Bob $C_A = (g^r, h^{r+\ell_A})$, where r is a random integer. On receiving $C_A = (c_1, c_2)$, Bob picks two random integers s, t and sends Alice: $C_B = (c_1^s g^t, c_2^s h^{(t-s\ell_B)})$. Finally, when Alice receives: $C_B = (u_1, u_2)$, she computes $R = u_2 u_1^{-x}$. If $R = 1$, then she deduces that $\ell_A = \ell_B$, otherwise R will be a random point of E.

3   The Proposed Protocol

3.1   Threat Model

Like most privacy-preserving techniques, we assume that users have a *honest but curious* (HBC) behavior. According to the HBC model, also known as *semi-honest*, users will follow the rules of the protocol (honesty), they will not act maliciously, nevertheless, they will try to extract as much information as possible from the other users. This threat model can be considered realistic as in most social LBS services, the users have some form of acquaintance (e.g. friends, colleagues) or want to have (case of mobile dating applications). Thus, users have no incentive to behave maliciously.

We assume probabilistic polynomial time (PPT) passive adversaries that are polynomially bounded and do not have the ability to break the underlying cryptographic primitives. Moreover, we assume that an adversary may monitor all the exchanged traffic of the users. Nevertheless, we do not consider active attacks; the exchanged messages in a execution of the protocol are authenticated and integrity protected, therefore an adversary cannot modify or inject fake messages making them seem legitimate.

3.2   Main Actors and Desiderata

In what follows, we use the grids of Narayanan et al. [23], to reduce private proximity testing to private equality testing. In this regard, we assume that we have divided the earth with a grid, where each square is marked as $\mathcal{L}_i$. Therefore, the scope of the protocol will be to determine whether two users, Alice and Bob are in the same square. The set of all possible squares is denoted as $\mathcal{L}$, so $\mathcal{L} = \{\mathcal{L}_1, \mathcal{L}_2, \ldots, \mathcal{L}_k\}$ where $|\mathcal{L}| = \mathcal{O}(2^{32})$.

Moreover, we assume that there is a bijection $\chi : \mathcal{L} \to L(x)$, where $L(x)$ is a set of polynomials in $\mathbb{Z}_q/(x^N - 1)$. The role of χ is to encode a square $\mathcal{L}_i$ to a polynomial ℓ_i in order to use it in the NTRU-based protocol. Therefore, for simplicity from now on when we refer to a location of an entity, we will represent it as ℓ_i. Clearly, this encoding is known to everyone.

Finally, we assume that each user constructs a NTRU key pair. Note that users do not need to share their public keys with others, but only n, p, q and the "noise" parameters. For the sake of simplicity, we assume that users have already agreed on the above, e.g. they use NTRU_EES439EP1 for 128 bits of security, and we call them *public parameters*. Clearly, this feature drastically decreases the communication cost as users do not need to store any additional information about their "friends". As it will become apparent, the knowledge of the actual public key does not add any additional value, since the operations that have to be made by the recipient are depend solely on the n, p, q and the "noise" parameters. Moreover, since NTRU is considered secure, the publication of the public key h does not jeopardize the security of the scheme.

3.3   The Protocol

Let Alice be located in ℓ_A and Bob in ℓ_B. Even if Bob does not know Alice's public key, he may perform some operations on Alice's encrypted location using the public parameters, to allow Alice determine whether he is within her proximity, that is $\ell_A = \ell_B$.

Initially, Alice sends the message $c_A = rh + \ell_A$ to Bob, where r is a random invertible polynomial in $\mathbb{Z}_q[x]/(x^N - 1)$. Then Bob picks a random polynomial ρ with small coefficients and sends Alice $c_B = \rho(c_A - \ell_B)$. Alice receives it and checks whether $r^{-1}c_B$ decrypts to zero.

3.4   Protocol Correctness

Let us assume that $l_A = l_B$. Then, in step 2, Bob computes:

$$c_B \equiv \rho(c_A - \ell_B) \equiv rh\rho$$

that he will sent to Alice. Thus, when Alice in step 3 decrypts:

$$r^{-1}c_B + m = r^{-1}rh\rho + m \equiv h\rho + m$$

the result will be m, otherwise it will be a random polynomial.

3.5   Security Analysis

We consider both external and internal adversaries. An external adversary represents all entities other than the users running the protocol, while an internal adversary represents an honest-but-curious user running the protocol. In any case, the goal of the adversary is on input the messages exchanged during a protocol run and (in case of internal adversaries the private keys of the adversary), to learn the private input of the honest user(s) running the protocol. In the following analysis we will first examine internal adversaries (either a curious Bob against Alice or a curious Alice against Bob). Obviously, the security arguments also hold for external adversaries.

Definition 1. *A function $\nu(\cdot)$ is negligible in x, or just negligible, if for every positive polynomial $p(\cdot)$ and any sufficiently large x it holds that:*

$$\nu(x) \leq \frac{1}{p(x)}$$

Private Input Indistinguishability. We formalize private input indistinguishability by a security experiment $DistExp$ in which the adversary $\mathcal{A}$ has access to an oracle $\mathcal{O}$ that on input: the low-entropy set of all possible private input $\mathcal{L}$, the public parameters of two users Alice and Bob n_A, n_B and a protocol run $[c_A, c_B, y]$, is used to extract information about the private input of Alice and/or Bob. In case on an internal adversary, then the oracle is also given the private keys $\mathcal{K}$ of the compromised user. If $\mathcal{O}^{dist}$ is able to distinguish the private input of a target user (l_A and/or l_B) from the set $\mathcal{L}$ using the given input (where $|\mathcal{L}|$ is the security parameter), then the output of the experiment is 1, else the output is 0.

Definition 2. [Private input indistinguishability]. *A protocol provides private input indistinguishability if $\forall$ PPT adversary $\mathcal{A}$, $\exists$ a negligible function ν such that:*

$$Advantage(\mathcal{A}) = \mid Pr[DistExp(|\mathcal{L}|) = 1] - \frac{1}{|\mathcal{L}|} \mid = \nu(|\mathcal{L}|)$$

Theorem 1. *The proposed PET protocol provides private input indistinguishability for Alice against a curious Bob, provided that the NTRU encryption algorithm is secure.*

Proof. Since Bob only learns the public key h of Alice and c_A which is the NTRU encryption of l_A with the key h, clearly Bob cannot learn the private input of Alice assuming that the NTRU cryptosystem is secure.   □

Theorem 2. *The proposed PET protocol provides private input indistinguishability for Bob against a curious Alice, provided that the NTRU encryption algorithm is secure.*

Proof. Let us assume that Alice wants to find Bob's location when $\ell_A \neq \ell_B$. Alice has c_A, c_B, as well as to her private keying material f and f_p and to the polynomial r. Since Bob is assumed honest, the structure of c_B will be of the form $c_B = \rho(rh + \ell_A - \ell_B)$.

Since the value ρ is only known to Bob, the only possible way for Alice to reveal ℓ_B is through brute forcing. Alice may attempt to calculate all $\delta_i = \ell_A - \ell_i$, for each possible $\ell_i \in \mathcal{L}$ (recall that $\mathcal{L}$ is a low entropy set). Then Alice would decrypt c_B in order to find which δ_i corresponds to the actual decrypted value and thus learn ℓ_i.

While the values $rh + \delta_i$ are known to Alice, trying to solve these equations in $\mathbb{Z}_q[x]/(x^N - 1)$ would not give her an actual advantage. We consider two cases: In the first case, if $rh + \delta_i$ in not an invertible polynomial, then Alice will not be able to recover ρ from c_B and thus she will not be able to test these values, without the knowledge of ρ.

In the second case, if $rh + \delta_i$ is invertible, then for each such ℓ_i, Alice would get $|K|$ additional possible values for ρ, without being able to distinguish the correct one. Therefore, Alice cannot distinguish the private input of Bob in case of private input inequality.

We should note that in either case; $rh + \delta_i$ being or not being invertible, Alice would have to brute force the polynomial which would requires $\mathcal{O}(c^N)$ attempts. For more details on the latter, the interested reader may refer to [12].   □

Note that while the original NTRU is not IND-CPA secure, like RSA without padding, the variant of Stehlé and Steinfeld [39] provides this feature and the adaption of the latter scheme is straightforward. Moreover, the paddings proposed in [14,15,25] make NTRU IND-CCA2-secure, with the latter making it IND-CCA2-secure in the random oracle model.

Theorem 3. *The proposed PET protocol provides private input indistinguishability against external adversaries, under the NTRU assumption.*

Proof. The proof is an immediate result of the previous proofs. Notice that external adversaries have no access to any keying material (e.g. of a curious party).   □

4   Comparison/Experimental Results

We compare the NTRU with the Narayanan et al. protocol in a machine with an Intel Core i3-2100 CPU at 3.1 GHz with 6 GB of RAM, running on Ubuntu 15.04 64 bit. The implementation in both cases is made in Sage[2]. For NTRU we have used the latest parameters proposed by SecurityInnovation [12]. The parameters are illustrated in Table 2. According to their recommendations, to generate f, we compute a polynomial $P(x)$ which is of the form $A_1(x)A_2(x) + A_3(x)$, where polynomial $A_i, i \in \{1, 2, 3\}$ have D_i coefficients set to 1 and D_i coefficients set

---

[2] sagemath.org.

to -1. Similarly, to construct polynomial g, we select a polynomial having D_g coefficients set to 1 and $D_g - 1$ coefficients set to -1. Finally, each message, when converted to polynomial must have at most D_m coefficients set to 1 and $D_m - 1$ coefficients set to -1. The code to perform the experiments is publicly available on Github[3].

Table 2. NTRU parameters for different security levels

Level (bits)	p	q	n	D_1	D_2	D_3	D_g	D_m
128	3	2048	439	9	8	5	146	112
192	3	2048	593	10	10	8	197	158
256	3	2048	743	11	11	15	247	204

The protocol of Narayanan et al. has been implemented over elliptic curves, as the original. To provide 128-bits of security, we used Curve25519 [3] well-known for its security and performance. Furthermore, to provide 192 and 256 bits security we used the curves M-383 and M-511 respectively, both described in [1]. Note that all these curves are renowned for their security and performance, so they were selected instead of random elliptic curves. The experiments report the averages of 1,000 executions of the protocol in a single thread.

Table 3 clearly illustrates that the proposed protocol is far more efficient than the protocol of Narayanan et al. More precisely, the protocol is approximately 20 times faster. The result can be considered expected, as the protocol of Narayanan et al. has to perform more and heavier computations. In Narayanan et al. Alice (the initiator of the protocol) has to perform 3 exponentiations and Bob 4 exponentiations. On the contrary, in the proposed protocol Alice has to perform 1 encryption and 1 decryption with NTRU, while Bob has to perform one polynomial addition and one polynomial multiplication. Therefore, in all security levels Bob's cost is below 2 ms. Further comparison to other schemes is illustrated in Table 5.

It has to be noted that implementing the protocols in another language like C would make the implementations far more efficient, mostly in favor of NTRU as its structure is rather lightweight and can receive many improvements, as highlighted in other works e.g. [10]. Nevertheless, the result can be considered in accordance with the reported results of other implementations e.g. NTRU project[4].

While Sage is based on Python, and there is already a Python implementation of Curve25519 available[5], the Sage implementation was far more efficient so it was used it for the experiments.

---

[3] https://github.com/kpatsakis/NTRU_Private_Proximity_Testing.
[4] http://tbuktu.github.io/ntru/.
[5] http://ed25519.cr.yp.to/software.html.

Table 3. Comparison of the Narayanan et al. protocol with the proposed. Time in ms and Security in bits. Ratio denotes the ratio of the total time of the Narayanan et al. protocol over the total time of the proposed protocol.

	Narayanan et al.			Proposed			Ratio
Security	Alice	Bob	Total	Alice	Bob	Total	
128	80.718	99.194	179.912	7.362	1.051	8.413	21.385
192	102.267	133.873	236.140	10.527	1.518	12.045	19.605
256	155.329	193.887	349.216	12.733	1.745	14.478	24.120

Table 4. Approximate communication cost in bytes. Security in bits.

Security	Narayanan et al.	Proposed
128	128	1208
192	192	1630
256	256	2044

Table 5. Comparison of our protocol with its peers.

Protocol	Efficiency
Pierre [42]	6exp+3 DL Bob: 6exp
NFP [5]	2 exp/user
EG-PET [23]	Alice: 3exp Bob: 4exp
DH-PET [21]	2 exp/user
Proposed	Alice: 3 mult
	Bob: 1 mult. 1 add

Table 5 provides an overview of the comparison of the proposed protocol with its peers, highlighting the "heavy" computations that each party needs to perform.

The major disadvantage of the protocol is that it has a significant bandwidth overhead, see Table 4. Since NTRU has far bigger keys and messages compared to elliptic curves, the exchanged messages are far bigger than the ones in Narayanan et al. so performance boost is balanced by the communication cost.

5   Conclusions

The continuous development of location-aware applications and services might provide users novel features and functionality, nevertheless, it implies serious privacy exposure. This exposure can be significantly reduced in many occasions, since users do not need to share their actual location, but their proximity to other entities, which is a single bit of information. Current state of the art contains several private proximity protocols to enable this functionality with the least, if any, user exposure as they diminish information leakage.

In this work we introduced a novel protocol which is far more efficient than its peers basing its security on lattice-based cryptography, and more precisely the well-known NTRU algorithm. To the best of our knowledge, this is the first private proximity testing protocol, and probably the first for private equality testing, using lattice-based cryptography. In the future, we plan to make a more optimized implementation, using a low level programming language to further examine the efficiency of the protocol. Furthermore, we plan to study the cost of converting the protocol according to the variant of Stehlé and Steinfeld [39] to provide CPA-security, as theoretically, the changes in the protocol can be easily made.

Acknowledgments. This work was supported by the European Commission under the Horizon 2020 Programme (H2020), as part of the *OPERANDO* and *TACTICS* projects (Grant Agreements no. 653704 and no. 285533 respectively) and is based upon work from COST Action *CRYPTACUS*, supported by COST (European Cooperation in Science and Technology).

The publication of this paper has been partly supported by the University of Piraeus Research Center.

References

1. Aranha, D.F., Barreto, P.S.L.M., Pereira, G.C.C.F., Ricardini, J.E.: A note on high-security general-purpose elliptic curves. Cryptology ePrint Archive, Report 2013/647 (2013). http://eprint.iacr.org/
2. Banks, W.D., Shparlinski, I.E.: A variant of NTRU with non-invertible polynomials. In: Menezes, A., Sarkar, P. (eds.) INDOCRYPT 2002. LNCS, vol. 2551, pp. 62–70. Springer, Heidelberg (2002)
3. Bernstein, D.J.: Curve25519: new Diffie-Hellman speed records. In: Yung, M., Dodis, Y., Kiayias, A., Malkin, T. (eds.) PKC 2006. LNCS, vol. 3958, pp. 207–228. Springer, Heidelberg (2006)
4. Brassil, J., Netravali, R., Haber, S., Manadhata, P., Rao, P.: Authenticating a mobile device's location using voice signatures. In: 2012 IEEE 8th International Conference on Wireless and Mobile Computing, Networking and Communications (WiMob), pp. 458–465. IEEE (2012)
5. Chatterjee, S., Karabina, K., Menezes, A.: A new protocol for the nearby friend problem. In: Parker, M.G. (ed.) Cryptography and Coding 2009. LNCS, vol. 5921, pp. 236–251. Springer, Heidelberg (2009)
6. Coglianese, M., Goi, B.-M.: MaTRU: a new NTRU-based cryptosystem. In: Maitra, S., Veni Madhavan, C.E., Venkatesan, R. (eds.) INDOCRYPT 2005. LNCS, vol. 3797, pp. 232–243. Springer, Heidelberg (2005)
7. Fluhrer, S.: Quantum cryptanalysis of ntru. Cryptology ePrint Archive, Report 2015/676 (2015). http://eprint.iacr.org/
8. Gentry, C.: A fully homomorphic encryption scheme. Ph.D. thesis, Stanford University (2009)

9. Halevi, T., Ma, D., Saxena, N., Xiang, T.: Secure proximity detection for NFC devices based on ambient sensor data. In: Foresti, S., Yung, M., Martinelli, F. (eds.) ESORICS 2012. LNCS, vol. 7459, pp. 379–396. Springer, Heidelberg (2012)
10. Hermans, J., Vercauteren, F., Preneel, B.: Speed records for NTRU. In: Pieprzyk, J. (ed.) CT-RSA 2010. LNCS, vol. 5985, pp. 73–88. Springer, Heidelberg (2010)
11. Hirschhorn, P.S., Hoffstein, J., Howgrave-Graham, N., Whyte, W.: Choosing NTRU encrypt parameters in light of combined lattice reduction and MITM approaches. In: Abdalla, M., Pointcheval, D., Fouque, P.-A., Vergnaud, D. (eds.) ACNS 2009. LNCS, vol. 5536, pp. 437–455. Springer, Heidelberg (2009)
12. Hoffstein, J., Pipher, J., Schanck, J.M., Silverman, J.H., Whyte, W., Zhang, Z.: Choosing parameters for ntruencrypt. Cryptology ePrint Archive, Report 2015/708 (2015). http://eprint.iacr.org/
13. Hoffstein, J., Pipher, J., Silverman, J.H.: NTRU: a ring-based public key cryptosystem. In: Buhler, J.P. (ed.) ANTS 1998. LNCS, vol. 1423, pp. 267–288. Springer, Heidelberg (1998)
14. Hojfstein, J., Silverman, J.: Protecting NTRU against chosen ciphertext and reaction attacks. Technical Report 16 (2000)
15. Hojfstein, J., Silverman, J.: Optimizations for ntru. In: Public-key cryptography and computational number theory. In: Proceedings of the International Conference organized by the Stefan Banach International Mathematical Center Warsaw, Poland, September 11–15, 2000, p. 77. Walter de Gruyter (2001)
16. Huberman, B.A., Franklin, M., Hogg, T.: Enhancing privacy and trust in electronic communities. In: Proceedings of the 1st ACM conference on Electronic commerce, pp. 78–86. ACM (1999)
17. Kotzanikolaou, P., Patsakis, C., Magkos, E., Korakakis, M.: Lightweight private proximity testing for geospatial social networks. Comput. Commun. (2015)
18. Li, M., Zhu, H., Gao, Z., Chen, S., Ren, K., Yu, L., Hu, S.: All your location are belong to us: breaking mobile social networks for automated user location tracking (2013, arXiv preprint). arXiv:1310.2547
19. Lin, Z., Foo Kune, D., Hopper, N.: Efficient private proximity testing with GSM location sketches. In: Keromytis, A.D. (ed.) FC 2012. LNCS, vol. 7397, pp. 73–88. Springer, Heidelberg (2012)
20. López-Alt, A., Tromer, E., Vaikuntanathan, V.: On-the-fly multiparty computation on the cloud via multikey fully homomorphic encryption. In: Proceedings of the forty-fourth annual ACM symposium on Theory of computing, pp. 1219–1234. ACM (2012)
21. Magkos, E., Kotzanikolaou, P., Magioladitis, M., Sioutas, S., Verykios, V.S.: Towards secure and practical location privacy through private equality testing. In: Domingo-Ferrer, J. (ed.) PSD 2014. LNCS, vol. 8744, pp. 312–325. Springer, Heidelberg (2014)
22. Mascetti, S., Freni, D., Bettini, C., Wang, X.S., Jajodia, S.: Privacy in geo-social networks: proximity notification with untrusted service providers and curious buddies. VLDB J. 20(4), 541–566 (2011)
23. Narayanan, A., Thiagarajan, N., Lakhani, M., Hamburg, M., Boneh, D.: Location privacy via private proximity testing. In: NDSS. The Internet Society (2011). http://www.isoc.org/isoc/conferences/ndss/11/
24. Nevins, M., Karimianpour, C., Miri, A.: NTRU over rings beyond $\mathbb{Z}$. Des. Codes Cryptogr. 56(1), 65–78 (2010)
25. Nguyên, P.Q., Pointcheval, D.: Analysis and improvements of NTRU encryption paddings. In: Yung, M. (ed.) CRYPTO 2002. LNCS, vol. 2442, p. 210. Springer, Heidelberg (2002)

26. Nielsen, J.D., Pagter, J.I., Stausholm, M.B.: Location privacy via actively secure private proximity testing. In: 2012 IEEE International Conference on Pervasive Computing and Communications Workshops (PERCOM Workshops), pp. 381–386. IEEE (2012)
27. Novak, E., Li, Q.: Near-pri: private, proximity based location sharing. In: 2014 Proceedings IEEE INFOCOM, pp. 37–45. IEEE (2014)
28. Palmieri, P., Calderoni, L., Maio, D.: Spatial bloom filters: enabling privacy in location-aware applications. In: Lin, D., Yung, M., Zhou, J. (eds.) Inscrypt 2014. LNCS, vol. 8957, pp. 16–36. Springer, Heidelberg (2015)
29. Patsakis, C., Zigomitros, A., Papageorgiou, A., Solanas, A.: Privacy and security for multimedia content shared on OSNs: issues and countermeasures. Comput. J. 58(4), 518–535 (2014). doi:10.1093/comjnl/bxu066
30. Patsakis, C., Zigomitros, A., Solanas, A.: Analysis of privacy and security exposure in mobile dating applications. In: Boumerdassi, S., Bouzefrane, S., Renault, E. (eds.) MSPN 2015. Springer, Heidelberg (2015)
31. Perlner, R.A., Cooper, D.A.: Quantum resistant public key cryptography: a survey. In: Proceedings of the 8th Symposium on Identity and Trust on the Internet, pp. 85–93. ACM (2009)
32. Popa, R.A., Blumberg, A.J., Balakrishnan, H., Li, F.H.: Privacy and accountability for location-based aggregate statistics. In: Proceedings of the 18th ACM conference on Computer and communications security, pp. 653–666. ACM (2011)
33. Puttaswamy, K.P., Wang, S., Steinbauer, T., Agrawal, D., El Abbadi, A., Kruegel, C., Zhao, B.Y.: Preserving location privacy in geosocial applications. IEEE Trans. Mob. Comput. 13(1), 159–173 (2014)
34. Qin, G., Patsakis, C., Bouroche, M.: Playing hide and seek with mobile dating applications. In: Cuppens-Boulahia, N., Cuppens, F., Jajodia, S., Abou El Kalam, A., Sans, T. (eds.) SEC 2014. IFIP AICT, vol. 428, pp. 185–196. Springer, Heidelberg (2014)
35. Regev, O.: On lattices, learning with errors, random linear codes, and cryptography. J. ACM (JACM) 56(6), 34 (2009)
36. Saldamli, G., Chow, R., Jin, H., Knijnenburg, B.: Private proximity testing with an untrusted server. In: Proceedings of the sixth ACM conference on Security and privacy in wireless and mobile networks, pp. 113–118. ACM (2013)
37. Šikšnys, L., Thomsen, J.R., Šaltenis, S., Yiu, M.L., Andersen, O.: A location privacy aware friend locator. In: Mamoulis, N., Seidl, T., Pedersen, T.B., Torp, K., Assent, I. (eds.) SSTD 2009. LNCS, vol. 5644, pp. 405–410. Springer, Heidelberg (2009)
38. Siksnys, L., Thomsen, J.R., Saltenis, S., Yiu, M.L.: Private and flexible proximity detection in mobile social networks. In: 2010 Eleventh International Conference on Mobile Data Management (MDM), pp. 75–84. IEEE (2010)
39. Stehlé, D., Steinfeld, R.: Making NTRU as secure as worst-case problems over ideal lattices. In: Paterson, K.G. (ed.) EUROCRYPT 2011. LNCS, vol. 6632, pp. 27–47. Springer, Heidelberg (2011)
40. Terrovitis, M.: Privacy preservation in the dissemination of location data. ACM SIGKDD Explor. Newsl. 13(1), 6–18 (2011)
41. Zheng, Y., Li, M., Lou, W., Hou, Y.T.: SHARP: private proximity test and secure handshake with cheat-proof location tags. In: Foresti, S., Yung, M., Martinelli, F. (eds.) ESORICS 2012. LNCS, vol. 7459, pp. 361–378. Springer, Heidelberg (2012)
42. Zhong, G., Goldberg, I., Hengartner, U.: Louis, Lester and Pierre: three protocols for location privacy. In: Borisov, N., Golle, P. (eds.) PET 2007. LNCS, vol. 4776, pp. 62–76. Springer, Heidelberg (2007)

Selecting a New Key Derivation Function for Disk Encryption

Milan Brož[✉] and Vashek Matyáš

Faculty of Informatics, Masaryk University, Brno, Czech Republic
{xbroz,matyas}@fi.muni.cz

Abstract. Many full disk encryption applications rely on a strong password-based key derivation function to process a passphrase. This article defines requirements for key derivation functions and analyzes recently presented password hashing functions (second round finalists of the Password Hashing Competition) for their suitability for disk encryption.

Keywords: Disk encryption · Key derivation · Password hashing

1 Introduction

Passwords are still a very common method to secure systems. Unfortunately, they usually contain little entropy, exhibit poor randomness characteristics and cannot be directly used as encryption keys. Password-based key derivation functions (PBKDF) are a common solution to this problem. One specific use of PBKDF is in full disk encryption (FDE) applications, where it is used to derive a decryption key from a user-provided passphrase.

As the only standardized form of PBKDF, *PBKDF2* [14] is designed to be a strictly sequential function which allows to set a number of iterations. The memory footprint of PBKDF2 is constant and small, which allows very efficient brute-force attacks to be performed on GPU or ASIC systems [8]. The only sufficiently scrutinized alternative is *scrypt* [15].

The problem with lack of algorithms that can effectively defeat massively parallel attacks led to the *Password Hashing Competition* (PHC) initiative [1]. The PHC is run by an independent panel of experts and the main goal is to identify and analyze new password hashing schemes. While PBKDF is not the main focus of the competition, some of the selected candidate functions are usable also as a PBKDF and could replace the frequently-used PBKDF2 in the future.

In this paper we evaluate suitability of PHC second round finalists for use in a KDF application. The main contributions are:

- a definition of requirements of KDF function for the FDE environment,
- description of common building blocks in submitted algorithms,
- measurements based on a real FDE use case,
- fixes of several implementation issues discovered by our tests [6].

© Springer International Publishing Switzerland 2015
S. Foresti (Ed.): STM 2015, LNCS 9331, pp. 185–199, 2015.
DOI: 10.1007/978-3-319-24858-5_12

Section 2.2 defines requirements for a KDF for the FDE environment. Section 3 contains an overview of common building blocks in PHC functions. The following Sect. 4 shortly describes a subset of newly submitted PHC algorithms that were selected for testing performed in Sect. 5 (as an extension to the PHC survey [13] and analyses [5,9]).

2   Requirements for a Key Derivation Function

2.1   Environment for Disk Encryption

FDE environment is not always friendly to all security features of a password hashing function.

Firstly, a disk encrypted on one machine must be often read (decrypted) on another machine where the processing power can be significantly different (not only in the sense of speed and number of CPU cores but also it can be a completely different computer platform, where some operations are slower or where an important acceleration feature is missing). For users, it is probably not a big problem if unlocking of a disk takes long time (within reasonable limits), but it can be a real usability problem if unlocking is not possible at all.

Secondly, a decryption environment can be very limited (an example is unlocking of a system disk in a bootloader, where we cannot use process or thread management or where strict memory limits are imposed).

While we are focusing on desktop or server platforms, requirements and even evaluation of algorithms can be directly applied to smart-phones or tablet computers. These FDE-capable devices have several CPU cores and a decent amount of memory. Requirements are also applicable to key management in the area of non-volatile RAM (persistent memory) encryption.

2.2   Requirements for a Disk Encryption Application

If a password-based key derivation function is used in a FDE environment, we propose the following requirements:

1. A key derivation function is a deterministic algorithm defined by the choice of a pseudo-random function [21]. It also must be a one-way, collision-resistant function.
2. It must be able to use resources in such a way that it allows users to unlock a device in an acceptable time and using acceptable resources. Resources can be the time of calculation, the level of parallelism or the amount of memory required.

    Overly long unlocking time can lead to a risk that users switch the encryption off to speed up their system start. The effort to harden security then would be counterproductive.
3. Possible configurations should cover high variety of systems from embedded systems to high-end storage servers.

4. The level of parallelism must not block the use of this function on systems where parallel processing is not available (there will be a time penalty but the function should be still usable).

   An example for requirements 3 and 4 is encryption of portable disk drives. Such a disk should be readable on the majority of systems. Some systems could be embedded or old devices without parallel processing capability. Unlocking time will be much longer on such systems, but users will still be able to access the encrypted data.
5. It should have predictable run-time calculations (to benchmark an algorithm on a particular machine and select attributes that fit best).

   This requirement copies current work-flow of some existing disk encryption systems that benchmark the system to achieve best approximation of the unlocking time. This is mainly useful for encryption of a boot or fixed disk where the disk is always unlocked on the same system.
6. Configured resources should not significantly influence each other. (For example, increasing computational time should not significantly affect memory requirements.)
7. Algorithms must be able to take input (password) of any length.
8. Maximal output length (keys) should not be significantly limited, so a function can derive multiple keys from single input.

   While there are options to seed another algorithm (like a stream cipher) with the fixed key, it is preferred to have one standardized key-derivation algorithm instead of chaining several different key generators. However, this requirement can add another final step (like iterated hashing) to the key-derivation algorithm.
9. Any change in running time caused by the change of input password size should be marginal. The running time must not provide information about password attributes (such as length).
10. Underlying cryptographic primitives should be upgradable, interchangeable and should be available in common cryptographic libraries.
11. Cryptographic algorithms should not be hard-coded in the function's design.

    The lifetime of an encrypted disk is usually years to decades. It should be possible to replace an underlying primitive even during its lifetime if a security problem is uncovered. Upgradable components also help to fine-tune for specific needs, typically for certified systems where only a limited set of algorithms is allowed. The downside of allowing interchangeable components is that users will sometimes select less secure combinations.
12. Algorithms must not be patent encumbered.

3   KDF Building Blocks

A key derivation function can be constructed either as a completely new cryptographic primitive or more often it can be built with existing cryptographic primitives as building blocks. Usually, it is a combination of both, where the newly designed part adds a memory requirement property while the computationally intensive part is based on utilizing existing cryptographic primitives.

The major problem with newly designed cryptographic primitives is that there is no adequate security analysis. If we are using a thoroughly analyzed hash function, security of a KDF can be derived from the security of the hash function. Since FDE is not a short-lifetime problem (some encrypted devices are already used for a decade without reformatting) the preference is to use proved cryptographic primitives in the design.

3.1 Cryptographic Primitives

- A *hash* function or a *block cipher* are commonly used. For hash functions, it is usually one of the SHA family or a sponge function [3] like BLAKE (often the 64-bit optimized variant BLAKE2b [2]). Only a single property of a function can be used (for example compression).
- *Reduced cryptographic primitives* are hash functions or block ciphers with a reduced number of rounds. These are often used where performance is an issue and repeated call of a full-round function is slowing down the whole algorithm above acceptable limits. Security of such a solution depends on the context where it is used. In general, this solution requires new security analysis similar to the situation when a new cryptographic primitive is used.

3.2 Concepts to Utilize Resources During Computation

The main intent is to complicate password search attacks.

- *Strictly sequential processing* prevents an attacker from using a massively parallel system to speed up function run.
- *Memory-hard function* [15] is the concept of using as much memory space as it is possible for a given number of operations. A *sequential memory-hard function* adds a property that it is not possible to achieve a significantly lower cost if a parallel function is used instead.
- *Paralellization* denotes the use of available parallel capabilities in a function (for example utilize common multi-core CPUs).
- *Server relief* is the possibility of delegating part of computation to another system (for subproblems where the system in question does not need to be trusted). This property is not important for FDE (disk unlocking often runs in an environment where it cannot easily communicate with other systems).
- *Client-independent upgrade* is the possibility of increasing resource usage (cost) without providing a password (upgrade password hashes without requiring to enter all related passwords). This property is not usable for a FDE because a hash (a secret key) is not available for an upgrade (without knowledge of the user input).

3.3   Ingredients

Attributes influencing the use of resources are often called ingredients.

- *Salt* is a unique sequence of random and public bits added to a user password before processing. The goal is to increase the cost of brute-force attacks (an attacker cannot build a common dictionary but has to build a table for every case separately).
- *Garlic* configures required memory cost. In reality, increasing the memory requirements also increases the running time (memory accesses take time).
- *Pepper* increases the time of processing by making some of the bits of salt secret, so the password-checking algorithm must verify more variants.

3.4   Processing Unlimited Input and Output

If a function is designed using an underlying cryptographic primitive with limited block size (a hash function usually dictates the block size), the input has to be compressed to the requested block size, while preserving entropy.

One know problem in PBKDF2 is that for the input exceeding the internal block size, the hash of the input is used instead. That leads to simple collisions (an input behaves the same as a hash of itself). When hashing is used, it should avoid such a collision problem by design (usually by adding some attribute value in initial hashing).

For unlimited output (used to derive multiple keys from a single password), hashing can be used as well. It is usually an iterative form of hashing (sequentially applying a hash function, possibly with the help of a counter).

4   PHC Candidates as KDF Algorithms

The following list is based on the PHC second-round candidates. We also include newly proposed algorithms (which were added in later rounds so it is not yet clear if they can be handled the same as original candidates). The main focus here is to compare them with our requirements described in Sect. 2.2.

A more detailed survey of candidates is available in [13], but it does not contain some more recently introduced functions (Argon2 or Catena instances).

4.1   Argon

There are two different algorithms *Argon* [4] (based on the original submission) and *Argon2* (in two variants *Argon2d* and *Argon2i*). Argon is designed mainly to maximize the cost when used on non-Intel 64-bit architectures. Authors suggest to use Argon2i for KDF applications.

Argon after the initial hashing phase (BLAKE2b) and initial permutation round (based on 5-round reduced AES-128 with a fixed key) creates a memory layout (a matrix of blocks, where size depends on memory cost). The round part then combines shuffling the rows and columns of the matrix, repeated according to the time cost parameter. The finalization part uses XOR of the matrix blocks for an iterated hashing step that produces an output of requested length.

Argon2 initially hashes the input and then fills the memory (matrices of blocks according to a parallel property). Every matrix is computed using a compression function (based on BLAKE2b round function). Input block indices are either selected randomly (in Argon2d, data-dependent version) or pseudo-randomly (in Argon2i, data-independent version). The whole procedure is repeated based on the time cost parameter. The final step is to use XOR applied to the matrix columns to calculate the final block. The output is generated from the final block using iterative hashing.

4.2   Battcrypt

Battcrypt (Blowfish All The Things) [19] constructs a memory-hard function using the Blowfish block cipher. Initially it hashes the password and salt using SHA-512 and uses the output as a Blowfish cipher key (with zeroed IV) in CBC mode. The memory is organised in blocks (the number depends on the memory cost parameter) and is initialized using Blowfish encryption. The work phase (repeated, based on the required time cost) then traverses the memory and modifies it using xor and Blowfish CBC encryption (the function is data-dependent). The output is then produced using one SHA-512 hash operation. There is also a separate KDF mode, where a variable output is provided by additional iterated hashing.

4.3   Catena

Catena [10] is a generic password hashing framework. The submitted version presents two instances of this framework, *Catena-Dragonfly* based on a bit-reversal graph and *Catena-Butterfly* based on a double-butterfly graph [10]. Catena uses a reduced-round BLAKE2b function.

Catena framework consists of an initialization, where a password is hashed (BLAKE2b) and one call of the *flap* function is performed. The work phase then iteratively calls the flap function and the hash function according to the garlic parameter. The flap function consists of sequential initialization of memory and applying a function that provides random memory accesses, followed by a call of a memory-hard function. For the given instances, *SaltMix* function (accessing memory according to provided salt) is used for the first part and bit-reversal hashing or double-butterfly hashing for the second memory-hard part. For a KDF, the algorithm uses *Catena-KG* mode that adds an iterative hashing step to producing a variable-length output.

4.4   Lyra2

Lyra2 [18] is a password hashing function based on the concept of cryptographic sponge [3] with duplex construction (operating in stateful mode). Lyra2 is constructed as a strictly sequential algorithm. The internal state of the sponge is never reset between algorithm phases. Except for the final wrap-up phase, a reduced-round sponge is used.

The initial password is absorbed by the underlying sponge (BLAKE2b). Then a matrix of blocks is constructed in memory (setup phase). The number of columns in the matrix is hard-coded in the algorithm while the number of rows is defined by the memory cost parameter. The memory is filled up using the sponge duplex function, XOR, and bit rotation. Next phase (wandering) is the most time consuming phase and is similar to the setup phase, just with an additional data-dependent operation and repetition based on the time cost parameter. Finally, the wrap-up phase contains one full round of sponge absorb over one fixed final memory cell. The output is generated using the sponge squeeze function.

4.5 Yescrypt

Yescrypt [16] is an extension of the *scrypt* [15] algorithm. The original *scrypt* design already supports both time and memory cost.

Initial PBKDF2 round (one iteration with SHA-256) processes the input password and generates input memory blocks (depends on parallel cost). Blocks are then processed by a sequential memory-hard function called *ROMix*, based on the internal *BlockMix* function. The processed blocks are used as a salt for the final PBKDF2 one-round iteration step that produces output of requested size.

Yescrypt extends scrypt using optional flags that can modify ROMix memory accesses from *write once, read-many* to *mostly read-write* operation. It also fixes usage of the initial PBKDF2 round (to avoid simple collisions) and allows to increase the processing time with the given memory cost (scrypt does not enable that independently). The parallelism present in scrypt on a high level is possible in yescrypt also inside the ROMix function. The Salsa20/8 cipher (used in scrypt BlockMix) is partially replaced by a *parallel wide transformation function* that is intended to utilize 64-bit single instruction, multiple data (SIMD) computations.

4.6 Algorithms Not Selected for Further Testing

MAKWA [17] is not designed as a memory-hard algorithm so it does not fit our criteria. The most interesting attribute is the introduction of delegation that means that a part of the processing cost can be delegated (offloaded) to external, untrusted systems.

Parallel [20] is a very straightforward function based on the underlying hash function (SHA-512). The design is comparable to PBKDF2 and does not allow to specify memory cost, and so it does not fit our needs.

POMELO [22] is designed as a new cryptographic primitive (not utilizing any existing cryptographic hash or cipher). It is built on the concept of a non-linear feedback function.

Table 1. Notes on cryptographic primitive use (requirements in Sect. 2.2).

Candidate	Notes
Argon	- design replaced with *Argon2*
	- uses reduced round *AES*
Argon2	- based on *BLAKE2*
	- need to use data-independent version *Argon2i*
battcrypt	- based on *Blowfish* only
	- KDF mode is separate
Catena	- possible use of reduced *BLAKE2*
Lyra2	- partial use of reduced *BLAKE2*
yescrypt	- compatibility with *scrypt*, adds complexity
	- requires *PBKDF2*
MAKWA	- not a memory-hard algorithm
Parallel	- not a memory-hard algorithm
POMELO	- new cryptographic primitive
Pufferfish	- uses own *Blowfish* implementation
	- *bcrypt* replacement only

Table 2. Cryptographic primitives used in candidate functions.

Candidate function	Cryptographic primitive	Modification for KDF	Unlimited input	Unlimited output
Argon	reduced AES-128 BLAKE2b	no	hashing	iterative hashing with XOR on init
Argon2i	BLAKE2b (compression)	no	hashing	iterative hashing
battcrypt	Blowfish SHA-512	yes	hashing	iterative hashing
Catena	BLAKE2b BLAKE2b-reduced	yes	hashing	iterative hashing
Lyra2	BLAKE2b	no	sponge absorbing	sponge squeeze
yescrypt	Salsa20/8 SHA-256	no	hashing PBKDF2	PBKDF2

Pufferfish [12] is designed to *extend life of bcrypt*. It rewrites the underlying Blowfish implementation to use 64-bit words to better utilize 64-bit platforms and provides for a variable length output by using iterative hashing (SHA-512). Considering the special Blowfish implementation and the narrow design goal, this algorithm was not selected for testing.

Table 1 summarizes the cryptographic primitives used in candidate functions based on description above and the requirements defined in Sect. 2.2.

4.7   Overview

Table 2 summarizes which cryptographic primitives are used in the described functions, whether code changes are needed for the KDF mode of operation and how unlimited input and output are processed.

For comparison, in the following tests we also include *POMELO*, even though the algorithm does not use any existing cryptographic primitives (our criteria prefer algorithms based on existing cryptographic primitives).

5   Run-Time Test

We ran a test that measures real memory use and run-time for the increasing memory or time cost parameter while the other parameters are fixed. The tests are described in more detail in Appendix A and in our test report [6].

The provided *PHC* interface does not allow to set parallel cost attribute at run-time. All algorithms are compiled without parallel attribute set to eliminate an advantage of algorithms that use internal parallel processing (in other words, it uses only one thread even if an algorithm allows for a parallel computation internally).

In the follow-up discussion to our tests [7], an alternative interface for parallel attribute testing was introduced. This interface slightly modifies the source code of the candidates (to expose the parallel attribute).

If the candidate provides an optimized variant, it is tested separately. Reference implementations are usually not optimized for speed but can be used to show how the algorithm will behave on a system that does not have required acceleration functions (AVX, SSE or AES-NI instructions in our case).

The overview plot of measurement of dependence of memory cost and run time is shown in Fig. 1.

Comparison based on the calculation of required memory and partially normalized by the number of rounds of underlying function calls is described in Appendix A and the output is shown in Fig. 2.

5.1   Specific Use Case Measurement

Some FDE systems already include machine benchmarks with the intention of fine-tuning KDF parameters to perform best on a particular machine. An example is to benchmark the iteration count for PBKDF2 in such a way that unlocking should take a specific time (on the same machine).

The following test tries to answer the question whether a function is able to provide usable parameters on the test machine for the given set of memory and time use conditions.

The test limits memory to 1 MB, 100 MB or 1 GB and also limits the runtime. The first run is the time minimum for the required memory limit, the second is an approximate 1 second run-time and the last one is run-time of approximate 20 seconds.

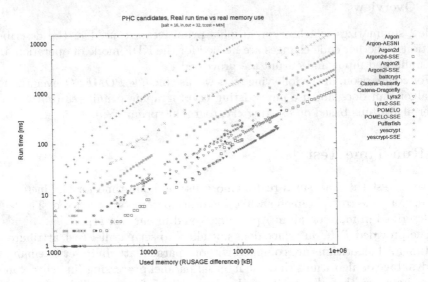

Fig. 1. Real used memory and run-time while increasing memory cost parameter.

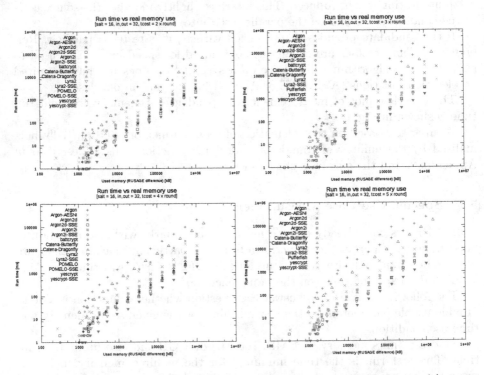

Fig. 2. Real used memory and run time (normalized to performed rounds).

Table 3. Ability to cover preset limits.

Candidate	Memory	Reference			Optimized		
		min	~1s	~20s	min	~1s	~20s
Argon	1MB	✓	✓	✓	✓	✓	✓
	100MB	[11.6s] ✓	×	✓	[1.8s] ✓	✓	✓
	1GB	[119.1s] ✓	×	×	[18.0s] ✓	×	✓
Argon2i	1MB	✓	✓	✓	✓	✓	✓
	100MB	✓	✓	✓	✓	✓	✓
	1GB	[6.6s] ✓	×	✓	[2.9s] ✓	×	✓
battcrypt	1MB	✓	✓	✓	n/a		
	100MB	[3.6s] ✓	×	✓			
	1GB	[28.8s] ✓	×	×			
Catena Butterfly	1MB	✓	✓	×	n/a		
	100MB	[1.8s] ✓	×	✓			
	1GB	[35.6s] ✓	×	×			
Catena Dragonfly	1MB	✓	×	×	n/a		
	100MB	✓	✓	✓			
	1GB	[2.9s] ✓	×	✓			
Lyra2	1MB	✓	✓	✓	✓	✓	✓
	100MB	✓	✓	✓	✓	✓	✓
	1GB	[1.6s] ✓	×	✓	✓	✓	✓
POMELO	1MB	✓	✓	✓	✓	✓	✓
	100MB	✓	✓	✓	✓	✓	✓
	1GB	[2.1s] ✓	×	✓	[1.8s] ✓	×	✓
yescrypt	1MB	✓	✓	✓	✓	✓	✓
	100MB	✓	✓	✓	✓	✓	✓
	1GB	[4.2s] ✓	×	✓	[1.2s] ✓	×	✓

The selection of one second simulates *the default iteration time used in the Linux Unified Key Setup (LUKS) FDE system* [11], and 20 seconds represent *the limit that is usually acceptable for users when waiting for unlocking a device.*

Measured time includes a complete run of the key-derivation, including all algorithm setup costs. It does not include the additional time needed for the operating system to boot or to initialize the required environment.

Since the attributes can be set in discrete steps only, the measured time and memory for different candidates are slightly different and cannot be directly compared to each other. The table shows only values when a particular combination is possible for a particular test case. A detailed description of the parameters used is included in our test report [6].

When a failure is listed in Table 3, the reason can be either that the function run-time is longer even for the minimum memory cost parameter, or because a function parameter limit was exceeded (for example, Catena seems to support only maximum cost value 255 that is not high enough for the required limits).

5.2   Fixed Implementation Issues

Our test framework discovered several issues with the proposed algorithms. Most of them are just implementation problems, but for cryptographic algorithms, it is very important that border cases are processed properly (even if it is just a reference implementation).

As examples, out testsuite found following notable issues:

- Several candidates (*Argon* family, *Lyra2*, *POMELO*, *Pufferfish*) were not ready for big-endian platforms (producing different output on platforms with different endianness).
- *Argon2* mixes C and C++ interfaces leading to a crash if used in plain C code.
- The optimized *Argon2d* implementation output differs from the reference implementation for certain parameter values (code bug).
- There were several missing parameter boundary tests (*Argon* produced a non-random hash for input longer than 255 characters).
- *Catena* allowed use of unsupported time cost parameters (leading to a less secure function).
- *Lyra2* crashes on certain parameter values (missing a lower bound check).

Most of these were fixed either as follow-up patches or just temporarily in our testsuite. *Argon2* authors fixed all of reported problems (and Argon2 was accepted as a replacement for the Argon algorithm eventually).

6   Conclusions and Open Issues

Based on the criteria defined in Sect. 2.2, we executed several run tests of selected password hashing candidates. We took advantage of the ongoing Password Hashing Competition and based our selection on the second round finalists. Some tests mentioned in [6] are just illustrative overviews of possible parameter configuration, but were also useful to discover code portability problems and some other issues in implementations. Some of the plots were discussed on the PHC list, providing new ideas for proper comparison of algorithms and also helped to fix some mistakes in tests.

Table 3 shows that some functions cannot provide valid attributes for our test cases (if the minimal run-time is higher than the requested one for the intended memory use, it means that the user will be forced to wait longer than the default interval). If the minimal time exceeds 20 seconds, the algorithm is practically not usable for the given memory limits (no user will probably accept such a long delay without any possibility of reducing it).

In general, for disk encryption environment, selection and tests were able to identify candidates that clearly do not fit the intended use. These include candidates that do not have the configurable memory property (MAKWA, Parallel) or are not aligned with our requirements (POMELO, Pufferfish). We have shown that some candidates are very slow in the presented form (and it is a question whether an optimization could bring the requisite speedup). Others would hardly be usable without changes in our scenario (Argon, battcrypt, Catena-Butterfly). Some of these issues would be probably solvable through a modification of the algorithms (for example, by replacing the underlying cryptographic primitive), but this was out of scope for this work.

Unfortunately, there were also implementation issues. Some candidates are still not prepared to run in the big-endian environment. However, these are technical problems that can be easily fixed later. However, we demonstrate that implementation of cryptographic functions brings new problems not easily detected on paper alone.

The most promising candidates identified in our tests appear to be *Argon2i*, *Lyra2* and *yescrypt*.

Recently – on June 20, 2015 – Password Hashing Competition panel announced *Argon2* as a basis for the final winner and gave special recognition to *Catena, Lyra2, Makwa* and *yescrypt* [1].

The next practical step would be designing a benchmarking application that can calculate cost parameters on a particular machine according to user needs (a similar tool is already part of the Catena framework).

From the user perspective, it is important that a derivation function is not only secure but also usable in real situations. If the minimal running time exceeds tens of seconds, only a very limited user base is likely to accept it.

The authors thank Geraint Price and Petr Ročkai for their help in reviewing this paper.

A   Appendix

A.1   PHC Candidate Implementation and Benchmarking Tests

These tests were run for all submitted candidates of the second round of the Password Hashing Competition [1], including new and fixed versions (tweaks of submitted candidates in the first round).

All tests were run on a Lenovo X230 notebook with i5 CPU and 16GB of memory. This machine represents a typical end-user machine (with additional memory). The Intel processor provides both AES-NI and SSE instructions so tests could be performed also for optimized variants.

Variable cost tests use a special utility that measures differences in the memory allocation using the *getrusage()* system call.

Run-time measurement used *clock_gettime(CLOCK_MONOTONIC)* on the Linux platform.

The test ran as a special forked process started for each test separately. Tests were repeated 5 times, and the arithmetic mean (for the time) or maximum (for the memory) of the measurements was used.

The tests are not performance tests of the candidates, their major purpose it to verify claimed memory and time configuration and to detect bugs and incompatibilities in reference implementations.

A.2   PHC Test Report

More measurement outputs were presented in the separate test report [6], including:

- Test vector generator and checker, intended to verify that functions behave the same on various platforms. As a part of this test we tried to compile the source code on a different endian platform. These tests uncovered that many of the reference implementations are written only for little-endian environments.
- Tests that try to detect limits (boundary checking) in functions (detection of crashes with wrong parameters, parameter overflows, etc.).
- Tests based on algorithm analysis where parameters are calculated for an exact numbers of rounds (calls of underlying cryptographic primitive) and several presets of used memory.
- Output randomness tests: the output should pass all basic randomness tests provided by the Dieharder testsuite. The test generates 32-byte hashes of a consecutive little-endian integer (4 bytes) with a fixed 16 byte salt. The output is written to a file that is passed to the Dieharder testsuite.
- The complete source code of tested candidate functions and test scripts.

References

1. Password hashing competition (2014). https://password-hashing.net/
2. Aumasson, J.-P., Neves, S., Wilcox-O'Hearn, Z., Winnerlein, C.: BLAKE2: simpler, smaller, fast as MD5. In: Jacobson, M., Locasto, M., Mohassel, P., Safavi-Naini, R. (eds.) ACNS 2013. LNCS, vol. 7954, pp. 119–135. Springer, Heidelberg (2013)
3. Bertoni, G., Daemen, J., Peeters, M., Assche, G.V.: Sponge functions. Ecrypt Hash Workshop 2007, May 2007
4. Biryukov, A., Khovratovich, D.: Argon and argon2, January 2015. https://password-hashing.net/submissions/specs/Argon-v2.pdf
5. Biryukov, A., Khovratovich, D.: Tradeoff cryptanalysis of memory-hard functions. Cryptology ePrint Archive, Report 2015/227 (2015). http://eprint.iacr.org/
6. Broz, M.: Password Hashing Competition second round candidates - tests Report Technical Report, April 2015. https://github.com/mbroz/PHCtest/raw/master/output/phc_round2.pdf
7. Cox, B.: Added multi-threading support to test suite. PHC mailing list archive, April 2015. http://article.gmane.org/gmane.comp.security.phc/2915
8. Dürmuth, M., Güneysu, T., Kasper, M., Paar, C., Yalcin, T., Zimmermann, R.: Evaluation of standardized password-based key derivation against parallel processing platforms. In: Foresti, S., Yung, M., Martinelli, F. (eds.) ESORICS 2012. LNCS, vol. 7459, pp. 716–733. Springer, Heidelberg (2012)

9. Forler, C., List, E., Lucks, S., Wenzel, J.: Overview of the candidates for the password hashing competition - and their resistance against garbage-collector attacks. Cryptology ePrint Archive, Report 2014/881 (2014). http://eprint.iacr.org/

10. Forler, C., Lucks, S., Wenzel, J.: The Catena Password-Scrambling Framework, January 2015. https://password-hashing.net/submissions/specs/Catena-v3.pdf

11. Fruhwirth, C.: New methods in hard disk encryption. Ph.D. thesis, Institute for Computer Languages Theory and Logic Group Vienna University of Technology (2005). http://clemens.endorphin.org/publications

12. Gosney, J.M.: The pufferfish password hashing scheme, March 2014. https://password-hashing.net/submissions/specs/Pufferfish-v0.pdf

13. Hatzivasilis, G., Papaefstathiou, I., Manifavas, C.: Password hashing competition - survey and benchmark. Cryptology ePrint Archive, Report 2015/265 (2015). http://eprint.iacr.org/

14. Kaliski, B.: PKCS #5: Password-Based Cryptography Specification Version 2.0. RFC 2898 (Informational), September 2000. http://www.ietf.org/rfc/rfc2898.txt

15. Percival, C.: Stronger key derivation via sequential memory-hard functions, May 2009. http://www.tarsnap.com/scrypt/scrypt.pdf

16. Peslyak, A.: yescrypt - a password hashing competition submission, January 2015. https://password-hashing.net/submissions/specs/yescrypt-v1.pdf

17. Pornin, T.: The MAKWA Password Hashing Function, March 2014. https://password-hashing.net/submissions/specs/Makwa-v0.pdf

18. Simplicio, M.A., Almeida, L.C., Andrade, E.R., Barreto, P.S.L.M.: The Lyra2 reference guide, January 2015. https://password-hashing.net/submissions/specs/Lyra2-v3.pdf

19. Thomas, S.: battcrypt (Blowfish All The Things), March 2014. https://password-hashing.net/submissions/specs/battcrypt-v0.pdf

20. Thomas, S.: Parallel, January 2015. https://password-hashing.net/submissions/specs/Parallel-v1.pdf

21. Turan, M.S., Barker, E.B., Burr, W.E., Chen, L.: SP 800–132. Recommendation for Password-Based Key Derivation: Part 1: Storage Applications. Technical Report, National Institute of Standards and Technology, Gaithersburg, MD, United States (2010)

22. Wu, H.: POMELO: A Password Hashing Algorithm, January 2015. https://password-hashing.net/submissions/specs/POMELO-v2.pdf

Controlling Data Release

It's My Privilege: Controlling Downgrading in DC-Labels

Lucas Waye[1](✉), Pablo Buiras[2], Dan King[1], Stephen Chong[1],
and Alejandro Russo[2]

[1] Harvard University, Cambridge, MA, USA
{lwaye,danking,chong}@seas.harvard.edu
[2] Chalmers University of Technology, Gothenburg, Sweden
{buiras,russo}@chalmers.se

Abstract. Disjunction Category Labels (DC-labels) are an expressive label format used to classify the sensitivity of data in information-flow control systems. DC-labels use capability-like *privileges* to downgrade information. Inappropriate use of privileges can compromise security, but DC-labels provide no mechanism to ensure appropriate use. We extend DC-labels with the novel notions of *bounded privileges* and *robust privileges*. Bounded privileges specify and enforce upper and lower bounds on the labels of data that may be downgraded. Bounded privileges are simple and intuitive, yet can express a rich set of desirable security policies. Robust privileges can be used only in downgrading operations that are *robust*, i.e., the code exercising privileges cannot be abused to release or certify more information than intended. Surprisingly, robust downgrades can be expressed in DC-labels as downgrading operations using a weakened privilege. We provide *sound and complete* run-time security checks to ensure downgrading operations are robust. We illustrate the applicability of bounded and robust privileges in a case study as well as by identifying a vulnerability in an existing DC-label-based application.

1 Introduction

Information-flow control (IFC) systems track the flow of information by associating *labels* with data. Disjunction Category Labels (DC-labels) are a practical and expressive label format that can capture the security concerns of principals. IFC systems and DC-labels can provide strong, expressive, and practical information security guarantees, preventing exploitation of, for example, cross-site scripting and code injection vulnerabilities [9,10,19,23,26].

IFC systems often need to *downgrade* information: *declassification* downgrades confidentiality, and *endorsement* downgrades integrity. Downgrading of

This work is supported in part by the National Science Foundation under Grants 1054172 and 1421770, DARPA CRASH under contract #N66001-10-2-4088, the Swedish research agencies VR and STINT, and the Barbro Osher Pro Suecia foundation.

A.Russo—Work done while visiting Stanford.

S. Foresti (Ed.): STM 2015, LNCS 9331, pp. 203–219, 2015.
DOI: 10.1007/978-3-319-24858-5_13

DC-labels occurs via operations that require unforgeable capability-like tokens known as *privileges*. Unfortunately, DC-labels offer no methodology to protect developers from the *discretionary* (i.e., unrestricted) exercise of privileges—even a minor mistake in handling privileges can compromise the whole system's security. For example, we found a one-line vulnerability in an existing DC-label application written by experts that enabled confidential information to be inappropriately released, thus violating the application's intended security properties.

To address this, we introduce *restricted privileges*: privileges that are limited in their ability to declassify and endorse information. By declaratively restricting the use of privileges, developers can reason about the security properties of the system, regardless of the code that may possess or use the restricted privileges. Thus, the developer's local declaration of restrictions enables the enforcement of global information security guarantees.

We present two kinds of restricted privileges: *bounded privileges* and *robust privileges*. A bounded privilege imposes upper and lower bounds on the DC-labels of data that is declassified or endorsed using that privilege. Robust privileges avoid the accidental or malicious use of privileges to declassify or endorse more information than intended, achieving a property known as *robustness* [16,25].

Bounded Privileges. A bounded privilege wraps an unrestricted privilege with two *immutable* labels that indicate upper and lower bounds for downgrading. DC-labels form a lattice structure (described in Sect. 2), and thus a bounded privilege restricts where in the lattice downgrading may occur. A bounded privilege also has a *mode*, indicating whether the bounded privilege may be used for declassification, endorsement, or both declassification and endorsement.

In terms of confidentiality, the upper bound limits the confidentiality of information that can be declassified using the privilege, and the lower bound limits the confidentiality of the information after declassification. For example, suppose principal `fb.com` passes a bounded privilege to `gogl.com`. If the lower bound of the bounded privilege is the label "`gogl.com`" then the privilege can be used to declassify information only from `fb.com` to `gogl.com`. Even if `gogl.com` passes the bounded privilege to another domain, say `evil.com`, the bounded privilege cannot be used to declassify information from `fb.com` to `evil.com`.

In terms of integrity, the upper bound of a bounded privilege indicates the least trustworthy level of information the privilege can be used to endorse, and the lower bound limits the integrity of the information after endorsement. For example, by setting the upper bound appropriately, `fb.com` can create a bounded privilege that can be used to endorse data only from `gogl.com`, and cannot be used to endorse other data, say from `evil.com`.

Robust Privileges. The security of a system might be at risk if an attacker is able to influence the decision to declassify or endorse information, or can influence what information is declassified. For example, consider a routine that receives a secret pair (`username,password`) and uses a privilege to declassify the first component of the pair. If an attacker (from another system component) can influence the pair to be (`password,username`) and trigger the declassification, the password will be leaked.

Robust declassification [25] and *qualified robustness* [16] are end-to-end semantic security guarantees that ensure that attackers are unable to inappropriately influence what information is revealed to them. These security conditions can be enforced by restricting declassification and endorsement operations. A robust privilege wraps a privilege and ensures that it is used only in declassification and endorsement operations that satisfy appropriate robustness checks.

This paper makes the following contributions: (i) We introduce bounded and robust privileges to limit the exercise of privileges for declassification and endorsement. (ii) We present a semantic characterization of how bounded privileges and robust privileges restrict declassification and endorsement operations. (iii) We define run-time security checks for bounded privileges and robust privileges that soundly and completely enforce the semantic characterization of restricted downgrading operations. The run-time checking for robust downgrading is effectively a weakening of the underlying unrestricted privilege: a surprisingly simple characterization of robustness. (iv) We illustrate the applicability of bounded and robust privileges via a case study. Moreover, use of restricted privileges identified a vulnerability in an existing DC-label-based application.

This paper is organized as follows. Section 2 introduces the DC-label model. Section 3 characterizes downgrading operations that use restricted privileges, and Sect. 4 provides the corresponding enforcement. Section 5 describes security properties in the presence of multiple restricted privileges. Case studies are given in Sect. 6. Section 7 examines related work and Sect. 8 concludes.

2   Background

We briefly define three concepts fundamental to our presentation: the DC-label model, privileges, and floating label systems.

Label Lattice. DC-labels [21] are pairs of confidentiality and integrity policies. Confidentiality polices describe who may learn information. Integrity polices describe who takes responsibility or vouches for information. Both confidentiality and integrity policies are positive propositional formulas in conjunctive normal form, where propositional constants represent *principals*. Let CNF denote the set of all positive propositional formulas in conjunctive normal form; we use the term *formula* to range over CNF. We assume that operations on formulas always reduce their results to conjunctive normal form.

Both confidentiality policies and integrity policies form lattices—see Figs. 1 and 2. We interpret $C_1 \sqsubseteq^c C_2$ as: C_2 is at least as confidential as C_1. For instance, Alice $\vee$ Bob $\sqsubseteq^c$ Alice, which means that data readable by either Alice or Bob is less confidential than data readable only by Alice. Conjunctions of principals represent the

$$C_1 \sqsubseteq^c C_2 \iff C_2 \Rightarrow C_1$$
$$C_1 \sqcup^c C_2 \iff C_1 \wedge C_2$$
$$C_1 \sqcap^c C_2 \iff C_1 \vee C_2$$
$$\perp^c \equiv True \qquad \top^c \equiv False$$

Fig. 1. Confidentiality lattice

$$I_1 \sqsubseteq^I I_2 \iff I_1 \Rightarrow I_2$$
$$I_1 \sqcup^I I_2 \iff I_1 \vee I_2$$
$$I_1 \sqcap^I I_2 \iff I_1 \wedge I_2$$
$$\perp^I \equiv False \qquad \top^I \equiv True$$

Fig. 2. Integrity lattice

multiple interest of principals to protect the data. Conversely, disjunctions of principals represent groups wherein any member may learn the information. The integrity lattice is dually defined [3]; we interpret $I_1 \sqsubseteq^I I_2$ as: I_1 is at least as trustworthy as I_2. For example, Alice $\wedge$ Bob $\sqsubseteq^I$ Alice, which indicates that data vouched for by Alice $\wedge$ Bob is more trustworthy than data vouched for only by Alice. In this case, conjunctions of principals represent groups whose members are independently responsible for the information. For example, data with integrity Alice $\wedge$ Bob means that Alice is completely responsible for the data, and so is Bob. Conversely, disjunctions of principals represent groups that collectively take responsibility for the information, however, no principal takes sole responsibility. For example, data with integrity Alice $\vee$ Bob means that Alice and Bob collectively are responsible for the data, i.e., both may have contributed to, or influenced the computation of the data.

Formally, a DC-label is a pair of a confidentiality policy C and an integrity policy I, written $\langle C, I \rangle$. DC-labels form a product lattice given in Fig. 3. The $\sqsubseteq$ relation is called the *can-flow-to* relation because it describes informa-

$$
\begin{aligned}
\langle C_1, I_1 \rangle \sqsubseteq \langle C_2, I_2 \rangle &\iff C_1 \sqsubseteq^c C_2 \text{ and } I_1 \sqsubseteq^I I_2 \\
\langle C_1, I_1 \rangle \sqcup \langle C_2, I_2 \rangle &\equiv \langle C_1 \sqcup^c C_2, I_1 \sqcup^I I_2 \rangle \\
\langle C_1, I_1 \rangle \sqcap \langle C_2, I_2 \rangle &\equiv \langle C_1 \sqcap^c C_2, I_1 \sqcap^I I_2 \rangle \\
\textsc{c}(\langle C, I \rangle) &\equiv C \qquad\qquad \textsc{i}(\langle C, I \rangle) \equiv I
\end{aligned}
$$

Fig. 3. Security lattice for DC-labels

tion flows that respect confidentiality and integrity policies. We write $\textsc{c}(\cdot)$ and $\textsc{i}(\cdot)$ for the projection of confidentiality and integrity components, respectively.

Downgrading. In the DC-label model, one security policy *downgrades* to another security policy if they do not satisfy the can-flow-to relation. Consider the pair of security labels in Fig. 4. The first security label enforces the policy that data is vouched for by Charlie. The second security

$\langle$Alice, Charlie$\rangle \not\sqsubseteq \langle$Alice, Charlie $\wedge$ Alice$\rangle$

Fig. 4. Downgrading integrity

$\langle$Alice $\wedge$ Bob, Charlie$\rangle \not\sqsubseteq \langle$Bob, Charlie$\rangle$

Fig. 5. Downgrading confidentiality

label enforces the policy that data is vouched for by Charlie and Alice, therefore a secure system cannot permit data to flow from the sources protected by the first policy to sinks protected by the second policy. This downgrade is an *endorsement*, since it downgrades only integrity, i.e., it makes a value more trustworthy. Dually, a *declassification* downgrades only confidentiality, i.e., it makes a value less confidential. Consider the pair of security labels in Fig. 5: The first security label enforces the policy that data is confidential to Alice $\wedge$ Bob. The second security label enforces that data is confidential to Bob. Permitting data to flow from a source protected by the first policy to a sink protected by the second policy violates the confidentiality expectations of the source.

Privileges. Practical systems must permit some downgrading. The DC-label model controls downgrading with *privileges*, where every principal has an associated privilege, and a principal's privilege enables downgrading. More precisely,

$$\langle C_1, I_1 \rangle \sqsubseteq_p \langle C_2, I_2 \rangle \iff C_1 \sqsubseteq_p^c C_2 \text{ and } I_1 \sqsubseteq_p^I I_2$$
$$\text{where} \quad C_1 \sqsubseteq_p^c C_2 \iff C_1 \sqsubseteq^c C_2 \sqcup^c p$$
$$I_1 \sqsubseteq_p^I I_2 \iff I_1 \sqcap^I p \sqsubseteq^I I_2$$

Fig. 6. Relation can-flow-to-with-privilege-p

given principal p, the *can-flow-to-with-privilege-p* relationship, written $\sqsubseteq_p$, describes the information flows permitted with p's privilege—see Fig. 6. Observe that both downgrading examples from the previous section are now permitted by the can-flow-to-with-privilege relationship for the principal Alice, i.e., $\langle \text{Alice}, \text{Charlie} \rangle \sqsubseteq_{\text{Alice}} \langle \text{Alice}, \text{Charlie} \wedge \text{Alice} \rangle$ and $\langle \text{Alice} \wedge \text{Bob}, \text{Charlie} \rangle \sqsubseteq_{\text{Alice}} \langle \text{Bob}, \text{Charlie} \rangle$.

Floating Label Systems. DC-labels are usually part of *floating label systems* like LIO [22], Hails [9], and COWL [23]. Such systems associate a *current label*, L_{pc}, with every computational task—this label plays a role similar to the *program counter* (PC) in more traditional language-based IFC approaches [19]. The current label denotes the fact that a computation depends only on data with labels bounded above by L_{pc}. When a task with current label L_{pc} observes information with label L_A, the current label after observation, L'_{pc}, must "float" above both the previous current label and the observed information's label, i.e., $L'_{pc} = L_{pc} \sqcup L_A$. Importantly, and to respect the security lattice, the current label restricts the subsequent writes to communication channels. Specifically, a task with current label L_{pc} is prevented from writing to channels protected by policy L_A if $L_{pc} \not\sqsubseteq L_A$.

Floating-label systems typically use some run-time representation of principals' privilege, and downgrading operations require the run-time representation of a principal p's privilege to be presented in order to use the can-flow-to-with-privilege-p relation, $\sqsubseteq_p$. Thus, the run-time representation of a principal's privilege acts like a capability to downgrade that principal's information. We write $p^{\mbox{\tiny ♛}}$ for the run-time representation of the privilege of principal p, and refer to this value as a *raw privilege* (to contrast it with the restricted privileges that we introduce in this paper).

3 Security Definitions

If a system contains $p^{\mbox{\tiny ♛}}$, then downgrading of data with policies involving p depends entirely on how $p^{\mbox{\tiny ♛}}$ is used in the system. Reasoning about what downgrading occurs may require reasoning about global properties of the system. Indeed, we found a vulnerability in a Hails example application [9] of a web-based rock-paper-scissors game where use of a raw privilege was localized to one component, but arbitrary data could be passed to this component to be downgraded. This motivates our work to restrict privileges, and enable local reasoning about downgrading that may occur in a system.

A *restricted privilege* is a raw privilege "wrapped" with limitations on its use. These limitations enable sound reasoning about the downgrading that may be performed using the restricted privilege, even if arbitrary code uses the restricted privilege. Thus, local reasoning that ensures $p^{\text{♛}}$ is always appropriately restricted provides global guarantees about the downgrading that can occur with respect to policies involving p.

We present two kinds of restricted privileges, *bounded privileges* and *robust privileges*, which provide simple declarative limitations on the use of raw privileges.

Bounded Privileges. A bounded privilege wraps a raw privilege with *downgrading bounds* and a downgrading mode. A downgrading bound is a pair of security lattice labels L_{high} and L_{low} that provide upper and lower bounds on downgrading, and the mode indicates whether the bounded privilege can be used to both declassify and endorse, only to declassify, or only to endorse.

Definition 1 (Downgrading Bounds). *An operation that downgrades from security policy L_{from} to security policy L_{to} in a computational context with current label L_{pc} satisfies downgrading bounds L_{high} and L_{low} if and only if $(L_{from} \sqcup L_{pc}) \sqsubseteq L_{high}$ and $L_{low} \sqsubseteq (L_{to} \sqcup L_{pc})$*

Definition 2 (Bounded Privileges). *A bounded privilege with bounds L_{high} and L_{low} and mode m on privilege $p^{\text{♛}}$, written $^{m}[p^{\text{♛}}]_{L_{low}}^{L_{high}}$, can be used only for downgrading operations with privilege $p^{\text{♛}}$ that satisfy downgrading bounds L_{high} and L_{low}. Mode m is one of* de, d, *or* e. *Declassification operations are permitted only if the mode is* de *or* d; *endorsement operations are permitted only if the mode is* de *or* e.

Figure 7 shows a visualization of bounded downgrading. The security lattice on the left is overlaid with a visualization of where bounded downgrading can occur (shaded) with respect to bounds L_{high} and L_{low}. The security lattice on the right shows an example of what labeled values can be declassified (shaded) with a

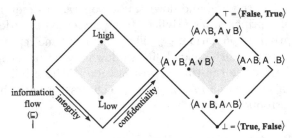

Fig. 7. Bounded downgrading

bounded declassification privilege with bounds $L_{high} = \langle \mathsf{A} \wedge \mathsf{B}, \mathsf{A} \vee \mathsf{B} \rangle$ and $L_{low} = \langle \mathsf{A} \vee \mathsf{B}, \mathsf{A} \wedge \mathsf{B} \rangle$.

In essence, the confidentiality lattice has collapsed $\mathrm{C}(L_{high})$ and $\mathrm{C}(L_{low})$ and all points in between: information that has confidentiality up to $\mathrm{C}(L_{high})$ may be declassified to confidentiality $\mathrm{C}(L_{low})$—all other points in the confidentiality lattice are not affected. Guarantees for endorsement with respect to bounded privileges are similar, but for integrity instead of confidentiality.

Example 1 (Policy: Only Bob controls Alice's privilege). Principal Alice allows Bob to declassify her data provided that Bob vouches for the data and the decision to declassify. In other words, information labeled with Alice can be declassified only after endorsement by Bob. This property can be captured by a bounded privilege with mode d and bounds: $L_{high} = \langle \top^C, \mathsf{Bob} \rangle, L_{low} = \langle \bot^C, \mathsf{Bob} \rangle$. If the privilege is used to declassify information that is not endorsed by Bob or in a context where the current label is not endorsed by Bob, then the declassification fails. In general, data must be vouched for by Bob (e.g., by using $\mathsf{Bob}^{\text{\textcircled{w}}}$ or another restricted privilege) before the bounded privilege for Alice can be used. For example, if a computational task has a current label $L_{pc} = \langle \mathsf{Alice}, \mathsf{Bob} \vee \mathsf{Charlie} \rangle$, the current label must be endorsed by Bob first. By endorsing the current label, Bob effectively vouches for any influence Charlie may have had on the computational task.

Example 2 (Policy: "A close source said..."). The bounded privilege $^{\mathsf{d}}[\mathsf{Alice}^{\text{\textcircled{w}}}]^{\langle \top^C, \top^I \rangle}_{\langle \bot^C, \top^I \rangle}$ or another restricted privilege) before requires that the integrity of data being declassified is $\top^I$, i.e., data that no principal takes responsibility for. Alice may wish to impose this restriction on declassification involving data confidential to her to ensure that she has plausible deniability regarding the source of the data released. That is, the bounded privilege can not be used to declassify data for which Alice is explicitly responsible.

Robust Privileges. *Robustness* [16,25] is a semantic security condition that limits downgrading based on which principals might benefit from the downgrading, and which principals have influenced the data to downgrade and the decision to downgrade.

Consider a declassification of information from a source protected by label L_{from} to a sink protected by label L_{to}. A formula A (representing a principal or party of principals) will benefit from the declassification if A cannot read from the source, but can read the sink, i.e., $\mathsf{c}(L_{from}) \not\sqsubseteq^C A$ and $\mathsf{c}(L_{to}) \sqsubseteq^C A$. A robust declassification does not permit any principal that benefits from it to influence either the decision to declassify or the data to declassify. A influences the decision to declassify if $A \sqsubseteq^I \mathsf{I}(L_{pc})$, and A influences the data to declassify if $A \sqsubseteq^I \mathsf{I}(L_{from})$.

Definition 3 (Robust Declassification). *A robust declassification using privilege $p^{\text{\textcircled{w}}}$ from a source protected by L_{from} to a sink protected by L_{to}, in a computational context with current label L_{pc} is a declassification (i.e., $\mathsf{c}(L_{from}) \sqsubseteq^C_p \mathsf{c}(L_{to})$) where $\forall A \in CNF.\, \mathsf{c}(L_{to}) \sqsubseteq^C A \wedge \mathsf{c}(L_{from}) \not\sqsubseteq^C A \Rightarrow A \not\sqsubseteq^I \mathsf{I}(L_{pc}) \wedge A \not\sqsubseteq^I \mathsf{I}(L_{from})$.*

For endorsement, a principal benifits if it may be held responsible for information from the source but is not held responsible for information from the sink. In other words, A benefits from an endorsement if A gets absolved of responsibility for a value, i.e., $A \sqsubseteq^I \mathsf{I}(L_{from}) \wedge A \not\sqsubseteq^I \mathsf{I}(L_{to})$. Robust endorsement does not permit principals that benefit from it to influence the decision to endorse.

Definition 4 (Robust Endorsement). *A robust endorsement using privilege* $p^{♛}$ *from a source protected by* L_{from} *to a sink protected by* L_{to}, *in a computational context with current label* L_{pc} *is an endorsement (i.e.,* $\textsc{i}(L_{from}) \sqsubseteq^{\textsc{i}}_{p} \textsc{i}(L_{to})$*) where* $\forall A \in CNF. A \sqsubseteq^{\textsc{i}} \textsc{i}(L_{from}) \land A \not\sqsubseteq^{\textsc{i}} \textsc{i}(L_{to}) \Rightarrow A \not\sqsubseteq^{\textsc{i}} \textsc{i}(L_{pc})$.

A *robust privilege* is a privilege that can only be used for robust downgrading operations.

Definition 5 (Robust Privilege). *A robust privilege with mode* m *on privilege* $p^{♛}$, *written* $rbst^{m}\{p^{♛}\}$, *restricts downgrading operations where it is used to those that are robust for* $p^{♛}$. *Mode* m *is one of* de, d, *or* e. *Declassification operations are permitted only if the mode is* de *or* d; *endorsement operations are permitted only if the mode is* de *or* e.

The definitions of robust declassification and endorsements both quantify over all formulas A in the (possibly infinite) set CNF. In Sect. 4, we consider how to implement efficient checks that do not use universal quantification.

Figure 8 shows a visualization of where robust declassification is allowed for a given robust privilege. The security lattice on the left is overlaid with a visualization of where a value with label L_{from} can be declassified to (shaded line) using a robust declassification privilege. (Note that the current label L_{pc} is not included in

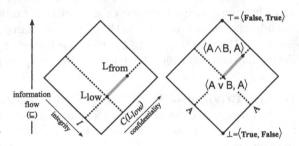

Fig. 8. Robust declassification

the diagram for brevity.) I represents the boolean formula for the integrity of the labeled value. L_{low} is one of the lowest points where L_{from} can be declassified to while still being a robust declassification, i.e., $L_{low} \sqsubseteq L_{to}$. That is, the integrity of the label of the value for declassification (together with the integrity of the current label of the process) is used as a lower bound for declassification. Intuitively, those who influence a declassification should not learn from it. In the right hand side of Fig. 8, the shaded line indicates to where a robust privilege may declassify the labeled value $\langle A \land B, A \rangle$. The declassification is robust if A is not able to learn from the declassification. As a result, the value could not be declassified to $\langle A \lor B, A \rangle$ as A would learn from a declassification that it influenced. In contrast, it is robust to declassify it to $\langle B, A \rangle$.

4   Enforcement for Robust Privileges

In this section we describe enforcement mechanisms for restricted privileges that satisfy their semantic characterizations described in Sect. 3. We have implemented these mechanisms in LIO and use them in our case study (see Sect. 6).

When a bounded privilege (Definition 2) is used at run time, it is simple to check that the downgrading operation satisfies the appropriate bounds, since the labels relevant to the downgrading (L_{from}, L_{to}, and L_{pc}) are all available at run time, and the label ordering relation can be easily checked dynamically.

Robust privileges (Definition 5) impose restrictions on downgrading operations which quantify over formulas A. However, attempting to explicitly check each possible formula A at run time is not feasible. We can however, derive simple and efficient run-time checks that are sound and complete with respect to their semantic characterizations. These checks are inspired by Chong and Meyers [6], who provide run-time checks for robustness that are sound but not complete.

The following theorem shows that the semantic characterization of robust declassification (Definition 3) is equivalent to two confidentiality-policy comparisons involving only L_{from}, L_{to}, and L_{pc}.

Theorem 1 (Robust Declassification Check). *A declassification using privilege $p^{\mathbb{W}}$ from a source protected by L_{from} to a sink protected by L_{to} in a computational context with current label L_{pc} is robust if and only if* $\mathrm{C}(L_{from}) \sqsubseteq_p^\mathrm{C} \mathrm{C}(L_{to})$, $\mathrm{C}(L_{from}) \sqsubseteq^\mathrm{C} \mathrm{C}(L_{to}) \sqcup^\mathrm{C} \mathrm{I}(L_{pc})$, *and* $\mathrm{C}(L_{from}) \sqsubseteq^\mathrm{C} \mathrm{C}(L_{to}) \sqcup^\mathrm{C} \mathrm{I}(L_{from})$.

The run-time check ensures that if there is any formula A that benefits from the declassification ($\mathrm{C}(L_{from}) \not\sqsubseteq^\mathrm{C} A$ and $\mathrm{C}(L_{to}) \sqsubseteq^\mathrm{C} A$) then $A \not\sqsubseteq^\mathrm{I} \mathrm{I}(L_{pc})$ (or, equivalently, $\mathrm{I}(L_{pc}) \not\sqsubseteq^\mathrm{C} A$), and similarly that $A \not\sqsubseteq^\mathrm{I} \mathrm{I}(L_{from})$. Thus, the run-time check converts a comparison of integrity policies to a comparison of integrity policies that does not involve A.

The next theorem describes a simple run-time check for robust endorsement.

Theorem 2 (Robust Endorsement Check). *An endorsement using privilege $p^{\mathbb{W}}$ from a source protected by L_{from} to a sink protected by L_{to}, in a computational context with current label L_{pc} is robust (Definition 4) if and only if* $\mathrm{I}(L_{from}) \sqsubseteq_p^\mathrm{I} \mathrm{I}(L_{to})$, *and* $\mathrm{I}(L_{pc}) \sqcap^\mathrm{I} \mathrm{I}(L_{from}) \sqsubseteq^\mathrm{I} \mathrm{I}(L_{to})$.

The run-time check that all formulas A that may be responsible for either the current label ($A \sqsubseteq^\mathrm{I} \mathrm{I}(L_{pc})$) or the data itself ($A \sqsubseteq^\mathrm{I} \mathrm{I}(L_{from})$) should also be responsible for the data after endorsement ($A \sqsubseteq^\mathrm{I} \mathrm{I}(L_{to})$). Proofs of Theorems 1 and 2 are omitted due to space limitations.

Alternative Formulation. In DC-labels, privileges can be arbitrary formulas, which can be stronger or weaker than privileges for individual principals. For example, a privilege for A ∧ B can downgrade more information than a privilege for A or B alone, whereas a privilege for A ∨ B can downgrade less information than a privilege for A or B alone. Leveraging this feature, we show how robust downgrading can be seen (and enforced) as normal downgrading operations that use a weakened privilege. That is, the privilege used in a downgrading operation is weakened so as to permit all and only robust downgrading operations.

The next corollaries follow from Theorems 1 and 2 and the definition for the *can-flow-to-with-privilege-p* relation.

Corollary 1. *A declassification using raw privilege $p^{\mathbb{W}}$ from a source protected by L_{from} to a sink protected by L_{to} in a computational context with current label L_{pc} is robust (Definition 3) if and only if $\mathrm{C}(L_{from}) \sqsubseteq^{\mathrm{C}}_{p\ \vee\ \mathrm{I}(L_{from})\ \vee\ \mathrm{I}(L_{pc})} \mathrm{C}(L_{to})$.*

This indicates that robust declassification can be achieved by simply weakening privilege $p^{\mathbb{W}}$ with the integrity labels of the current label and the data to be released, i.e., $p \vee \mathrm{I}(L_{from}) \vee \mathrm{I}(L_{pc})$. Robust endorsement has a similar corollary.

Corollary 2. *An endorsement using raw privilege $p^{\mathbb{W}}$ from a source protected by L_{from} to a sink protected by L_{to} in a computational context with current label L_{pc} is robust (Definition 3) if and only if $\mathrm{I}(L_{from}) \sqsubseteq^{\mathrm{I}}_{p\ \vee\ \mathrm{I}(L_{pc})} \mathrm{I}(L_{to})$.*

The proof of Corollary 1 is omitted due to space limitations; the proof of Corollary 2 is similar.

The current implementation of DC-labels [21] provides the ability to infer appropriate L_{to} labels of downgrading operations given a privilege p. By expressing the runtime checks for robust downgrading operations as a standard downgrading operation with a weakened privilege, we can take advantage of this feature and automatically infer a suitable L_{to} label if one exists. This reduces the burden on the programmer.

5   Interaction Among Restricted Privileges

We can extend restricted privileges to allow them to be composed, i.e., by allowing bounded privileges and robust privileges to wrap around other restricted privileges, as well as raw privileges. The guarantee provided by the composition of restricted privileges is the intersection of their individual guarantees. For example, a bounded privilege composed with another bounded privilege will require that downgrading operations satisfy the bounds of both privileges. A bounded privilege composed with a robust privilege (and vice-versa) requires the downgrading both to be robust and satisfy the downgrading bounds. Robust privileges are idempotent: a robust privilege composed with a robust privilege will simply require all downgrade operations to be robust.

Privileges might also interact because a system has multiple privileges available. Unlike composed privileges (which further restrict possible information flows), multiple privileges enable additional information flows. In the remainder of the section, we discuss the guarantees that result from the use of multiple restricted privileges. In the accompanying figures, bounded privileges are depicted as a shaded rectangle corresponding to their bounds. Robust declassification privileges are depicted as a pair of dashed lines: one line represents the integrity of the source and the

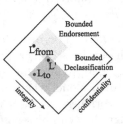

Fig. 9. Multiple bounds.

other line represents the lower bound to which data may be declassified. Labels are depicted as points along with their names.

Bounded Declassification and Bounded Endorsement. Figure 9 depicts two bounded privileges, one for declassification and one for endorsement, as well as a label, L_{from} that is outside the bounds of the declassification privilege. Because the bounds of the privileges overlap, data can transitively flow from L_{from} to L_{to}. The endorsement privilege enables data from L_{from} to be endorsed to L'. The bounded declassification privilege can then declassify data from L' to L_{to}.

Bounded Declassification and Robust Declassification.
Figure 10 depicts two declassification privileges, one robust and one bounded, and a label that is outside the bounds of the bounded declassification privilege. Neither privilege alone permits a flow from L_{from} to L_{to}. However, when used together, the robust declassification privilege permits declassification of data from L_{from} to L' and the bounded declassification permits a flow from L' to L_{to}, completing a flow from L_{from} to L_{to}.

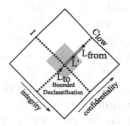

Fig. 10. Bounded and robust declassification.

Endorsement and Robust Declassification. In a system with unrestricted endorsement, robust declassification provides almost no protection against attackers influencing what they learn. Intuitively, the endorsement of data by p can make the data trustworthy enough to make a subsequent declassification robust. Consider a declassification of a value from label $L_{from} = \langle A \wedge B, A \rangle$ to $L = \langle A, A \rangle$ using the robust privilege $rbst^d\{B^{\text{♛}}\}$. This declassification is not robust: principal A, who benefits from this declassification, may be held responsible for the value, i.e., A may have decided what gets declassified. However, an unrestricted endorsement privilege $B^{\text{♛}}$ could be used to endorse the value— effectively endorsing any possible influence by A. In other words, $\langle A \wedge B, A \rangle$ can be endorsed to $\langle A \wedge B, B \rangle$, and a subsequent declassification from $\langle A \wedge B, B \rangle$ to $\langle A, B \rangle$ is robust.

Bounded endorsement effectively limits the aforementioned deletrious effects of unrestricted endorsement to the bounded area of the lattice, Fig. 11 depicts this situation. Besides mitigating the effects of unrestricted endorsement, bounded endorsement is useful to relax robust declassification so that it succeeds for principals collaborating in achieving a common goal—see, for example, Sect. 6.

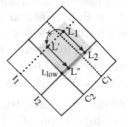

Fig. 11. Bounded endorsement and robust declassification.

Bounded and Robust Declassification. Figure 10 shows the guarantees when a robust declassification-only privilege (i.e., $rbst^d\{p^{\text{♛}}\}$) and a bounded declassification-only privilege (i.e., $[p^{\text{♛}}]^{L_{high}}_{L_{low}}$) for the same principal are both available in the system. Intuitively, p's information can be declassified from L_{from} to L' using the robust privilege. The information can then be declassified again to L_{to} using the bounded privilege, even though L_{from} is below the threshold imposed by robust declassification (i.e., the lowest possible label that robust declassification could declassify label L_{from}). Thus, the presence of a bounded declassification-only privilege can bypass the guarantees provided by robust declassification.

Several Bounded Privileges. Multiple robust privileges for the same principal do not add any additional complexity, as all robust privileges are equivalent (up to their modes). Bounded privileges, however, may differ on the bounds they impose. The presence of multiple bounded privileges in a system for principal p collapses the label lattice for principal p in complex ways. For instance, the left diagram of Fig. 9 illustrates an example where there is a bounded endorsement-only privilege and a bounded declassification-only privilege with different bounds. It may be possible for a value labeled L_{from} to be relabeled to L_{to} via an endorsement to L' followed by a declassification. Thus, labels between L_{from} and L' and between L' and L_{to} are effectively collapsed, since the bounded privileges allow a value with any of these labels to be relabeled to any other of these labels. More generally, as more overlapping bounded privileges exist for a given principal, data can be downgraded in more possible ways.

6   Case Studies

6.1   Calendar Case Study

We have extended LIO [22] with support for bounded privileges and robust privileges, and used them to develop a Calendar application to explore and illustrate the utility of restricted privileges. The application allows users to view their appointments, and schedule appointments with each other. DC-label principals are the calendar users. A user's appointments are confidential to that user.

We consider a setting where principals belong to groups and a principal is willing to disclose her availability to all and only members of her groups. For example, if Bob wants to schedule an appointment with Alice at time t, the application will check Alice's calendar and inform Bob whether Alice is available at that time. This operation, which declassifies Alice's availability at time t to Bob, should succeed only if Alice and Bob are in the same group.

Each user A has a robust declassification privilege $rbst^d\{A^{\text{♛}}\}$, and, for each group G that A belongs to, a bounded endorsement privilege ${}^e[A^{\text{♛}}]_{\langle \bot^c, \bot^i \rangle}^{\langle \top^c, G \rangle}$, where G is the disjunction of all users in the group. These are the only privileges available in the system for user A, and thus all endorsements must be bounded appropriately, and all declassifications must be robust.

Joint scheduling between A and B works as follows:

1. User B sends a scheduling request for time t labeled $\langle B, B \rangle$ to user A.
2. User A computes her availability for time t. Because the context that computes the availability reads data labeled $\langle A, A \rangle$ and $\langle B, A \rangle$, the label of the availability result is $\langle A \wedge B, A \vee B \rangle$.

3. If A and B are both in some group G, then A uses her bounded privilege to endorse the availability result to $\langle A \wedge B, A \rangle$, since she is prepared to take sole responsibility for the availability result. Since both A and B are in the same group, the endorsement satisfies the bounds (i.e., $A \vee B \sqsubseteq^l G$). If there is no group for which both A and B are members, then A has no bounded endorsement privilege for which the bounds will be satisfied.
4. User A uses her robust privilege to declassify the availability result to $\langle B, A \rangle$. The declassification is robust.
5. User A sends the declassified value to B.

Because all downgrading in the system relevant to user A must use A's restricted privileges, we obtain strong system-wide guarantees, even if A's restricted privileges manage to escape from the scheduling component, and even if B sends malicious scheduling requests. Section 5 (Fig. 11) discusses in more detail the system-wide guarantees that hold when both a bounded endorsement privilege and a robust declassification privilege are available.

6.2   Restricted Privileges in Existing Applications

Using our restricted privileges, we found a security vulnerability in an application written using Haskell Automatic Information Labeling System (Hails) [9]. Hails is a web framework built on LIO that extends the traditional Model-View-Controller paradigm to Model-Policy-View-Controller. The policy module specifies all models and describes the labels for data fetched from the database. When data is stored in the database, Hails checks labels against the policy module to ensure appropriate data integrity. The policy module has access to a privilege that can declassify all models. As a design pattern, policy modules export functions that perform declassification for untrusted applications using the privilege; untrusted applications never have direct access to the privilege.

Rock-Paper-Scissors[1] is a Hails application that contains a security vulnerability due to misuse of the policy privilege, despite being written by security experts who developed Hails.

The policy module includes a function to get the outcome of a match given a particular move by a player. This function can be exploited to reveal the opponent's move before the player has actually committed to a move by submitting it to the database. As a result, a player can always win a match by exploiting this function to determine which move will win, and then committing to that winning move. When we replaced the policy module's raw privilege with a robust privilege, the robust declassification check signalled a potential security vulnerability. To fix the vulnerability, we added code that checks whether a player had committed to a move (i.e., the move is in the database), and, if so, endorses the submitted move. This endorsement allows the robust declassification check to succeed. Endorsing only when the player has committed to his move fixes the security vulnerability.

---

[1] https://github.com/scslab/hails/tree/master/examples/hails-rock.

7   Related Work

Declassification can be characterized into different dimensions: *who, what, where,* and *when* [20]. Our work can be considering as restricting *where* in the security lattice downgrading may occur (bounded downgrading) and *who* may influence downgrading (robustness). Almeida Matos and Boudol [1] introduce a construct **flow** $p \prec q$ **in** c to indicate *where* additional information flows are allowed within a lexical scope. Intransitive noninterference [11,12,18] posits a non-transitive information flow ordering which describes *what* downgrading operations are permitted. Mantel and Sands [11] combine intransitive noninterference with language techniques that use declassification annotations to explicitly identify non-transitive information flows. In our bounded declassification mechanism, violating the normal ordering of security levels is tied to a runtime value, and not lexically scoped or marked by annotations.

In Jif [13], declassifications may explicitly state where in the security lattice the declassification occurs. By contrast, our bounded mechanisms declare this restriction on the run-time value that authorizes downgrading. Jif uses a form of access control to restrict which code may downgrade information, coined *selective declassification* by Pottier and Conchon [17]. Specifically, a downgrading operation that may compromise the security of principal p may only occur in code that has been (statically or dynamically) authorized by p. Similarly, the authority to declassify or endorse information in Asbestos [7], HiStar [26], Flume [10], and COWL [23] must come from the creator of the exercised privileges. By contrast, LIO associates the authority to declassify or endorse a principal's information with a run-time value. This capability-like approach to authorizing downgrading enables our local declarative approach to restrict downgrading. Birgisson et al. [4] use capabilities to restrict the ability to read and write memory locations, but do not consider the use of capabilities to restrict downgrading.

Zdancewic and Myers [25] introduce the semantic security condition of *robust declassification*, and Myers et al. [16] enforce robust declassification with a security type system [19,24], and introduce *qualified robustness*, which extends the concept to reason about endorsement. Askarov and Myers [2] subsequently present a semantic framework for downgrading, and present a crisper version of qualified robustness. Chong and Myers [6] extend the notion of robust declassification to the Decentralized Label Model [14,15]. The run-time checks used in this work to enforce robustness are analogous to the run-time checks Chong and Myers introduce for the DLM. In other work, Chong and Myers [5] note that the semantic security condition for robust declassification applies to information flow of confidential information generally, including, for example, information erasure, and is more general than just declassification. If the only privilege for p available in the system is a robust privilege with mode d then the system will be robust for p. If the privilege for that mode is de (i.e., robust declassification operations and robust endorsement operations are possible), then the end-to-end security guarantee is *qualified robustness* [2,16]. A system satisfies qualified robustness if the only way an attacker can influence what information is released to it is via robust endorsement operations.

Foley et al. incorporate bounds constraints on a system with relabeling operations on objects [8]. Our model performs relabeling based on the use of capability-like tokens rather than with respect to a particular subject. Bound restrictions can be placed per privilege rather than on all relabeling operations, so the guarantees of this work are more dependent on what sorts of privileges are available for use, but do not require changes to the trusted computing base.

The system HiStar [26] provides the notion of gates: entities designed to encapsulate privileges so that processes can safely switch their current label by exercising them through the gate. Gates have a clearance component which imposes an upper bound on the label that results from using it. Gates can be leveraged to restrict the use of privileges similar to upper bounds in bounded privileges. Similar to our approach, Flume [10] distinguishes privileges used for declassification (symbol −) and endorsement (symbol +).

8 Conclusion

Restricted privileges are a new mechanism to control declassification and endorsement in DC-labels that is simple and intuitive yet expresses a rich set of desirable policies. Bounded privileges impose upper and lower bounds on data that is declassified or endorsed. Robust privileges help prevent the accidental or malicious exercise of privileges to downgrade more information than intended, and can provide the end-to-end security guarantees of robustness and qualified robustness. We provide sound and complete efficient security checks for downgrading using restricted privileges. We note that robust downgrading operations can be viewed as privileged downgrading with a weakened privilege. We explore the guarantees provided by combining the use of bounded and robust privileges as well as their composition in a case study. This work establishes a basis for better design of IFC systems that use privileges for downgrading information.

References

1. Almeida Matos, A., Boudol, G.: On declassification and the non-disclosure policy. In: Proceedingsof the 18th IEEE Computer Security Foundations Workshop, pp. 226–240 (2005)
2. Askarov, A., Myers, A.: A semantic framework for declassification and endorsement. In: Proceedings of the 19th European Symposium on Programming (2010)
3. Biba, K.J.: Integrity considerations for secure computer systems. ESD-TR-76-372 (1977)
4. Birgisson, A., Russo, A., Sabelfeld, A.: Capabilities for information flow. In: Proceedings of the 6th Workshop on Programming Languages and Analysis for Security (2011)
5. Chong, S., Myers, A.C.: Language-based information erasure. In: Proceeding of the 18th IEEE Computer Security Foundations Workshop, pp. 241–254, June 2005
6. Chong, S., Myers, A.C.: Decentralized robustness. In: Proceedings of the 19th IEEE Workshop on Computer Security Foundations, pp. 242–256 (2006)

7. Efstathopoulos, P., Krohn, M., VanDeBogart, S., Frey, C., Ziegler, D., Kohler, E., Mazières, D., Kaashoek, F., Morris, R.: Labels and event processes in the Asbestos operating system. In: Proceedings of the 20th ACM Symposium on Operating Systems Principles (2005)

8. Foley, S., Gong, L., Qian, X.: A security model of dynamic labeling providing a tiered approach to verification. In: Proceedings of the 1996 IEEE Symposium on Security and Privacy, pp. 142–158 (1996)

9. Giffin, D.B., Levy, A., Stefan, D., Terei, D., Mazières, D., Mitchell, J., Russo, A.: Hails: Protecting data privacy in untrusted web applications. In: Proceedings of the Symposium on Operating Systems Design and Implementation (2012)

10. Krohn, M., Yip, A., Brodsky, M., Cliffer, N., Kaashoek, M.F., Kohler, E., Morris, R.: Information flow control for standard OS abstractions. In: Proceedings of the 21st Symposium on Operating Systems Principles, October 2007

11. Mantel, H., Sands, D.: Controlled declassification based on intransitive noninterference. In: Chin, W.-N. (ed.) APLAS 2004. LNCS, vol. 3302, pp. 129–145. Springer, Heidelberg (2004)

12. van der Meyden, R.: What, indeed, is intransitive noninterference? In: Biskup, J., López, J. (eds.) ESORICS 2007. LNCS, vol. 4734, pp. 235–250. Springer, Heidelberg (2007)

13. Myers, A.C., Zheng, L., Zdancewic, S., Chong, S., Nystrom, N.: Jif: Java Information Flow (2001-), software release. http://www.cs.cornell.edu/jif

14. Myers, A.C., Liskov, B.: A decentralized model for information flow control. In: Proceedings of the 16th ACM Symposium on Operating System Principles, pp. 129–142. New York, NY, USA (1997)

15. Myers, A.C., Liskov, B.: Complete, safe information flow with decentralized labels. In: Proceedings of the IEEE Symposium on Security and Privacy, pp. 186–197, May 1998

16. Myers, A.C., Sabelfeld, A., Zdancewic, S.: Enforcing robust declassification and qualified robustness. J. Comput. Secur. 14(2), 157–196 (2006)

17. Pottier, F., Conchon, S.: Information flow inference for free. In: Proceedings of the 5th ACM SIGPLAN International Conference on Functional Programming, pp. 46–57. New York, NY, USA (2000)

18. Roscoe, A.W., Goldsmith, M.H.: What is intransitive noninterference? In: Proceedings of the 12th IEEE Computer Security Foundations Workshop (1999)

19. Sabelfeld, A., Myers, A.C.: Language-based information-flow security. IEEE J. Sel. Areas Commun. 21(1), 5–19 (2003)

20. Sabelfeld, A., Sands, D.: Dimensions and principles of declassification. In: Proceedings of the 18th IEEE Computer Security Foundations Workshop, pp. 255–269, June 2005

21. Stefan, D., Russo, A., Mazières, D., Mitchell, J.C.: Disjunction category labels. In: Laud, P. (ed.) NordSec 2011. LNCS, vol. 7161, pp. 223–239. Springer, Heidelberg (2012)

22. Stefan, D., Russo, A., Mitchell, J.C., Mazières, D.: Flexible Dynamic Information Flow Control in Haskell. In: Proceedings of the 4th ACM Symposium on Haskell, pp. 95–106. New York, NY, USA (2011)

23. Stefan, D., Yang, E.Z., Marchenko, P., Russo, A., Herman, D., Karp, B., Mazières, D.: Protecting users by confining JavaScript with COWL. In: Proceedings of the 11th Symposium on Operating Systems Design and Implementation, October 2014

24. Volpano, D., Smith, G., Irvine, C.: A sound type system for secure flow analysis. J. Comput. Secur. 4(3), 167–187 (1996)

25. Zdancewic, S., Myers, A.C.: Robust declassification. In: Proceedings of the 14th IEEE Computer Security Foundations Workshop, pp. 15–23, Jun 2001
26. Zeldovich, N., Boyd-Wickizer, S., Kohler, E., Mazières, D.: Making information flow explicit in HiStar. In: Proceedings of the 7th Symposium on Operating Systems Design and Implementation, pp. 263–278 (2006)

Obligations in PTaCL

Jason Crampton[✉] and Conrad Williams

Royal Holloway, University of London, London, UK
{Jason.Crampton,Conrad.Williams.2010}@rhul.ac.uk

Abstract. Obligations play an increasingly important role in authorization systems and are supported by languages such as XACML. However, our understanding of how to handle obligations in languages such as XACML, particularly in exceptional circumstances, is hampered by a lack of formality and rigor in the existing literature, including the XACML standard. PTaCL is an attribute-based policy language that makes use of tree-structured policies and targets, like XACML. However, PTaCL is more general than XACML and has rigorous operational semantics for request evaluation, from which a policy decision point can be implemented. In this paper, we enhance PTaCL by extending the policy syntax to include obligations and defining the obligations that should be associated with an authorization decision. Our final contribution is to extend our analysis to cases where policy evaluation may return an indeterminate value. We demonstrate that obligation semantics for PTaCL coincide with those of XACML when there is no indeterminacy. More importantly, we show that our obligation semantics provide a principled method for determining obligations for any policy-combining algorithm and the set of possible obligations in the presence of indeterminacy, thereby providing considerable advantages over existing approaches.

1 Introduction

There has been considerable work in recent years on defining authorization policies for "open" systems which need to make access control decisions based on user attributes, instead of identities. An authorization policy is typically defined by a target, a set of child policies and a decision-combining algorithm. The target, either implicitly or explicitly, identifies a set of requests. The policy is said to be "applicable" if the access request belongs to (or "matches") the policy's target. If a policy is applicable, then its child policies are evaluated and the results returned by those child policies are combined using the decision-combining algorithm. The most commonly used language of this type, particularly in real-world implementations, is XACML [16]. Despite its widespread use, the XACML standard is somewhat vague and inconsistent in its articulation of policy evaluation, making it unsuitable for formal analysis and leading to counterintuitive authorization decisions (notably when errors in policy evaluation occur) [13,15].

C. Williams—This research was supported by the EPSRC and the UK government as part of the Centre for Doctoral Training in Cyber Security at Royal Holloway, University of London (EP/K035584/1).

© Springer International Publishing Switzerland 2015
S. Foresti (Ed.): STM 2015, LNCS 9331, pp. 220–235, 2015.
DOI: 10.1007/978-3-319-24858-5_14

An important aspect of authorization policies, and the focus of this paper, is obligations and the methods for returning them. An obligation is a mandate on what must be carried out before or after an access is approved or denied, and they are used to meet formal requirements of systems such as non-repudiation. One example of an obligation would be to log access to a resource when an access request is made. Usually, each access control policy will have associated obligations, rather than having obligations as separate functions, so obligations may be thought of as a function of the access request. The XACML 2.0 standard defines how to compute the set of obligations returned when policy evaluation occurs; however, like much of the standard, the definition lacks rigor.

There is some work that define methods for returning obligations in policy-combining languages [1,13]. However, like XACML this work also lacks formal semantics and uses weak methods to return obligations in exceptional circumstances. The lack of a formal deterministic method for computing the appropriate obligation associated with an authorization decision motivates us to develop new methods that can provide this functionality and provide default ways of returning obligations.

To tackle some of the shortcomings of XACML, Crampton and Morisset defined the policy language PTaCL [6]. PTaCL defines three basic policy-combining operators, which can be used to represent all other policy-combining operators. PTaCL also provides a concise syntax for policy targets and precise semantics for policy evaluation. XACML policies (without obligations and conditions) can be encoded using PTaCL, which allows XACML to be analyzed within a more formal environment. In this paper, we extend the PTaCL syntax to incorporate obligations and define which obligations should be returned when evaluating an access request with respect to a PTaCL policy. We then show how to extend the PTaCL decision set so that we can handle errors in policy evaluation and demonstrate that our approach has advantages over existing approaches in the literature. The insights this provides suggests alternative ways of returning obligations in XACML. Thus the main contributions of this paper are:

- the specification of syntax extensions for PTaCL to incorporate obligations;
- the specification of "obligation semantics" for a PTaCL policy, defining precisely what obligations are returned for a given authorization request and PTaCL policy;
- a systematic extension of PTaCL to compute possible obligations in the presence of incomplete information; and
- a comparison of our approach with those in the literature and concrete proposals to improve how XACML handles obligations, particularly in the presence of indeterminate authorization decisions.

In the following section we provide an overview of PTaCL and introduce an example of a policy that we will use throughout the paper. In Sect. 3, we extend PTaCL policy syntax to include obligations and show how obligations can be evaluated in XACML by encoding policies in PTaCL. In Sect. 4, we explain how

PTaCL semantics can be extended to account for indeterminacy in target and policy evaluation. We conclude the paper with a comparison and discussion of related work and ideas for future work.

2 PTaCL

PTaCL is intended to provide a generic framework for specifying target-based policy languages. In particular, it may be used to provide a more formal representation of XACML, thereby facilitating the analysis of XACML and identifying weaknesses in its specification.

PTaCL defines a *policy target language* (PTL), for specifying targets in terms of attributes (of users and resources), and a *policy combining language* (PCL), for combining (the decisions associated with the evaluation of) sub-policies [6]. For the purposes of this paper it is sufficient to understand that a policy target t is evaluated with respect to an access request q. This evaluation, which we denote by $[t](q)$, may return true or false, which we denote by 1_T and 0_T, respectively. If $[t](q) = 1_T$, we say the target is *applicable* to the request (and *inapplicable* if $[t](q) = 0_T$).

2.1 Syntax and Semantics

PTaCL policies are defined inductively with respect to a set of policy decisions D. We assume that D contains decisions 1 and 0, corresponding to "allow" and "deny", respectively. For now, we assume $D = \{0, 1, \bot\}$, where the decision $\bot$ denotes that a policy is not applicable to a request. (We consider more complex decision sets in Sect. 4.) Then 0 and 1 are (atomic) policies. Moreover, if p, p_1 and p_2 are policies and t is a target, then the following are policies:

$$\neg p \text{ (negation)} \qquad p_1 \wedge p_2 \text{ (join)}$$
$$\sim p \text{ (deny-by-default)} \qquad (t, p) \text{ (selection)}$$

The semantics of a PTaCL policy are defined by applying the operators $\neg$, $\sim$ and $\wedge$ (defined on the set of decisions) to the decisions returned by the evaluation of sub-policies. The evaluation tables for $\neg$, $\sim$ and $\wedge$ are shown in Fig. 1a, b. The unary operators $\neg$ and $\sim$ simply modify the decision: the former switches the values of 0 and 1, leaving $\bot$ unchanged; the latter transforms $\bot$ to 0, leaving 0 and 1 unchanged. These operators are used to implement policy negation and deny-by-default policies, respectively. The binary operator $\wedge$ is strong conjunction in the Kleene three-valued logic [11]. It returns 0 if at least one of the operands is 0, 1 if both operands are 1, and $\bot$ otherwise. Given a request q, we write $\Delta(p, q)$ to denote the decision returned by policy p for request q. The semantics of PTaCL policies are defined in Fig. 1c.

Policy Trees. Any PTaCL policy may be represented as a *policy tree*, in which leaf nodes are 0 or 1 decisions and internal nodes may be a target, one of the unary operators $\neg$ or $\sim$, or the binary operator $\wedge$. We introduce a special target

$$\Delta(0, q) = 0$$
$$\Delta(1, q) = 1$$
$$\Delta(\neg p, q) = \neg(\Delta(p, q))$$
$$\Delta(\sim p, q) = \sim(\Delta(p, q))$$
$$\Delta(p_1 \wedge p_2, q) = \Delta(p_1, q) \wedge \Delta(p_2, q)$$

$\wedge$	0	1	$\perp$
0	0	0	0
1	0	1	$\perp$
$\perp$	0	$\perp$	$\perp$

d	$\neg d$	$\sim d$
0	1	0
1	0	1
$\perp$	$\perp$	0

$$\Delta((t, p), q) = \begin{cases} \Delta(p, q) & \text{if } [\![t]\!](q) = 1 \\ \perp & \text{otherwise} \end{cases}$$

(a) $\wedge$ (b) $\neg$ and $\sim$ (c) Policy semantics

Fig. 1. Decision operators and policy semantics in PTaCL

$$\sim\Big(t_5, \big(\neg(t_3, (t_1, 1) \wedge (t_2, 0)) \wedge (t_4, 1)\big)\Big).$$

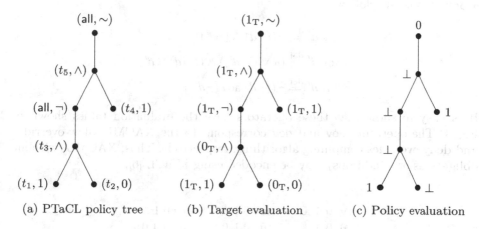

(a) PTaCL policy tree   (b) Target evaluation   (c) Policy evaluation

Fig. 2. Evaluating a PTaCL policy

all which is applicable to every request. Thus, we may assume that every policy has the form (t, p). Figure 2a shows the policy tree representing the policy

$$\sim\Big(t_5, \big(\neg(t_3, (t_1, 1) \wedge (t_2, 0)) \wedge (t_4, 1)\big)\Big).$$

Request Evaluation. Request evaluation may be described in terms of policy trees and comprises two phases. The first phase *evaluates the targets*. The second phase *propagates the decisions* of sub-policies up to the root of the policy tree using the policy-combining operators at the internal nodes and the semantics defined in Fig. 1.

Consider the policy depicted in Fig. 2a and suppose that

$$[t_1](q) = [t_4](q) = [t_5](q) = 1_T \text{ and } [t_2](q) = [t_3](q) = 0_T.$$

The first phase of request evaluation results in the tree shown in Fig. 2b; recall that the targets for $\sim$ and $\neg$ are all and thus necessarily evaluate to 1_T. The second phase of policy evaluation is shown in Fig. 2c. Note that the evaluation of the sub-trees with roots t_3 and t_5 consider the combination of a 1 and $\perp$ decision, and $\perp \wedge 1 = \perp$. At the root, the $\sim$ operator converts the $\perp$ decision into a 0 decision, which is the final decision returned for this policy.

2.2   Additional Operators

Crampton and Morisset showed that PTaCL is functionally complete [6]. In practical terms, this means we can introduce new binary operators to combine policies, which act as syntactic sugar, knowing that any such operator may be constructed using the PTaCL operators. In particular, we define three new operators: $\vee$, aov and dov, where

$$d \vee d' \stackrel{\text{def}}{=} \neg((\neg d) \wedge (\neg d'))$$

$$d \text{ aov } d' \stackrel{\text{def}}{=} (d \vee (\sim d')) \wedge ((\sim d) \vee d')$$

$$d \text{ dov } d' \stackrel{\text{def}}{=} \neg((\neg d) \text{ aov } (\neg d'))$$

It is easy to show that these operators have the evaluation tables shown in Fig. 3. The operators aov and dov correspond to the XACML allow-overrides and deny-overrides combining algorithms, respectively. Thus, XACML (without obligations or conditions) may be encoded using PTaCL [6].

$\vee$	0	1	$\perp$
0	0	1	$\perp$
1	1	1	1
$\perp$	$\perp$	1	$\perp$

aov	0	1	$\perp$
0	0	1	0
1	1	1	1
$\perp$	0	1	$\perp$

dov	0	1	$\perp$
0	0	0	0
1	0	1	1
$\perp$	0	1	$\perp$

Fig. 3. Supplementary decision operators for PTaCL

To illustrate how the various techniques we develop may be applied in practice, and to demonstrate some shortcomings in XACML, we will use a running example due to Li et al. [13]. We cast their example in the syntax of PTaCL in the interests of brevity; the resulting policy and policy tree is shown in Fig. 4. The obligations (represented o_1, o_2, o_5) are not present in Li et al.'s original example; we include them to illustrate our methods for returning obligations alongside decisions.

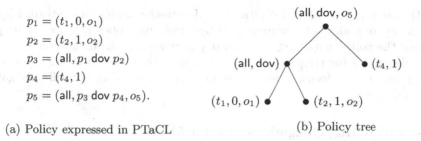

$$p_1 = (t_1, 0, o_1)$$
$$p_2 = (t_2, 1, o_2)$$
$$p_3 = (\text{all}, p_1 \text{ dov } p_2)$$
$$p_4 = (t_4, 1)$$
$$p_5 = (\text{all}, p_3 \text{ dov } p_4, o_5).$$

(a) Policy expressed in PTaCL   (b) Policy tree

Fig. 4. Motivating example policy and policy tree

3   Obligations in PTaCL

In this section we define the method for incorporating obligations in PTaCL. In this paper, we are not concerned with the specific types of obligations, how they will be provided by the policy information point, or how they will be enforced by the policy enforcement point. Instead, we focus on how they will be combined by the policy decision point (following the approach taken by the XACML standard). Thus, we simply assume the existence of some "abstract" set of obligations O.

The method we define for computing obligations in PTaCL is inspired by the XACML standard, and one of our results shows that the obligations returned by a PTaCL policy will be the same as those returned by an equivalent XACML policy. While recognizing that there may be other ways of computing obligations, we make the assumption that the behavior specified by the XACML standard is that expected by the practitioners who designed it and is, therefore, a reasonable proxy for the required behavior of an obligations-combining strategy.

3.1   Defining Obligations in PTaCL

In XACML, each policy or policy set may be associated with one or more obligations. An obligation is associated with an effect (a decision in PTaCL), which may be Permit or Deny (denoted by 1 and 0, respectively, in PTaCL). Thus, the obligation associated with Permit is applied when the effect of a policy is Permit for a particular request. Informally, then, the result of evaluating a request in XACML is a pair comprising a decision and an obligation. Thus, we extend PTaCL syntax in the following ways.

- The PTaCL policy d, where $d \in \{0, 1\}$, may only return d, so it suffices to extend the syntax for such policies to (d, o) (where $o \in O$).
- The unary policy operators $\sim$ and $\neg$ are used only to eliminate or switch policy decisions, so we will assume that obligations are not associated with these operators. When evaluating policies with the operators $\sim$ and $\neg$ the obligations from child nodes are passed up with no change.
- All other policies (generated using $\wedge$ or targets) may return 0 or 1, so we extend the syntax for a policy p to (p, o_0, o_1), where $o_i \in O$ is the obligation that should be returned if the evaluation of p returns decision $i \in \{0, 1\}$.

Henceforth, we will write $\Omega(p,q)$ to denote the obligations returned by the evaluation of policy p for request q. When depicting policy trees, we write p_i to denote the policy with target t_i and $o_{i,j}$ to represent the obligation associated with decision j for target t_i. We may not wish to specify obligations for every policy and every decision, so we assume the existence of a "null" obligation, denoted by ϵ.

3.2   Computing Obligations in PTaCL

In general terms, when a policy language includes obligations, the policy decision point will return a decision and a set of obligations as a result of evaluating an access request. In terms of our notation, then, request evaluation will return the pair $(\Delta(p,q), \Omega(p,q))$: $\Delta(p,q)$ is an element of D, as we have seen, and is determined by applying the relevant binary operator to the decisions returned by the child policies; $\Omega(p,q)$ is a subset of O and, informally, is determined by taking the union of the sets of obligations associated with particular child policies (together with any relevant obligation for the parent policy). This method leverages the tree-structured, bottom-up evaluation strategy of PTaCL (and XACML) to return obligations from the nodes in the policy tree that influence the final decision returned by policy evaluation.

More formally, PTaCL obligation semantics are shown in Fig. 5a. The interesting case is policy conjunction, where we only take the obligations from child policies that return a decision equal to that of the parent policy. Thus we take obligations from both child policies if they return the same decision (as well as the relevant obligation from the parent policy), and if child policy p_i returns 0 and the other does not then we return $\{o_0\} \cup \Omega(p_i, q)$. (In all other cases, the decision returned is $\bot$ and the obligation set is empty.) We interpret $\{\epsilon\}$ as the empty set $\emptyset$.

By an abuse of notation, we can build an evaluation table for $\wedge$, as shown in Fig. 5b (with the understanding that the relevant obligation needs to be included from the parent policy, the set of obligations associated with the decisions indexing the rows is O_1 and the set of obligations indexing the columns is O_2).

3.3   Computing Obligations for Derived Policy Operators

Given that (i) we can define arbitrary policy operators in terms of $\sim$, $\neg$ and $\wedge$ and (ii) we have defined how obligations are computed for these operators, we can extend our method of computing obligations to arbitrary policy operators. For example, we can define the obligations that should be returned by $\vee$, dov and aov, as shown in Fig. 6. (As in Fig. 5b for $\wedge$, we assume that the relevant obligation from the parent policy will be included during policy evaluation; O_1 and O_2 are the obligations associated with the evaluation of p_1 and p_2, respectively.)

Consider the policy shown in Fig. 4b taken from our running example, and assume that all targets are applicable for a request q. (Where obligations are not shown, they are assumed to be ϵ.) The result of evaluating the policy with respect to q is $(0, \{o_1, o_5\})$, as illustrated in Fig. 7b. In particular,

$$\Omega((0,o),q) = \Omega((1,o),q) = \{o\}$$
$$\Omega(\neg p,q) = \Omega(\sim p,q) = \Omega(p,q)$$

$$\Omega((p_1 \wedge p_2, o_0, o_1), q) = \begin{cases} \{o_0\} \cup \Omega(p_1,q) & \text{if } \Delta(p_1,q)=0 \text{ and } \Delta(p_2,q) \neq 0 \\ \{o_0\} \cup \Omega(p_2,q) & \text{if } \Delta(p_1,q) \neq 0 \text{ and } \Delta(p_2,q)=0 \\ \{o_0\} \cup \Omega(p_1,q) \cup \Omega(p_2,q) & \text{if } \Delta(p_1,q)=0 \text{ and } \Delta(p_2,q)=0 \\ \{o_1\} \cup \Omega(p_1,q) \cup \Omega(p_2,q) & \text{if } \Delta(p_1,q)=1 \text{ and } \Delta(p_2,q)=1 \\ \emptyset & \text{otherwise} \end{cases}$$

$$\Omega((t,p,o_0,o_1),q) = \begin{cases} \{o_0\} \cup \Omega(p,q) & \text{if } t \text{ is applicable to } q \text{ and } \Delta(p,q)=0 \\ \{o_1\} \cup \Omega(p,q) & \text{if } t \text{ is applicable to } q \text{ and } \Delta(p,q)=1 \\ \emptyset & \text{otherwise} \end{cases}$$

(a) Obligation semantics in PTaCL

	0	1	$\perp$
0	$(0,\{O_1,O_2\})$	$(0,\{O_1\})$	$(0,\{O_1\})$
1	$(0,\{O_2\})$	$(1,\{O_1,O_2\})$	$(\perp,\emptyset)$
$\perp$	$(0,\{O_2\})$	$(\perp,\emptyset)$	$(\perp,\emptyset)$

(b) A look-up table for $\wedge$ with decision-obligation pairs

Fig. 5. Obligation semantics and look-up table

p_1	p_2	$p_1 \vee p_2$	$p_1 \vee \sim p_2$	$\sim p_1 \vee p_2$	$p_1 \text{ aov } p_2$	$p_1 \text{ dov } p_2$
0	0	$(0,\{O_1,O_2\})$	$(0,\{O_1,O_2\})$	$(0,\{O_1,O_2\})$	$(0,\{O_1,O_2\})$	$(0,\{O_1,O_2\}))$
0	1	$(1,\{O_2\})$	$(1,\{O_2\})$	$(1,\{O_2\})$	$(1,\{O_2\})$	$(0,\{O_1\})$
0	$\perp$	$(\perp,\emptyset)$	$(0,\{O_1\})$	$(\perp,\emptyset)$	$(0,\{O_1\})$	$(0,\{O_1\})$
1	0	$(1,\{O_1\})$	$(1,\{O_1\})$	$(1,\{O_1\})$	$(1,\{O_1\})$	$(0,\{O_2\})$
1	1	$(1,\{O_1,O_2\})$	$(1,\{O_1,O_2\})$	$(1,\{O_1,O_2\})$	$(1,\{O_1,O_2\})$	$(1,\{O_1,O_2\})$
1	$\perp$	$(1,\{O_1\})$	$(1,\{O_1\})$	$(1,\{O_1\})$	$(1,\{O_1\})$	$(1,\{O_1\})$
$\perp$	0	$(\perp,\emptyset)$	$(\perp,\emptyset)$	$(0,\{O_2\})$	$(0,\{O_2\})$	$(0,\{O_2\})$
$\perp$	1	$(1\{O_2\})$	$(1,\{O_2\})$	$(1,\{O_2\})$	$(1,\{O_2\})$	$(1,\{O_2\})$
$\perp$	$\perp$	$(\perp,\emptyset)$	$(\perp,\emptyset)$	$(\perp,\emptyset)$	$(\perp,\emptyset)$	$(\perp,\emptyset)$

Fig. 6. Decisions and obligations for the PTaCL $\vee$, aov and dov operators

$(0,\{o_1\}) \text{ dov } (1,\{o_2\}) = (0,\{o_1\})$. The root policy has an obligation o_5, which is always returned (irrespective of the decision), so we return the set of obligations $\{o_1, o_5\}$ along with the 0 decision.

Our approach to obligations thus provides considerably greater flexibility than XACML, which only specifies how obligations should be computed for the pre-defined rule- and policy combining algorithms. Moreover, it is easy to

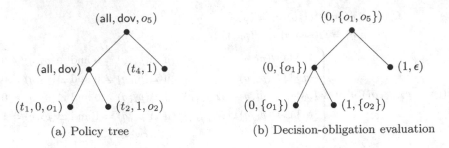

(a) Policy tree   (b) Decision-obligation evaluation

Fig. 7. PTaCL policy evaluation with obligations

show that the obligations computed by PTaCL for the aov and dov operators are identical to those computed by XACML. In other words, PTaCL is (i) consistent with XACML in terms of the obligations returned for standard operators, and (ii) provides an extensible mechanism for computing obligations for arbitrary policy operators.

4 Indeterminacy in PTaCL

Thus far, we have assumed that target evaluation will return either 1_T or 0_T. In fact, PTaCL recognizes (like XACML) that target evaluation might fail and return $?_T$. The full semantics for PTaCL are shown in Fig. 8.

$$\Delta(\neg p, q) = \{\neg d : d \in \Delta(p, q)\}$$
$$\Delta(\sim p, q) = \{\sim d : d \in \Delta(p, q)\}$$
$$\Delta(p_1 \wedge p_2, q) = \{d_1 \wedge d_2 : d_i \in \Delta(p_i, q)\}$$
$$\Delta((t, p), q) = \begin{cases} \Delta(p, q) & \text{if } [\![t]\!]_T(q) = 1_T \\ \{\bot\} & \text{if } [\![t]\!]_T(q) = 0_T \\ \{\bot\} \cup \Delta(p, q) & \text{if } [\![t]\!]_T(q) = ?_T \end{cases}$$

Fig. 8. PTaCL decisions in the presence of indeterminacy

The interesting case here is for policies of the form (t, p) when target evaluation returns $?_T$. Informally, PTaCL assumes that either one of 1_T and 0_T could have been returned. Thus policy evaluation may return a set of decisions (reflecting the indeterminacy). The semantics for the other operators operate on sets, rather than single decisions, in the natural way. A simple inductive argument establishes that if we can guarantee that $[\![t]\!](q) \in \{1_T, 0_T\}$, then $\Delta(p, q) = \{d\}$ for some $d \in D$; moreover, d is the decision that would be returned by the original PTaCL semantics [6].

We now revisit the example in Fig. 4 and suppose that $[t_1](q) = 0_T$ and $[t_2](q) = ?_T$. Li et al. used this example to demonstrate flaws in the way in which XACML 2.0 computed decisions in the presence of indeterminacy [13]. Specifically, for this request, a deny decision would be returned, when one would expect an allow decision (since if t_2 had evaluated to either 0_T or 1_T the root policy would evaluate to 1). The evaluation of the same policy for the same request in PTaCL is shown in Fig. 9. The set-based semantics mean that additional information is based up the tree during evaluation, resulting in the expected decision.

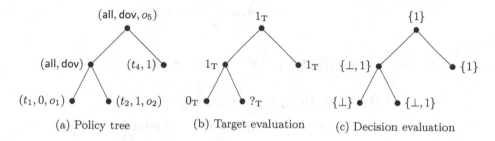

(a) Policy tree   (b) Target evaluation   (c) Decision evaluation

Fig. 9. PTaCL policy evaluation with indeterminacy

4.1 Failure of Target Evaluation

When target evaluation fails, PTaCL returns a decision set as opposed to a single decision. We can extend this method when obligations are included in PTaCL. Without indeterminacy, request evaluation returns a decision-obligation pair; with indeterminacy, therefore, it returns a set of decision-obligation pairs. If the evaluation of target t fails, for example, the leaf policy $(t, (d, o))$ evaluates to $\{(\bot, \emptyset), (d, \{o\})\}$.

We once again revisit our running example, again assuming that $[t_1](q) = ?_T$ and $[t_2](q) = 1_T$, as in Fig. 9. The resulting policy evaluation is shown in Fig. 10a and returns $\{(1, \{o_5\}), (1, \{o_2, o_5\})\}$. We see on this occasion that policy evaluation returns the same decision but different obligation sets.

Let us now consider request q' such that $[t_1](q') = ?_T$ and $[t_i](q') = 1_T$ for all other i. The resulting policy evaluation is shown in Fig. 10b. In this case, different decisions and different obligation sets are obtained.

Thus, in many situations we will be faced with a set of decision-obligation pairs. The behavior of the policy enforcement point would need to be defined for such situations. One possibility is to adopt use the idea of a resolution function, as described by Crampton and Huth [5]. This is a topic for future research.

4.2 Failure of Policy Retrieval

In the previous section, we explored the scenarios that arise when target evaluation fails, in which case we considered the possibilities that the target evaluated to 1_T and 0_T. In handling indeterminacy, the XACML standard makes the

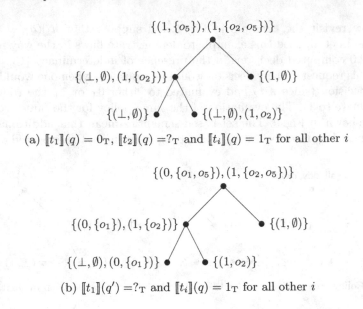

(a) $\llbracket t_1 \rrbracket(q) = 0_\mathrm{T}$, $\llbracket t_2 \rrbracket(q) = ?_\mathrm{T}$ and $\llbracket t_i \rrbracket(q) = 1_\mathrm{T}$ for all other i

(b) $\llbracket t_1 \rrbracket(q') = ?_\mathrm{T}$ and $\llbracket t_i \rrbracket(q) = 1_\mathrm{T}$ for all other i

Fig. 10. PTaCL policy evaluation with indeterminacy and obligations

assumption that the contents or effect of a sub-policy or rule may be retrieved and inspected, and this influences the type of indeterminate decision returned (in XACML 3.0). However, it is not always possible to retrieve a sub-policy, or inspect a rule. This may occur if a policy is not self-contained: a policy may, for example, reference a sub-policy that is located on a remote server that has crashed. Even in these circumstances, we would still like to attempt to evaluate the root policy, despite lacking a complete policy tree. In the XACML standard, this scenario is not considered at all.

Under normal circumstances, the evaluation of policy with respect to a request q may return a $0, 1$ or $\bot$ decision. However when a policy may not be retrieved, we only know that the policy could have evaluated to one of the three basic decisions 0, 1 or $\bot$. Hence, when we can not retrieve a policy, we return the set $\{0, 1, \bot\}$ in place of the policy.

We now consider how we should handle obligations in this scenario. Given that obligations are part of the policy specification, we will have no information about the obligations that should be returned. To handle this lack of information, we consider two methods. Firstly, return the empty set of obligations with each of the three possible decisions. Thus the set of decision-obligations pairs for an irretrievable (sub)policy is then $\{(0, \emptyset), (1, \emptyset), (\bot, \emptyset)\}$. Alternatively, return "error" obligation $o!$ alongside each decision, rather than the empty set. In an implementation, the later option has merit as more information is provided and it highlights that an error occurred in policy evaluation, which can in turn be handled by the policy enforcement point.

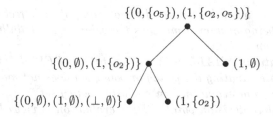

Fig. 11. Policy evaluation when p_1 is irretrievable

Returning to our running example, suppose policy p_1 is irretrievable and all the remaining targets are applicable for a request q. Policy evaluation under the first method is shown in Fig. 11 and results in the set $\{(0, \{o_5\}), (1, \{o_2, o_5\})\}$. Clearly, in this situation we are not able to return the correct set of obligations, even if policy evaluation returns a conclusive decision. Policy evaluation using the "error" obligation in the same example would return $\{(0, \{o!, o_5\}), (1, \{o!, o_2, o_5\})\}$.

5 XACML and Other Related Work

Informally, a policy written in XACML may be viewed as a tree in which the leaf nodes are XACML *rules*, nodes whose children are rules are XACML *policies*, and all other nodes are XACML *policy sets*. Each node has a *target*, defined in terms of user and resource attributes. A target determines whether a rule, policy or policy set is evaluated for a given access request. Each rule is associated with an *effect* (an authorization decision), which may be either "Permit" or "Deny". Each policy node is associated with a *rule-combining algorithm* (RCA), which is used during request evaluation to combine the decisions of the policy's rules that are applicable to the request. Each policy set node is associated with a *policy-combining algorithm* (PCA), which is used to combine the decisions of its applicable child policies. Thus, an XACML rule corresponds to leaf nodes (atomic policies) in a PTaCL policy tree; and XACML policies and policy sets are non-leaf nodes in a PTaCL policy tree.

In addition, each XACML policy and policy set (but not rules) may be associated with one or more *obligations*[1]. An obligation is defined by the FulfillOn attribute (whose value is either "Permit" or "Deny") and an action (such as "create audit entry"). Policy evaluation returns a decision and a set of obligations to the policy enforcement point, which is required to enforce the decision and execute any obligations. The XACML 2.0 and 3.0 standards [14,16] define how this set of obligations is computed:

> "*When such a policy or policy set is evaluated, an obligation SHALL be passed up to the next level of evaluation (the enclosing or referencing*

---

[1] XACML 3.0 allows obligations to be associated with rules.

policy, policy set or authorization decision) only if the effect of the policy or policy set being evaluated matches the value of the FulfillOn attribute of the obligation... "

"... no obligations SHALL be returned to the PEP if... the decision resulting from evaluating the policy or policy set does not match the decision resulting from evaluating an enclosing policy set."

"... If the [policy decision point] PDP's evaluation is viewed as a tree of policy sets and policies, each of which returns "Permit" or "Deny", then the set of obligations returned by the PDP to the [policy enforcement point] PEP will include only the obligations associated with those paths where the effect at each level of evaluation is the same as the effect being returned by the PDP."

Like much of the XACML standard, this statement lacks formality and prior work has indicated that the way in which policy-combining algorithms and the way of computing obligations produces some counterintuitive results [13].

The XACML 2.0 standard [14] defines how obligations are returned when target evaluation fails:

"... no obligations SHALL be returned to the PEP if the policies or policy sets from which they are drawn are not evaluated, or if their evaluated result is "Indeterminate" or "NotApplicable"... "

Thus, obligations from any policy that evaluates to "Indeterminate" are lost in the evaluation process. The XACML 3.0 standard has improved the way in which decisions are computed in the presence of indeterminacy [16], but has not changed how obligations are computed.

The specification and computation of obligations in PTaCL has some similarities to, and some notable differences, from XACML, which we summarize in Table 1. We also include a comparison with the work on obligations by Li et al. [13], discussed below.

Arguably the two greatest improvements offered by the approach we propose are (i) the ability to return obligations when policy evaluation is indeterminate, and (ii) the ability to compute the set of obligations for any policy, irrespective

Table 1. Comparison of XACML and PTaCL

Feature	XACML	PCA [13]	PTaCL
Obligations associated with different policy decisions	Yes	Yes	Yes
Selective "inheritance" of obligations from child policies by parent	No	Yes	No
Computation of obligations rigorously defined	No	Yes	Yes
Obligations associated with rules	Yes	No	Yes
Obligations returned when policy evaluation is indeterminate	No	No	Yes
Obligations defined for all policy combining algorithms	No	No	Yes

of the operators used. In the first case, it seems natural to allow obligations to be returned even for indeterminate policies (and these could be considered as "default obligations") and provides more fine-grained control over which requests are subject to indeterminacy. In the second case, we believe it is important to specify the computation of obligations as completely and unambiguously as possible, thus minimizing the likelihood that an implementation will be incorrect.

Other work exists that define methods for handling obligations in XACML. Alqatawna et al. [1] introduce a way of using obligations to implement a discretionary overriding mechanism in XACML. They do this by using two algorithms, an effects-combining algorithm which is similar to standard policy-combining algorithms and an obligations-combining algorithm, the implementation of the latter being left to the discretion of the policy author. We believe it will be more useful, in general, to provide, as we have done, standardized mechanisms for combining obligations that are natural extensions of the existing decision-combining algorithms.

Li et al. defined semantics for handling obligations in XACML, largely following the definition in the XACML standard where obligations are returned only from paths which "contribute" to the final decision returned by the PDP [13]. Li et al. do define an algorithm for computing the set of obligations for an arbitrary policy operator, although this algorithm requires the operator to have certain properties. In contrast, our approach to obligations is completely general: any policy operator can be defined using PTaCL and a decision and a set of obligations can be computed. Like our definition of obligations in PTaCL, if the outcome of policy evaluation is not-applicable then the set of obligations is defined to be empty. Like XACML, if the outcome of policy evaluation is indeterminate, then the set of obligations is defined to be indeterminate. We would argue that it is more useful to return as much information as possible to the PEP, which can then decide what obligations, if any, should be enforced. The work Li et al. differs when combining obligations from two sub-policies that return the same decision, by allowing for three different methods to be specified in the policy combining language: both, first and either, leaving the choice to the policy author.

Subsequently, Li et al. [12] developed an architecture extending the XACML architecture in order to handle access control policies with different types of obligations. The focus of their work is how to enforcing the obligations once they have been returned to the PEP, while we focus on which obligations should be returned in the first place. A combination of our Li et al.'s architecture and our method for returning obligations may be an interesting and beneficial solution to some of the issues in XACML. Finally, we note that there exists work on dependencies between obligations and the effect these might have on the ability to fulfil obligations [8,9]. These considerations are outside the scope of this paper, but may prove fruitful areas for future research.

6   Conclusion

The need to support obligations in a policy language is important for many real-world situations. It is recognized, for example, that obligations will play an important part in systems that use context-sensitive policies, where controlled overrides of policy decisions are required [2,3], and risk-aware policies [4,7,10].

We extend the PTaCL language to incorporate syntax for specifying obligations and semantics for computing obligations as part of policy evaluation. We compare our method for returning obligations with the way they are returned in the XACML 2.0 standard, as well as comparing them with other work in the field [1,13]. In doing so, we highlight a number of shortcomings in the XACML specification and computation of obligations, and in subsequent attempts to "patch" XACML.

One deficiency in the XACML standard is the way in which XACML handles indeterminacy, not least because the rule- and policy-combining algorithms behave differently. We show how decision sets can be used in PTaCL to handle indeterminacy and illustrate its effectiveness using an example from the literature. We further extend PTaCL semantics to handle obligations when there is indeterminacy, which results in a set of decision-obligation pairs. This is more informative and expressive than previous attempts to handle obligations when indeterminacy arises [13].

In summary, we have provided a principled method for computing decisions and obligations in PTaCL. These methods provide a rigorous foundation for attribute-based access control languages, including XACML.

In this paper we were not concerned with the specific type or scope of obligations, nor how they are handled by the system after evaluation. This is however an important aspect of obligations within authorization systems, and there has been extensive research into this area [8,9,12]. Future work could extend PTaCL to handle different types of obligations and model the behaviour that occurs after a decision-obligation pair has been returned to the PEP. Another natural extension for future work would be to implement a custom XACML policy decision point that is capable of handling PTaCL policies, or implementing a compiler that can translate policies expressed in PTaCL into XACML.

References

1. Alqatawna, J., Rissanen, E., Firozabadi, B.S.: Overriding of access control in XACML. In: 8th IEEE International Workshop on Policies for Distributed Systems and Networks (POLICY 2007), pp. 87–95. IEEE Computer Society (2007). http://doi.ieeecomputersociety.org/10.1109/POLICY.2007.31
2. Ardagna, C.A., di Vimercati, S.D.C., Foresti, S., Grandison, T., Jajodia, S., Samarati, P.: Access control for smarter healthcare using policy spaces. Comput. Secur. 29(8), 848–858 (2010). http://dx.doi.org/10.1016/j.cose.2010.07.001
3. Brucker, A.D., Petritsch, H.: Extending access control models with break-glass. In: Proceedings of the 14th ACM Symposium on Access Control Models and Technologies, pp. 197–206 (2009)

4. Cheng, P., Rohatgi, P., Keser, C., Karger, P.A., Wagner, G.M., Reninger, A.S.: Fuzzy multi-level security: An experiment on quantified risk-adaptive access control. In: 2007 IEEE Symposium on Security and Privacy (S&P 2007), pp. 222–230. IEEE Computer Society (2007). http://dx.doi.org/10.1109/SP.2007.21

5. Crampton, J., Huth, M.: An authorization framework resilient to policy evaluation failures. In: Gritzalis, D., Preneel, B., Theoharidou, M. (eds.) ESORICS 2010. LNCS, vol. 6345, pp. 472–487. Springer, Heidelberg (2010)

6. Crampton, J., Morisset, C.: PTaCL: a language for attribute-based access control in open systems. In: Degano, P., Guttman, J.D. (eds.) Principles of Security and Trust. LNCS, vol. 7215, pp. 390–409. Springer, Heidelberg (2012)

7. Dimmock, N., Belokosztolszki, A., Eyers, D.M., Bacon, J., Moody, K.: Using trust and risk in role-based access control policies. In: Proceedings of the 9th ACM Symposium on Access Control Models and Technologies, pp. 156–162 (2004)

8. Hilty, M., Basin, D., Pretschner, A.: On obligations. In: di Vimercati, S.C., Syverson, P.F., Gollmann, D. (eds.) ESORICS 2005. LNCS, vol. 3679, pp. 98–117. Springer, Heidelberg (2005)

9. Irwin, K., Yu, T., Winsborough, W.H.: On the modeling and analysis of obligations. In: Juels, A., Wright, R.N., di Vimercati, S.D.C. (eds.) Proceedings of the 13th ACM Conference on Computer and Communications Security, CCS 2006, pp. 134–143. ACM (2006). http://doi.acm.org/10.1145/1180405.1180423

10. JASON Program Office: Horizontal integration: Broader access models for realizing information dominance. Technical Report JSR-04-132, MITRE Corporation (2004)

11. Kleene, S.: Introduction to Metamathematics. D. Van Nostrand, Princeton (1950)

12. Li, N., Chen, H., Bertino, E.: On practical specification and enforcement of obligations. In: Bertino, E., Sandhu, R.S. (eds.) Second ACM Conference on Data and Application Security and Privacy, CODASPY 2012, pp. 71–82. ACM (2012). http://doi.acm.org/10.1145/2133601.2133611

13. Li, N., Wang, Q., Qardaji, W.H., Bertino, E., Rao, P., Lobo, J., Lin, D.: Access control policy combining: theory meets practice. In: Carminati, B., Joshi, J. (eds.) SACMAT 2009, 14th ACM Symposium on Access Control Models and Technologies, Proceedings, pp. 135–144. ACM (2009). http://doi.acm.org/10.1145/1542207.1542229

14. Moses, T.: eXtensible Access Control Markup Language (XACML) Version 2.0 OASIS Standard (2005). http://docs.oasis-open.org/xacml/2.0/access-control-xacml-2.0-core-spec-os.pdf

15. Ni, Q., Bertino, E., Lobo, J.: D-algebra for composing access control policy decisions. In: Proceedings of the 4th International Symposium on Information, Computer, and Communications Security, pp. 298–309. ACM (2009)

16. Rissanen, E.: eXtensible Access Control Markup Language (XACML) Version 3.0 OASIS Standard (2012). http://docs.oasis-open.org/xacml/3.0/xacml-3.0-core-os-en.html

Content and Key Management to Trace Traitors in Broadcasting Services

Kazuto Ogawa[1]([✉]), Goichiro Hanaoka[2], and Hideki Imai[3]

[1] Japan Broadcasting Corporation, Setagaya, Japan
ogawa.k-cm@nhk.or.jp
[2] National Institute of Advanced Industrial Science and Technology, Koto, Japan
hanaoka-goichiro@aist.go.jp
[3] The University of Tokyo, Meguro, Japan
imai@iis.u-tokyo.ac.jp

Abstract. Traitor tracing encryption schemes are a type of broadcasting encryption and have been developed for broadcasting services. There are multiple distinct decryption keys for each encryption key, and each service subscriber is given a unique decryption key. Any subscriber that redistributes his or her decryption key to a third party or who uses it to make a pirate receiver ($\mathcal{PR}$) can be identified using the schemes. However, almost all previous schemes are effective against only those $\mathcal{PR}$s with only one decryption key. We first discuss an attack (*content comparison attack*) against the above encryption schemes. The attack involves multiple distinct decryption keys and content-data comparison mechanism. We have developed a *content and key management method* (*CKM*) that makes traitor tracing schemes secure against the content comparison attack. Its use makes it impossible for $\mathcal{PR}$s to distinguish ordinary content data from test data and makes traitor tracing schemes effective against all $\mathcal{PR}$s. The CKM makes the broadcasting services secure.

1 Introduction

1.1 Background

Broadcasting and cable TV services encrypt their content before distributing to their subscribers. Each subscriber needs a decoder with a decryption module for decrypting the content. If a malicious subscriber extracts the decryption key from the module and uses it and maybe other keys to make a pirate receiver ($\mathcal{PR}$), anyone using the $\mathcal{PR}$ can decrypt the content and view it. Many traitor tracing encryption schemes (*TTE schemes*) [3,4,7,13,15–17,20] have been developed as a countermeasure against such attacks. Moreover, a conditional access system of broadcasting service that has a traitor tracing mechanism (*TTM*) is standardized [1] and practically used in Japan. A TTM is not a TTE scheme and is constructed with multiple symmetric encryption schemes.

In the TTE schemes, there are multiple distinct decryption keys for each encryption key, and each subscriber is given a unique decryption key. Distributed

S. Foresti (Ed.): STM 2015, LNCS 9331, pp. 236–252, 2015.
DOI: 10.1007/978-3-319-24858-5_15

content is encrypted with a symmetric encryption scheme and its key (*content key*) is encrypted with a TTE scheme. Every subscriber that has a decryption key of the TTE scheme can watch the content.

In Japanese TTM, there are multiple distinct keys (*device keys*) for each model of receivers. The models are divided into at most 254 groups and a distinct device key is preset in each receiver. Broadcasters assign a distinct work key for each group and encrypts the work key using a corresponding device key. When a broadcaster sends content to receivers, it encrypts the content using a content key and encrypts the content key using the work keys. Since there are multiple work keys, multiple ciphertexts corresponding to a content key are generated.

There exists only one ciphertext for the content key in the TTE schemes and multiple ciphertexts in the TTM. Hence, the TTE schemes are more efficient in terms of transmission bit rate than the TTM. On the other hand, the TTE schemes are asymmetric encryption schemes and the mechanism uses only symmetric encryption schemes. In general, encryption and decryption costs of asymmetric encryption schemes are ten or one hundred times higher than those of symmetric encryption schemes, and thus, the TTM is more efficient in terms of CPU cost than the TTE schemes.

In any TTE scheme, when a $\mathcal{PR}$ is found, a tracer of the service can use the scheme's tracing algorithm to analyze the decryption key(s) and identify the traitor. That is, the tracer can identify the decryption key(s) in the $\mathcal{PR}$. In the TTM, when a $\mathcal{PR}$ is found, the tracer can use the mechanism's tracing algorithm to analyze the device key(s) and identify the model.

As far as we know, all previous TTE schemes, and as far as we guess, the TTM are effective against $\mathcal{PR}$s only if one or more of three conditions is met: the decryption key(s) can be extracted from the $\mathcal{PR}$, the $\mathcal{PR}$ has only one decryption module, and the $\mathcal{PR}$ has a reset function even if it has multiple decryption modules. The first condition is particularly advantageous for the tracer because it means that the tracer can disassemble the $\mathcal{PR}$ and extract the decryption key(s). That is, the $\mathcal{PR}$s do not have a self-destruction mechanism for protection against disassembly, which would disrupt the tracer's efforts. If the $\mathcal{PR}$ cannot be disassembled, it has to be treated as a black-box, which means that either the second or third condition (or both) must hold for the tracer to be successful.

With any TTE schemes and with the TTM, identical content is distributed to all subscribers (receivers) in an ordinal service. Only one content key is used to encrypt the content, and only one piece of encrypted content is generated for each piece of content.

Previous TTE schemes that treat a $\mathcal{PR}$ as a black-box use multiple pieces of content and multiple content keys to identify the decryption key(s) in the $\mathcal{PR}$. The tracer encrypts content M with a content key k_s, $Enc(k_s, M)$. The tracer generates two encrypted content keys, $Enc(sk_1, k_s)$ and $Enc(sk_2, rnd)$, where sk_1 and sk_2 are distinct secret keys of TTE scheme and rnd denotes a random number. The tracer inputs $(Enc(k_s, M), Enc(sk_1, k_s))$ or $(Enc(k_s, M), Enc(sk_2, rnd))$ into the $\mathcal{PR}$ and analyzes its output. If the $\mathcal{PR}$ has sk_1, it can obtain k_s and thus can output M. If it has sk_2, it cannot obtain

k_s and thus cannot output M. From this result, the tracer can determine which decryption key is installed in the $\mathcal{PR}$.

The TTM might perform a similar algorithm to analyze and identify the device key(s) in the $\mathcal{PR}$.

1.2 Related Works

Chor, Fiat and Naor proposed the first TTE scheme [7] based on combinatorics. Following this, Kiayias and Yung proposed another scheme with improved security [13]. Naor, Naor and Lotspiech's scheme [17] employs tree-based key derivation. Kurosawa and Desmedt proposed an algebraic method based on an ElGamal-like structure [15]. Mitsunari, Sakai and Kasahara proposed another algebraic construction [16] in which a bilinear map was introduced. Boneh, Sahai and Waters proposed a scheme [4] based on a bilinear map of composite order, which is efficient and secure against collusion attacks involving $N - 1$ traitors, where N denotes the number of users. Boneh and Naor proposed a scheme with constant size ciphertext [3]. Moreover, a lot of attribute-based encryption and functional encryption schemes have been proposed [2, 9, 18, 19, 23, 26] and those schemes can be used for this purpose.

Another kind of traitor tracing schemes have been developed to trace traitors that decrypt the content and rebroadcast it to a third party illegally through networks. They use watermarked content (*TTW scheme*). Fiat and Tassa proposed a framework of dynamic TTW scheme (DTT) [8]. DTT assigns each user to a certain subset in order to trace illegal redistributors dynamically in real-time in accordance with the illegally redistributed content. Safavi-Naini and Wang took an alternative approach (STT) that uses predefined watermark allocation. It does not need to dynamically assign watermarks and is secure against a delayed redistribution attack [24]. Ogawa, Ohtake, Hanaoka, and Imai proposed an another scheme (TrTT) [21] whose network cost is lower than STT's. Jin and Lotspiech claimed that protection should not increase the bandwidth by more than 10 % and proposed a tracing method over several content [12]. Kiayias and Pehlivanoglu proposed a message-trace and revoke scheme that does not have limitation on revoked users [14]. Phan, Pointcheval, and Strefler proposed a scheme with constant ciphertext size (*PPS scheme*) [22].

The TTM standardized for Japanese broadcasting services [1] uses multiple symmetric encryption schemes. The details of its tracing algorithm is not described in the draft. However, its CPU cost would be low because only symmetric encryption schemes are used.

1.3 Our Contributions

We show an attack (*content comparison attack*) against previous TTE schemes and Japanese TTM. We then propose a traitor tracing method (*content and key management method (CKM)*) to complement security of both previous TTE schemes and the TTM as a countermeasure against the content comparison attack.

The CKM is a modified and simplified version of PPS scheme. PPS scheme uses random permutation and the positions for certain information to be embedded is kept secret to be secure against Pirates 2.0-attack [6]. However, the vector information related to the permutation is disclosed and colluding traitors can know the positions from the information. This means that the permutation does not work well and PPS scheme is not secure against Pirates 2.0-attack as described in Remark 4 of [22]. If there are other primitives except for permutation, we should consider the security against Pirates 2.0-attack, but actually, keeping such permutation secret is quite difficult. We then may not consider the security against Pirates 2.0-attack here. That is, we can remove the some parts of PPS scheme that are added for security against Pirates 2.0-attack.

Basically, TTW schemes assume that the traitors do not construct a $\mathcal{PR}$ [8]. Currently, this assumption does not stand. In addition, the schemes assume that there is an efficient group key management scheme that allows the service providers to efficiently regroup the receivers, and need large capacity of broadcast channel to distribute multiple content. However, key management is not easy for broadcasters and broadcasters do not have enough transmission capacity. That is, the schemes are not appropriate for broadcasting services through the air.

The TTE schemes/TTM are more appropriate to trace traitors that make a $\mathcal{PR}$ for broadcasting services through the air than the TTW schemes. However, their tracing algorithms are effective against only $\mathcal{PR}$s from which the decryption key(s) can be extracted, that have only one decryption module, or that have a reset mechanism even if they have multiple decryption modules. That is, it works well if the $\mathcal{PR}$ cannot determine whether a tracing algorithm is being run or if the $\mathcal{PR}$ does not take any countermeasure against a tracing algorithm. Installing multiple decryption modules, each with a distinct decryption key, into a $\mathcal{PR}$ increases the probability that the $\mathcal{PR}$ can resist a tracing algorithm. This is because the $\mathcal{PR}$ can compare the outputs of the multiple modules. In an ordinal content distribution service, the decrypted content is identical while, with the tracing algorithm, the decrypted content depends on the decryption key used. If the $\mathcal{PR}$ detects a difference in the outputs among its multiple modules, it knows that it is being subjected to tracing analysis. It can then self-destruct and thereby prevent its decryption keys from being identified.

The CKM can overcome this problem. It combines watermarking technology with the TTE schemes/TTM and have a characteristic of TTW schemes, such that multiple content is distributed.

The normally distributed content is modified and content providers transmit at least two versions of their content in ordinary services so that $\mathcal{PR}$ cannot distinguish between ordinary service and tracing analysis. The modification method is important but in the PPS scheme, the modification method is not described. We then propose the modification method considering the current broadcasting system. Distinct content keys are distributed, and each receiver obtains one of them in accordance with the decryption key(s) installed. The distinct decryption keys generate multiple versions of the content. These versions make that the tracing algorithm effective against a "smart $\mathcal{PR}$".

In particular, we focus on tracing traitors that make a $\mathcal{PR}$ for broadcasting services through the air. In addition, we take its practical use into account. We then construct a CKM based on a TTM considering the actual broadcasting system and describe the CKM using MPEG-2 video coding [11] and MPEG systems [10]. The CKM based on Japaneses standard does not use any asymmetric encryption schemes and uses only symmetric encryption schemes. It is also secure against the content comparison attacks. It should be noted that the CKM can be used with small modification for the services through networks.

Furthermore, we propose a transmission method not to increase the transmission rate for the modified content distribution service so much. The rate does not increase in proportion to the number of content and it is possible to distribute multiple versions of content in a transmission channel that has small capacity. In order to make sure of its practicality, we calculate its necessary transmission bit rate referring to the actual bit rate of the current broadcasting services. Concretely, the transmission bit rate is about 20 Mbps in the ordinary service and the transmission data only sometimes increases 188 byte. That is, it is useful even if the transmission capacity is limited like broadcasting services.

It should be remarked that the CKM employs only essential techniques so that the CKM is quite simple.

After first giving the background to our work, we present the CKM and describe how it makes traitor tracing schemes effective against all $\mathcal{PR}$s, even those with multiple distinct decryption keys and a self-destruct mechanism.

2   Preparation: Traitor Tracing Mechanism in [1]

We propose a CKM based on the TTM as a practical example in this paper. We then show the TTM here. We assume that video content is compressed using MPEG-2 coding [11] and that the compressed video is transmitted using MPEG systems [10]. Those are used most commonly in the world content distribution services. Particularly, almost systems for the broadcasting service through the air uses them and the number of receivers is enormous.

In the standard for Japanese broadcasting services [1], the details of tracing algorithm are not described. However, we can imagine the algorithm.

In the basic principle of the broadcasting system, a distinct device key k_d is assigned to each model of receivers. The k_d is preset in a receiver by a manufacturer. Content is encrypted (scrambled) by using a content key k_s at a TV station. k_s is encrypted using a work key k_w and k_w is encrypted using multiple device keys k_d. The encrypted k_w is included in individual information EMM and the encrypted k_s is included in program information ECM. The encrypted content, ECM, and EMM are multiplexed and transmitted from the TV station to receivers. Each receiver demultiplexes them and gets the encrypted content, ECM, and EMM. The receiver uses the preset k_d, decrypts the encrypted k_w in a EMM, and obtains k_w. The receiver then uses the k_w, decrypts the encrypted k_s in a ECM, and obtains k_s. The receiver finally uses the k_s, decrypts the encrypted content and obtains the plain content. It should be noted that a single work key is common to all receivers in this basic principle.

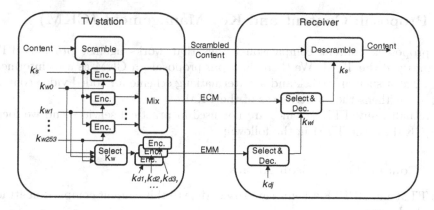

Fig. 1. Japanese standard: system structure extended for k_w leak source detection. Enc. and Dec. denote encryption and decryption blocks, respectively.

The draft, then, describes the extension of the basic principle shown in Fig. 1. The draft includes the TTM, and we can guess its tracing algorithm as follows:

(a) Each model of receivers has a preassigned unique key (device key $k_{d_j} \in \{k_{d_1}, \cdots, k_{d_m}\}$).

(b) A tracer assumes that one device key (k_{d_A}) would be installed in a $\mathcal{PR}$.

(c) The tracer divides the models into multiple groups $g_0, \cdots, g_{253}$ and a distinct work key $k_{w_i} \in \{k_{w_0}, \cdots, k_{w_{253}}\}$ is distributed to each group.

(d) The tracer repeats the following procedure from $l = 0$ to $l = 253$.
- The tracer encrypts content using k_s.
- The tracer encrypts k_s using every $k_{w_i} \in \{k_{w_0}, \cdots, k_{w_{253}}\}\backslash k_{w_l}$ and generates 253 encrypted k_s.
- The tracer picks a random number r and encrypts r using k_{w_l}.
- The encrypted k_ss and the encrypted r are multiplexed and fed into the $\mathcal{PR}$.

(e) The tracer identifies the work key k_{w_l}, that is installed into $\mathcal{PR}$, from the output of $\mathcal{PR}$ and its corresponding group g_l.

(f) The tracer assigns the groups dynamically in such a way that the group g_l is divided into smaller groups as follows:
- The device keys in the groups that do not hold k_{w_l} join in a group g_0.
- The device keys in the group g_l are divided into 253 groups $\{g_1, \cdots, g_{253}\}$.

(g) The tracer repeats from (d)–(f) until it determines a device key k_{d_A} in $\mathcal{PR}$.

It remarks that, if the $\mathcal{PR}$ holds k_{w_l}, it cannot decrypt the content because it cannot decrypt k_s. The tracers can identify g_l and finally identify a single device key in the $\mathcal{PR}$ as described in [1].

3   Proposal: Content and Key Management (CKM)

We propose a content comparison attack that works against previous TTE schemes and the TTM. We then show our proposals, a CKM as a countermeasure against such an attack and a watermarking scheme for coded video content that strengthens the effectiveness of the CKM.

Actually, any TTE schemes are not used in practical services and we focus on a CKM for the TTM in the following.

3.1   Content Comparison Attack

The TTM and all TTE schemes are susceptible to this content comparison attack described below.

1. An adversary ($\mathcal{A}$) extracts multiple decryption keys from authorized receivers.
2. $\mathcal{A}$ makes a $\mathcal{PR}$ using the extracted decryption keys. The $\mathcal{PR}$ has multiple decryption modules and can run them simultaneously.
3. If the $\mathcal{PR}$ is disassembled, it self-destructs, erasing its decryption keys.
4. If the $\mathcal{PR}$ is not disassembled and a signal is input into it, it selects one of two steps in accordance with the data output by its decryption modules.
   4-a: If all data are identical, the $\mathcal{PR}$ outputs the data.
   4-b: Otherwise, the $\mathcal{PR}$ self-destructs, erasing its decryption keys.

A self-destruction mechanism is installed into the $\mathcal{PR}$, and in the steps 3 and 4-b, the $\mathcal{PR}$ determines that it is being analyzed by a tracer and self-destructs, which means that its decryption keys can no longer be used and that the $\mathcal{PR}$ can no longer work. The tracer therefore cannot analyze the $\mathcal{PR}$. This self-destruction causes the tracing algorithm to fail, making it difficult for the tracer to identify the traitor(s). In step 4-a, the $\mathcal{PR}$ determines that it is receiving content normally, not test data from a tracer, and outputs the decrypted data.

Here we assume that multiple users (traitors) collude to make the $\mathcal{PR}$. This assumption is common among researchers of TTE schemes, but we guess it would not be taken into account in the TTM.

The $\mathcal{PR}$ can distinguish between service data from a content provider and test data from a tracer. This is because, when content providers distribute content, they distribute a unique key k_s, while the tracer uses two types of keys (k_s and k'_s). In accordance with the decryption key it holds, a receiver can obtain one of these keys (k_s or k'_s). That is, when the tracing algorithm is used, the keys held by the receivers differ. By detecting this difference, the $\mathcal{PR}$ can distinguish between ordinary service data and test data.

3.2   Content Management: Slight Modification of Coded Content

The service providers need to generate multiple versions of content. The difference among these versions should be as slight as possible from the viewpoint of service quality. We then use a watermarking technique as the content management method to meet the requirement of the service providers. Generally

Table 1. Example Codes: s denotes a sign of a DCT coefficient.

code		zero run length	Quantized DCT coefficient
$c_{1,0}$	0010 0110 s	0	5
$c_{1,1}$	0010 0001 s	0	6
$c_{2,0}$	0000 0001 1101 s	0	8
$c_{2,1}$	0000 0001 1000 s	0	9
$c_{3,0}$	0000 0001 0011 s	0	10
$c_{3,1}$	0000 0001 0000 s	0	11
$c_{4,0}$	0000 0000 1101 0s	0	12
$c_{4,1}$	0000 0000 1100 1s	0	13
$c_{5,0}$	0000 0000 1100 0s	0	14
$c_{5,1}$	0000 0000 1011 1s	0	15
$c_{6,0}$	0000 0000 1011 0s	1	6
$c_{6,1}$	0000 0000 1010 1s	1	7

speaking, the CPU costs of watermarking techniques may not be light, but such techniques are absolutely necessary for the content management. In addition, our technique is not so heavy since it is not a base-band watermarking technique.

In the current broadcasting services, MPEG-2 coding is used, and in the coding protocols, the pixels in each block are transformed into DCT coefficients by using two-dimensional DCT. Each coefficient and its zero run length are encoded, and all the codes are mixed to form an elementary stream (ES). Some codes have the same bit length, and are created from the same zero run length. Examples of such codes are shown in Table 1. We assign a symbol $c_{i,j}(i \in \{1, 2, \cdots\}, j \in \{0, 1\})$ to each code. We treat the two codes with an identical index i as *a code pair*. Codes in a code pair have a difference of only one after they are quantized.

Our watermarking scheme uses this code pair. For example, let a code pair (0010 0110 s and 0010 0001 s) be used. To embed the symbol 0 into the coded video content, the code 0010 0110 s is used, and to embed the symbol 1, the code 0010 0001 s is used. We use this scheme to modify the coded video content.

Embedding a bit is a four-step procedure.

1. The content provider determines special codes $\{c_{1,0}, c_{1,1}, c_{2,0}, c_{2,1}, \cdots, c_{m,0}, c_{m,1}\}$ and sets code pairs $\{(c_{1,0}, c_{1,1}), (c_{2,0}, c_{2,1}), \cdots, (c_{m,0}, c_{m,1})\}$.
2. The video content is encoded and an ES is generated.
3. The provider searches for every special code $c_{i,j} \in \{c_{1,0}, c_{1,1}, c_{2,0}, c_{2,1}, \cdots, c_{m,0}, c_{m,1}\}$ in the ES.
4. When the provider embeds a bit $b \in \{0, 1\}$, it replaces special code $c_{i,j}$ with code $c_{i,b}$ in accordance with the value of b.

The bit detection procedure comprises two steps.

1. A search is made for every special code $c_{i,j} \in \{(c_{1,0}, c_{1,1}), (c_{2,0}, c_{2,1}),$ $\cdots, (c_{m,0}, c_{m,1})\}$ in the ES.
2. The bit embedded as special code is detected:
   if $j = 0$, $b = 0$; else $b = 1$.

The embedded bit can be detected through analysis of the ES.

This watermarking scheme is not perfect. The difference between original and watermarked content may be perceptible in certain content. However, there is no problem even if the difference is perceptible. We use the technique to generate content that is different from its original content.

3.3   Content and Key Management Method

In the CKM, content providers transmit two different versions of their content in ordinary service. The version recovered by each receiver depends on the decryption key it holds. This will enable TTM to detect traitors without disassembling the $\mathcal{PR}$ and do not need to follow the step 3 of the attack procedure. The two versions' transmission means that the $\mathcal{PR}$ self-destructs and comes to a halt in the ordinary service. As a result, tracing traitors does not succeed, but $\mathcal{PR}$s are eliminated. This elimination is good for content providers.

Any $\mathcal{PR}$ that does not have the data-output comparison mechanism described in step 4-b can be analyzed using the tracing algorithm many times and at least one traitor can be identified. This success of tracing is also good for the content providers.

The CKM does not require any large increase in the transmission bit rate and enables the above protection against the content comparison attack. It uses the TTM [1] and the watermarking scheme shown in Sect. 3.2. It consists of five protocols {Distribution of Decryption Keys, Distribution of Content Keys, Content Distribution, Content Recovery, and Tracing}.

Distribution of Decryption Keys. Let $\Gamma = \{d^{(1)}, \cdots, d^{(N)}\}$ be a collusion-resistant fingerprinting code [5,25] and m be the bit length of one codeword, where $d^{(i)}$ $(1 \leq i \leq N)$ is a codeword and N is the number of device keys. Let $\{k_{w_{1,0}}, k_{w_{1,1}}, \cdots, k_{w_{m,0}}, k_{w_{m,1}}\}$ be $2m$ work keys.

1. Define a set of work keys $\{k_{w_{1,0}}, k_{w_{1,1}}, \cdots, k_{w_{m,0}}, k_{w_{m,1}}\}$.
2. Define a work-key set for a device key $k_{w_{ID}} \mapsto (d^{(ID)}, k_{w_{1,d_1^{(ID)}}}, \cdots, k_{w_{m,d_m^{(ID)}}})$
   and distribute $k_{w_{ID}}$ to the receiver which holds a device key $k_{d_{ID}}$.

Distribution of Content Keys. The content provider distributes content keys as follows:

1. Choose bit number $i \in \{1, \cdots, m\}$ for encryption of content keys.
2. Encrypt a common content key k_{s_c} and two distinct content keys k_{s_0} and k_{s_1}:
   $Enc(k_{w_{i,0}}, (k_{s_c}, k_{s_0}))$ and $Enc(k_{w_{i,1}}, (k_{s_c}, k_{s_1}))$.

3. Transmit ciphertext $C_{key} = (i\,,\, Enc(k_{w_{i,0}}\,,\, (k_{s_c},\, k_{s_0})),\, Enc(k_{w_{i,1}}, (k_{s_c}, k_{s_1})))$
   to all receivers.

Each receiver obtains a content key set as follows:

4. Receive ciphertext $C_{key} = (i, C_0, C_1)$.
5. Decrypt a content key set $k_{ss} = (\,k_{s_c}\,,\, k_{s_{d_i^{(ID)}}}\,) = Dec(k_{w_{i,d_i^{(ID)}}}, C_{d_i^{(ID)}})$ in
   accordance with the ith bit $d_i^{(ID)}$ of codeword $d^{(ID)}$ for a device key $k_{d_{ID}}$.

Content Distribution. The content provider distributes content as follows:

1. Encode content using a compression coding scheme such as MPEG-2.
2. Search for all special codes.
3. Make TS packets in accordance with the characteristics of each packetized
   part (including/not including a special code $c_{x,y}$).
   including: Two distinct TS packets are generated. One is generated as
   follows. A special code $c_{x,0}$ is inserted at the position where a special code $c_{x,y}$ is found, and the entire packetized part is encrypted
   $C_{M_0} = Enc(k_{s_0}, M_0)$ using k_{s_0}, where M_0 denotes a part of encoded
   content. A TS packet identifier $T_{ID} = 10$, which indicates that the content key is k_{s_0}, and a TS packet header is added, and a TS packet is
   generated. The other TS packet is generated as follows. A special code
   $c_{x,1}$ is inserted at the position where a special code $c_{x,y}$ is found, and
   the entire packetized part is encrypted $C_{M_1} = Enc(k_{s_1}, M_1)$ using k_{s_1}.
   A TS packet identifier $T_{ID} = 11$, which indicates that the content key is
   k_{s_1}, and a TS packet header is added, and a TS packet is generated.
   not including: The packetized part is encrypted $C_{M_c} = Enc(k_{s_c}, M_c)$ using
   k_{s_c}. A TS packet identifier $T_{ID} = 00$, which indicates that the content
   key is k_{s_c}, and a TS packet header is added, and a TS packet is generated.
4. All TS packets are multiplexed and distributed.

Content Recovery. Each receiver obtains content as follows:

1. Pick one of three procedures in accordance with the TS packet identifier
   $T_{ID} \in \{00, 10, 11\}$ in the received TS packet.
   00: Decrypt a part of the content using k_{s_c}.
   10: Decrypt a part of the content using k_{s_0}, if it has a content key k_{s_0}.
   11: Decrypt a part of the content using k_{s_1}, if it has a content key k_{s_1}.
2. Multiplex all decrypted parts and make an ES.
3. Decode the ES and obtain content.

Tracing. Let M_0 and M_1 be content, where they are different. A tracer identifies
at least a codeword as follows:

(a) For each $j \in \{1, \cdots, m\}$
   1. $C_{M_0} \leftarrow Enc(k_{s_0}, M_0)$, $C_{M_1} \leftarrow Enc(k_{s_1}, M_1)$.
   2. $C_0 \leftarrow Enc(k_{w_{j,0}}, k_{s_0})$, $C_1 \leftarrow Enc(k_{w_{j,1}}, k_{s_1})$.
   3. $C^* \leftarrow (j, C_0, C_1)$.

4. $M_b \leftarrow \mathcal{PR}(\mathcal{C}^*, \mathcal{C}_{M_0}, \mathcal{C}_{M_1})$.
5. $d_j^{(*)} = l$ if $M_l = M_b$, where $l \in \{0,1\}$, and $d_j^{(*)} = 0$ if $M_b \neq M_0$ and if $M_b \neq M_1$.

(b) Reconstruct $d^{(*)} = d_1^{(*)} \cdots d_m^{(*)}$.
(c) Identify $d \in \Gamma$ from $d^{(*)}$ using a tracing algorithm of a fingerprinting code.

In Distribution of Content Keys protocol, each receiver can receives a content key set, (k_{s_c}, k_{s_0}) or (k_{s_c}, k_{s_1}), without fail since $d_i^{(ID)} \in \{0,1\}$.

In Content Distribution protocol, three types of TS packets are generated: the packet includes the content encrypted using k_{s_c}, the packet includes the content encrypted using k_{s_0}, and the packet includes the content encrypted using k_{s_1}. In order to distinguish the three types, the content providers must add an identifier $T_{ID} \in \{00, 10, 11\}$ to each TS packet. These identifiers are not encrypted. A transport stream generated with this protocol is shown in Fig. 2.

It should be noted that content providers must distribute two packets when a special code is found and that the transmission bit rate must be doubled.

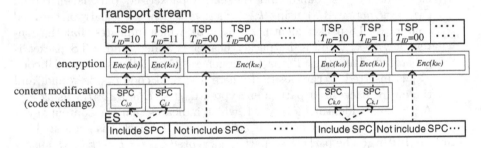

Fig. 2. Transport stream generated using a CKM: TSP, SPC, and $Enc(k)$ denote a TS packet, a special code, and encryption using key k, respectively. Include SPC denotes a part of the ES that includes a special code, and Not Include SPC denotes parts without a special code, and $C_{i,j}$ denotes a special code.

In Content Recovery protocol, a receiver that has k_{s_0} decodes the ES that includes special code $c_{x,0}$. One that has k_{s_1} decodes the ES that includes special code $c_{x,1}$. These two versions of content differ; however, the difference is almost imperceptible to the viewer. This means that these two types of content have the same service quality.

The Tracing protocol is applied to the $\mathcal{PR}$ that does not have self-destruction mechanism. When $\mathcal{PR}$ has two decryption keys, it can select one from two input versions of content and output it, or the $\mathcal{PR}$ can output content that is different from both input versions of content. In the latter case, the tracer cannot determine whether $d_j = 0$ or $d_j = 1$ immediately. The tracer then sets $d_j = 0$ temporarily as described in the item (a) 1–5. In collusion-resistant fingerprinting codes, such a situation is taken into account and the tracing algorithm of the code can work effectively. Thus, the tracer can determine d^* as described in the item (c) by using the tracing algorithm.

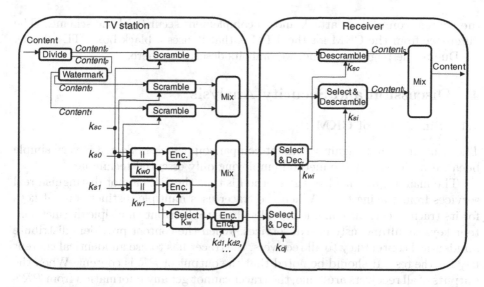

Fig. 3. CKM with symmetric encryption: $Content_c$ and $Content_p$ denote common and private segment of content, respectively. $Content_0$ and $Content_1$ denote watermarked content. k_{s_c}, k_{s_0}, and k_{s_1} denote content keys. k_{w_0} and k_{w_1} denote work keys. || denotes concatenation.

3.4   Actual Content and Key Management System

We show the actual broadcasting system using a CKM in Fig. 3. It is based on Japanese TTM [1] and its characteristics are as follows.

1. Content is divided into common and private segment ($Content_c$ and $Content_p$).
2. It uses a watermarking technique and generates two versions of private segment ($Content_0$ and $Content_1$).
3. Each receiver can get common segment and one version of private segment.
4. It uses three content keys: one (k_{s_c}) for common segment and two (k_{s_0} and k_{s_1}) for private segment.
5. k_{s_c} and k_{s_0} are concatenated, and k_{s_c} and k_{s_1} are concatenated.
6. Each codeword of a collusion-resistant fingerprinting code is assigned to each receiver (not describe in Fig. 3).
7. Content providers have to be a trusted entities.

The item 7 is a unique characteristic of the CKM for TTM and not that for TTE scheme.

3.5   Content and Key Management Method for TTE

A CKM based on asymmetric encryption schemes is useful when arbitrary entities become content providers. The CKM makes TTE schemes effective against the content comparison attack and to complement security of the schemes. The difference from the CKM for the TTM is that it uses a black-box TTE scheme.

Due to the page limitation, we omit its description here.

4 Discussion and Security Analysis

4.1 Simplicity of CKM

The countermeasure against content comparison attack in Sect. 3 is very simple because we construct the method employing only essential techniques.

The main requirement to the method is that the $\mathcal{PR}$ cannot distinguish real services from tracing tests. When the tracer uses multiple distinct content keys for its tracing test, the content providers have to distribute multiple distinct content keys simultaneously in real services. When the content providers distribute an identical content key to all receivers, the tracer has to use an identical content key for the test. It should be noted that the output of $\mathcal{PR}$ is content. When the outputs of all receivers are same, the tracer cannot get any information from $\mathcal{PR}$'s output. Hence, the distinct versions of content are used for the tracing test. That is, the outputs of the $\mathcal{PR}$ are various according to the content keys that the $\mathcal{PR}$ holds. It means that multiple distinct versions of content should be used in real services. That makes it possible that the views from adversaries become same.

Content providers require that quality of service should be same for all subscribers. Watermarking techniques can meet these requirements.

In addition, it is better to embed information into coded content than to embed into content. When n multiple distinct versions of content are generated with the latter technique and are transmitted simultaneously, transmission bit rate would be n times higher than that of single version of content. The rate is restricted by the capacity of the transmission channel and such rate increase is not acceptable. Even if the information is embedded into only small segment of content, the bit rate control is difficult. The former technique can control the bit rate easier and can make its transmission bit rate smaller than the latter technique. Hence, we employ the watermarking technique that embed information into coded content.

In addition, the embedded information must be resist against collusion attacks and we employ collusion-resistant fingerprinting code. We use its codewords as identifiers of device keys. This enables that the tracer identifies a codeword from the output of $\mathcal{PR}$ that is combined with multiple versions of content.

Next, the method must enforce the receivers that they reconstruct content that the content providers assign. For this purpose, encryption technique is employed. Particularly, since the TTM has distinct decryption key for each subscriber, it fits the purpose. On that basis, we employ the tracing algorithm of the TTM as a broadcasting algorithm. That makes it possible to distribute distinct content keys to each subscribers. The content providers generate distinct encrypted content from distinct content by using distinct content keys and distribute them simultaneously. Each receiver has one content key, that is decrypted using its device and work keys, and can reconstruct content assigned by a content provider.

TTM, watermarking techniques, and collusion-resistant fingerprinting codes are essential and indispensable for efficient broadcasting and tracing.

4.2   Security

The CKM has two purposes: to enable a TTM to be used and to prevent a $\mathcal{PR}$ from distinguishing between data from a content provider and data from a tracer. That is, it makes the TTM secure against a content comparison attack and complement security of the TTM. Here we show that the CKM fulfills these purposes.

It is possible to make a $\mathcal{PR}$ that disables the tracing algorithm of a previous TTM. Such a $\mathcal{PR}$ resists open-box tracing, such as disassembly and key extraction, by self-destruction. It can distinguish ordinal services from tracer's checks because it has multiple work and device keys and can distinguish between data from a content provider and data from a tracer by using the keys. This is because the multiple types of output data are the same when the data are sent by a content provider and are not the same when they are sent by a tracer.

With the CKM, however, even in ordinary service, distinct content keys are distributed in accordance with each receiver's identifier, and distinct parts of the content are distributed. That is, multiple versions of content and content keys are distributed by content providers, so the $\mathcal{PR}$ cannot distinguish ordinary content data from test data. The most effective way to use a tracing algorithm is to use data from content providers as data for tracing because it eliminates the need for special data for tracing. The use of special data enables a $\mathcal{PR}$ to easily distinguish the two types of data. If the same data is used, the provability of the distinguishing is zero.

With the CKM, $\mathcal{PR}$s with multiple distinct content keys and a self-destruction mechanism will self-destruct even if the data are from a content provider. That is, the $\mathcal{PR}$s cannot be used to obtain service and can be harmless to content providers, copyright holders, and legal honest subscribers. In addition, $\mathcal{PR}$s that do not have a self-destruction mechanism will continue to work even when receiving test data. This enables the tracer to send test data multiple times until one or more traitors is identified.

4.3   Transmission Bit Rate

We consider the transmission bit rate with the CKM. Previous studies focused on only one content key, which is the situation for current broadcasting and multicast services. In contrast, CKM uses three content keys (k_{s_c}, k_{s_1}, and k_{s_2}). When k_{s_c} is used, the rate is the same as that for current methods; when k_{s_1} or k_{s_2} is used, twice the rate is required because two distinct versions are generated for each content part.

As shown in Fig. 2, at least two TS packets must be used when a special code is included. That is, the transmission rate must be increased to handle an additional 188 byte. The rate increase depends on the occurrence probability of special codes. However, content providers do not need to use all the special codes.

Content providers and tracers simply need to determine the frequency, i.e., how often the parts are used. A large frequency is better for a tracer. It enables the tracer to more quickly identify traitors. On the other hand, a lower frequency is better for content providers because a smaller increase in the transmission rate is preferable to them. Destroying a $\mathcal{PR}$ that has a self-destruction mechanism once a day should be sufficient. For $\mathcal{PR}$s that use the frequency difference between tracing tests and ordinary services, the frequencies of the tracing tests and ordinary services should be the same. It will be up to content providers and tracers to find an appropriate frequency. In any case, it should be noted that current content distribution services through the air use a transmission bit rate of 10–20 Mbps and several 188 bytes increase would not be a big problem.

5   Conclusion

Our proposed attack, which uses content comparison and self-destruction mechanism, is very effective against previous TTM/TTE schemes. We then proposed a CKM using watermarking and TTM/TTE schemes to trace traitors. It is simple and secure against a content comparison attack. It works by having content providers transmit multiple versions of their content and multiple content keys so that $\mathcal{PR}$ cannot distinguish ordinary content data from test data. In addition, its transmission bit rate is not so large and acceptable.

That is, the CKM can use the full ability of TTM/TTE schemes and is a useful mean to preserve copyright of content.

For both broadcasting services and network-based content distribution services, it is important to trace traitors in order to protect the rights of copyright holders and authorized subscribers. As far as we know, any current broadcasting system does not employ any traitor tracing encryption schemes. Replacing current systems without a traitor tracing encryption scheme with a new system is naturally difficult due to the existence of strict standards and previously used security modules. However, when a current system is updated or replaced, it should not be too difficult to introduce CKM, which will lead to more efficient tracing of traitors.

References

1. ARIB, Conditional Access System Specifications for Digital Broadcasting, ARIB STD-B25 (2007). http://www.arib.or.jp/english/html/overview/doc/6-STD-B25v5_0-E1.pdf
2. Attrapadung, N., Libert, B., de Panafieu, E.: Expressive key-policy attribute-based encryption with constant-size ciphertexts. In: Catalano, D., Fazio, N., Gennaro, R., Nicolosi, A. (eds.) PKC 2011. LNCS, vol. 6571, pp. 90–108. Springer, Heidelberg (2011)
3. Boneh, D., Naor, M.: Traitor Tracing with Constant Size Ciphertext. In: Proceedings of ACM CCS 2008, pp. 501–510 (2008)

4. Boneh, D., Sahai, A., Waters, B.: Fully collusion resistant traitor tracing with short ciphertexts and private keys. In: Vaudenay, S. (ed.) EUROCRYPT 2006. LNCS, vol. 4004, pp. 573–592. Springer, Heidelberg (2006)
5. Boneh, D., Shaw, J.: Collusion secure fingerprinting for digital data. IEEE Trans. Inf. Theory **44**(5), 1897–1905 (1998)
6. Billet, O., Phan, D.H.: Traitors collaborating in public: pirates 2.0. In: Joux, A. (ed.) EUROCRYPT 2009. LNCS, vol. 5479, pp. 189–205. Springer, Heidelberg (2009)
7. Chor, B., Fiat, A., Naor, M., Pinkas, B.: Tracing traitors. IEEE Trans. Inf. Theory **46**(3), 893–910 (2000)
8. Fiat, A., Tassa, T.: Dynamic traitor tracing. J. cryptol. **14**(3), 211–223 (2001)
9. Goyal, V., Pandey, O., Sahai, A., Waters, B.: Attribute-based encryption for fine-grained access control of encrypted data. In: Proceedings of ACM CCS 2006, pp. 89–98 (2006)
10. ISO/IEC, 13818-1 Information technology-Generic coding of moving pictures and associated audio information - part1: Systems (2007)
11. ISO/IEC, 13818-1 Information technology-Generic coding of moving pictures and associated audio information - part2: Video (2000)
12. Jin, H., Lotspiech, J.: Renewable traitor tracing: a trace-revoke-trace system for anonymous attack. In: Biskup, J., López, J. (eds.) ESORICS 2007. LNCS, vol. 4734, pp. 563–577. Springer, Heidelberg (2007)
13. Kiayias, A., Yung, M.: On crafty pirates and foxy tracers. In: Sander, T. (ed.) DRM 2001. LNCS, vol. 2320, p. 22. Springer, Heidelberg (2002)
14. Kiayias, A., Pehlivanoglu, S.: Tracing and revoking pirate rebroadcasts. In: Abdalla, M., Pointcheval, D., Fouque, P.-A., Vergnaud, D. (eds.) ACNS 2009. LNCS, vol. 5536, pp. 253–271. Springer, Heidelberg (2009)
15. Kurosawa, K., Desmedt, Y.G.: Optimum traitor tracing and asymmetric schemes. In: Nyberg, K. (ed.) EUROCRYPT 1998. LNCS, vol. 1403, pp. 145–157. Springer, Heidelberg (1998)
16. Mitsunari, S., Sakai, R., Kasahara, M.: A new traitor tracing. IEICE Trans. Fundam. **E85−A**(2), 481–484 (2002)
17. Naor, D., Naor, M., Lotspiech, J.: Revocation and tracing schemes for stateless receivers. In: Kilian, J. (ed.) CRYPTO 2001. LNCS, vol. 2139, p. 41. Springer, Heidelberg (2001)
18. Okamoto, T., Takashima, K.: Fully secure functional encryption with general relations from the decisional linear assumption. In: Rabin, T. (ed.) CRYPTO 2010. LNCS, vol. 6223, pp. 191–208. Springer, Heidelberg (2010)
19. Okamoto, T., Takashima, K.: Fully secure unbounded inner-product and attribute-based encryption. In: Wang, X., Sako, K. (eds.) ASIACRYPT 2012. LNCS, vol. 7658, pp. 349–366. Springer, Heidelberg (2012)
20. Ogawa, K., Hanaoka, G., Imai, H.: Traitor tracing scheme secure against key exposure and its application to anywhere TV service. IEICE Trans. Fundam. **E90−A**(5), 1000–1011 (2007)
21. Ohtake, G., Ogawa, K., Hanaoka, G., Imai, H.: A trade-off traitor tracing scheme. IEICE Trans. Inf. Syst. **E92−D**(5), 859–875 (2009)
22. Phan, D.H., Pointcheval, D., Strefler, M.: Message-based traitor tracing with optimal ciphertext rate. In: Hevia, A., Neven, G. (eds.) LatinCrypt 2012. LNCS, vol. 7533, pp. 56–77. Springer, Heidelberg (2012)
23. Rouselakis, Y., Waters, B.: Practical constructions and new proof methods for large universe attribute-based encryption. In: Proceedings of ACM CCS 2013, pp. 463–474 (2013)

24. Safavi-Naini, R., Wang, Y.: Sequential traitor tracing. IEEE Trans. Inf. Theory **49**(5), 1319–1326 (2003)
25. Tardos, G.: Optimal probabilistic fingerprint codes. In: Proceedings of STOC 2003, pp. 116–125 (2003)
26. Waters, B.: Ciphertext-policy attribute-based encryption: an expressive, efficient, and provably secure realization. In: Catalano, D., Fazio, N., Gennaro, R., Nicolosi, A. (eds.) PKC 2011. LNCS, vol. 6571, pp. 53–70. Springer, Heidelberg (2011)

Security Analysis, Risk Management, and Usability

In Cyber-Space No One Can Hear You S·CREAM

A Root Cause Analysis for Socio-Technical Security

Ana Ferreira[1], Jean-Louis Huynen[2]([⊠]), Vincent Koenig[2], and Gabriele Lenzini[2]

[1] CINTESIS, University of Porto, Porto, Portugal
[2] SnT and COSA, University of Luxembourg, Luxembourg City, Luxembourg
`Jean-Louis.huynen@uni.lu`

Abstract. Inspired by the root cause analysis techniques that in the field of safety research and practice help investigators understand the reasons of an incident, this paper investigates the use of root cause analysis in security. We aim at providing a systematic method for the security analyst to identify the socio-technical attack modes that can potentially endanger a system's security.

Keywords: Root Cause Analysis · Security analysis · Socio-technical security

1 Introduction

Accounting for the impact of a user in a system's security incident is a complex matter. In safety, this impact is usually studied by applying *Human Reliability Analysis* to predict how reliable a system is or *Root Cause Analysis (RCA)* to understand the reasons of an incident where humans are involved. These techniques are not practised in security, but we argue that they should. They would help understanding why security fails in the presence of humans. However, applying RCA in security is not straightforward, it needs some adjustments.

The primary cause of any security incident is unsurprisingly the attacker. But the success of an attacker's Socio-Technical Attacks—attacks that rely at least partially on the presence of human users—also depends on the system, the user, and the context: users can err and create security failures by executing *security critical actions* (e.g., clicking on an infected attachment), whereas human factors (e.g., carelessness), usability problems, and disturbances in the human environment (e.g., noise, psychological pressure) catalyse such situations. These untangled factors are pre-conditions for the attacker's ability to trigger what is often dismissed as "human errors". But if this is the conclusion of a security analysis, no one would know how to secure the system except by extruding completely the user. This drastic solution is obviously severely limited. In the field of safety-critical systems instead, a "human error" is not a conclusion but a start, a symptom of further underlying causes that calls for investigating its

© Springer International Publishing Switzerland 2015
S. Foresti (Ed.): STM 2015, LNCS 9331, pp. 255–264, 2015.
DOI: 10.1007/978-3-319-24858-5_16

"root causes". This is what an insightful security analysis should also do. To this concern we hypothesize that cascades of events that lead to the success of user-mediated attacks are comparable to the ones studied in safety and that it is possible, in a socio-technical analysis of security, to retrieve a root cause more informative than the mere "human error".

Contribution. Inspired by the RCA techniques that are used in the field of safety research and practice, we devise a method to compile a *catalog of Socio-Technical Attack Modes (AMs)*.[1] These are events injected by the attacker that may drive the user to err (e.g., trusting a malicious link) while executing a critical action (e.g., clicking on a link) and initiating a cascade of steps eventually ending with the attacker harming a system's security. AMs actually exploit Error Modes (i.e., ways to err) and reveal the complex interplay among the user, the system, and the context.

The catalog we present could serve (a) to analyze the user-system interactions in search for patterns that are known to trigger Error Modes and eventually harm the system's security, and (b) to identify realistic vulnerabilities of socio-technical nature in those interactions under an extended threat model that accounts for the effect of the intruder's action on the user. From the attacker's capabilities one can determine what effect s/he has on the system and consequently what controls can be applied in defence.

Overall, this paper answers two research questions. Does applying RCA give original insights into the cause of success of existing attacks? Can we find new attacks thanks to RCA techniques? Given the space constraints of this short paper, we can only sum up how we customized a RCA technique to build a small catalog of Attack Modes. A description of the whole methodology and the compilation of a comprehensive catalog of attacks will be developed in an extended version of this paper.

Related Works. The most relevant works related to this paper's objectives are: Cranor et al. work on security-related communications [1], Curzon et al.'s *Cognitive Framework* [2], and Carlos et al. [3] proposal of a taxonomy of human-protocol weaknesses. They all discuss the role of users in security and, from different perspectives, explain how human features may affect security. Our work can be seen as a re-elaboration of those discussions, extended and integrated in our methodology of analysis for the search of root cause analysis in security.

2   Methods

Our methodology combines socio-technical security analysis with Root Cause Analysis (RCA) as inspired from the safety field. First we select and adapt a RCA technique for security; then we use this technique to build a catalog of generic *(socio-technical) Attack Modes (AMs)* observed in actual attacks. We draw our

---

[1] For improved readability, we do not spell out 'socio-technical' in the following while it has to be systematically assumed.

sample of actual attacks from the CAPEC [4] attack library. We use the adapted RCA to explain the success of known attacks and to check if it covers explanations from the literature. We also augment our explanation with the causes brought up by the analysis of root causes.

Selecting an RCA Technique and Adapting it for Security. We selected Cognitive Reliability and Error Analysis Method (CREAM) [5] as our preferred RCA. CREAM is a 2nd generation Human Reliability Analysis; it focuses on errors whereas more recent techniques consider human performance as a continuum [6]. By considering cognitive causes of errors, CREAM brings a great deal of details in the analysis of an accident and because of such richness in details it has been criticized in Human Reliability Analysis [7]. However, such richness is what makes CREAM a great candidate for computer security: a security analysis should identify all factors that an attacker can use to push a human to err. Among other criteria, the most important aspect of CREAM is that it offers retrospective and prospective analysis. Thus, it provides us with bi-directional links between causes and effects. This allows us to build a catalog of AMs that can be used in both ways: in detecting attacks (starting from observed effects) and in predicting attacks (starting from a threat model).

CREAM relies on two pillars: (1) a classification of erroneous actions (this is represented in tables linked together by causal relationships), and (2) a method that describes how to follow those links back to the human, the contextual and the technological factors at the origin of an "event". An event is caused by the manifestation of an "erroneous action", and is called the phenotype [5]. The confluence of underlying factors that made the erroneous action arise is called its genotype. CREAM's tables of causal relationships between antecedent (cause of errors) and consequent (effect of errors) link a phenotype with its genotype [5]. Following these causal relationships, it is possible to find what caused an erroneous action and the root cause(s) of an event.

CREAM is a building block of our method, but it needs to be customized for security. We call the result S·CREAM, which stands for "Security CREAM".

Applying the RCA and Building a Catalog of AMs. We apply our RCA to build a catalog of AMs. We take as input a library of known attack patterns which we got from Common Attack Pattern Enumeration and Classification (CAPEC) [4]. This library contains attacks "generated from in-depth analysis of specific real-world exploit examples".[2] It is maintained by MITRE Coorporation, and it is the only detailed classification scheme where attacks centered on the user are compiled and documented. We use CAPEC's repository to extract and select those Attack Patterns whose success relies on a critical action of the user. The CAPEC taxonomy contains descriptions of social-engineering Attack Patterns, together with their pre-requisites, mechanisms and possible mitigations.

---

[2] See https://capec.mitre.org/.

3   S·CREAM: An RCA for Computer Security

We describe S·CREAM, the technique we devise by customizing CREAM and that we propose as the way to identify root causes of socio-technical attacks.

3.1   Adapting CREAM as an RCA Technique for Security

S·CREAM's retrospective analysis draws on CREAM, but it needed adaptations because of our computer security focus.

In CREAM's retrospective analysis, one first defines common performance conditions to describe the analyzed event, then the Error Modes to investigate. This investigation is a process where the analyst searches for the antecedents of each Error Mode. This process is recursive: each antecedent an analyst finds can be investigated in turn. Antecedents justified by other antecedents are called "generic"; those which are "sufficient in themselves" are called "specific". To avoid following "generic antecedents" endlessly, one must stop the investigation on the current branch when a "specific antecedent" is found to be the most likely cause of the event.

The computer security context in which we intend to use CREAM's retrospective analysis calls for a different procedure because of three main singularities that make it peculiar: (a) we already know that an attacker is the initiator of the cascade of events and what message s/he has sent the user, (b) erroneous actions are already defined, and (c) we lack contextual information as we operate from a generic description of Attack Patterns. Two adaptations to CREAM's retrospective analysis methods are therefore needed. First, we customize the phase preceding the investigation: instead of formalizing the context in common performance conditions, S·CREAM uses its own description of the event focusing on the information flowing between the attacker and the user; we describe this part in the next section. Second, S·CREAM uses a less restrictive stop rule. Doing so we avoid pointing invariably to the attacker's action, and we investigate additional contributing antecedents. So, where CREAM stops as soon as a specific antecedent is found being a likely cause of the event, S·CREAM lists all likely specific antecedents for the event plus the specific antecedents that are contained into sibling generic antecedents, it then stops the investigation of the current branch.

To choose between the different possible antecedents that CREAM's tables propose, we look at the Attack Pattern's description that we built before the analysis and we stick to the attacker's actions we described.

3.2   Using S·CREAM

As stated previously, S·CREAM needs a description of the Attack Patterns under scrutiny. The most important aspect is that this description should enable us to choose objectively among the different paths possible through the antecedent-consequent links. To describe each Attack Pattern before the analysis, we follow what has been proposed in [8]: describing Attack Patterns as a set of messages flowing between the attacker and the victim prior to the manifestation of the critical action. Thus, this first event that initiates the attack is described through common properties shared by the messages sent from the attacker to the user. In synthesis: (1) a source, that is the principal that the user believes to be interacting with, (2) an identity split into a declared identity (i.e., who the attacker says he is, like the from field of an email) and imitated identity (i.e., who the attacker imitates by stealing a logo for instance), (3) a command for the user to execute, (4) an action description, to state for instance if the action is booby-trapped or spoofed, (5) a sequence that describes the temporal situation of the message, and (6) a medium (web, phone, paper).

Running S·CREAM on Identified Attack Patterns. Once an Attack Pattern is described, we perform the S·CREAM analyses on the critical actions carried out by the victim (those with an effect on the system's security). We have at least one Error Mode for each Attack Pattern. Additional Error Modes may have to be analysed in the course of events that lead to the critical action, for instance when the victim first encounters the attacker and misidentifies him/her as being trustworthy.

From Error Modes to AMs. Attack Modes are ways to exploit Error Modes that stem from the interaction between the user, the system and the surrounding context. For instance, an AM can state that an attacker, who can send messages to the user of a system that displays ambiguous symbols may be able to usurp somebody else's identity (this is the effect on the system's security). AMs are readily usable links between Threat Models and possible security-harming effects enabled by particular user-system interactions.

4 Building the Catalog of Attack Modes

To start we need to have a database of known existing Attack Patterns, and we chose to look for them in CAPEC. Applying S·CREAM is about reconstructing the chain of events that lead to harming a system's security. The results of the S·CREAM analyses unveil contributing factors to those events that, thanks to the bi-directional nature of CREAM's causation links, we could turn into a catalog of AMs. We identified 16 Attack Patterns out of CAPEC where the user is at the source of the success of the attack. For the sake of space, we only report on one Attack Pattern, the CAPEC-195 "Principal Spoofing". This Attack Pattern is not considered an issue from a sole technical point of view: its root cause mostly depends on the user's weaknesses and technical factors only increase its likelihood. We first detail how we translate this Attack Pattern into our framework, then we perform a S·CREAM analysis of its causes of success.

Translation of CAPEC-195 "Principal Spoofing" into S·CREAM. In the CAPEC-195 "Principal Spoofing" Attack Pattern, the attacker pretends to be one more actor in the interaction. This attack relies on the content of the message to appear that it reflects an honest identity. Its translation into our

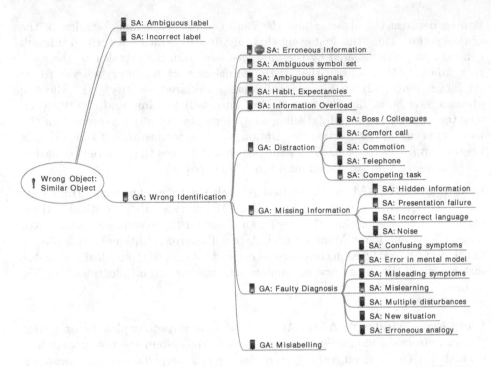

Fig. 1. Part of S·CREAM's investigation of the "Wrong Object" Error Mode (EM) observed in CAPEC-195. A green traffic light means that we consider the specific antecedent as being a contributor or that we expand the generic antecedent. A red traffic light means that we do not consider that the antecedent contributes to the EM. An additional stop sign means that we encountered a specific antecedent that is a probable cause in the current branch and that the stop rule is now engaged. Additional sibling generic antecedents of "Wrong identification" are not displayed and specific antecedents and generic antecedents are abbreviated as SA and GA (Color figure online).

framework can be summed up by the following: (1) the source is another principal that the target knows, (2) the imitated identity is used because the appearance of the message is crafted to reflect the source's identity, (3) the command is not specified, (4) the attacker is the initiator of the non-spoofed action "disclose information" or "perform action on behalf of the attacker", (5) the message is a continuation of a previous interaction as the target must know the principal, and (6) the medium can be on screen or paper, in person or by phone ("either written, verbal, or visual").

Detailed Root Cause Analyses. In the following, the EM is analyzed using Serwy et al.'s [9] implementation of CREAM's tables. The main EM of this Attack Pattern is the misidentification of the attacker for another principal, we identify it as being a "Wrong object:Similar Object" EM. Figure 1 shows among

Table 1. Justifications of the selections of contributors for the "Wrong identification" generic antecedent. Specific antecedents inside generic antecedents are not named and specific antecedents and generic antecedents are abbreviated as SA and GA.

Antecedent	Justification
SA "Ambiguous Signals and Symbols"	The usability of the interface can contribute to this Error Mode.
SA "Habit and Expectancies"	As the message sent by the attacker is a continuation from a previous interaction we can reasonably consider that this antecedent plays a role in the target's behavior.
GA "Distraction"	We don't have additional information regarding the SAs contained in this GA in our description. But it is likely that the user was performing a main task while assessing the identity of the attacker, so we consider SA "Competing task" as an additional contributor.
GA "Missing Information"	The attacker deliberately hides its real identity and the presentation fails to clearly state the sender identity. So we consider the corresponding SAs as contributors.
GA "Faulty Diagnosis"	The user may have a wrong mental model about how to assess identity, or misunderstood previous explanations.

the possible antecedents for this EM, which path we follow: as the declared identity is not used in this attack, the specific antecedents related to the labeling do not contribute to the behavior. Therefore, we continue the analysis by looking at the generic antecedents: following the generic antecedent "Wrong identification:Incorrect identification", the specific antecedent 'Erroneous information' is selected as contributor because the imitated identity is spoofed. This root cause provided by S·CREAM is the same as the explanation provided by CAPEC: the wrong information furnished by the attacker tricks the user. As shown in Table 1, we follow our custom stop rule and consider the other specific antecedents and sibling generic antecedents for this branch.

Following the analysis out of this branch, the next generic antecedent "Communication failure" leads to the specific antecedent "inattention". The last generic antecedent is "Observation missed" where the specific antecedent "multiple signal" is likely if the attack is run on a computerized medium.

Results. The analyses we performed with S·CREAM on the set of 16 Attack Patterns that we extracted from CAPEC yielded numerous antecedents; assuming that CREAM's bi-directional links of causation can be trusted, we consider that these antecedents can be exploited by an attacker to facilitate the occurrence of critical actions. For the sake of space, we only report on the AMs whose effect is to give the attacker the ability to *usurp another actor's identity*. Most of the following AMs were built by listing the specific antecedents resulting from the S·CREAM analysis of CAPEC-195: "Principal Spoofing" and CAPEC-194 "Fake source of data".

Table 2. AMs an attacker can use to usurp an identity. AMs that only require the attacker to be able to send a message are not shown for the sake of space, namely: *Bad mental Models*, *Mislearning*, *Inattention*, and *Multiple Signals*.

Attack mode	Prerequisites system	Attacker
Incorrect label	Amendable messages	Change sender's field in a message
Erroneous Information	Displayed information is not verified	Can send a message with falsified information or the visual identity of another actor
Ambiguous symbol	Bad usability, symbols are confusing	Can send a message that uses said symbols to convey misleading signals
Habits and Expectancies	Use is monotonous or repetitive	Can send/replay/mimic a message. Knows about previous user's interactions.
Competing task	Main task, or sub tasks	Can send a message
Hidden information	Provides amendable info	Can alter the information provided in messages
Presentation failure	Amendable interface	Can send a message that abuses presentation

Table 2 compiles the AMs that an attacker with certain capabilities can use against a system working under specific conditions. Because those AMs are built from the data provided by CAPEC, there are no assumptions about the users.

5   Discussion

The example we develop in §4 shows that an RCA-based technique like S·CREAM improves our understanding of known attacks without the need of looking each time into the literature or performing user studies ourselves. We believe that in this regard, S·CREAM is an effective tool for security practitioners who want to investigate specific user-mediated attacks at a lesser cost. Furthermore, S·CREAM identifies contributors to the success of an attack that are not considered in taxonomies such as CAPEC.

The contribution of S·CREAM to research is also substantial. E.g., it is well known that the Wi-Fi selection process suffers from security issues bound to the misconceptions that people have about the meaning of the different symbols used in the graphical user interface [10]. Where user-studies and surveys had been performed to investigate this problem from scratch, preliminary answers could have been readily obtained through an S·CREAM analysis to support the design of those studies. S·CREAM proposes an additional input allowing to triangulate findings and thus contributes to validating such findings. Such a combination of methods and data sources is an invaluable asset contributing to consolidating the relatively young field of socio-technical security research.

Even if the exploitation of psychological characteristics in socio-technical attacks arises (e.g., tabnabbing attack [11]), these remain mainly focused on the user's observation mistakes. S·CREAM and our catalog of AMs can help anticipating more advanced attacks because S·CREAM yields new means to trick users to err while performing security-critical actions; and our catalog lists the potential attacks that can be fomented. S·CREAM can help refining attacks, and adding information about the user and the context of the attack can open new doors. Of course, the sheer possibility of an AM in a system does not guarantee that an attack will happen, but it constitutes an additional entry point to the system's attack surface.

We think S·CREAM can be further specialized for computer security to bring more specific information about the threat model required for each AM. We can, for instance, map the concertina model of an existing framework for a socio-technical analysis (see [8]) into what CREAM categorizes as the "Man-Technology-Organization" triad, systematically linking where the attacker can strike in the concertina interaction layers.

6   Conclusion

We have illustrated how to adapt RCA, a technique used in safety to investigate the cause of "human errors", to security. The resulting technique, named S·CREAM, is a valuable tool to identify the factors that contribute to damage a system' security by inappropriate, security critical user actions. We used S·CREAM to build an initial catalog of socio-technical Attack Modes (AMs). This is only a first step: there is a need to apply S·CREAM on more socio-technical attacks and attack patterns to improve the way it models them and the information it provides. We believe that the AMs catalog we started building will lead to define a more realistic threat model,, that is, one that integrates user-mediated capabilities. Still, our catalog is preliminary. Expanding its scope is future work: we intend to list additional AMs by using results we could not report here. We also plan modifications to the S·CREAM method to guarantee more objectivity in the analysis process, and in support to that, the creation of a computer assisted tool to help the security analyst performing his/her tasks.

Acknowledgments. This research is supported by FNR Luxembourg, project I2R-APS-PFN-11STAS.

References

1. Cranor, L.F.: A framework for reasoning about the human in the loop. Proc. First Conf. Usability Psychol. Secur. 1–15 (2008). http://portal.acm.org/citation.cfm?id=1387650
2. Curzon, P., Ruksenas, R., Blandford, A.: An approach to formal verification of humancomputer interaction. Form. Aspects Comput. **19**(4), 513–550 (2007)

3. Carlos, M., Price, G.: Understanding the weaknesses of human-protocol interaction. In: Blyth, J., Dietrich, S., Camp, L.J. (eds.) FC 2012. LNCS, vol. 7398, pp. 13–26. Springer, Heidelberg (2012)
4. Corporation, M.: CAPEC - Common Attack Pattern Enumeration and Classification (2014). https://capec.mitre.org/
5. Hollnagel, E.: Cognitive reliability and error analysis method CREAM. Elsevier, Oxford (1998)
6. Hollnagel, H.: FRAM: The Functional Resonance Analysis Method: Modelling Complex Socio-technical Systems. MPG Books Group (2012)
7. Cacciabue, P.C.: Guide to Applying Human Factors Methods - Human Error and Accident Management in Safety-Critical Systems. Springer, Heidelberg (2004)
8. Ferreira, A., Huynen, J.-L., Koenig, V., Lenzini, G.: A conceptual framework to study socio-technical security. In: Tryfonas, T., Askoxylakis, I. (eds.) HAS 2014. LNCS, vol. 8533, pp. 318–329. Springer, Heidelberg (2014)
9. Serwy, R.D., Rantanen, E.M.: Evaluation of a software implementation of the cognitive reliability and error analysis method (CREAM). Proc. Hum. Factors Ergonomics Soc. Ann. Meet. **51**(18), 1249–1253 (2007)
10. Ferreira, A., Huynen, J.-L., Koenig, V., Lenzini, G., Rivas, S.: Do graphical cues effectively inform users? In: Tryfonas, T., Askoxylakis, I. (eds.) HAS 2015. LNCS, vol. 9190, pp. 323–334. Springer, Heidelberg (2015)
11. Raskin, A.: Tabnabbing: A New Type of Phishing Attack. http://www.azarask.in/blog/post/a-new-type-of-phishing-attack/

A Socio-Technical Investigation into Smartphone Security

Melanie Volkamer[1,3], Karen Renaud[2(✉)], Oksana Kulyk[1], and Sinem Emeröz[1]

[1] Technische Universität Darmstadt, Darmstadt, Germany
{melanie.volkamer,oksana.kulyk}@secuso.org
emeroez@rbg.informatik.tu-darmstadt.de
[2] University of Glasgow, Glasgow, Scotland
karen.renaud@glasgow.ac.uk
[3] Karlstad University, Karlstad, Sweden

Abstract. Many people do not deliberately act to protect the data on their Smartphones. The most obvious explanation for a failure to behave securely is that the appropriate mechanisms are unusable. Does this mean usable mechanisms will automatically be adopted? Probably not! Poor usability certainly plays a role, but other factors also contribute to non-adoption of precautionary mechanisms and behaviours. We carried out a series of interviews to determine justifications for non-adoption of security precautions, specifically in the smartphone context, and developed a model of Smartphone precaution non-adoption. We propose that future work should investigate the use of media campaigns in raising awareness of these issues.

1 Introduction

The usable security field initially identified poor usability as the primary obstacle preventing adoption of privacy and security measures [28]. Improving usability, on its own, while necessary, has not proved sufficient in many contexts [10,11, 23]. It is necessary to investigate other justifications for non-adoption in the smartphone context [27].

We carried out a series of semi-structured interviews to explore possible explanations for non-adoption of smartphone precautions. We derived a model depicting the progression towards smartphone precaution adoption and report on it in this paper.

2 Methodology

We conducted a series of semi-structured interviews either in person or via Skype, which took, on average, 41 minutes.

© Springer International Publishing Switzerland 2015
S. Foresti (Ed.): STM 2015, LNCS 9331, pp. 265–273, 2015.
DOI: 10.1007/978-3-319-24858-5_17

2.1   Interview Protocol

Phase 1: Introduction. Welcome, explain what the study is about, gather demographic data and general information about smartphone experiences.

Phase 2: General security threats. Which security threats they were aware of, which countermeasures could mitigate, how effective they are, and whether they had used them. Their vulnerability to attack was explored, as well as their own experiences of security problems. We also asked about data stored on smartphones, and responsibility for security.

Phase 3: Specific countermeasures. We explored mechanisms used to protect sensitive data.

Phase 4: Specific threats. Specific threats were explored, based upon the guidelines from Federal Office for Information Security[1].

2.2   Participants

Twenty Smartphone owners were recruited via email, according to the snowball principle, with a perfect gender balance ranging from 12 to 65 years of age, with a mean age of 33.2 years. Ethical requirements for research involving human participants are provided by an ethics commission at Darmstadt. Participants were initially told that the study was about smartphone usage and debriefed afterwards about the real nature of the investigation. Permission was gained from adults or parents, where applicable, to record the interview anonymously.

2.3   Analysis

To support an interpretative phenomenological analysis (IPA) of our interviews we needed a set of pre-existing themes. Researchers have reported a number of non-usability related factors that are likely to hinder the adoption of security and privacy solutions *in other contexts* [10,11,23,24]. We synthesised a number of deterrents to adoption and usage: (1) Lack of awareness, (2) Lack of concern, (3) Lack of self-efficacy, (4) Lack of compulsion and (5) Lack of perseverance.

3   Results

The interviews were transcribed, and responses were analysed using semi-open coding using the categories enumerated in the previous Section. Two authors independently reviewed the transcripts and assigned explanations to codes and codes to categories.

---

[1] https://www.bsi-fuer-buerger.de/SharedDocs/Downloads/DE/BSI/Grundschutz/ Download/Ueberblickspapier_Smartphone_pdf.

3.1   Lack of Awareness

Participants were either completely unaware, or only aware of threats that required physical access to their smartphone: *"No, I wouldn't know where I could have problems here. There might be something, but nothing comes to mind at the moment"* We identified a number of possible explanations for lack of awareness:

It's a Phone, not a Computer. Participants had not made the mental connection to the need for precautions, e.g.: *"Yes, I consider it more of a phone. So, you can make phone calls, write short messages, and it also has the advantage that you can access the Internet. But, yes, it is mostly for communicating, and is not like a laptop, where one works or writes stuff, so, I use it in a different way."*

Poor Media Coverage. Participants complained that attacks on smartphones did not get as much media coverage as threats to laptops or desktops. Most had heard about malware on PCs, but not on smartphones: *"I have heard, or maybe one has heard, on the TV, or has read about, some attacks on companies, some hackers, but I haven't heard that this also happens in private life"*

3.2   Lack of Concern

Their Own Insignificance. Participants believed that they were not important enough to interest attackers, or that they did not have any interesting data on their smartphones: *"Honestly, I personally think that no one would target me, because I believe that I do not have anything important on my smartphone"*

Low Probability of Becoming a Victim. Some participants underestimated their vulnerability; this led to their not behaving securely and not using privacy-protecting tools: *"I simply believe that out of number of internet-banking users, the number of people that have experienced problems is so small that it results in small percentage"*

Underestimating Consequences. Participants did not seem to anticipate the concrete harm that could result: *"Honestly, I do not have concerns, because this data may be important for me, mostly personal stuff, but there are no state secrets in my emails, if someone wants to read them or something, he, in my opinion, does not get much from it [..]*

Some Privacy Violations are Acceptable. For example: *"If it is an app that I absolutely need, then I need to ponder. Then I say, I take it, even though it is not secure."*

Trust Someone Else to Take Responsibility. Participants named developers, smartphone providers, play stores and state institutions, as being responsible: *"Ahm, ok, basically, if there are extreme vulnerabilities, also problems, then I think, it should be regulated legally.[..] that the manufacturers develop the devices in a way that it is not possible."*

In particular, some overestimated the level of scrutiny by either Apple or Google. Assuming that malicious apps could not enter the store, they did not take precautions: *"So, I hope at least, that they do this [check the apps], that they have some filter criteria, so that they do not sell apps that are dubious, but how well they pay attention to to privacy, I honestly do not know."*

Device Loss is More Worrying Than Privacy. No one mentioned privacy and only a few mentioned security. Instead a number said that the main problem would be losing the device itself: *"As long as it is not stolen, I do not worry."*; *"So, honestly, I think for me the device itself is more important, because I think, oh no, it cost so much. I would only think about the data sometime later, and then worry about my contacts and my images."*

Several mentioned an adversary using their smartphone to make calls or send text messages, that also would cost them something: *"Good, I would immediately lock the card. So that no one can use it. [...] I would also go to the police, but I believe this has nothing to do with it."*

3.3   Lack of Self-Efficacy

People can still fail to act defensively if they do not possess the know-how or self confidence to take action.

Lack of Knowledge. Some did not seem to know how to protect themselves, or what actions to take against threats: *"I do not know how I could protect myself from it."*; *"I cannot judge at all whether an app is secure or not."*

Others complained about the level of pre-existing security-related knowledge that was required: *"I do not find it very obvious, also what they write about security, it is never very clear or understandable for laymen, what is allowed and what is not allowed."* More advanced measures, such as the option to remotely track the stolen device or wiping data from it, or encryption, were hardly ever mentioned.

Other participants, demonstrated misconceptions with respect to specific threats, such as using non-secured WLAN: *"I do not have the feeling that anyone can access my computer or my phone better on non-secured WLAN than on secured."*

Misplaced Faith in Efficacy of Solutions. Participants believed that they already used their smartphones securely, and that they did not require additional measures. For example, they did not use the screen lock since they always had their phone on their person: *"I have my phone always in my pants pocket, and I believe that no one can easily get it."*

They did not use antivirus software because they believed that their careful usage of their phone (i.e. not installing many apps) prevented them from getting a virus: *"I consider antivirus software to be important when you download stuff that you might install on your computer or with which you do something. I do not do this on the phone at all. So, I read emails, or read news and go on the internet to look something up, but I never install stuff on my phone."*

Some believed that since they had not experienced any security issues so far, it meant that their way of using the smartphone must be secure: *"I did not have any negative experiences on my smartphone, that some trojans or something was installed on smartphones because there were no antivurus. I can't recall reading anything about it. Therefore I didn't consider it to be important."*

Futility of Precautions. Participants were sceptical about whether the existing precautionary measures were indeed capable of protecting them. *"I think that at least these big players [Apple, Google, Windows, Blackberry], or one of them, could attack me if they wanted to."*

Lack of Confidence. Some did not have the confidence to engage with precautionary measures: *"I would need to ask someone to download or install it for me."*

3.4   Lack of Compulsion

Some, despite being aware of the threats and of the precautionary measures, cited other factors that kept them from adopting those measures.

Inconvenience. Many referred to the effort that would be required that would hinder their usage of their smartphone: *"Because I am irritated that I have to constantly enter this, around 50 times a day."; "I think it is more secure than the PIN, but it is too effortful."; "I can suggest that I would not do it out of a desire for convenience. That is, out of convenience or forgetfulness, that I forget that I have to do this."; "Besides, one has to think of new passwords every time; this is horrible."*

Finally, some did not install essential updates to their operating systems even though they knew they should. They cited inconvenience: *"Yes, since I also have to work with the device or use it. It is not so, that complete functions are not available, instead, I can still work with it, and when I have a quiet minute, then I do the update."*

Negative Past Experiences. Participants expressed concern about existing solutions hindering the functionality of their smartphones, such as a loss of data as a result of an update, or antivirus software making the phone work too slowly: *"Antivirus software makes my phone too slow if it runs in the background all the time, therefore I decline to use it."*

Financial Cost. *"There might be some antivirus software that one has to pay for, I leave it alone. If I somehow find free antivirus software, and I read that it delivers value, then I would install it".*

3.5   Lack of Perseverance

I Trust What My Friends Do. *"Apps that I have on it are just the apps used by many people, also by many in my social circle. And somehow it creates trust, so that one thinks, ok, if they all have it, than it must be secure and not do anything bad."*

Not Wanting to be Paranoid. *"On one hand, it to some extent naïvety, and on the other side, it is to some extent, one can not permanently go on with such* *distrust, and always with these thoughts in head, I have to be absolutely sure, that no data falls in wrong hands. One can also become paranoid with it."; "The problem is, that one does not understand the things that they write there, unless one becomes acquainted with the topic of security, so one could only trust that whatever is written there is secure."*

4   Model of Precaution Adoption

Based on our findings we have derived a model of smartphone precaution adoption, as depicted in Fig. 1[2]. (The subcategory *poor media coverage of smartphone security issues* is new.)

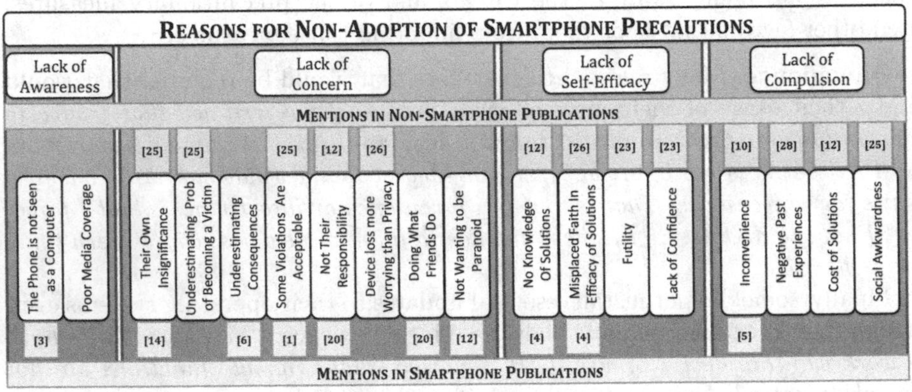

Fig. 1. Categories of explanations for non-adoption in a Smartphone context. Citations for Sub-categories are those who mentioned a related finding in a different context. [1–6, 10, 12–14, 20, 21, 23, 25, 26]

Not many papers in usable security seem to mention the role of the media. Some notable exceptions are Furnell and Evangelatos [9,18] who do mention the media's role with respect to public awareness of biometrics. Certainly this is an area for future focus if we are to make users more aware of the existence of smartphone-related threats, and the appropriate precautions to take.

5   Related Work

A study to evaluate how users protect their data on their smartphones was conducted by Muslukhov et al. [19]. The researchers reported that users tend to store various types of sensitive data on their smartphones yet many do not actively protect their data. Lazou and Weir [16] conducted a quantitative study

---

[2] This list of references is not exhaustive due to lack of space.

to evaluate the security practices of smartphone users, the types of sensitive data stored on the smartphones, and users' security awareness but did not look into the reasons for either lack of awareness or failure to use the tools. Other quantitative studies with similar goals were conducted in [8,21,22].

A great deal of research has been carried out examining app permissions [7,15,17]. Their results include usability and understandability issues as well as reasons for non-consideration of permissionsbut they did not address other smartphone threats.

6 Conclusions and Future Work

We have known for at least the last 15 years that poor usability deters use of security-related software. Yet other factors also deter adoption and it is important to understand the nature of these factors too so that we can address them. We identified five context-neutral causative categories from the non-smartphone literature. We then conducted interviews and analysed them to determine whether these same categories manifested in the smartphone arena. We did confirm them, and – more interestingly – identified an exhaustive list of sub-categories in each of the four meta-categories.

Acknowledgements. This paper has been developed within the project 'ZertApps', which is funded by the German Federal Ministry of Education and Research (BMBF) under grant no. 16KIS0073. The authors assume responsibility for the content.

References

1. Botha, R.A., Furnell, S.M., Clarke, N.L.: From desktop to mobile: examining the security experience. Comput. Secur. **28**(3), 130–137 (2009)
2. Campbell, M.: Phone invaders. New Sci. **223**(2977), 32–35 (2014)
3. Canova, G., Volkamer, M., Bergmann, C., Borza, R.: NoPhish: an anti-phishing education app. In: Mauw, S., Jensen, C.D. (eds.) STM 2014. LNCS, vol. 8743, pp. 188–192. Springer, Heidelberg (2014)
4. Clark, S., Goodspeed, T., Metzger, P., Wasserman, Z., Xu, K., Blaze, M.: Why (special agent) johnny (still) can't encrypt: a security analysis of the APCO project 25 two-way radio system. In: USENIX Security Symposium (2011)
5. Debatin, B., Lovejoy, J.P., Horn, A.K., Hughes, B.N.: Facebook and online privacy: attitudes, behaviors, and unintended consequences. J. Comput. Mediat. Commun. **15**(1), 83–108 (2009)
6. Bursztein, E.: Survey: most people don't lock their android phones - but should (2014). https://www.elie.net/blog/survey-most-people-dont-lock-their-android-phones-but-should
7. Felt, A.P., Egelman, S., Wagner, D.: I've got 99 problems, but vibration ain't one: a survey of smartphone users' concerns. In: 2nd ACM Workshop on Security and Privacy in Smartphones and Mobile Devices, pp. 33–44. ACM (2012)
8. Ferreira, A., Huynen, J.-L., Koenig, V., Lenzini, G.: Socio-technical security analysis of wireless hotspots. In: Tryfonas, T., Askoxylakis, I. (eds.) HAS 2014. LNCS, vol. 8533, pp. 306–317. Springer, Heidelberg (2014)

9. Furnell, S., Evangelatos, K.: Public awareness and perceptions of biometrics. Comput. Fraud Secur. **2007**(1), 8–13 (2007)
10. Gaw, S., Felten, E.W., Fernandez-Kelly, P.: Secrecy, flagging, and paranoia: adoption criteria in encrypted email. In: SIGCHI Conference on Human Factors in Computing Systems, CHI 2006, pp. 591–600 (2006)
11. Harbach, M., Fahl, S., Rieger, M., Smith, M.: On the acceptance of privacy-preserving authentication technology: the curious case of national identity cards. In: De Cristofaro, E., Wright, M. (eds.) PETS 2013. LNCS, vol. 7981, pp. 245–264. Springer, Heidelberg (2013)
12. Harbach, M., Hettig, M., Weber, S., Smith, M.: Using personal examples to improve risk communication for security & privacy decisions. In: 32nd Annual ACM Conference on Human Factors in Computing Systems, CHI 2014, pp. 2647–2656. ACM (2014). http://doi.acm.org/10.1145/2556288.2556978
13. Harbach, M., von Zezschwitz, E., Fichtner, A., De Luca, A., Smith, M.: It's a hard lock life: a field study of smartphone (un) locking behavior and risk perception. In: Symposium on Usable Privacy and Security (SOUPS) (2014)
14. Herath, T., Rao, H.R.: Encouraging information security behaviors in organizations: role of penalties, pressures and perceived effectiveness. Decis. Support Syst. **47**(2), 154–165 (2009)
15. Kelley, P.G., Consolvo, S., Cranor, L.F., Jung, J., Sadeh, N., Wetherall, D.: A conundrum of permissions: installing applications on an android smartphone. In: Blyth, J., Dietrich, S., Camp, L.J. (eds.) FC 2012. LNCS, vol. 7398, pp. 68–79. Springer, Heidelberg (2012)
16. Lazou, A., Weir, G.R.: Perceived risk and sensitive data on mobile devices. In: Cyberforensics, pp. 183–196. University of Strathclyde (2011)
17. Lin, J., Amini, S., Hong, J.I., Sadeh, N., Lindqvist, J., Zhang, J.: Expectation and purpose: understanding users' mental models of mobile app privacy through crowdsourcing. In: ACM Conference on Ubiquitous Computing, UbiComp 2012, pp. 501–510. ACM (2012). http://doi.acm.org/10.1145/2370216.2370290
18. Liu, S., Silverman, M.: A practical guide to biometric security technology. IT Prof. **3**(1), 27–32 (2001)
19. Muslukhov, I., Boshmaf, Y., Kuo, C., Lester, J., Beznosov, K.: Understanding users' requirements for data protection in smartphones. In: Data Engineering Workshops (ICDEW), pp. 228–235. IEEE (2012)
20. Mylonas, A.: Security and privacy in the smartphones ecosystem. Technical report. AUEB-CIS/REV-0313, Athens University of Economics and Business (2013)
21. Ophoff, J., Robinson, M.: Exploring end-user smartphone security awareness within a South African context. In: Information Security for South Africa (ISSA 2014), pp. 1–7. IEEE (2014)
22. Pramod, D., Raman, R.: A study on the user perception and awareness of smartphone security. Int. J. Appl. Eng. Res. ISSN **9**(23), 19133–19144 (2014)
23. Renaud, K., Volkamer, M., Renkema-Padmos, A.: Why doesn't jane protect her privacy? In: De Cristofaro, E., Murdoch, S.J. (eds.) PETS 2014. LNCS, vol. 8555, pp. 244–262. Springer, Heidelberg (2014)
24. Sasse, M.A., Flechais, I.: Usable security: what is it? how do we get it?. In: Security and usability: designing secure systems that people can use. pp. 13–30. O'Reilly Books (2005)
25. Smith, S.W.: Humans in the loop: human-computer interaction and security. IEEE Secur. Priv. **1**(3), 75–79 (2003)

26. Solove, D.J.: "I've got nothing to hide" and other misunderstandings of privacy. San Diego law Rev. **44**, 745 (2007)
27. Wash, R.: Folk models of home computer security. In: Proceedings of the Sixth Symposium on Usable Privacy and Security, p. 11. ACM, Redmond, WA (2010)
28. Whitten, A., Tygar, J.D.: Why Johnny can't encrypt: a usability evaluation of PGP 5.0. In: 8th USENIX Security Symposium, SSYM 1999, vol. 8, pp. 169–184 (1999)

A Game Theoretic Framework for Modeling Adversarial Cyber Security Game Among Attackers, Defenders, and Users

Tatyana Ryutov[1(✉)], Michael Orosz[1],
James Blythe[1], and Detlof von Winterfeldt[2]

[1] USC Information Sciences Institute, Marina del Rey, USA
{tryutov,mdorosz,blythe}@isi.edu
[2] USC, Los Angeles, USA
winterfe@usc.edu

Abstract. This paper models interactions in the cyber environment as a three-way security game between attacker, defender, and user. The paper focuses on understanding and modeling the roles, motivations and conflicting objectives of the players. Unlike most research in cyber security, this paper studies not only technological but also psychosocial aspects of the interactions. The paper develops recommendations for selecting games that have relevant features for representing cyber security interactions and outlines directions for future research.

1 Introduction

Cyber security can be seen as an adversarial game comprising multiple players: attackers, defenders and users who have different objectives and choose their course of action based on some rationale (e.g., cost-benefit analysis). Attackers choose their targets and attack strategies by balancing the effort spent and expected reward. Defenders define security policies and implement security measures according to the evaluated risk to the organization resources and mission. Users have to balance the constraints set by the security policies against the level of effort required.

Game theoretic approaches [8, 10] have been employed to solve security problems in computer and communication networks. One of the challenges is choosing the appropriate game model for a given security problem. In this paper we develop a game theoretic framework that captures the fundamental characteristics of typical adversarial interactions between representative stakeholders. We include often overlooked psychosocial aspects of the cyber security interactions, such as actors' beliefs and values and outline the potential parameters that must be considered to model such interactions. Our framework introduces the user as an independent player, rather than simply an asset or extension of the defender. Our framework shows the inherent relationship between the features of adversarial interactions and different types of game models and identifies the conditions under which a specific game type is suitable.

The next section describes the 3-way security game. It presents game theoretic representation the objectives, tradeoffs and strategies of the attacker, defender and user

S. Foresti (Ed.): STM 2015, LNCS 9331, pp. 274–282, 2015.
DOI: 10.1007/978-3-319-24858-5_18

and provides some concrete game examples. Section 3 outlines related research. Lastly, Sect. 4 summarizes the contributions and describes next research steps.

2 Cyber Security Game

We classify computer **users** as individual users and organizational users. **Defenders** are security professionals who are in charge of protecting a computer system. **Attackers** can be categorized as foreign government, foreign military, non-state combatant, business, criminal, hacker, and terrorist.

The security game (Fig. 1) represents a cycle starting with user-defender interaction (stage 1). The defender attempts to minimize risks by conducting security training, making protection mechanisms available to users, etc. Users may or may not follow the requirements. In situations where the user also plays the role of defender of his home system, this step corresponds to obtaining security information from public websites, IT professionals, and friends or relatives. The game proceeds (stage 2) with the attacker performing an attack against the user (e.g., send a phishing email). User may be fooled and let the attack succeed. The final step (stage 3) shows attacker attempting to attack defender. Successful attacks against users are typically not the final goal for attackers. Attackers often use the obtained sensitive information to attack or gain access to another target. Detected or successful attack may trigger stage 1 (defender implements stricter security policy), and so on. During this game players perform information gathering and analysis (indicated by the loop arrows).

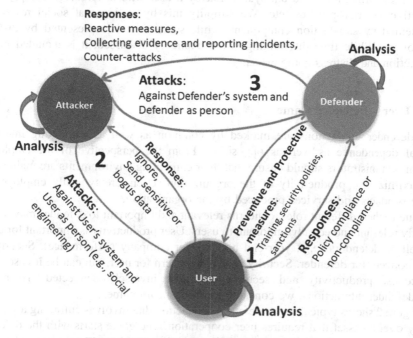

Fig. 1. 3-Way adversarial cyber security game.

2.1 Player Objectives

The defender's primary objective is to decide what security policies to implement based on assessed risk. The preferred defense strategy strikes the balance between minimizing risk while minimizing costs and impact on business operations and productivity. In addition, the defender attempts to maximize satisfaction and minimize distress (e.g., annoyance due to complains).

The attacker's main objective is to decide whether to commit a cyber-attack and of what nature. The type of attack strategy selected varies based on different motivations for expected rewards which can vary from getting publicity to sabotaging competitors to financial gain. For the attacker, this process also involves minimizing costs and distress (e.g., fear of getting caught), maximizing satisfaction (e.g., enhancing personal reputation within the attacker community) and victim's distress (e.g., cause terror).

The user's primary objective is to continue their business and leisure activities by maximizing the number of available resources and services, minimizing costs due to successful attacks on user private information, while maximizing convenience. Users are also concerned with maximizing and minimizing distress. We represent each actor objectives and trade-offs by a utility function:

$$Utility = Reward + Satisfaction - Cost - Distress \qquad (1)$$

Reward and cost represent material constituents expressed in terms of money, time, effort, etc. The social constituents of the utility function may involve psychosocial factors, such as anger and fear experienced by attack victims; pride and pleasure felt by the attacker, frustration and annoyance felt by a user who is forced to comply with restrictive security policies, etc. We simplify this by stating that social reward is represented by satisfaction component, while social cost is represented by distress component. While time discounting is not explicitly discussed, it is included in the satisfaction and distress components.

2.2 User – Defender Game

User-defender interactions are marked by common as well as conflicting interests, mutual dependence as well as opposition. From the perspective of the employer, system administrators should ensure that their computing environments are maintained to maximize the productivity of the organization. Users are typically employed to create products and services produced by the organization.

Due to their different roles, concerns relevant and important to defender may not be directly relevant and equally important to users. User productivity is important for users as well as defenders (e.g., year-end bonuses for company performance). Security is main concern for defender. Security is also a concern for user, but can be less so. This is because productivity and security are often inversely connected. To model user-defender interactions, we consider a non-zero sum game.

Figure 2 shows typical user – defender interaction that involves enforcing a security policy over an asset that requires user cooperation. The game starts with the defender making a decision whether to request policy compliance. The user next has a choice to comply or do not comply. The defender next decides to revoke or not the access to resource in the case of non-compliance. In addition to revoking resource, the defender can sanction the user.

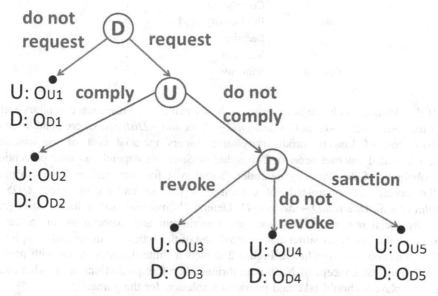

Fig. 2. User-Defender extended form game.

We next discuss outcome values for each leaf node in the game tree. If defender does not request policy compliance, user gets access to the resource without hindrance. We assume that the material reward of acquiring access to the resource is increased user productivity (denoted by *Value*), while the material cost is possible loss due to successful attack denoted by Security. Thus user outcome is $OU1 = ValueU - SecurityU$. Similarly, defender's outcome is $OD1 = ValueD - SecurityD$. However, as discussed earlier $SecurityD \geq SecurityU$ due to diverse user and defender roles. In addition, the value of *Secuirty* depends on the probability of an attack as perceived by user and defender. Typically, the probability is higher for defender due to better understanding of cyber security threats.

If defender requests policy compliance and user follows, the user outcome is $OU2 = -ProductivityU + SecurityU + SatisfactionU$. For the user material cost is the loss of productivity. Social reward is represented by satisfaction from reinforced ability to use security tools and following norms (expectations of superiors, peers, and IT personnel) [20]. Defender's outcome is $OD2 = -ProductivityU + SecurityS$.

If user chooses not to comply and defender decides to revoke the access, user and defender payoffs are $OU3 = -ValueU + SecurityU$ and $OD3 = -ValueD + SecurityD$, respectively. In case defender chooses not to revoke access, the outcomes are: $OU4 = ValueU - SecurityU$ and $OD4 = ValueD - SecurityD$.

Table 1. Values of utility components in User-Defender game.

Variable Type	Variable Name	Defender	User
Reward	Value	2	6
Satisfaction	Retribution	1	–
	Compliance	–	1
Cost	Productivity	1	5
	Security	6	2
	Sanction	–	1
Distress	Violation	–	3

If the defender's choice is to sanction the user in case of user non-compliance, the outcomes are: $OU5 = -ValueU + SecurityU - Sanction - Distress$, where in addition to material cost of loss of productivity, user incurs material cost of the sanction (e.g., suspended internet access). The value of *Sanction* depends on user perception of probability of detection by defender. Social cost for user derives from violation of the norms and organizational commitment [6]. Defender's outcome: $OD5 = -ValueD + SatisfactionD + SecurityD$. Defender's material cost is loss of user productivity social reward derives from just punishment and expectation for increased future compliance. We assume that material cost of the actions (request and comply) as well as sanction is insignificant. Figure 2 depicts a finite dynamic game with perfect information. The concept of Nash equilibrium [4] offers predictions as to what strategies the players should take and provides a solution for the game.

Game analysis (sub-game perfect Nash equilibria) given concrete values listed in Table 1 predicts that the actor strategies are: defender *{request, sanction}*, user *{comply}*. Note that if the value of *SecurityD* is low for defender, such as 2, defender strategy changes to {do not request}. Low values of the lost value and sanction can result in *{do not comply}* strategy for the user.

This game represents situations where the user and defender can observe each other's actions and are aware of each other's utility values. In cases where it is not true, the type of the game changes to imperfect information game. So in the game tree shown in Fig. 2, the nodes corresponding to the results of user actions after the defender's first move will become equivalence classes since defender does not know the actual user action. So, the defender has a choice of actions: revoke, do not revoke, and sanction. Thus, the game analysis becomes that of game of imperfect information.

2.3   User-Attacker Game

Figure 3 shows representative user – attacker interactions. We show the outcome for each node in the figure. The game begins with the attacker either attempting to trick the user (e.g., send phishing email) or not. User responds with ignore, report attempt, respond with genuine information, or cheat (respond with fake information). Reporting an attack incurs some cost for the user, e.g., filing formal report, but provides satisfaction from compliance with the obligation to report incidents.

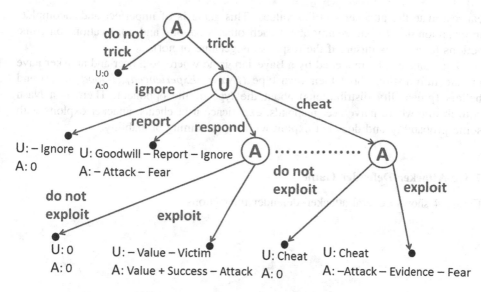

Fig. 3. User-Attacker extended form game.

User response depends on the ability of the attacker to craft the message that looks authentic as well as the user type. Users are classified into two types: Naïve – who believe email/malicious software is genuine and therefore the attacker is "good". Experienced users believe the message is fake (attacker type is "bad") and represents an attack. Table 2 contains possible assignments of the utility components related to the two user types. Note that for Naïve users the cost of ignoring the message is high, while the values of goodwill, report, and satisfaction from cheating are 0. Since naive user believes the message is genuine (i.e., it is not an attack), the user does not want to fail to react to critical situation. In addition, naïve users can believe that the utility of exploiting sensitive information as well as risk from reveal/evidence and fear of being caught for the opponent is low. Experienced users believe that the attacker is "bad" and

Table 2. Values of utility components in User-Attacker game.

Variable Type	Variable Name	Attacker	Naïve User	Experienced User
Reward	Value	10	10	10
Satisfaction	Cheat	–	– 3	3
	Goodwill	–	0	2
	Success	2	–	–
Cost	Attack	3	–	–
	Report	–	1	1
	Ignore	–	9	0
	Reveal	2	0	2
	Evidence	5	0	5
Distress	Victim	–	0	8
	Fear	3	0	3

can estimate the attacker's utility values. This game is of imperfect and incomplete information due to uncertainty about each other's payoffs and observations on some actions (attacker is unsure if the response is genuine or not).

The game can be modelled by a Bayesian game where both user and attacker have private information about their own type (*{Naïve, Experienced}, {Good, Bad}*) and beliefs (probability distributions) about the type of the opponent. There is a Nash equilibrium where naïve user responds, experience user cheats, attacker exploits with some probability and does not exploit with the remaining probability.

2.4   Attacker-Defender Game

Figure 4 shows general attacker–defender interactions.

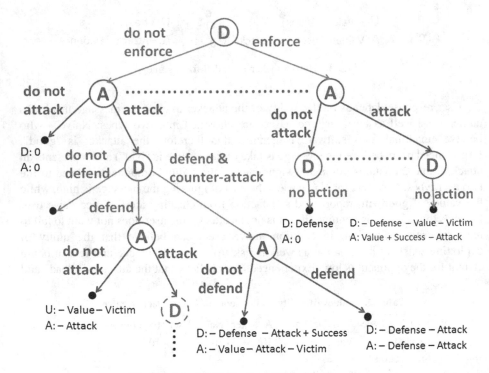

Fig. 4. Attacker-Defender extended form game.

Compromise of a resource or a set of resources incurs a cost to defender and his organization while the attacker gets a reward. Execution of an attack incurs some cost to attacker, e.g., conducting reconnaissance with the intentions of identifying vulnerabilities. The game starts with the defender deciding to enforce or not a set of security policies. In practice, trade-offs have to be made between security and usability and a system may have to remain in operation despite known vulnerabilities. The attacker may be unaware of the active defense mechanisms (represented by the top dotted line that indicates equivalence classes). The attacker decides whether to execute an attack. Defenders use various sensors (e.g., Intrusion Detection System) to observe the status of the system. However, due to known limitations of such sensors, the defender is not always able to detect an attack (represented by the dotted line and no action defender's action). When an attack is detected, the defender decides whether to defend and even fight back. The attacker next stops or responds with a new attack. The game can continue a finite number of steps. In the case of counter-attack, the attacker can employ defense measures.

This game is of imperfect and incomplete information since the players are not certain about the action sets and the payoffs of others. General-sum stochastic games are well suited for modeling such interactions [12]. Since general-sum games often result in non-linear often intractable solutions for even moderately sized problems, a zero-sum approximation of players' optimal strategies is often used in practice [3, 7].

3   Related Work

Game theory offers a unique body of techniques to analyze the interaction and the outcomes, dictated by the rational interests of all involved parties [1].

[8] gives a survey of the flexibility of game theory as a modeling paradigm of diverse security situations, including but not limited to: security of the physical and MAC layers, security of self-organizing networks, intrusion detection systems, anonymity and privacy, economics of network security, and cryptography. [10] presents a dual taxonomy; they give examples of cyber security research where different classes of games are used in the modeling; static or dynamic games, games with complete or incomplete information, games with perfect or imperfect information. In fact, many games of particular interest have emerged through the analysis of some cyber security concerns [8]. [12] surveys a large body of theoretical papers with respect to the underlying assumptions and validity of the quantified security approach and points to the lack of repeated large-sample empirical validation. [2] propose approach to evaluate effectiveness and profitability of countermeasures their effect on attackers.

Our work differs from the research discussed above in that we present a general game theoretic framework that focuses on the actors' incentives and behavior rather than specific attack–defense scenarios. We considered three players in our security games, which is not typical in the related works.

4   Conclusions

This paper models interactions in the cyber environment as a three-way adversarial security game between attacker, defender, and user. We (1) conducted a comprehensive survey of the literature to determine objectives, tradeoffs and strategies of the attacker, defender and user, (2) developed a general game theoretic framework, and (3) presented specific game studies and discussed conditions under which different types of game models are suitable. The utility components of presented games were made up to demonstrate how different actor's beliefs influence the game solutions. Modeling actor motivations in a more realistic way requires a thorough understanding of their incentives and trade-offs. As a part of ongoing NSF project we are conducting studies with human subjects to capture risk preferences and trade-offs among conflicting objectives to infer parameters for our utility functions. This framework serves as a guideline and gives us structure for developing such studies. Next step is to examine a range of concrete cyber-security scenarios, formally represent them and determine if the model fits. Step after that is to develop a set of cyber security games involving actual actors, conduct experiments and compare outcomes to the developed models.

Acknowledgments. The authors would like to thank Richard John and Heather Rosoff for discussions and feedback that helped develop the ideas expressed in this paper. This research was supported by funding the National Science Foundation under award No. 1314644.

References

1. Anderson, R., Moore, T.: The economics of information security. Science **314**, 610–613 (2006)
2. Bistarelli, S., Fioravanti, F., Peretti, P.: Defense trees for economic evaluation of security investments, Availability, Reliability and Security, IEEE Computer Society (2006)
3. Ibidunmoye, E.O., Alese, B.K., Ogundele, O.S.: A Game-theoretic scenario for modelling the attacker-defender interaction. J. Comput. Eng. Inf. Technol. **2**(1), 27–32 (2013)
4. Funderberg, D., Tirole, J.: Game Theory. MIT Press, Cambridge (1992)
5. Herath, T., Rao, H.: Protection motivation and deterrence: a framework for security policy compliance in organisations. Eur. J. Inf. Syst. **18**(2), 106–125 (2010)
6. Furnell, S., Bryant, P., Phippen, A.: Assessing the Security Perceptions of Personal Internet Users. Comput. Secur. **26**(5), 410–417 (2007)
7. Lye, K., Wing, J.: Game strategies in network security. In: Proceedings of the Foundations of Computer Security (2002)
8. Manshaei, H., Zhu, Q., Alpcan, T., Basar, T., Hubaux, J.P.: Game theory meets network security and privacy. ACM Trans. Comput. Logic **5** (2011)
9. Perry, T.S., Wallich, P.: Can computer crime be stopped? IEEE Spectr. **21**(5), 34–45 (1984)
10. Roy, S., Ellis, C., Shiva, S., Dasgupta, D., Shandilya, V., Wu, Q.: A survey of game theory as applied to network security. In: System Sciences (HICSS) (2010)
11. Shapley, L.S.: Stochastic Games. In: Proceedings of the National Academy of Science USA 39: 1095-1100 (1953)
12. Verendel, V.: Quantified security is a weak hypothesis: a critical survey of results and assumptions. In: Proceedings of the workshop on new security paradigms workshop. ACM (2009)

Design, Demonstration, and Evaluation of an Information Security Contract and Trading Mechanism to Hedge Information Security Risks

Pankaj Pandey[1,2]([⊠]) and Steven De Haes[2]

[1] Gjovik University College, Gjovik, Norway
pankaj.pandey2@hig.no
[2] University of Antwerp, Antwerp, Belgium
{pankaj.pandey,steven.dehaes}@uantwerpen.be

Abstract. Cyber-insurance products are the only financial instrument available as a risk-transfer mechanism in the information security domain. Furthermore, cyber-insurance markets are unable or unwilling to facilitate the transfer of risks, particularly those with a high probability and high intensity of loss. Thus, there is a need for a new mechanism to address the variety of information security risks. This article addresses the shortcomings in the existing information security risk hedging market. The article presents a financial instrument and a corresponding trading mechanism to be used for risk hedging in an information security prediction market. Also, the article uses an imaginary case to demonstrate the application of the contract. Furthermore, an evaluation of the contract and trading mechanism in its usefulness in hedging the underlying risks is presented. In our analysis, we found that information security contracts can be a solution (at least to some extent) to the problems in the existing risk hedging mechanisms in the information security domain.

Keywords: Information security · Security economics · Risk management · Financial instruments · Prediction markets

1 Introduction

A large number of financial instruments, such as insurance, forwards, futures, options, swaps, etc., have emerged to allow hedging of risks associated with the underlying assets, whether it is a commodity, real estate or economic indicators [3]. In the information security domain, cyber-insurance policies are the only financial instrument providing a risk-transfer mechanism. Furthermore, the cyber-insurance markets are unable or unwilling to facilitate the transfer of risks, particularly those with a high probability and high intensity of loss [6,9,11]. The currently available cyber-insurance products fail to address the problems such as [1,6,9]: (i) inadequate diversity of products; (ii) high transaction costs;

S. Foresti (Ed.): STM 2015, LNCS 9331, pp. 283–292, 2015.
DOI: 10.1007/978-3-319-24858-5_19

(iii) inadequate real-time communication capabilities; (iv) illiquidity; and (v) risks to insurance providers in case of high probability and high intensity events. Thus, there is a need for a new market mechanism to address the shortcomings in the existing information security risk hedging market [18]. The article presents an Information Security Contract (ISC) and corresponding Trading Mechanism (TM) for an Information Security Prediction Market (ISPM).

The remainder of the paper is structured as follows: Sect. 2 presents the related work. Section 3 identifies the requirements for ISC and TM in ISPM. Section 4 explains the design and development of ISC and TM. Section 5 demonstrates the use of ISC in information security risk hedging. Section 6 presents an evaluation of ISC and TM in ISPM. Section 7 concludes the article with conclusion.

2   Related Work

The efficiency and effectiveness of the market in achieving the specific objectives depends upon the design and implementation of the market. Spann proposed a taxonomy for the implementation of (prediction) markets [16]. This taxonomy has five elements with several sub-components, namely Market Strategy, Market Design, Information Design, Market Operations and Data Interpretation. Weinhardt and Gimpel proposed a 'Market Engineering Framework' to define a structured, systematic and theoretically grounded process of design, implementation, evaluation and introduction of market platforms [19]. Plott and Chen [15], Luckner [10], Sripawatakul and Sutivong [17] also present guidelines on the design and implementation of prediction markets. However, due to various legal, intellectual property and security reasons [4] the design and implementation issues discussed in the above articles do not suffice to address the specific requirements and objectives of the ISPM. Furthermore, the limitations in existing information security market mechanisms [13] need to be addressed in ISPM.

3   Requirements for ISC and TM

Based on a systematic review of literature on information security market methods [4,13], prediction markets [7,10] and risk-hedging financial instruments [3], we have identified the following requirements for ISC and TM in ISPM:

Information Security Contracts (Financial Instruments)

1. Using contracts to hedge risks associated with underlying information security events or conditions.
2. The contracts are manipulation resistant, so that the market price can be used as a forward looking indicator (probability) of occurrence or non-occurrence of the underlying event.

Trading Mechanism

1. Continuous incorporation of information in the contract. Traders are allowed to adjust their bets/position based on any new information available to them.
2. The payout depends on the status of betting at the time of the trade.
3. The market guarantees liquidity to the participants.
4. There is no or limited risk to the market operator.

4 Design and Development of ISC and TM

This section presents the design and development of contracts and trading mechanism, and is divided into two respective subsections.

4.1 Information Security Contract

The contracts are designed to be used with reasonable predictability by security stakeholders (participants) to neutralize (at least reduce) their risk exposure with respect to the underlying event. Thus like in other financial (asset) markets, ISCs trading in ISPM are intended to be used as a mechanism to transfer risk. The ISCs can be designed in at least three forms: (i) Fixed Payout Contract; (ii) Variable Payout Contract; (iii) Contract Bundle (Fixed or Variable Payout Instruments). This article presents a fixed payout type of bundle contracts and other forms of ISCs are beyond the scope of the article.

ISCs are a bundle of 'futures' contracts that are designed to pay an aggregate fixed sum at the contract expiry and each of the constituent futures contract pays the fixed sum at maturity depending upon the occurrence of the future possible outcome of the underlying event in that particular contract. On the other hand, on non-occurrence of the future possible outcome of the underlying event, the contract pays a zero sum at the maturity.

A bundle of ISC is a collection of contracts whose aggregate payoff at expiry date 'Ed' in any *state* is '$D'. A *state* of event 'Se' is a possible outcome of the underlying event realized at the contract expiry date. The event's states 's' and 's′' are mutually exclusive if and only if they cannot occur together. A set of event states, $S_e = (s_1, s_2, \ldots, s_n)$ is complete if: (i) All the members of the set are mutually exclusive, and (ii) Every possible final outcome of the underlying event is a set member. The number of states in S_e must be at least 2 and can be any number equal to and greater than 2. For example, a contract bundle is designed with a collection of contracts (C_1, C_2, C_3) with the complete set of event's states being $S_e = (s_1, s_2, s_3)$. The contract expiry date is E_d and pays $D in respective state else it pays zero. Then at E_d: (i) C_1 pays $D for s_1 else 0; (ii) C_2 pays $D for s_2 else 0; (iii) C_3 pays $D for s_3 else 0.

Now, consider a potential hedger who is exposed to a risk with payoff $P(s_x)$ dollars in state s_x. $P(s_x)$ could be positive or negative. Let us say the payoffs are arranged in the order of magnitude such that:

$$P(s_1) > P(s_x) \quad \forall\, x > 1 \tag{1}$$

Without hedging, the potential hedger is exposed to the risk of 'unfavorable' outcome s_x of the underlying event. However, if there is a bundle of future contracts $(C_1, C_2, ..., C_x)$ and the contract pays \$D if and only if $(s_1, s_2, ..., s_x)$ occurs respectively. Then to completely hedge the risk exposure and obtain a risk-free position, the hedger should buy the following position:

$$\text{Number of shares for } C_2 = \{P(s_1) - P(s_2)\}/D$$

$$\text{Number of shares for } C_3 = \{P(s_1) - P(s_3)\}/D \tag{2}$$

$$....$$

$$\text{Number of shares for } C_x = \{P(s_1) - P(s_x)\}/D$$

This position assures the hedger a completely risk-less position with profit exposure (minus transaction costs) of:

$$P_r = P_r(s_1)P(s_1) + P_r(s_2)P(s_2) + ... + P_r(s_x)P(s_x) \tag{3}$$

where P_r is the profit from the trade.

4.2   Trading Mechanism

This article considers the Dynamic Pari-mutuel Mechanism (DPM) [14] as the suitable trading mechanism for the ISPM. A DPM combines many benefits of other trading mechanisms. In DPM traders can purchase shares at anytime from the automated market-maker and the market prices are set continuously by the market-maker. The market prices are set according to the current state of betting. If many traders are buying a contract then they will drive up the contract price, and if a contract is unpopular then the market price will go down. This is achieved through an automatic system based on a *price function* and the market prices will reflect all the information known to the market participants.

The Trading Mechanism (TM) in ISPM will enable the transactions (matching of orders) related to the bundles of futures contracts. The TM facilitates the transaction of bundles of ISC, includes purchase and sale of complete bundles from the 'clearing house' (market operator), which stands as a guarantee for sale and purchase of contracts at a fixed and pre-stated price. In addition to this, the clearing house will have the absolute authority and ability to issue contracts, decide on settlement of contracts, authorize the trading limit of traders, and perform verification of market participants.

The TM also facilitates trading of individual futures contracts. Those in possession of contracts may place limit orders to sell the contracts, and potential buyers may place limit orders to buy contracts at the specified price. Furthermore, ISPM may enable trading of bundle of ISC or a combination of ISC bundles into one contract. The combinatorial trading may be required to gauge the interdependent nature of the underlying events. Furthermore, it is cost effective to electronically reproduce the ISC to facilitate the trading of highly specialized information security risk hedging financial instruments; including the instruments with extremely low popularity and trading interests. In such a scenario, two or more counterparties (at least one buyer and one seller) may trade a futures contract at ISPM to hedge their shared risk. This is beneficial for the counterparties as well as for the third party observers, by revealing the information about the traders' expectations.

5   Demonastration: ISC to Hedge Underlying Risk

In this section, we demonstrate the application of ISC in hedging the security risk.

Let us say, there is a company 'C' listed at the stock exchange of the country. The company stores and processes customer data for its client companies in banking and healthcare sectors. If the company suffers a major cyber-attack and loses its customer's data then the investors in the company may suffer loses due to loss of clients, fine by regulatory body and so on. In such a scenario, ISPM may list a bundle of futures contract to enable hedging of risk exposure which may arise due to loss of customer data. In the event of company suffering a cyber-attack, the states which define the possible outcomes are: *no data loss* (s_1), *loss of less than or equal to 100,000 customer records* (s_2), *loss of 100,001 or more customer records* (s_3). Thus, the complete set of outcomes in this case is, S=(s_1,s_2,s_3). Therefore, the contracts bundle consists of 3 contracts C_1,C_2,C_3. Let us say, the contract sells for $100 where:

- C_1 paysoff $100 if and only if s_1 occurs
- C_2 paysoff $100 if and only if s_2 occurs
- C_3 paysoff $100 if and only if s_3 occurs

The contracts can be designed for any period, such as for every quarter of the calender year. Furthermore, the contract specification clearly defines the 'customer data loss', i.e., what constitutes the loss of data, whether it is deletion of customer records, theft of customer credit card information, and so on. The contract specification also mentions the (decision)source which will be used for the settlement of the contract. The source on the decision criteria information could be the company's filling of such incidents to the stock exchange or other regulatory bodies. The contract settlement date may not be same as the contract expiry date. The settlement may take after several days of contract expiry, this time gap may be required to obtain the relevant information from the source specified in the contract's specification.

Let us say, an investor has an investment position in company 'C' which is worth $500,000. Though, the investor is confident about the security system at the company but is concerned about the risk exposure and volatility in the share price of the company, which may occur if the company suffers a cyber-attack. The investor is worried if the company loses customer data, in the event of a cyber-attack, then the company's share price will fall. Then the investors unhedged investment position will be worth one of the following:

- $550,000 if the company suffers no cyber-attack or it loses no data if an attack occurs
- $450,000 if the company loses 100,000 or less customer records
- $400,000 if the company loses 100,001 or more customer records

Though, the expected value of the investor's investment is $500,000 but after the announcement of a cyber-attack on the company, the value of the investment may range from $400,000 to $550,000. Thus, the position is potentially volatile and to fully hedge the position, the investor will buy the ISCs as:

- (550,000-450,000)/100 -> 1000 shares of C_2 contracts
- (550,000-400,000)/100 -> 1500 shares of C_3 contracts

Let us say, the market predicts that there are 55 % chance that the company will not lose any customer record, 35 % chance that the company will lose 100,000 or less customer records, and 10 % chance that the company will lose 100,001 or more customer records. Then, the hedger will pay (1000*100*0.35=)$35000 for 1000 shares of C_2 contract, and (1500*100*0.1=)$15000 for 1500 shares of C_3 contract. So, the cost of risk management strategy is $50000 ($35000+$15000). The profit or loss on the hedge position is the number of contracts held, times the payoff per contract. The payoff per contract in the given case is $100. Therefore, after hedging the position the investor is guaranteed a risk-less investment value of $500,000.

6   Evaluation

This section presents an evaluation of ISC and TM against the previously identified requirements for the same.

Contracts to Hedge Information Security Risks. The ISCs can be designed for narrowly defined security events, thus may provide flexibility in hedging the risks associated with specific/specialized underlying events. In comparison to cyber-insurance products, ISCs can be used for a wide range of risks and thus provide diversity in risk hedging products. Furthermore, the cyber-insurance products are often customized to meet client objectives, yet the fine print of the insurance contract includes many exclusions. This leads to opaqueness (high cost) in pricing of the products and the products may not provide the risk coverage as expected by the customer. On the other hand, due to economics of scale the ISCs may incur lower transaction costs and traders can dynamically adjust there position in real time. The current price of ISC in the market will indicate belief of the traders on the future outcome of the underlying event. This will be useful for organizations in formulation of their risk management strategy, decisions on investments in relevant information security controls/tools, and pricing of cyber-(re)insurance products.

Manipulation Resistance. In ISPM traders may be interested in 'manipulating' the market prices to influence the actions of other traders or market observers. This is of great concern when the market prices are to be used for other purposes, such as if it is to be used to make strategic decisions related to deployment of information security controls, as a risk hedging tool to hedge the financial impact of occurrence of the underlying event, using the market data for pricing and formulation of cyber-insurance products. In such a scenario, a manipulator may be willing to suffer loss to distort the prices to indirectly affect the objectives of traders and observers.

The literature [2,5,8] provides explanation that despite all these problems prediction markets are remarkably accurate in forecasting future events and so could be true for ISPM. As explained in [2,5,8] the prices are not set by the average traders who have those shortcoming but the prices are set by marginal traders who are much more rational and tend to make less errors than the average traders. On the other hand, as the ISPM does not aims to prohibit 'insider trading', i.e., participation of traders who may have direct information on the underlying event, such as a developer who has worked on the development of a software and is the subject of underlying event in the contract. The advantage of this is that it could increase the predictive (forward looking indicator) power of the market, thus allowing incorporation of more meaningful and truthful information into prices. However, the trading (financial) limit of an individual trader should be limited to avoid any huge change in the prices. At the same time, other traders in the market must be careful to decide if the change in price is due to some private information or due to a manipulator.

Continuous Incorporation of Information. As the ISPM is meant to provide hedging of a range of information security risks, the mechanism must facilitate incorporation of any 'new' information available to traders. This will allow the traders to dynamically adjust their positions based on the new information available to them. The new information helps the traders in formulation of their belief with respect to the underlying event and this new information is reflected in the market prices. The market prices carry information from the more informed traders to less informed traders. Thus, the receivers of the information signal will revise their market position accordingly. This leads to convergence of trader's beliefs on the potential outcome of the underlying event. Thus, the DPM in the present setting enables adjustment of bids and asks based on the new information which a trader may have. Therefore, the automated market-maker in DPM facilitates trading of contracts in real-time. An inability to continuously incorporate any new information will hamper the risk hedging strategy and the whole idea of hedging risk in ISPM will fail.

Time Dependent Payout. The payout in DPM depends on the status of betting at the time of taking a position, thus the market can react to any new information in a meaningful and reasonable way. A key property of the information security events or conditions is 'time-sensitivity'. This makes it important to have time dependent payout in the ISPM. For instance, Ozment made an important point that the possibility of independent rediscovery of vulnerability is non-trivial [12]. This implies that it is likely that two or more researchers working independently on a particular product may discover the same vulnerability almost at the same time. So, the researcher who first reports/signals the information by purchasing the relevant contract at the lower price will benefit more compared to others who purchase the contract after the prices have shot up. So, for a researcher expecting to make profit for the discovery, it is extremely important to be able to buy the contracts at the earliest possible time. The payout in DPM is time-dependent, thus the trader who purchases the contract first (at lower price) will benefit more than others.

Liquidity. As the ISPM is expected to facilitate trading in narrowly defined and a wide range of ISC, the liquidity in the market may be limited. Thus, the DPM is the chosen mechanism for the market, as it provides virtually infinite liquidity. The automated market maker in DPM will quote a price for the ISCs. Thus, at anytime a trader may buy from the market maker as long as he is willing to purchase the contracts at the quoted price. However, DPM's automated market maker will not buy-back the contracts. Thus, the selling of the contract is through the continuous double auction. Thus, the liquidity on the sell side is limited.

Bounded Risk to Market Operator. The benefit of liquidity comes at a cost. The automated market maker can lose money. However,the risk to the market operator is bounded, and may be considered as the cost of running the business. Furthermore, the cost of transaction charged by the market operator can be priced in such a way that the total money received as transaction cost across the market is higher than the total risk exposure of the market maker. This will limit the total risk exposure of the market operator and the market operator can generate consistent profit from the market.

7 Conclusion

The cyber-insurance products fail to address the needs of information security stakeholders. Therefore, we have presented an ISC and TM for an ISPM. The security stakeholders can participate in ISPM and transact with each other in real time, i.e., as and when new information is available, at low transaction cost. The DPM provides virtually infinite liquidity in the market. We have used an imaginary case to demonstrate the application of the ISC and evaluated the ISC and TM against the identified requirements. Further, the ISPM can be a source of aggregated information on the underlying security events and indicate the probability of (non-)occurrence of the underlying event in the future. Thus, the ISPM can provide authentic data on various information security events, which can be used for risk assessment and management. The data can be used to formulate the information security policy, strategy on investments on and deployment of security controls, and pricing of cyber-insurance products. Thus, the ISCs can be a solution (at least to some extent) to the problems in the existing risk hedging mechanisms in information security domain.

The article has three limitations: (i) ISC explained in the article is only one type of contract among the various other possible types, such as catastrophic derivatives, insurance-linked derivatives, etc., (ii) The article covers only two elements of ISPM, however other elements of ISPM may have a significant impact on the performance of the market. (iii) The demonstration and evaluation of ISC and TM is based on an imaginary case; however the implementation of the same in a naturalistic setting may face some obstacles.

References

1. Managing cyber security as a business risk: Cyber insurance in the digital age. Technical Report, Ponemon Institute, LLC, August 2013
2. Dimitrov, S., Sami, R.: Composition of markets with conflicting incentives. In: Proceedings of the 11th ACM Conference on Electronic Commerce, pp. 53–62. EC 2010, ACM, New York, NY, USA (2010)
3. Fabozzi, F.J.: The Handbook of Financial Instruments. Wiley, Hoboken (2002)
4. Fidler, M.: Anarchy of Regulation: Controlling the Global Trade in Zero-Day Vulnerabilities. Ph.D. thesis, Stanford University, May 2014
5. Forsythe, R., Rietz, T.A., Ross, T.W.: Wishes, expectations and actions: a survey on price formation in election stock markets. J. Econ. Behav. Organ. 39(1), 83–110 (1999)
6. Gray, A.: Government resists calls to fund backstop for cyber disaster losses, April 2015. http://www.ft.com/cms/s/0/7f9d8326-d096-11e4-a840-00144feab7de.html. Accessed 19 June 2015
7. Hanson, R.: Designing real terrorism futures. Public Choice 128(1–2), 257–274 (2006)
8. Hanson, R., Oprea, R.: A manipulator can aid prediction market accuracy. Economica 76(302), 304–314 (2009)
9. King, R.: Cyber insurance capacity is very small: Aig ceo. CIO Journal, Apr 2015. http://blogs.wsj.com/cio/2015/04/02/cyber-insurance-capacity-is-very-small-aig-ceo/. Accessed 19 June 2015
10. Luckner, S.: Prediction markets: Fundamentals, key design elements, and applications. The 21st Bled eConference, eCollaboration: Overcoming Boundaries Through Multi-Channel Interaction, June 2008
11. NewYork Supreme Court: Zurich American Insurance Company vs Sony Corporation of America, no. No. 651982/2011, July 2011
12. Ozment, A.: The likelihood of vulnerability rediscovery and the social utility of vulnerability hunting. In: Workshop on Economics and Information Security (2005)
13. Pandey, P., Snekkenes, E.A.: An assessment of market methods for information security risk management. In: 16th IEEE International Conference on High Performance and Communications, WiP track (2014)
14. Pennock, D.M.: A dynamic pari-mutuel market for hedging, wagering, and information aggregation. In: Proceedings of the 5th ACM Conf. on Electronic Commerce, pp. 170–179 (2004)

15. Plott, C.R., Chen, K.Y.: Information aggregation mechanisms: Concept, design and implementation for a sales forecasting problem. W.P. 1131, California Institute of Technology (2002)
16. Spann, M.: Virtuelle Börsen Als Instrument Zur Marktforschung. Deutscher Universitäts-Verlag (2002)
17. Sripawatakul, P., Sutivong, D.: Decision framework for constructing prediction markets. In: The 2nd IEEE International Conference on Information Management and Engineering, April 2010
18. WEF, Partner: Risk and responsibility in a hyperconnected world. Technical Report, World Economic Forum in collaboration with McKinsey and Company, January 2014
19. Weinhardt, C., Gimpel, H.: Market engineering: An interdisciplinary research challenge. In: Jennings, N., Kersten, G., Ockenfels, A., Weinhardt, C. (eds.) Negotiation and Market Engineering. No. 06461, IBFI, Germany (2007)

Author Index

Printed in the United States
By Bookmasters